AOL Keyboard Shortcuts

Windows Keyboard Shortcuts

Keyboard Shortcuts for Windows

Function	Keyboard Shortcut
Cancel an action	Esc
Cascade windows	Shift+F5
Check spelling	Ctrl+=
Close a window	Ctrl+F4
Compose mail	Ctrl+M
Copy	Ctrl+C
Cut	Ctrl+X
Find in top window	Ctrl+F
Get member profile	Ctrl+G
Keyword (go to)	Ctrl+K
Locate a member online	Ctrl+L
Move to next button	Tab
Move to next window	Ctrl+F6
Move to previous button	Shift+Tab
My Shortcuts menu	Ctrl+1 through Ctrl+0
Open a new text file	Ctrl+N
Open an existing file	Ctrl+O
Open Keyword window	Ctrl+K
Open Mail window	Ctrl+M
Paste	Ctrl+V
Print Document	Ctrl+P
Read mail	Ctrl+R
Save a file	Ctrl+S
Scroll down a page	Page Down
Scroll up a page	Page Up
Send an instant message	Ctrl+I
Send instant message or email	Ctrl+Enter
Tile windows	Shift+F4
Undo action	Ctrl+Z

Using America Online 4.0© by Que® Corporation.

Mac Keyboard Shortcuts

Macintosh keyboard shortcuts

Function	Keyboard Shortcut
AOL guide	⌘-?
Add to Favorite Places	⌘-+
Bold	⌘-B
Check spelling	⌘-=
Close window	⌘-W
Compose mail	⌘-M
Copy	⌘-C
Cut	⌘-X
Find (People, Places, or Things)	⌘-F
Get member's profile	⌘-G
Locate a member online	⌘-L
Move to next entry field	Tab
New memo	⌘-N
Open an existing file	⌘-O
Open keyword window	⌘-K
Paste	⌘-V
Paste as quotation	⌘-Option-V
Plain text	⌘-T
Print	⌘-P
Quit application	⌘-Q
Read new mail	⌘-R
Save a file	⌘-S
Send an instant message	⌘-I
Speak text	⌘-H
Stop speaking	⌘-.
Underline text	⌘-Underline
Undo	⌘-Z

Using
America
Online® 4.0

Gene Steinberg

A Division of Macmillan Computer Publishing, USA
201 W. 103rd Street
Indianapolis, Indiana 46290

Contents at a Glance

Using America Online® 4.0

Library of Congress Catalog No.: 97-68689

ISBN: 0-7897-1424-8

00 99 98   6 5 4 3 2 1

Interpretation of the printing code: the rightmost double-digit number is the year of the book's printing; the rightmost single-digit number, the number of the book's printing. For example, a printing code of 98-1 shows that the first printing of the book occurred in 1998.

All terms mentioned in this book that are known to be trademarks or service marks have been appropriately capitalized. Que cannot attest to the accuracy of this information. Use of a term in this book should not be regarded as affecting the validity of any trademark or service mark.

Screen reproductions in this book were created using SnapzPro from Ambrosia Software, Inc. and edited in Graphic Converter from Lemke Software and Adobe Photoshop from Adobe Systems, Inc.

This book was written based on beta release software of America Online 4.0.

Credits

Executive Editor
Angie Wethington

Acquisitions Editor
Stephanie J. McComb

Development Editor
John Gosney

Technical Editors
John Purdum
Kim Tedrow

Managing Editor
Thomas F. Hayes

Project Editor
Gina Brown

Copy Editor
Julie McNamee

Indexer
Tim Tate

Production Team
Laura A. Knox

Contents

About the Author

Gene Steinberg is an inveterate desktop computer user who first joined America Online in 1989. He quickly became addicted to the online service and finally earned positions in its Computing channel. He currently runs the AOL Portrait Gallery (which features photos of members and their families).

In his regular life, Gene has worked at several occupations. He first studied broadcasting and then worked for a number of years as a disc jockey and newscaster. Gene is now a full-time writer (fact and fiction) and computer software and systems consultant. His published work includes *Using America Online*, *Using America Online With Your Mac*, *Using America Online With Windows 95*, and *Special Edition Using the Macintosh* for Que Corporation, and feature articles and product reviews for such magazines as MacAddict, MacUser, and Macworld.

About the Technical Editor

Kim Tedrow majored in literature/creative writing and rhetoric/technical writing at the University of Minnesota. She joined the online community in 1992, where she subsequently moderated a real-time writing workshop, and coordinated volunteers for AOL's Learning and Reference. She has performed technical edits of several previous editions of *Using America Online*, as well as other books on AOL and the Internet. Kim lives with her daughter in the Washington D.C. area, where she is the Director of Web Services at www.writersclub.com.

Dedication

The book you hold in your hands is almost encyclopedic in size, and although my name is shown as the author, it is not a project a sane or almost sane person can do alone. I am grateful for the assistance of many, working behind the scenes, who made this book possible.

First, I should like to thank the folks in AOLs corporate communications area for letting me see the future of the service. I'd also like to give special praise to Jennifer Watson for her assistance in maintaining an up-to-date list of the service's keyword shortcuts and Jonathan Bird for his help in compiling a list of AOL software tips and tricks.

I'd like to express my appreciation to AOL's Tim Barwick for getting me involved in their forums to begin with and for his ongoing friendship and support.

A number of experts in the computing industry have provided special assistance in researching several chapters of this book. They include Rick Barron of Affinity Microsystems (publishers of Tempo II Plus), Donald Brown of CE Software (publisher of QuicKeys), Clayton Cowgill and Doug Little of the Supra division of Diamond Multimedia, Heidi Palmer of Global Village Communications, Mike Beltrano and Lauri Lentz of 3-Com/U.S. Robotics, Ray Zamagni of Zoom Telephonics, Brian Grove of Connectix Corp. (publishers of Virtual PC), Joanne Sperans Hartzell of Insignia Solutions (publishers of SoftWindows 95), and Peter Paulson, one of Intels top webmasters.

Somehow, despite the long hours in front of my computer to write this manuscript, my forum on AOL managed to keep rolling anyway. For that I must give heartfelt praise to my staff at the AOL Portrait Gallery (A.J., Alex, Dave, Dimitri, Julie, Kathie, Mike, and Paul).

I must give special praise to the team at Que Corporation for putting up with my many eccentricities and for allowing me a great deal of latitude in outlining and writing this book. They include Gina Brown, John Gosney, Stephanie McComb, Julie McNamee, and Angie Wethington. Que's dedicated, fearless technical editors, John Purdum and Kim Tedrow, deserve to be singled out for pouring through every written word and every illustration to verify that they were absolutely correct to the last, minute detail.

And last, I wish to offer a heartfelt, loving thank you to my wonderful, beautiful wife Barbara and my extraordinary son Grayson for putting up with the long hours I spent chained to my computer so that my work could be done on schedule.

We'd Like to Hear from You!

Que Corporation has a long-standing reputation for high-quality books and products. To ensure your continued satisfaction, we also understand the importance of customer service and support.

Tech Support

If you need assistance with the information in this book or you have feedback for us about the book, please contact Macmillan Technical Support by phone at 317-581-3833 or via email at support@mcp.com.

Orders, Catalogs, and Customer Service

To order other Que or Macmillan Computer Publishing books, catalogs, or products, please contact our Customer Service Department:

Phone: 1-800-428-5331
Fax: 1-800-835-3202
International Fax: 1-317-228-4400
Or visit our online bookstore: http://www.mcp.cpm/

Introduction

On August 7, 1996, millions of people learned just how important an online service has become to our daily lives.

Every couple of weeks America Online shuts down the service for a couple of hours for routine maintenance. They upgrade equipment and software, and add new features. At 4:00 a.m. on August 7th, the service shutdown started off normally. Then things went awry. Due to a procession of system glitches, they didn't get back online for nearly 19 hours.

Havoc ensued. Six million people suddenly found themselves without access to their email, their favorite online meeting places, their favorite forums, and the hundreds of computing industry companies who provide free support on the world's largest online service.

The story made the front pages of newspapers worldwide. It was the lead story on the evening broadcast news programsÑbeating out the presidential campaign and other important issues.

The growing importance of the online world in our daily lives was brought front and center that day.

The History of America Online

The dream of building a global Information Superhighway probably wasn't even a glimmer in anyone's eye in 1985, when America Online was founded as Quantum Computer Services. In that year, the Apple Macintosh was just a low-powered niche computer, and Microsoft Windows didn't exist. The Commodore computer was king, however, and a new, easy-to-use and affordable telecommunications service was established called Q-Link.

Q-Link might best be compared to a national Bulletin Board Service (BBS) where computer owners could communicate with one another. Members with a specific interest, such as a special type of software, could congregate in a single meeting place called a *forum*. Members could meet for interactive conversations called *chats*.

From this humble beginning, support was added for other computer platforms, such as Apple II and Tandy's DeskMate. The Apple platforms, platforms such as Apple II and Tandy's DeskMate. The Apple Macintosh, IBM PC, and compatibles soon followed.

Today America Online is a publicly owned company that offers an online community for over ten million members (with millions more joining each year). The service offers online shopping, information services such as daily newspapers and magazines, and even virtual reference books, such as encyclopedias. America Online also allows you to reach out beyond the borders of its service, by providing a direct gateway to the Internet, which serves tens of millions of computer users across the world.

Just as important, America Online is like a huge city, with many people hanging out and communicating with one another on a host of subjects, from the time of day and the weather, to the state of the nation and the world. The online experience is unlike any you've ever had. After you have been introduced to America Online, you'll undoubtedly want to stick around.

Stumbling Along the Information Superhighway

Being the largest online service isn't easy. In December, 1996, AOL opened the floodgates in a big way by instituting flat-rate pricing. Prior to flat-rate pricing, you paid for a basic 5 or 20 hours per month (depending on the pricing plan you chose) and every hour you spent online above that was charged at the regular hourly rate. Many of you watched the clocks carefully while on AOL, and kept your visits as short as possible.

When the pricing changed to cover an unlimited number of hours, however, many folks stayed on for much longer periods. AOL's network capacity was clogged to capacity day and night. Millions of users tried to log on, but found the lines busy.

The situation was particularly bad at night, when (as with TV's prime time) most folks tried to get connected. I remember spending 40 minutes trying to get online to host an online conference. Fortunately, I started quite early and was only a few minutes late for the session.

Because many members use AOL for their businesses, their complaints were loud and voluminous. Some threatened to file class action lawsuits. Various state governments got involved, and AOL finally reached an agreement with the attorney generals of many states to provide partial refunds to users who couldn't connect.

At the same time, AOL committed hundreds of millions of dollars to expand network capacity and to add more network modems so that you could call up AOL without a busy signal.

As this book was being written, AOL was at the end of the first stage of their expansion program. Many of the problems that plagued the service are history now, and you can usually get online with one or two tries at any hour of the day or night (even Sunday, when online traffic is at its highest level).

The system expansion, however, is just the first step in providing an expanded range of online services. The second stage is to roll out new software and new online features. Chief among them is interactive multimedia, the capability to insert pictures in AOL's email and online slide shows. AOL is also building upon its promise of seamless integration with the Internet so that you can access AOL's own exclusive online resources or an Internet-based resource with the same actions, using the same convenient software.

With the largest online capacity in the industry, AOL was also gearing up major promotional campaigns, promising 11 to 12 million members by the end of 1997. It's possible you are reading this book right after you signed up with AOL as a result of seeing one of their fancy TV ads.

Why This Book?

Have you ever purchased a Using book from Que? The Using books have proven invaluable to readers as both learning guides and as references for many years. The Using series is an industry leader, and has practically become an industry standard. We encourage and receive feedback from readers all the time and we consider and implement their suggestions whenever possible.

Using America Online 4.0 incorporates fresh new ideas and approaches to the Using series. New features include

- *Improved Index.* *To help you find information the first time you look!* What do you call tasks and features? As we wrote, we anticipated every possible name or description of a task that we've heard people call it.

- *Reference or Tutorial.* You can learn to quickly perform a task using step-by-step instructions, or you can investigate the why and wherefore of a task with the discussions preceding each task.

- *Wise Investment.* Lastly, pay the right price for the right book. We won't waste your valuable bookshelf real estate with redundant or irrelevant material, nor do we assume you "know it all" or need to "know it all." Here is what you need, when you need it, how you need it, with an appropriate price tag.

- *Easy-to-find procedures.* Every numbered step-by-step procedure in the book has a short title explaining exactly what it does. This saves you time by making it easier to find the exact steps you need to accomplish a task.

- *Cross referencing, to give to additional, related information.* We've looked for all the tasks and topics that are related to a topic at hand and referenced those for you. So, if you need to look for coverage that leads up to what you are working on, or if you want to build on the new skill you just mastered, you have the references to easily find the right coverage in the book.

- *Sidebar elements with quick-read headlines save you time.* Often times, we'll want to give you a little tip or note about how to make something work best. Or we'll need to give you a caution or warning about a problem you may encounter.

How This Book Is Organized

Part I: An AOL Quickstart

The first part of this book introduces you to AOL and offers the latest information about the newest versions of the software. From there you'll discover tips and tricks to get the most out of your online experience. You'll take a brief tour around the service, to get a taste of what's available.

Because many of you have laptop computers, a special chapter on how to get local phone access numbers and how to reach AOL on the road is included. You'll learn how to introduce your kids to the online experience, and how to use AOL's help forums as well.

With the growing popularity of low-cost, high-speed modems, and the availability of high-speed access to America Online, you'll also learn tips and tricks for improved connections and faster throughput. You'll find information on how to tweak your modem for best performance and how best to deal with connection problems. You'll even learn about those new 56KB modems and how AOL is rolling out support for the new protocol that'll let you download files and see Web sites almost twice as fast as you can with a conventional 28.8KB and 33.6KB modem.

Part II: Communicating Online

Because America Online is so close in concept to a large city, communications skills are important. In Part II, "Communicating Online," you learn how to meet other America Online members, participate in real-time chats and conferences, and use the service's advanced electronic mail and *instant messaging* capability (the latter is a feature that lets you communicate with fellow members while they are onlineÑon a one-to-one basis). As you probably know, some of the world's most famous personalities (from the business, literary, political, and entertainment worlds) have appeared at AOL's popular interactive conferences.

You also learn the most effective methods of using America Online's active message boards. The elements of a message board are dissected, piece by piece, and you learn how to locate messages of interest and how you can get involved in some of these online discussions. Helpful information on the rules of the road is also available, so that you can learn the elements of online etiquette and present your messages in the most effective manner.

Part III: AOL as an Internet Service Provider

One of the hallmarks of AOL is its near-transparent Internet access. In this part, you'll learn how to tap this global resource for information and discussion areas from America Online.

You'll find extensive coverage of such features as Internet email, database searches, Internet chatting, Usenet discussion groups, and the latestÑand perhaps the fastest growing Internet resourceÑthe World Wide Web. All these features, and more, are available to you when you log on to America Online.

You'll also learn how you can access the World Wide Web on AOL while continuing to use other browser software, such as Netscape.

Part IV: Setting Up Your Personal Web Page on AOL

The personal Web page feature is so cool it's worth a part all by itself. In this brief section, you'll learn how to create your own Web page on AOL in just five minutes. You'll learn some guidelines regarding how you can expand your Web authoring capabilities using free software available on AOL.

Part V: A Wealth of Information: AOL's Channels

America Online has a huge amount of information resources. In Part V, you'll begin to turn AOL's channel selector and explore the major online departments. You'll discover AOL's popular entertainment and sports forums. Coverage is also included of areas devoted to lifestyles and interests, ranging from hobbies to special information areas you might want to visit often. You'll find forums devoted to board games, computer games, and video games.

AOL isn't just a place for entertainment. It can serve as your daily newspaper, your corner newsstand, and an encyclopedia too. You'll find resources that cover such topics as the top news stories of the day, the latest weather forecasts in cities across the world, business news, entertainment news, and more. The contents of many of your favorite magazines and newspapers can also be seen online, sometimes before the issues hit the stands.

You'll also visit AOL's Reference Desk, where you can tap the resources of huge libraries, and your kids can get help with their homework.

Because you interact with America Online through a personal computer, it's nice to know that a tremendous amount of support for computer users is available in AOL's Computing channel. You also learn how to search AOL's huge databases, consisting of tens of thousands of Windows and Mac OS files, to find the software you want.

Online shopping is also popular on AOL, and they've taken steps to make your online transactions safe. You'll not only read about the secrets of online shopping, but you'll learn how to check the latest stock market prices, and research the firms you want to add to your portfolio. A chapter is also devoted to AOL's Workplace forums, where you can learn about online tools to help you expand your business, and learn how to use AOL's PrimeHost feature to establish a full-featured commercial Web site.

When it comes time to travel for business or pleasure, you'll find that AOL's Travel channel is a great resource for the information you need. You'll also learn about AOL's own travel agencies, where you can shop for good prices on air travel, car rentals, and popular hotel accommodations.

Part VI: Appendixes

Don't forget Part VI, especially if you're new to AOL. You'll learn how to install your new software, and get a full description of all the important features of AOL's Windows and Mac OS software. Special sections cover popular AOL keywords and Members ChoiceÑthe 50 most popular AOL hot spots.

Conventions Used in This Book

Commands, directions and explanations in this book are presented in the clearest format possible. The following items are some of the features that will make this book easier for you to use:

- *Menu and dialog box commands and options.* You can easily find the onscreen menu and dialog box commands by looking for bold text like you see in this direction: Open the **File** menu and click **Save**.

- *Hotkeys for commands.* The underlined keys onscreen that activate commands and options are also underlined in the book as shown in the previous example.

- *Combination and shortcut keystrokes.* Text that directs you to hold down several keys simultaneously is connected with a plus sign (+), such as Ctrl+P. For the Mac, text that directs you to hold down several keys simultaneously is connected with a minus sign (-), such as Command-P.

- *Cross references.* If there's a related topic that is prerequisite to the section or steps you are reading, or a topic that builds further on what you are reading, you'll find the cross reference to it after the steps or at the end of the section like this:

SEE ALSO

➤ *To learn more about email and instant messages, see page 157*

- *Sidebars.* Information related to the task at hand, or "inside" information from the author is offset in sidebars as not to interfere with the task at hand and to make it easy to find this valuable information. Each of these sidebars has a short title to help you quickly identify the information you'll find there. You'll find the same kind of information in these that you might find in notes, tips, or warnings in other books but here, the titles should be more informative.

Faster Than a Speeding Screenshot

Since 1994, I have written several books about America Online. Every time I revise one of my books, or write a new one, I've observed vast changes and improvements in the way the service is run and the way it looks.

America Online is growing and changing constantly and the under construction sign is always up. You will find that the service's look and feel develops and improves still further over time. Some of the places pictured in this book might look different on your screen, but the information in these pages will be useful for a long time.

As you begin to explore the online community, keep this book at hand. When you have a question or want to learn more about a particular place, you can move directly to that chapter for the information you need.

I began writing books about America Online as an experienced visitor to the service. As the writing progressed, however, I explored many of the nooks and crannies in the online city that I had never visited before. The process has been a tremendous, rewarding, learning experience.

The online community has, over the years, become my second home. It's a place where I can meet and interact with my friends and even conduct business. I've made deals and started work projects with people whom I know only by email.

Indeed, the dream of the Information Superhighway has, to me, become an up-close and personal reality, and I want you to share that dream, too. Let the pages that follow be your starting point on the road to a learning experience that might be unlike any other you've ever had.

Gene Steinberg Scottsdale, Arizona America Online address:
gene@aol.com

An AOL Quickstart

CHAPTER

1

Getting Past the Opening Screen

Mac and Windows AOL features

What you get when you upgrade

Where to get your upgrade

AOL's new software

Windows 95 versus Windows 3.1 AOL users

AOL's Software is Simple Yet Powerful

America Online has become the biggest online service on Earth for good reason. The software is relatively easy to use, and the online interface is friendly and accommodating.

Behind its simple, accessible interface, America Online's software offers a wealth of powerful features that enable you to enjoy a huge array of services and to explore the vast, uncharted waters of the worldwide Internet network.

If You Are New to America Online

AOL offers are almost everywhere

You'd be surprised where an AOL ad will turn up. A case in point is singer Celine Dion's best-selling CD from Sony Music, *Let's Talk About Love*. When you open the CD's case, you'll find a little insert with one of AOL's introductory offers. And, sure enough, when you pop the disc in your computer's CD drive, you'll find (in addition to the music of course) an installer for AOL's software.

This book is written with the assumption that you are already an AOL member and that you have your software installed so that you're ready to go out and enjoy your experiences in cyberspace.

Whether you want to use an online service for business, entertainment, or both, you will find that AOL has the resources you want, and most everything is just a mouse click or two away.

I hope that this book whets your appetite to explore the service, taking advantage of one of those free-trial disks or CDs to experience America Online firsthand. If you haven't received one of those disks (or the disks that you find in a magazine are for a PC, and you have a Mac, for example), you can call America Online directly and ask for a sign-up kit. The number is 800-827-6364.

See you online!

For AOL Beginners Only: Your First Bold Steps to Get Online

If you haven't established an account and signed on, *read the back of this book first*. Seriously! The first two appendixes are designed to be a full-featured tutorial for America Online.

- Appendix A, "The First Steps to Get Online," takes you through the process of installing your new software, logging on to America Online for the first time, creating your online account, and taking a brief tour of the service.

■ In Appendix B, "Setting Up AOL's Software," I dissect the Apple Macintosh and Windows versions of AOL's software, covering all the hidden features that you won't see described fully in the help menus.

After reading those sections, you'll soon become adept at using AOL's Mac and Windows software to navigate the service, and you'll be ready for the main event. In the rest of this book, I take you through every channel of America Online and provide detailed coverage of all the newest Internet access features.

Differences Between AOL for Macintosh and AOL for Windows

With a few exceptions here and there, I've included illustrations and instructions for the Macintosh and Windows versions of AOL software interchangeably. That's because the programs are meant to interface with you, the member, in a similar manner. AOL's software development teams have also worked hard to make both Mac and Windows offer a similar user experience.

AOL has also gone to the major manufacturers from both computing platforms to acquire technology and software. For example, you find that AOL has licensed Apple's QuickTime and QuickTime VR technology, and Microsoft's ActiveX and popular Internet Explorer Web browser.

If you routinely switch between computing platforms, however, you encounter some differences. To a great extent, these differences are due to ways in which document windows and dialog boxes are displayed.

The following sections show the differences in the features of the Mac and Windows versions of AOL software.

Windows-Only Features

The following features of Windows version 4.0 of the AOL software are not duplicated (or available in a different form) in the Macintosh version. I won't detail the minor differences in the graphic formats supported (such as PICT on the Mac and BMP on the PC).

- *Graphics editing tools.* When you have a graphic image open in your AOL software, you see a toolbar at the top of the image document window that enables you to rotate, scale, and make minor adjustments in a graphic file. You also are able to print or save the document using the buttons at the bottom of the document window.
- *Windows help.* Windows online help enables you to print help text windows for later review.

Macintosh-Only Features

Feature parity

Because AOL's Mac and Windows software is in a constant state of development, you can expect that one platform's feature set occasionally leap-frogs the other, and vice versa.

The following features of Macintosh version 4.0 of the AOL software are not duplicated in the Windows version. Minor differences exist in the graphic formats supported (such as PICT on the Mac and BMP on the PC), but I won't detail them here.

- *Text-to-speech capability.* This feature uses Apple's PlainTalk and Speech Manager technologies that enable text windows, chats, and instant messages to be spoken in voices that you select.
- *Apple Guide Help.* Apple's interactive help feature, Apple Guide, is fully supported on your Mac AOL software.
- *AppleScript Support.* Apple's own scripting capability makes it possible to develop automated routines using your AOL software.
- *Link to graphics software.* Although the Mac version of AOL software doesn't have built-in picture editing tools, it does enable you to link up to your favorite picture editing software, so you can use that software to touch up your pictures before you send them to other members. One especially good choice is a shareware program, GraphicConverter, which greatly helped in editing the illustrations for this book. It is located in AOL's software libraries.

AOL Software Features

The descriptions and illustrations shown in this book reflect the newest versions of the software. When you see them, you can see why I strongly recommend that you upgrade. Just take a look at the list of new features offered and you see many compelling reasons to get that AOL upgrade.

AOL 4.0, Code-Named Casablanca

In early 1998, AOL made some major changes to its Mac and Windows software. In previous versions, the user interface differed between the two platforms. The Windows version might leapfrog the Mac version in new features, and sometimes the reverse would occur. In general, however, there was a delay of many months before a Mac version of new AOL software would come out.

As this book is written, AOL promised to deliver its new version 4.0 software in both Mac and Windows form just weeks apart and to continue to work toward full-feature parity for both computing platforms.

Audio and Video

The hallmark of the new AOL software is the multimedia experience. AOL has integrated the latest audio and video streaming and graphic technologies to merge sounds and moving pictures into your AOL software. You are able to communicate with your online friends with sound and video, and you can create multimedia slideshows.

In the next few pages, I summarize some of these new features. In the coming chapters, you'll learn more about them and how to use them to your best advantage.

- *Streaming video and sound.* At the very top of the list is multimedia. AOL has incorporated video and sound into your online experience, using Apple's QuickTime, Microsoft's ActiveX and RealAudio, and Macromedia's Shockwave.

    You can experience multimedia presentations throughout the service, and make slideshows of your own, for your personal entertainment or for your friends and clients. Figure 1.1 shows one of those slideshows in action.

Upgrade to the latest AOL software

This book is written with the assumption that you want to use the very latest AOL software, which at this writing is version 4.0. AOL's software upgrades are always available online, free of charge, and this book has plenty of helpful information to guide you through all the new features.

AOL is kid-safe

AOL has considered safety uppermost in offering the new multimedia features. You're able to restrict access to this feature via AOL's Parental Controls. (See Chapter 7, "Parental Issues and Internet Access," for more information on how to customize your child's online account.)

FIGURE 1.1

Create and view slideshows with the newest AOL software.

① Click the **Resume** button to pick up where the presentation left off.

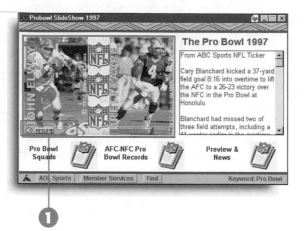

■ *AOL Picture Gallery.* If you are getting into digital photography, you might want to take advantage of AOL's Picture Gallery feature (see Figure 1.2). You can assemble pictures from your library of digital photos, or from a Kodak Picture Disk and collect them in a special file so that you can access them within seconds.

FIGURE 1.2

You can create an online photo album with AOL's Picture Gallery.

① Click an image to bring it up full size on your PC.

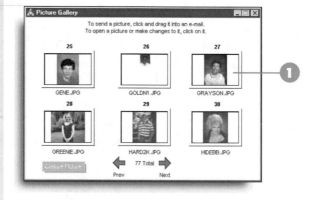

Preview images

You see miniature or thumbnail images of your picture collection (see Figure 1.2). You can crop, scale, and enhance the quality of the photo using AOL's handy image editing toolbar (or, in the Mac version, your favorite image editing software).

■ *Photo email.* After you've collected your online photos, you can insert pictures in to your AOL email (just as you see in Figure 1.3). You'll find this feature a great advantage when you want to show your friends a picture of a new family member or your brand new car.

FIGURE 1.3

Place photos in your email or use artwork as a background for a fancy look.

1 Scroll through the message window to see the rest of the picture.

AOL Email Enhancements

Beginning with AOL 4.0, you will find some big improvements to AOL's email features. The following is a rundown of those features:

- *Multiple email attachments.* This is a feature Mac users have enjoyed for a while, but it's just appearing in the Windows versions of AOL software. You can attach multiple files to your email. Windows users are able to compress the files into a single zip archive before the files are sent. Mac users can take advantage of the StuffIt compression technology. As with existing versions of AOL software, when you log off AOL, compressed files in most popular formats will be automatically expanded.

- *Expanded Address Book.* AOL's personal Rolodex file has grown in features as well. You can add personal data about your AOL contacts in your new Address Book. You're also able to store photos and then send them to your online friends (see Figure 1.4 for an example).

FIGURE 1.4

AOL's Address Book adds pictures and notes to your list of online contacts.

1 Click **Select Picture** to choose a photo for your Address Book.

- *Styled text.* In addition to using your full roster of fonts in your email messages, you also can use those fonts in your chat room text and message board postings (see Figure 1.5). In addition, message boards support hyperlinks; you can talk about your favorite online forum and provide a **Favorite Places** link so that your fellow members can get there with a single mouse click.

FIGURE 1.5

Use a full array of fonts and styles to enhance your chat room visits.

1 Choose your font styles from the handy toolbar.

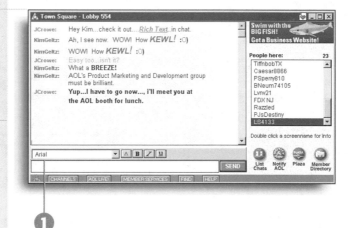

- *Instant screen name switching.* In past versions of AOL software (and for other online services), to use another online name, you had to disconnect and log on again. This was true even if you just wanted to check the email you received from another screen name. AOL's new **Switch Screen Name** feature enables you or members of your family to switch to another screen name on the same account without disconnecting.

Don't forget your password

To switch a screen name without disconnecting, you must enter the screen name and the correct password (if it's not already stored in the program). This is done for your added account security.

- *Longer screen names.* As this book was written, AOL had ten million members and was growing fast. You can stretch a 10-letter email address or screen name possibilities only so far, so AOL was planning to add the capability to create screen names with up to 16 characters. This extends your capability to use your full name for your online account. (Unfortunately it wasn't ready for me to try out with my own name, with a lucky 13 characters in it.)

- *Send greeting cards online.* In keeping with the new multimedia emphasis on AOL, version 4.0 includes the capability to send greeting cards to your online friends. You can have cards sent automatically on that special occasion, so you no longer have to remember to get to that card shop before it's too late.

Advanced Text Formatting Features

Taking a clue from your favorite word processing software, AOL has added new flexibility to the way you handle the text you write online:

- *New Formatting toolbar.* Windows users can now use different fonts in their AOL email (a feature that Mac users have previously enjoyed). The new Formatting toolbar (shown in Figure 1.6) also enables you to activate other new features, such as adding images to your email or a Favorite Places selection or to do a spell check.

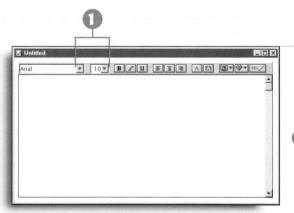

FIGURE 1.6

AOL's Formatting toolbar begins to look more and more like the one you find in a word processing program.

❶ The drop-down menus enable you to select a font and the font size.

- *Handy, customizable toolbar.* AOL's toolbar (see Figure 1.7) has been enhanced to include both the major online features, plus easy navigation for both Web sites and AOL forums. You can customize this toolbar to include some of your favorite AOL spots or move it to another portion of your screen for a better view.

FIGURE 1.7

Move between AOL forums and Web sites seamlessly with the customizable AOL program toolbar.

 The toolbar icons with arrows have drop-down menus.

- *Check grammar and spelling.* I have previously recommended that you use your word processor's spell check before sending your AOL email or forum messages. That's no longer necessary. AOL has added both grammar and spell checking features to version 4.0. Both grammar and spelling features can be customized to your taste.

Improved Navigation and Security

In addition to a beefed-up feature set, AOL has made it easier for you to move around the service and has greatly improved online security with the following:

- *Drop-down list of recently visited online areas.* The new toolbar (shown in Figure 1.7) has an added feature: a drop-down menu that shows the last 25 areas you visited (it's sometimes called a "history menu"), including AOL's own forums and Internet sites. You no longer have to keep track of a sometimes-convoluted path to a specific forum or discussion area. AOL's software remembers it for you.

■ *Improved account security.* AOL now supports *Secure Sockets Layer (SSL)* standards for your account, so you log in, even via a separate Internet provider, under state-of-the-art security. In addition, AOL members in the United States and Canada can enjoy 128-bit SSL encryption for online transactions either via AOL's own shopping areas, or for Internet commerce—as long as the Internet server is secure too.

Coming Soon from AOL

Not all the features promised for AOL 4.0 were included in the software in time for its release, but they are promised for the near future (perhaps by the time you read this book). The following are three of the most significant features that you may expect:

■ *Instant Images.* In previous versions of AOL software, you could exchange instant messages with your online friends. You were able to select fonts and sounds to enhance the appearance of your instant message texts. For version 4.0, you have a new feature called Instant Images. You'll be able to embed pictures from your graphics library or your digital camera.

■ *AOL Talk.* You are not limited to online pictures. You'll be able to harness the power of your multimedia Mac or PC in other ways, too, such as being able to actually talk with another member while online. The AOL Talk feature enables you to transmit sounds in addition to your text.

■ *Integration with Microsoft Outlook Express.* AOL will be including Outlook Express technology in its email software. So you'll not only be able to take advantage of such features as Dynamic HTML, and an expanded Address Book, but you'll be able to use Outlook Express software to send and retrieve your AOL email.

■ *Support for Eudora.* Future versions of both the Mac and Windows versions of the Eudora email program from Qualcomm will support AOL's email system.

You need a powerful PC for multimedia

Video and sound consumes lots of CPU horsepower. AOL requires a Pentium PC for the Windows 95 version of AOL 4.0. Mac users can use an 040 Mac (such as a Quadra or Centris), but a model with a PowerPC CPU is recommended for good performance.

Quick Installation Tips

Installing the newest AOL software is almost always just a double-click away. AOL's software installers, both the Mac and Windows versions, take you through the process quickly, and the software is up and running within a few minutes. Consider the following helpful advice when you upgrade.

- *For Windows users only*. All your program settings (including modem and phone access number setups), account information, and downloaded artwork can be transferred to the new version during the installation process. Just choose the option to upgrade from the earlier version of your AOL software, which is offered when the new installation begins.

- *For Mac users only*. If you're upgrading from a previous version of the software on a Mac, you have your upgrade option after your installation is complete, when you launch the program for the first time.

- *For Mac and Windows users*. If you have experienced crashes or other problems with your old AOL software, you may prefer to do a clean installation instead. In that way, a new version of the program is installed, and nothing is carried over from the previous installation. You only need to enter your screen name and password where the new member certificate number information is requested to restore your account information to the new software version.

Don't lose your file downloads

Files you've downloaded from AOL's software libraries may not always be transferred to the new version of AOL's client software when you install it. If you intend to delete the older version of AOL's software, be sure you move the downloaded files to a new location; otherwise, you'll delete them, too. The files are generally located in the Downloads folder or directory (it's called Online Downloads in the Mac version) unless you've chosen another location in your AOL software's preferences. AOL's Windows software installer offers you the option of moving these files to the new software's directory.

Windows 3.1 Versus Windows 95—Does It Make Any Difference for AOL?

The version of AOL software described in this book is the 32-bit or Windows 95 version, which has a basic set of features and performance similar to the 16-bit Windows 3.1 version. If you are upgrading to Windows 95, you want to download and install the new version to enjoy full support for the major features of your operating system software.

AOL's Keywords: The Fastest Route from Here to There

Throughout this book, I want you to get used to some simple steps that enable you to navigate easily AOL's vast landscape via keystrokes. I often describe a particular area's location by its *key-word*, a keyboard instruction that you can specify *only* while you're connected to America Online. Keywords take you just about anywhere on America Online, even if you don't know the exact route.

To use a keyword, press ⌘-K if you're using a Macintosh or Ctrl+K for Windows. Then enter the keyword in the entry field of the Keyword dialog box (see Figure 1.8). Press Enter, and in just a few seconds you are transported to the place you want to visit. If the keyword that you enter is wrong, you see a message to that effect, and you then have the option to search some alternate keywords to see which one is correct.

Does your new software look the same as the old version?

Help! I downloaded the new AOL software, but when I logged on to AOL, I didn't see any difference. I checked and I'm still running the old version. What went wrong? Downloading an AOL software update is only half the battle. The next step is to actually install the software so that you can take advantage of the new features. Installation steps are described in Appendix A, "The First Steps to Get Online."

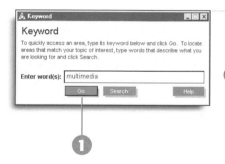

FIGURE 1.8

Use a keyword to go to a specific spot on America Online.

1 Enter your search word and click **Go**.

This book is filled with tips and tricks for making your online visits more fun and productive. In addition, many chapters contain helpful troubleshooting advice, so if you run into a problem, you can find a simple solution. America Online has its own support area, too, where you get support from both AOL's technical support staff and members.

If you run into chronic problems in getting and staying online, read Chapter 4, "Secrets of High-Speed Access on AOL," for advice on coping with such difficulties and on configuring your modem for best performance.

If you still have a problem getting connected consistently, use the keyword Help; it takes you to AOL's customer service area where you can get further assistance via an extensive list of text-based information. You also have access to an area called *Tech Live*, where you can have an online conversation with an AOL representative about your problem.

Getting the Most from Your AOL Software

Reduce online time

Discover hidden features

Secret tips and tricks

There's More to AOL's Software Than Meets the Eye

You probably don't pay a lot of attention to AOL's software. Using it is pretty simple. You log on, you visit your favorite parts of the service, and then you log off. More than likely, you tend to ignore the underlying software you've used, which can be coaxed into doing lots of cool stuff when you probe its secrets or add some enhancements. In this chapter, you see just how far you can stretch the software's boundaries to provide a superior online experience and make your visits more productive.

How to Plan Your Online Visits

Many of your online visits are, no doubt, motivated by the thrill of discovery and adventure. I'm not one to pour cold water on the fun of just hanging out and looking around. But if you take a few moments to plan where you're going and what you're going to do, you can definitely make your logins more productive and (if you still pay for AOL by the hour) save a few bucks, too.

The best way to make your online visits more fun is to have a plan of action before you log on. Decide in advance the areas you want to visit and what you want to do when you get there.

Planning online visits

1. Check your email.
2. Send previously composed email.
3. Check messages in your favorite online forum(s).
4. Respond to messages that interest you.
5. Attend an online conference featuring a famous show business figure.
6. Choose software to download, using the **Download Later** option.
7. Set an Automatic AOL session to receive files.
8. Log off.

AOL gets sluggish during prime time

The quality of AOL performance depends on the time of day you connect. In the evening prime time hours, for example, you find network traffic is high, and performance can bog down. If you want to download software, or just get through your session as quickly as possible, you may want to choose the early morning hours when fewer folks are online (unless you really want to attend a specific online event in the evening).

Getting There Faster with the Favorite Places Feature

One of the quickest ways to speed up travel around AOL is to add your favorite AOL spots (see Figure 2.1) to the list of Favorite Places. Do this by clicking the heart-shaped icon ♥ at the upper-right corner of an area's title bar, which opens a request for you to confirm where you want the area added (see Figure 2.2).

Bypassing the Favorite Places confirmation box

You can bypass a confirmation dialog box and get an area added right to your Favorite Places list by dragging the heart directly to the Favorites toolbar.

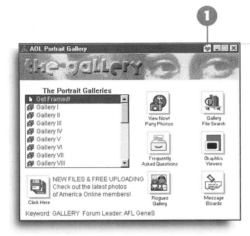

FIGURE 2.1

Click the heart-shaped icon on the right side of the title bar to add this area to your list of Favorite Places.

① Favorite Places icon

FIGURE 2.2

If you do want your Favorite Places selection added to the list, choose the third option and a sound confirms your selection (at least on the Windows AOL software).

① Add to your Favorite Places, email, or instant message.

You can open your Favorite Places directory at any time while using your AOL software by clicking the heart-shaped folder icon in the middle of the program's toolbar. After you've added an item to your personal Favorite Places listing (see Figure 2.3), you can go to a specific site by double-clicking its entry, even on Internet newsgroups and Web sites.

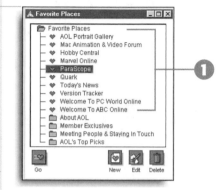

FIGURE 2.3

Your personal Favorite Places window displays the online areas you've added. You can move the selections around as you see fit by selecting and dragging an item to its new position.

 Your custom Favorite Places listing.

Use the Toolbar for Fast Access

Mess up your toolbar?

If you make a mistake in customizing your toolbar, or just want to restore it to its normal state, hold down the Ctrl key and drag the icons, one at a time, off the toolbar. The Mac version also has a toolbar preference labeled Restore Original Buttons, which puts it in its original state.

What do those icons mean?

If you forget what one of those new toolbar icons that you added means, hold the mouse cursor above the icon. You see a label indicating the area that is accessed by that icon (it's called a ToolTip).

The bottom half of your AOL program toolbar is used for navigation. Click the down arrow next to the **Go** button to bring up a list of up to 25 previously visited online areas, including Internet sites (shown in Figure 2.4).

You also can add some of these spots to the right side of the toolbar's top row. Just click a Favorite Places heart and drag it to the toolbar. Pick an icon to accompany your selection from the screen that appears, and then click the **OK** button.

Within seconds, the toolbar expands to accommodate the additional selection (up to the width of your screen). In the example shown in Figure 2.5, you see one icon added at the right side of the toolbar. Unfortunately, with a standard 800×600 PC screen, you won't be able to add those additional icons because the standard toolbar is so wide.

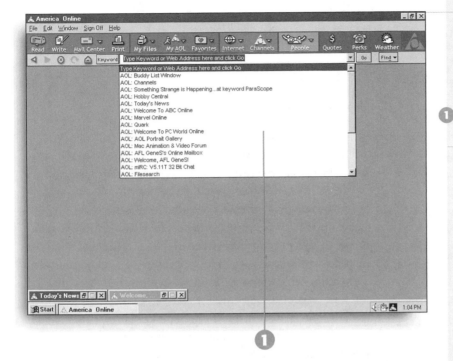

FIGURE 2.4

Whether you know the route or not, choosing a recently visited place in this drop-down menu returns you to that place—fast.

1 The drop-down menu shows the online places you visited.

FIGURE 2.5

You can easily customize the toolbar to include new selections. I added one item here, which appears at the right side.

Making Your AOL Software Work Faster

Enjoyment of your online visits can be much greater if you can get your AOL software to work better. Not every step I'm about to describe comes free; some of it involves getting new hardware. But by considering these options, you may be able to fine-tune your AOL software for the maximum possible performance on your PC. You also want to read the section following this one, "AOL Software Add-Ons," for brief descriptions of some very popular software that makes your online visits go more quickly and more efficiently.

You can speed up your AOL software by doing one or more of the following:

A final 56K standard is coming soon

As this book goes to press, it appears that a final V.pcm 56K standard had been agreed upon, incorporating elements of X2 and K56flex, which was expected to be ratified in the latter part of 1998. Before you buy a modem you want to make sure the product you purchase is eligible for a free or low-cost upgrade to the final standard. Even then, don't expect to connect at the highest possible speeds. Local phone lines sometimes prevent access at any of the higher 56K speeds, and even when they work, speeds of 40–46,000bps are often the best you can expect.

- *Get a faster modem.* America Online supports connection speeds up to 33,600 bps (V.34) in many U.S. cities. AOL is also field-testing two iterations of a proposed V.pcm 56K service (X2 and K56flex) to speed the download of Web pages and software to your computer. If you have a high-speed access number in your city, a faster modem more than pays for itself in reduced online time (and charges if you pay for hour by the hour or a toll charge for your telephone connection). It also makes your AOL software perform at a much higher level, not only for software downloads and uploads, but for text display, too. The keyword Access enables you to review the latest telephone connection numbers. (You learn more about getting the best possible performance from your modem in Chapter 4, "Secrets of High-Speed Access to AOL.")

- *Get a faster computer.* If you have more than one PC at your home or work site, installing AOL software on the fastest computer offers speedier screen redraws, faster application launching, and other performance enhancements. If you have an older model, the new low-cost Pentium PCs (or PowerPC Mac OS computers) and their extraordinary higher speed capability, can be quite attractive items to consider.

- *Get more RAM.* Viewing graphic files is RAM-intensive, and using AOL's integrated Web browser with its image-caching routine can also eat up additional memory. Computer manufacturers, striving to keep costs down, often supply the bare minimum amount of memory with their models. You may want to consider a RAM upgrade at the earliest opportunity.

- *Operating system fine-tuning.* A huge number of software products are available that are designed to add functions to the Mac and Windows operating systems, or add cute little effects—visual and sound. Some of these programs, however, may also rob your computer of the best possible performance or cause incompatibilities with other software. You should always select system enhancements with care and see whether they really do improve the way your computer runs, and not the reverse. Product reviews in your favorite computing magazine (many of which have forums on AOL) are a good resource on this subject.

AOL Software Add-Ons

AOL's own software provides an enormous degree of flexibility, enabling you to automate a number of online functions. The capability to easily include your regular online spots as part of your custom Favorite Sites listing or your program toolbar, for example, makes for fast navigation around the network. Some convenient tools are available, however, that not only provide some features missing from AOL's software, but add extraordinary power to help automate your online visits. Before you try out those tools, please consider the following:

- To locate any file in the software libraries of AOL's Computing channel, including the ones that are described in this chapter, click the **Find** button on the bottom row of your AOL toolbar and select the option to search for software. When the search window opens, enter the name or subject of your file search in the list field. A complete list of the selections that match your search appears in a few seconds. To get more information about a file and to download the file, double-click the name of a file that interests you from the listings you receive.

- Whenever a new version of AOL software is released, many of the add-on programs need to be updated as well. Although you can expect most of the ones I'm describing here are available in versions compatible with AOL 4.0, you should first check the file description for compatibility information before you try any of these products.

A popular source for AOL add-ons

You find these and other handy programs listed in the Windows AOL Add-Ons library of the Windows forum (keyword: `Windows forum`). The BPS Software products described here are also available via keyword `BPS`.

- Before downloading any of these handy Windows AOL utilities, be sure to check the file descriptions about hardware and software needs. Some of these programs require that you install Visual Basic Runtime Version 3.0, a free program available in AOL's software libraries, which can be located using the File Search tool.

- Although the programs described in this chapter are very popular with users of the Windows version of AOL software, they are not officially supported or endorsed by America Online, Inc. You are therefore using such software at your own risk. Should you have any problems in using this software, your best resources for support are the publishers or authors of the programs. AOL forum staff routinely checks all files for the presence of computer viruses before posting, but installing current virus protection software is a good idea as well.

In the next few pages, I cover a few of the most popular Windows AOL add-ons. Unfortunately, the programs have not been made available in Mac versions. But Mac users don't despair. You have other options to enhance your online visits, such as handy commercial macro utilities from Affinity Microsystems (Tempo II Plus), CE Software (QuicKeys), and WestCode Software (OneClick). These products can enhance just about any Mac program, and they're available from many software dealers.

SEE ALSO

➤ *Finding and downloading software, see page 437*

PICPOP

Author: Compunik Creations

This is a shareware program that adds exciting multimedia possibilities to your online visits. It works with your email, instant messages, message board postings, and chat room postings. After it's installed, type the following in the material you send:

```
{p picfile soundfile}
```

Does your friend have problems using PICPOP sounds and pictures?

To see the pictures and hear the sounds, your recipient also has to have a copy of PICPOP installed, along with the corresponding picture and sound files.

(*picfile* refers to the name of your picture file, and *soundfile* refers to the name of your sound file.) When the recipient opens this material, a picture pops up on the recipient's screen, and a sound plays. The program supports BMP and GIF image file formats and the WAV sound format.

You change the default sounds of Windows AOL just like you change any other sound association: through the Sounds Control Panel.

SWEETALK

Author: Compunik Creations

SWEETALK (see Figure 2.6) attaches fixed sounds and images to your online messages, but this program goes one step further. The authors tell me that this shareware program is dedicated to online romantics. It offers the following features:

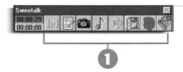

FIGURE 2.6

SWEETALK puts up a movable button bar that can be used to access its features.

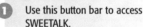 Use this button bar to access SWEETALK.

- When SWEETALK is started (or closed), Windows AOL automatically opens and closes, too.

- SWEETALK enables you to send a sound (or a WAV) to say sweet stuff to your online friend or sweetheart (male or female equally implied).

- SWEETALK enables you to send phrases (sweet nothings) up to 1,000 characters without typing them.

- SWEETALK saves that special email or posted message to a file with the click of a button.

- When you go online, clicking a button called Who's-On-First very quickly indicates whether your friends are online and where. Then a couple of clicks enable you to send

Instant Messages to the ones that are online. This feature bears more than a passing resemblance to AOL's own Buddy List.

- For those times when someone is sending you not-so-sweet instant messages (IMs), you have a virtual switch that automatically turns IMs off and on.

- SWEETALK also offers meters that display how long you have been sweet-talking in the pay areas and free areas of AOL. This is a useful feature if you pay for AOL by the hour.

- SWEETALK gives you a convenient scrollable list of sounds and phrases.

PowerTools for AOL

Author: BPS SoftWare

By far, the most popular AOL add-on is probably PowerTools. More than 110,000 AOL members have downloaded various versions of this shareware program as of the time this book was being prepared. The program offers a set of very powerful enhancements for AOL's program (see Figure 2.7). The major features include a colorized chat room, a macro "phrase" manager, an instant answering machine, and a wide array of other tools. The product's Control Panel attaches to the bottom of your AOL window and provides buttons and controls for many common and special tasks. A wide variety of add-on modules greatly increases the program's flexibility.

FIGURE 2.7

When you install PowerTools, the entire look and feel of your AOL software undergoes many changes, typified by the new expanded toolbar functions shown here.

1 PowerTools adds a custom toolbar to your AOL software.

The following are some of the major features of this program:

- PowerTools gives you many options with which to customize both its own toolbars and AOL's.

- A Hotlist Manager replaces AOL's Favorite Places feature and enables you to store additional locations to revisit, such as your favorite People Connection rooms, FTP sites, and more.

- The Status bar's screen name panel features a pop-up menu to enable the user to quickly switch screen names, while online or offline. To get the pop-up menu, right click your screen name on the right side of the Status bar.

- PowerTools replaces AOL's chat room window with its own Color Chat window, which enables you to assign colors for member names, extract chat text by member name, and enhance your logging options.

- PowerTools incorporates a **Get In** button that keeps trying to enter a crowded chat room until someone leaves, enabling you to automatically enter.

- You can establish a library of standard text phrases, organize them by category, and use the program's Phrase Manager to play them as you like. You can even insert variables within your stored phrases, so phrases can be linked. The phrases can be sent as part of your email, instant messages, or message board postings.

- An IM Manager can be configured to return instant messages with preselected phrases, arrange IM windows neatly on your desktop, selectively ignore messages, and log the messages to a file complete with your comments.

- Additional features enable you to manage your text messages, send WAV files from a pop-up list, and keep an accurate billing log of your online sessions that covers all screen names so that you can keep precise records of your accumulated online time.

PowerTools has enhancements for just about everything you do online (and perhaps many of the things you only imagined doing more efficiently). Because it is shareware, you can try it before you buy—and it may become an indispensable tool for you.

Whale Express

Author: Bill Pytlovany (Tartan Software)

Whale Express is a scripting utility that enables you to create automatic routines to sign-on, sign-off, retrieve and send email, send and capture text and posts, and more. The version posted on AOL is a trial version that enables you to store up to 10 commands. When you download Whale Express, you find ordering information in the README file.

Whale Express comes with sample scripts and Windows-based help that assists you in writing powerful online scripts (something like a small program) to automate your AOL visit. Even capturing email from multiple screen names is possible with the NewScreenName command.

Email can be created while you are offline using the Whale Express integrated editor, and sent via the SendMail script command. Online lectures can be prepared and reused over and over using the SendText command. Entire message boards can now be read and captured in a text file with the intelligent ReadList command.

The scripting language is easy to understand and requires no knowledge of complex programming structure. Error handling and calling other scripts can all be done with simple commands.

Windows Keyboard Power

Even if you haven't enhanced your capability to navigate through AOL's software with some of the handy macro utilities I discussed in this chapter, a good basic set of keyboard commands is available that you should keep in mind.

AOL for OS/2 and NT?

If you're a user of OS/2 or Windows NT, you might be hoping that a version of America Online's software specifically tailored for these workstation class operating systems might come some day. It isn't something for which you should hold your breath, however. Although, as I explain in Chapter 25, "Visiting the Computing Channel," very active forums do indeed cater to both operating systems on AOL, and they had to get online somehow to write about it. When you check those areas, you discover tips and tricks on getting the existing versions of AOL software to run with those operating systems. (It's not always easy, but it can be done.)

Table 2.1 is a list of many of the keyboard shortcuts available
with your America Online Windows software. They are based
on the version of AOL software available at the time this book
was written. Future software versions may offer additional shortcuts.

TABLE 2.1 **Keyboard shortcuts for windows**

Function	Keyboard Shortcut
Cancel an action	Esc
Cascade windows	Shift+F5
Check spelling	Ctrl+=
Close a window	Ctrl+F4
Compose mail	Ctrl+M
Copy	Ctrl+C
Cut	Ctrl+X
Find in Top Window	Ctrl+F
Get member profile	Ctrl+G
Keyword (go to)	Ctrl+K
Locate a member online	Ctrl+L
Move to next button	Tab
Move to next window	Ctrl+F6
Move to previous button	Shift+Tab
My Shortcuts menu	Ctrl+1 through Ctrl+0
Open a new text file	Ctrl+N
Open an existing file	Ctrl+O
Open Keyword window	Ctrl+K
Open Mail window	Ctrl+M
Paste	Ctrl+V
Print Document	Ctrl+P
Read mail	Ctrl+R

continues…

TABLE 2.1 **Continued**

Function	Keyboard Shortcut
Save a file	Ctrl+S
Scroll down a page	Page Down
Scroll up a page	Page Up
Send an instant message	Ctrl+I
Send instant message or email	Ctrl+Enter
Tile windows	Shift+F4
Undo action	Ctrl+Z

Mac Keyboard Power

On a Mac, you can enhance your online shortcuts with two convenient macro programs, QuicKeys from CE Software and Tempo II Plus from Affinity Microsystems. Another program, OneClick, from WestCode Software, puts your shortcuts on a custom toolbar.

Table 2.2 lists many of the keyboard shortcuts available with your America Online Macintosh software. They are based on AOL version 4.0, which became available at the time this book was written. Future versions may offer additional shortcuts.

TABLE 2.2 **Macintosh keyboard shortcuts**

Function	Keyboard Shortcut
AOL guide	⌘-?
Add to Favorite Places	⌘-+
Bold	⌘-B
Check spelling	⌘-=
Close window	⌘-W
Compose mail	⌘-M
Copy	⌘-C

Function	Keyboard Shortcut
Cut	⌘-X
Find (People, Places or Things)	⌘-F
Get member's profile	⌘-G
Locate a member online	⌘-L
Move to next entry field	Tab
New memo	⌘-N
Open an existing file	⌘-O
Open keyword window	⌘-K
Paste	⌘-V
Paste as quotation	⌘-Option-V
Plain text	⌘-T
Print	⌘-P
Quit application	⌘-Q
Read new mail	⌘-R
Save a file	⌘-S
Send an instant message	⌘-I
Speak Text	⌘-H
Stop Speaking	⌘-.
Underline text	⌘-Underline
Undo	⌘-Z

Teach Yourself: Secrets of the Right Mouse Button

AOL's software provides full support for that other mouse key that you may not use very often. When you click the message window of an email form, new memo form, or message board window, the right mouse button offers a new set of options (see Figure 2.8).

Right mouse buttons: The Mac user's alternative

Mac users need not feel cheated from a context-sensitive menu. If you're using Mac OS 8 or 8.1, you can take advantage of Apple's Contextual Menus feature, which pops up a menu when you Control-click an item that supports the feature. AOL offers a wide variety of Contextual Menus when you access different features of the software. In addition, AOL's software libraries include many freeware and shareware enhancements to this feature.

FIGURE 2.8

The right mouse button is fully supported by your AOL software.

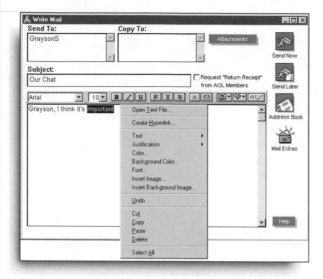

Right mouse button limits

If you select text that cannot be edited, such as in a forum information screen or posted message, your right mouse button options are limited to the standard Edit menu selection and copying commands.

You might notice in Figure 2.8 that many of the same text editing functions available in your AOL formatting toolbar are accessible via the right mouse button. It's up to you to decide which is easier to use. Such commands as **Open Text File**, **Create HyperLink**, **Font**, **Image**, and **Background Image**, open a dialog box with further choices. The **Text** and **Justification** commands have submenus with additional options.

Tips and Tricks from AOL Users

Before you try out those tips

The following tips mostly apply to both the Mac and Windows versions of AOL software. If they're platform-specific, it is noted at the beginning of the tip. I should also point out that because AOL software is often upgraded and online areas are nearly as often changed, I cannot guarantee that each and every tip works as presented in all instances.

The best source for ways to make AOL software run better and the coolest places to visit come from your fellow AOL members. When preparing this book, I put out a call far and wide for the favorite tips from my online friends and other active, savvy AOL members. I'm especially grateful to Jonathan Bird, an AOL Community Leader who works in AOL's Upgrade support area, for helping me to compile some of the most useful information that's included in this section.

- *AOL in the news tip.* It seems that hardly a day passes without a news item about AOL. Whether it's a new feature, an email outage, or the latest AOL financial statement, you find the news at keyword Press.

- *AOL network status tip.* Why is the chat room not working? Is there a reason some of your access numbers won't connect? You find the latest list of access numbers, new features, and the status of AOL's regular online maintenance program via the keyword AOL Insider.

- *AOL software upgrade tip.* AOL software upgrades are always available via keyword Upgrade. If you're not on AOL at the time and accessing the Internet via another Internet provider, you can also find current AOL software by pointing your Web browser to ftp://ftp.aol.com or to http://www.aol.com.

- *AOL Web page tip.* Your AOL Web page can include both Web links and links to your favorite areas on AOL. Your Personal Publisher Web creation form (as described in Chapter 18, "Become a Web Publisher on AOL") tells you how.

- *AOL's helping hand.* Not sure where to click your mouse? Look for your mouse cursor to change into a "helping hand," and click that spot. That's the key that the area you want is just one click away.

- *Chat room tip.* Can't stay in front of your computer to see the online conference you wanted to attend? No problem— choose **Log Manager** from the My Files toolbar's drop-down menu and open a chat room log. All the text from the chat is captured to a text file that you can view later.

- *Chat room tip.* If another member is annoying you with offensive chat room text, just double-click the member's name in the People Here window and check the **Ignore** option from the screen that appears. You won't be bothered by that member's chat text for as long as you remain in that chat room.

- *Chat room tip*. See someone in a chat room you want to meet? Well, double-click his or her name in the **People Here** window in the chat room screen. Click **Get Profile** to see his or her profile, and click **Send Message** to send an instant message.

- *Child's access tip*. You can easily customize your child's AOL user experience. First, connect to AOL using the screen name you used when you first joined the service—the one at the very top of the drop-down list of screen names on your Sign On screen (it's also known as your *master account*). Then choose **Parental Controls** from the My AOL toolbar's drop-down menu and select the screen name of the member for whom you want to change user settings. (You find more information about this feature in Chapter 7, "Parental Issues and Internet Access.")

- *Computing tip*. If you have a problem using your PC, use the keyword Help Desk to access AOL's Computing & Software assistance forum.

- *Cool Mac keyword*. Try this one. Use the keyword: aol://4344:378.aollink.5856596.543718745. (Hint: This keyword takes you to an area where you can learn more about using AOL Link—the system extension used to link AOL's Mac software with its Web browser and other Internet software.)

- *Cool Mac tip*. Drag a Favorite Place heart to your Mac's desktop or to a folder. When you double-click it, AOL launches if it's not yet running; you're signed on automatically and go right to the area you clicked. Just remember that you need to store your password in your AOL software to use this tip.

- *Cool Mac tip*. One fast way to download a file attached to your email is to click and drag the file listed from your email form to the desktop or a folder on the desktop.

- *Email tip*. To add a person's name to your AOL Address Book, double-click the underlined name to open a new mail form addressed to that person. *To use this feature, you must set your AOL Mail preferences to show addresses as hyperlinks (available only in the Windows version when this book was written).*

- *Family member access tip.* You can add up to four additional screen names to your online account. This feature enables you to give your other family members their own online identity. To create a new screen name, log on using your master account name (the one at the very top of the drop-down menu of screen names). Use the keyword Names to open the options to create or delete additional names on your account. You can also use the keyword Parental Controls to customize access and offer the safest possible online experience for your kids.

- *Fast stock quotes tip.* Learn how your stock portfolio is doing, or how your company is faring on the market. Use the keyword Quotes to access that information, along with profiles of a company in which you might want to invest.

- *Find a member tip.* If you want to see whether your friend is an AOL member, choose **Member Directory** from **Members** menu. You can search for your friend by his or her real name. (This feature only works if your friend has created an AOL member profile.)

- *Graphic viewing tip.* You can open and view image files created in GIF and JPEG format. In addition, Windows users can open BMP files, and Mac users PICT files with AOL's software. If you have files that cannot be read by AOL software, use the keyword Viewers to access a library where you can get other graphic viewing software.

- *Hobby help tip.* Having trouble rebuilding that old furniture or fixing up an old car? Use AOL's Hobby Central channel to find a forum where you can get assistance. The keyword is Hobby.

- *Instant Internet access tip.* When you want to open AOL's Web browser, click the globe-shaped icon on the program's toolbar and select **Go to the Web** from the drop-down menu, or type the keyword www. In seconds, you access

AOL's home page on the World Wide Web and you're ready to surf the Net.

- *Instant message tip.* Are you busy online, and you don't want to talk to a friend or stranger? You can turn off the instant message feature by sending a message to $im_off. (You have to type something in the message field—a single letter works.) If you want to restore your instant messages, send a message to $im_on. (again with at least a single letter in the message field). Your instant message feature is also reset to its normal state by logging off AOL. You also can customize the capability to receive instant message preferences by using the **Privacy Preferences** option in your Buddy List setup box.

- *Internet email trick.* If you access the Net via a third-party Web browser, such as Netscape, you can still use the automatic email tags. Just enter compuserve.com as your SMTP mail server in your browser preferences (sorry about that, CompuServe). Just be sure you include your AOL address in the **Reply To** field.

- *Internet searching tip.* To search the Internet, use the keyword NetFind, which opens AOL's handy Internet search tool.

- *Live conference tip.* Is your favorite author, show business figure, or politician appearing on AOL? Find out from the AOL Live conference center. The keyword is Live.

- *New feature tip.* AOL is always adding new or improved features to the service. For the rundown, use the keyword New.

- *Online assistance tip.* If you have a problem with your AOL software, or your latest bill, use the keyword Help to get assistance from AOL's Member Services area.

- *Private chat room trick.* You can send a hyperlink for a private chat room that hasn't been created yet. Create a Favorite Place link entered as aol:2719:2-2<name of room here>. This tip is especially useful if you're inviting your online friends to a future meeting and haven't created the room yet. (But remember to try to use a name unique enough so that someone else will not duplicate it by accident.)

- *Safe computing tip*. AOL's staff never asks you for your online password or credit card number. So even if you get a message from someone claiming to work for AOL, don't answer it. Use the keyword `Notify AOL` to open a screen where you can report the offender.

- *Safe computing tip*. Although AOL's software is checked for viruses, the same cannot be said about files you download from Internet sources. Use virus software to check those files before you use them. *(And don't download files sent by people you do not know.)*

- *Software download tip*. If you don't have time to finish a software download right now, you can resume it later. Click the **Finish Later** button in the download progress window. You can resume the download later by choosing **Download Manager** from the **My Files** submenu and clicking the **Download** button. (Just remember: Don't delete or move the partially downloaded file until the download is complete.)

- *Your AOL Internet address*. You already have an Internet address. It consists of your screen name and `@aol.com`. So, for example, my AOL screen name is `Gene`, and my Internet address (the very same one I use on my business cards) is `gene@aol.com`. If you need to insert a space in an Internet address, use an underscore instead (_).

SEE ALSO

➤ *For detailed information about the services AOL has to offer, see page 72*

➤ *AOL's support forums and common software problems, see page 101*

➤ *For more information about children using AOL, see page 116*

➤ *For more information about AOL's software, see page 509*

Connecting to AOL

Getting Ready to Take AOL on the Road

Ordinarily, connecting to AOL is a pretty cut and dried process. When you first join the service, you choose from a selection of connection numbers, perhaps make a modem setting or two, and continue to enjoy your online experience. But if you travel a lot, or jumble online connections between home and office, you find you need to do more to ensure the best possible performance from AOL.

How to Find Local Access Numbers

Online services are quite competitive. And AOL jumped right into the fray when it went with unlimited pricing. But even if your AOL bill isn't getting any higher when you spend extra time online, you may be paying extra charges to your phone company when you dial up AOL, if you happen to dial a long-distance exchange or their 800 or 888 numbers.

Although not every location in the United States has a local access number, most do, and those are the ones you want to use. In addition, through AOL's GlobalNet access network, you can hook up to America Online in other parts of the world.

Teach Yourself: Getting that New Local Number

If the numbers aren't already available

AOL usually stores a database of its available phone numbers on your computer's drive. If the file becomes unreadable or need to be updated, AOL has to dial in to its access center (a toll-free number in the USA) to retrieve the latest listing, which may take a few minutes to complete. If AOL cannot locate a number for the area you select, you see a screen and are given the chance to choose another area code or country.

In the latest releases of America Online's Mac and Windows software, you can find a local access number not only while you're online or when you're first configuring your America Online software (see Appendix B, "Setting Up AOL's Software"), but anytime you find yourself wanting to call America Online from a location where you are not certain of your local access number.

If you have not already done so, open the America Online program. You want to make a new Location setting for each city or area code for which you're choosing numbers.

Selecting a new access number is easy

1. Open your AOL software and click the **Setup** button.

2. Click the **Add Location** button, which opens the screen shown in Figure 3.1.

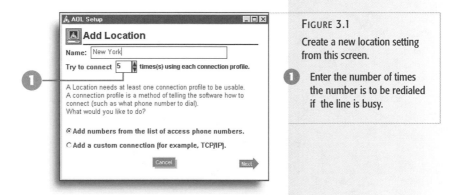

FIGURE 3.1

Create a new location setting from this screen.

① Enter the number of times the number is to be redialed if the line is busy.

3. Name your Location setting. You probably want to enter the city for which the numbers apply, as I did in Figure 3.1.

4. Click the **Next** button (see Figure 3.2) to search AOL's list of access numbers.

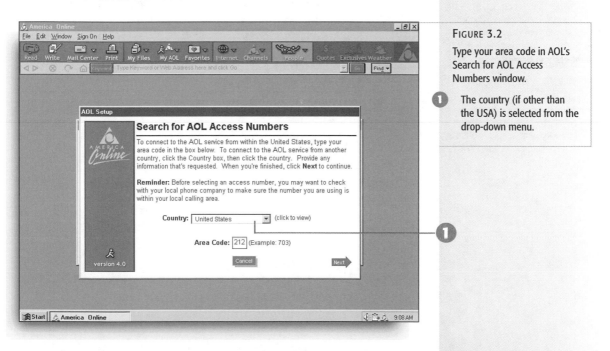

FIGURE 3.2

Type your area code in AOL's Search for AOL Access Numbers window.

① The country (if other than the USA) is selected from the drop-down menu.

5. On the Search for AOL Access Numbers screen, enter the area code or Country for which you want a number. (You have to call the phone company if you don't know the area code.) Then click the **Next** button to bring up the list of available numbers (see Figure 3.3).

FIGURE 3.3

Choose from the list of AOL access numbers in the **AOL access phone numbers** area.

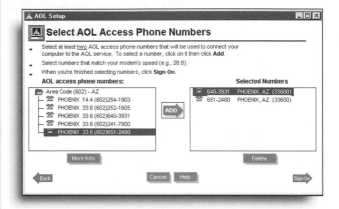

Changing locations is easy

You can switch the Location to which your selected numbers apply by clicking the drop-down menu under the item labeled **Selected numbers will be added to**.

Create separate Location setups for each city

Before you take your laptop computer on a trip, you want to create a separate Location profile for each city you're planning to visit.

6. Click a number once to select it, and then click the **Add** button, which puts the number on the right side of the screen. Be sure to okay the acknowledgment screen that appears next.

7. Repeat this process for each phone number that you want to select.

8. To remove a number, select it from the list on the right and click **Remove**.

9. Click **Done** to complete the process and store your new access numbers in your copy of AOL's software.

SEE ALSO

➤ *Adapting AOL's software to your new modem, see page 52*

How to Find Numbers When You're Already Signed On

Great! You like to plan ahead, which is better than a last-minute scramble to take care of forgotten details. If you're already online and want to find local access numbers, enter the keyword Access. You then are quickly taken to an online area that contains a database of all the access phone numbers that you could ever need while on your worldwide excursions (see Figure. 3.4).

FIGURE 3.4

Use America Online's **Search Access Numbers** feature to find a local connection.

1 Click **Search Access Numbers**.

These numbers are generally considered local telephone calls from most cities and do not incur toll charges from most residential telephones. If the nearest access number is not a local call, your local telephone service adds the per-minute charges to your phone bill. These charges are separate from the America Online connect time charges that apply if you're still paying for access by the hour. You might want to call the phone company in the city you're visiting to learn what toll charges you might incur. This may be important if you're connecting from a hotel, where you may be charged an extra fee for long-distance access.

After you arrive at the Accessing America Online screen, click the **Search Access Numbers** item, and press Return or Enter on your keyboard to open the Search Access Numbers screen (see Figure. 3.5).

FIGURE 3.5

The Search Access Numbers screen enables you to check for the latest available AOL numbers while you're online.

1 Enter the area code or city here.

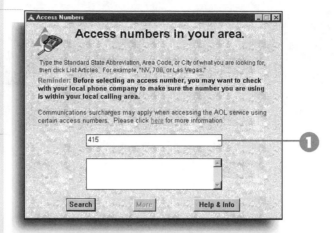

If you don't know the area code

You can find the area code for your city at keyword **Phone Book**.

One is never enough

You might want to get more than one number, just in case the primary number you try is busy for some reason. Using the steps described earlier in this chapter, you can easily add phone numbers to any Location setup you created.

A text entry field, which is the smaller of the two panes in the window, is set up for you to enter the location or area code from which you are calling.

America Online has arranged the telephone number database into a collection of searchable documents arranged by area code. Entering the area code from which you're calling is the fastest way to locate a nearby access number. In Figure 3.5, 415 has been entered as the area code from which to connect to America Online. Click the **Search** button or press Return or Enter to display a list of search documents for you to check. Double-click an entry to see the list of numbers (see Figure 3.6).

FIGURE 3.6

Double-click the search result to see the results of your quest for a list of access numbers.

1 Double-click the title to see the list.

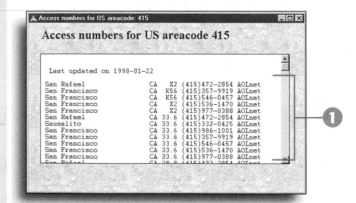

If you want to view the numbers, double-click the title to open a window containing the actual list of telephone numbers and the cities in which they are located. The listing shows the highest speed supported by the number and whether either of the two 56K high-speed protocols, K56flex or X2, are supported. (I'll tell you more about 56K in the next chapter.)

Getting Ready for the Road

Taking everything that you need for efficient computing with you on a trip is clearly difficult, if not impossible. Later in this chapter, in the section "Hard-Won Tips for Computing on the Road," I describe some of the essential preparations you should make when you pack your bag. The important watchword in personal computing, though, is backup. You should back up all your critical documents on another disk, if possible. That way, if your computer breaks down or your hard drive fails for some reason, you have another copy of your document on which to work.

Having an extra drive or two on the road isn't always practical, but America Online gives you a convenient outlet to back up your most important work—the service's email feature. Attach any file on which you work to a piece of America Online email (see Chapter 9, "Using AOL's EMail"), and send it to yourself. The file will be waiting safely in your America Online mailbox when you arrive home. It waits up to one month for your arrival (after a month, or when you have received 550 emails, older email is automatically deleted from your online mailbox).

America Online and Cellular Phones

They are found all over the countryside. Cellular telephones are used by millions of people on the road to stay in touch with the office or home. Almost every part of the country can support cellular connections. Sometimes you travel to places where no telephone line is handy, but you still need to stay in touch. You may want to consider attaching a modem to your cellular

AOL's 800 and 888 numbers are not free

An extra charge is incurred for using AOL's 800 and 888 phone number, some AOL numbers in Canada, and AOL's GlobalNet service in other parts of the world. Check the updated rates shown in the Access area before using any of these numbers so that you won't see any unexpected surprises added to your AOL bill. At the time this book was written, 800 and 888 access resulted in a surcharge of $6.00 per hour (or 10 cents per minute—or a fraction thereof).

You can search numbers by city name too

You also can search for an access number by typing a city name, the communications carrier (AOLNet, GlobalNet or SprintNet), or even the first three digits of the telephone number. You want to try to use an AOLNet number where possible in the USA, as they're the only ones to provide 33,600bps and 56,000bps access.

A cool way to back up your files

If you plan a long trip, you may want to create a second screen name to access this backup email. Then send the backup files to the other screen name so that you're not disturbed by extra "You've Got Mail" notices. (I'll tell you how to add new names to your account in Chapter 8, "AOL's People Connection.")

Calling from a plane

You'll encounter similar problems to cellular phones if you hook up your computer's modem to an airborne phone, such as an AirPhone (in addition to facing those hefty per-minute charges).

Get rid of those extra "You've Got Mail" notices

To avoid getting a `Mail Waiting` notice every time you log on while on vacation, you can create an alternate screen name and have mail you don't want to read right away addressed to your alternate screen name.

telephone so that you can connect to your favorite online service—America Online. Unfortunately, cellular phones, although quite reliable in regular use, present unique problems in maintaining stable connections.

Connecting Your Modem to a Cellular Telephone

The important thing to realize is that, although the technology behind them is truly a wonderful achievement, cellular telephone connections aren't nearly as stable as your regular home telephone. As you travel from place to place, the signal from your telephone is passed off from one cellular center to another. The quality of the signal can vary as you drive past tall buildings and hills. To cope with this occurrence, Microcom, a developer of the technology for modem error correction schemes, has a more robust error correction protocol, MNP-10 (or cellular), that's supported by some modems. The manual for your modem should indicate whether this compression scheme is supported.

A modem that doesn't have MNP-10 most likely works, but at reduced efficiency. You also need an interface of some sort to hook up directly to a cellular telephone. For example, Global Village, a manufacturer of popular Mac and PC modems, has a product that is designed to provide improved cellular connections. Called the PowerPort Coupler, this product is a base to which you can attach the headset of your cellular phone (or even a pay phone). The other end hooks into your laptop's modem. This acoustic coupler promises reliable transmissions at up to 9,600bps.

Many PC-card modems include support for MNP-10 (or cellular protocol). If you have a PC laptop or a recent Macintosh PowerBook computer (or a similar model), you may want to check into one of these products. Two manufacturers of cellular-compatible, high-speed modems are Apex and Megahertz (a division of U.S. Robotics). Many PC-card modems designed for a PC work on a Mac that supports this interface, although you may need different software. Check with the manufacturer about compatibility issues.

Wireless Modems

One solution to this dilemma is the arrival of devices that incorporate a cellular telephone and a modem—wireless modems. Manufacturers such as Motorola have introduced these units that, although presenting the utmost in convenience while traveling, are higher priced than a separate phone and modem.

Yet another type of wireless modem, one that operates similarly to your stereo or TV's remote control, includes a transmission/receiving device that attaches to your standard phone line (or even the modem jack on a cellular phone) and to a convenient AC outlet. The modem itself looks similar to a regular PC-card modem but has a small rectangular module attached to it that exchanges signals with the device that's hooked up to your phone line.

Hard-Won Tips for Computing on the Road

I know that business trips sometimes come on short notice, and you don't have much time to plan in advance. If, however, you take a few moments to assemble your computing equipment and add a few extras, your mobile personal computing experience and your visits to America Online are fast, efficient, and relatively trouble-free. A few ideas follow to make computing on the road easier.

When you book your hotel reservation, it is a good idea to ask if the phones in the rooms have a data port—a euphemism for a modem line. Some hotel phones still do not have such a connection, although just about all those in the larger cities do. If the room doesn't have a modem connection but it has a standard modular (RJ-11) phone plug, you can disconnect that plug from the telephone and attach it directly to your modem (I've done it often).

The important part is to double-check to see whether the hotel is using a PBX (digital) telephone system. A PBX system provides state-of-the-art service (and many automatic dialing

Hotels don't have call waiting

If you experience sudden disconnections while you're online, it may be because someone is trying to reach you on the hotel phone. Before beginning your AOL session, you may want to ask the hotel operator to hold your calls (if possible) until you're done to avoid this problem. Some hotels, fortunately, offer a second line for modem connections.

options), but it's also a serious problem for an analog telephone device, such as your computer's modem. Hooking up your modem to a PBX line may damage the modem. If the hotel uses a PBX installation, contact the manufacturer of your modem to find out whether they have a special interface card or module for use with such services. Global Village Corporation has such an interface available; the device is designed for use with their modems, but may work with other models, too, on both a Mac and a PC. Another product you might consider is the Data-Dapter from Konexx, which is designed to work with any modem.

A final bit of advice: Some hotels exact a large surcharge for telephone calls that you make from your room (even local calls in many cases). You may find, after your arrival, that another access number for America Online runs up a lower surcharge. At the very least, you may want to be more careful about the amount of time you spend online if the hotel adds a per-minute charge for your call.

Before leaving on a trip, you probably want to get some useful accessories that are bound to make your laptop computer work more effectively on the road.

Modem—Internal or External?

Many modems work on both Macs and PCs

External modems generally work on both a Macintosh or a PC. The only difference is the modem cable and the software. However, internal modems (except for PC-card models) are usually designed to support a specific computing platform or model. Make sure a modem is fully compatible with your laptop before you purchase it.

If you're buying a new laptop computer, you may want to consider the convenience of having it equipped with an internal modem. Although it may cost a few bucks extra, you don't need to pack an extra device in your storage case. Because America Online is adding 33,600bps (V.34) and new 56,000bps connection numbers throughout the country, consider a high-speed modem. It will also help you save money because your online sessions will be shorter, and, if you connect with a long-distance call or with a cellular phone, your phone bills also will be reduced.

Digital Phone Switch

One of the manufacturers of Macintosh PowerBook modems, Global Village, offers a phone switch that provides an interface between a PBX digital phone system and your laptop's modem. It works on any Mac or PC.

Connecting Overseas

Many laptops provide power adapters that work in both North America and most European countries. And the larger European cities do provide the same sort of flexible access to a modem jack that's offered in many USA hotels.

But when you travel to the far-flung corners of the world, you'll find that things aren't always so easy. Consider the following:

- Check with the hotel or your travel agent about power requirements in the cities that you intend to visit. You may need a special power adapter to be compatible, although it's true that many laptops have power adapters that handle the 220 volt connections that you often find overseas. I won't begin to suggest what one does in the jungle, other than to have a lot of batteries around and maybe access to a power generator.

- If you don't have a phone jack in your room, you may need to have the hotel wire one to its phone line at an extra charge. If the hotel isn't able to help, you may try a product called WorldPak, which consists of a set of 37 adapters for various phone jack configurations. Call Magellan's at 805-568-5400 for more information. Last I heard this product carried a $495 price tag for the whole set, but individual adapters are also available.

- If a phone jack doesn't succeed, you may have to resort to the technique used to attach your modem to a phone in the early days of personal computers—an acoustic coupler. You can find one for $150 (the price set when this book was written) from TeleAdapt at 408-370-5105.

Don't worry about airport x-rays

Although computer makers generally suggest caution when running your laptop computer and disks through the x-ray devices at an airport security check-in, the chances are almost nonexistent that you would be at risk of damage to your data (I've done it for years without any trouble). If in doubt, insist on a manual inspection. Some laptops, such as the Macintosh PowerBook, can be placed in an idle or sleep mode, rather than shut off so that it can be quickly activated for the benefit of skeptical airport security personnel.

Even with all this expensive gear, don't be surprised if you just
cannot get a satisfactory connection in some far-flung corners of
the world. Sometimes you may have to learn to survive for a
while without your online access (as hard as that may seem).

Backup Drives

Having a backup of your important files travel with you is a sure
protection in case something happens back at your home or at
the office to damage your computer. And it also gives you quick
access to the files you need. You may want to consider one of the
popular removable drives, such as Iomega's Jaz or Zip, or
SyQuest's SyJet. Later model Apple PowerBook and PC laptops
have expansion bay slots that support a wide range of drives,
such as the Zip100 Drive from VST Technologies Incorporated.
One important benefit is that such a drive can be put inside your
laptop, and you don't need accessory power adapters or batteries
to use it.

SEE ALSO

➤ *Meeting AOL members, see page 139*

➤ *AOL's email, see page 158*

➤ *Navigating message boards, post messages, and searching for responses, see page 206*

➤ *Planning trips, see page 472*

Secrets of High-Speed
Access to AOL

Secrets of ultra-fast performance

K56flex, x2, and beyond

How to set up your modem for best performance

Silence that modem

If the squawking and squealing sounds your modem makes when it is connecting disturbs you or others, you can turn the noise off by entering an M0 (that's always a zero) in your modem setup string. If you just want to make the sounds lower, check your modem manual.

Is the modem compatible?

A high-speed modem sends data at a greater speed through your computer's serial port. Although 14,400bps modems work okay on most recent Macs and PCs, you might want to contact the modem manufacturer about compatibility of its higher speed external models with your computer. Some older personal computers might need expansion cards to support the higher connection speeds without losing data or disconnecting.

AOL performance got you down?

As AOL continues to grow at an incredible rate, you might find performance slow, or connections difficult, from 8 P.M. until midnight. Schedule long online visits early in the morning or before dinner.

Making Sense of Modem Technology

Unless you have signed up with a regular Internet provider, and have connected to AOL through TCP/IP (as described in Chapter 12, "Using AOL's Internet Services"), you will log on to AOL in the same way I do. You'll need your personal computer, a telephone line, and a little box with some flashing lights, known as a modem, to connect to AOL's huge network and to send and receive data. (Sometimes that little box is located inside your computer, but what it does is still the same.)

The little box that squawks and squeaks when you connect to another telephone line is the gateway to a vast world. It not only affords you access to America Online but, through that service, opens a direct gateway to a huge, seemingly intangible body known as the *Internet*.

Increasing Connection Speeds

When America Online first appeared on the scene, the fastest connection speed available was 2,400bps (you'll read more about what that means later in this chapter). Just as computers have become cheaper and more powerful, the same holds true for modems. Today, modems that support 14,400bps are commonly available for less than $50, and models offering 28,800bps and 33,600bps (V.34) can be had for prices beginning at less than $100. In addition, the next generation of 56,000bps modems, now appearing on the landscape, are priced only slightly above the regular V.34 versions (and some V.34 units are eligible for free or low-cost upgrades to the higher speed).

To provide improved service to its members, America Online has established *AOLNet*, a high-speed fiber-optic access network that supports modem speeds of up to 56,000bps in many U.S. cities and, via the GlobalNet network, in major cities around the world. To find out whether your city has such an access number, use the keyword Access to examine the latest listing. If an AOLNet number isn't available in your city yet, you may find other high-speed options, such as 14,400bps.

I cover more details about changing modem access numbers in Chapter 3, "Connecting to AOL."

For a faster connection to AOL, you need:

- *A faster modem*. Modem technology has advanced to the point where the fastest modems are very affordable now. And they more than pay for themselves in performance and convenience.

- *A faster connection number*. Use the keyword Access to locate a higher speed connection number to AOL while you're online. You'll read more about changing AOL connection numbers in Chapter 3.

- *An updated modem profile*. AOL is always working with modem manufacturers to find ways to make your modem work faster and more efficiently. Use the keyword Modem to reach AOL's Modems & Connections support area for the latest modem files and advice on how to get the best possible performance from your modem.

The Sad Facts of High-Speed Hookups

Even the best 33,600bps modems have difficulty achieving consistent high-speed connections. In general, most phone lines in the United States seem capable of supporting at least 21,600bps. Many more work at 24,000bps. Many newer systems complete calls at 26,400 or even 28,800bps. If you find connections more consistent at the lower end of the spectrum, however, you can try the following suggestions, with no guarantee for success:

- *Modem hardware bugs*. Contact the modem maker and see whether a later product update is available that might make for more efficient connections.

- *Phone service problems*. Check for bogeymen in your local phone system that can sabotage the prospects for consistent high-speed connections. These include the following problems:

AOL is sometimes not available

America Online routinely shuts down all or part of the service for system maintenance every week or two during the early morning hours, usually from 4 to 7 A.M. eastern time. If you try to connect to AOL during these hours and you're not successful, try again later. Sometimes you'll get a message window about the maintenance procedure, sometimes you won't. For information about scheduled system outages, use the keyword AOL Insider.

Can't find support for your modem?

If you cannot find an up-to-date modem file for the modem you have, contact the manufacturer's technical support people. They might be able to provide an updated connection file, advise you about using another modem file, or help you tweak the file with new commands that will provide more efficient connections. Many of the top modem manufacturers already have support areas on AOL (the Modems & Connections support area has the latest listing).

What does hardware compression do for you?

Files that are already compressed do not benefit from V.42bps hardware compression.

Some computers are modems too

Some modems also rely, in part, on the processing power of your computer's CPU to do their work. One common example of this is Apple's GeoPort interface, which lets the computer act as a modem.

Many modems are cross-platform compatible

When it comes to an external modem, the nice thing is that most modems that work on a PC also work on a Mac. You need to change the cable and use communications software that's compatible with the specific computing platform. Ask the manufacturer for details. Some users are known to switch modems back and forth regularly between their PCs and Macs.

A possible phone wiring solution?

One solution is possible for poor or old phone wiring: If you think you have old wiring, have it replaced with data grade twisted pair. Data grade wire has a shield that protects it from crosstalk, and it is generally of higher quality than old solid-core phone wire. Your local telephone company is usually the best resource for information about the condition of your phone wiring.

- *Old wiring.* Older phone system wiring in a home or business can make the difference between getting a 33,600bps connection and not connecting at all. Such phone wiring is solid-core copper. Over time, the copper oxidizes and the solid-core wires wear thin and break when bent. Both of these conditions result in unpredictable signals traveling through the wires that can wreak havoc with high-speed modems. In addition, standard telephone wiring is usually *twisted pair* (a pair of wires run together beside each other). Signals from one wire often distort signals on the other, causing further difficulties with clear communications.

- *Old phone equipment.* Not every phone company has the latest in all-digital telephone switching equipment. Older telephone companies (particularly in smaller, rural areas) often use analog equipment, sometimes with mechanical relays for switching. The more analog interference between your modem and your destination, the lower your chances of a high-speed connection. Modern phone switches cost millions of dollars, so getting your phone company to upgrade their equipment is a tricky matter, and you might just be stuck with the service you get. Be assured that if and when service is improved, your phone bill improves too, to the phone company's benefit.

- *New phone equipment.* Just when you thought technological progress had come to your rescue, virtually all long distance and most local telephone calls are now conducted in a digital environment. Digital transmission provides a nearly loss-free medium for transmitting data, and for the phone company it provides an opportunity. Because the digital data in a telephone call is no different than the digital data on your computer, it can be compressed in the same manner. To the telephone company, compressing the digital voices of telephone calls means they can fit more calls onto those multimillion-dollar pieces of equipment.

The technique the telephone company uses to compress the data in a phone call is called *ADPCM* (which stands for *Adaptive Differential Pulse Code Modulation*). Although ADPCM can compress the sounds made by a human voice almost undetectably, when the beeps and squeaks a modem makes are compressed, information is lost. When faced with ADPCM phone lines, often 33,600bps modems will not connect, or will connect at only a fraction of their maximum potential (such as 14,400bps or 16,800bps). If your home wiring is good, your phone company uses digital equipment, and you're still having trouble with the connection, check with the phone company to see whether you are connected to an ADPCM compressed line. If you are, have the company move you to a noncompressed line (if they can).

■ *Other phones in your home or office.* Every telephone connected to a particular number at your home or office is taking a little bit of signal and introducing a little bit more interference onto that phone line. If your modem is using the same phone line as several telephones in your house, the combined effect of the noise and signal loss to the other phones can cause connection and data transfer problems. Luckily, this problem is easy to test for.

If you're having problems, unplug all the telephones that are on the same line as the modem (even if they're in different rooms).

If the problem goes away when only the modem is on the line, add the other phones back one at a time (checking that the modem still functions at each step). When the modem stops working, you have found the problem phone. Replace that phone or disconnect it when you're using the modem. (I once traced connection troubles to a second modem on one phone line; disconnecting either modem fixed the problem.)

Be especially suspicious of cordless phones or novelty phones (such as the ones with neon lights in them), because they seem to produce the most interference to other devices on the phone line.

Getting a response from your phone company isn't always easy

Take it from the author's personal experience; when you complain about the quality of your phone line, you can bet you'll go through several levels of customer support before someone is ready to listen to you. Most phone repair people are trained to deal with the common problems of lost dial tones and disconnects, and not with the arcane issues of getting a modem to work properly at a higher speed.

New modems are easy to upgrade

Many of the newer V.34 and 56K modems offer the capability of doing firmware updates via *FlashROM*. This is accomplished by a software program that you receive from the modem's manufacturer (you might even find it on America Online or at the manufacturer's own BBS). The software program examines the modem and then downloads the new code to its ROM chips, and in a few moments your modem is up-to-date and ready to use.

Another way to connect to AOL

If your efforts to hook up at a satisfactory speed to AOL's access numbers don't work, you might try signing up with an Internet services provider (such as EarthLink, Netcom, or AT&T WorldNet), and accessing AOL through those services. If you choose to connect to AOL exclusively through those services, you'll be eligible for AOL's "Bring Your Own Access" billing plan. Use the keyword `Billing` to consult current rates and requirements.

- *Cables.* Check whether the cord that connects your modem to the wall plug for the telephone is in good shape. Also ensure that the modem's power cable and serial cable are in good condition. A worn or frayed cord not only hampers your attempts at high-speed communication, but also poses a safety hazard.

- *Old firmware in your modem.* Firmware is the computer program that runs inside your modem that makes it act like a modem. Typically, this program is stored on a ROM (read-only memory) chip inside your modem. With new standards such as V.34 and the new 56K protocols, modem manufacturers often upgrade the firmware inside their modems for better performance over time.

Refer to your modem manual to see how to determine which version of ROM firmware your modem has. You usually need to enter an ATI3 (the letter I) in a telecommunications program, such as Microphone, and see what information is displayed.

Armed with the knowledge of what firmware version you have, contact your modem manufacturer by email or at its BBS and ask whether a newer version is available. Most modems purchased new off the shelf will be up-to-date, but with the newer standards such as V.34 and the two flavors of 56K, changes are often frequent and can make quite a difference in connection speeds and reliability.

Remember, even if your best efforts don't get you the highest speed connections, logging on at a somewhat slower speed still gets you much faster performance on America Online than 14,400bps and slower speeds. This is especially helpful when you are surfing the Internet using America Online's Web browser.

56K Technology—Making a Little Bit Go Twice as Far

As this book was being written, AOL had begun to phase in another technique to get your modem to run faster—U.S. Robotic's x2 technology and Lucent and Rockwell's K56flex.

PART **I**

x2 and K56flex—Which One to Choose? CHAPTER **4**

57

These new protocols are designed to get you speeds of up to 56,000bps. Let's see how it's done.

You may recall that I said that the present modem connection speeds of 33,600bps are rarely achieved with our existing phone lines. So by what form of magic do modem makers stretch this to 56,000? Well, first of all, it's a one-way trip. The new technology can send the data to you at a higher speed, but the data you send back still only travels at a maximum speed of 33,600bps.

The new 56K schemes take advantage of the fact that AOL and other online services use digital-based networks to send out data to telephone systems. A digital encoding technology is used to pass more data through the phone lines, and if you have a modem compatible with the standard, you can receive it faster too (so long as you use an access number with this capability).

These new protocols are based on a logical premise: The data you'll send via a modem (other than files to AOL's software libraries or your online friends) usually consists of short messages, mouse clicks, and simple keyboard commands. You'll be receiving a lot more data, however, such as multimedia files, graphic images from the World Wide Web, and other large files. If you can get that data to your modem more quickly, you'll get more out of your online experience. Web pages will draw on your screen in accelerated fashion, files will reach your PC in record time, and you'll be able to better enjoy the new multimedia features of AOL 4.0.

x2 and K56flex—Which One to Choose?

It's a sad fact that not all 56K-capable modems are the same. Two technologies are vying for approval by the ITU. If you have one type of modem, it won't achieve higher speeds if the connection number supports the other standard. It brings to mind the first 28,800bps protocol V.Fast, which was supported with modems using Rockwell chips. It quickly disappeared when the

How to join the 56K world…

First, you need a modem that supports either x2 or K56flex. Many existing 33,600 bps modems can get upgraded via software or hardware, to one or the other protocol.

Second, you have to connect to a number that offers this capability. AOL will be offering a list of access numbers as their high-speed network grows. You'll find the latest via the keyword **Access**. When you bring up a list of available numbers, you'll see whether x2 or K56flex is supported.

real V.34 (the final 28.800/33.600bps standard) came out, and existing modems required upgrades to talk with most modems that supported the final standard (although a few did retain support for V.Fast).

To make matters more confusing, some modem makers have chosen to play both sides of the fence. For example, Global Village is providing both x2 and K56fFlex modems. Hayes, a supporter of K56flex, is offering x2 capability via its Practical Peripherals subsidiary.

Eventually, a final standard will be agreed upon, and they were very close to a standard that would include elements of both x2 and K56flex as this book was written. After that happens, you should be able to upgrade most of the existing 56K modems to the final standard. Check with the manufacturer of the modem to find out whether it'll be a free or extra-cost upgrade.

Consider the following before jumping aboard this new technology:

- Not all phone lines can support 56K connections. U.S. Robotics, for example, offers a special BBS where you can dial and check your lines to see if such high speed connections are possible.

- Even if you can achieve higher speed, 56,000bps is a pipe dream. That's because current FCC regulations limit data transfers to roughly 53,000bps, and this situation won't change until these rulings are modified.

- Although your phone lines may handle higher speed transfers, expect connection normal rates in the low- to mid-40K range.

- If you want 56K performance from AOL, first check to see that an access number for one protocol or the other is available in your area.

- No clear winner has emerged in 56K performance. Some computer magazines rate x2 modems as superior, others rate K56flex as better.

Two 56K standards are supported by AOL

As this book was written, AOL had converted most of its AOLNet access network to support either x2 or K56flex, and they will upgrade these numbers to the final standard when it is available.

- If AOL doesn't have a 56K number in your city, you may want to check out a separate Internet access service, such as AT&T WorldNet or EarthLink, and access AOL via those services. Generally, such Internet providers only support one of the two standards in any given area, so you'll want to check which one is supported before you buy a new modem.

So long as the modem you buy can be upgraded to the final protocol after it's approved, you may just want to wait and see what sort of upgrade path is available, and, of course, how much the upgrade will cost.

Getting AOL's Software to Work with Your New Modem

After buying that new high-speed modem, no doubt you're ready to log onto AOL and watch those Web pages fill your screen at a rapid pace. Before you do, you'll want to make sure your AOL software is set up to work best with the new modem. In this section, I'll tell you how to locate custom modem profiles for your modem and how to use AOL's auto detection feature to set up the program for most popular models.

Adapting AOL's Software to Your New Modem

Adjusting AOL's software to work with your modem

1. Click the **Setup** button on the main America Online window, and then click the **Connections** tab.

2. Click **Auto Add** on the next screen to bring up the AOL Setup screen, which probes your modem to find out the make and model (see Figure 4.1).

3. If the search is successful, you'll see a Select Your Connection screen (see Figure 4.2) identifying the kind of modem that was located.

AOL checks your modem

When you first install AOL software, the program checks your computer's serial port to verify the type of modem that's installed, but it won't necessarily select the exact make and model; sometimes a default setting is used.

FIGURE **4.1**

AOL checks your modem to get the information it needs.

FIGURE **4.2**

AOL's software manages to detect most popular makes and modems without any extra help.

❶ If the choice is correct, click the **Next** button.

4. If the correct modem isn't selected, click the **Change Connection** button at the bottom of the screen and select a choice from the options shown (see Figure 4.3).

5. After you've selected a modem, click the **Settings** button to check whether the proper Com Port is selected (for Windows users, of course). You should also choose a maximum port speed from the drop-down menu (twice the maximum connection speed, if available, is recommended).

6. Click the **OK** button to return to the Select Your Connection setup box. Click the **Next** button.

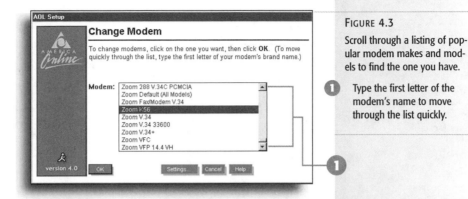

FIGURE 4.3

Scroll through a listing of popular modem makes and models to find the one you have.

1 Type the first letter of the modem's name to move through the list quickly.

7. If you want to add new access numbers, you'll have a chance to do so here. Otherwise, click **Cancel** to stop the process. You'll have to **OK** the next message about aborting the connection setup process, but don't worry about that, your modem settings will take anyway. You'll read more about choosing new access numbers in Chapter 3.

If the modems displayed in the **Change Modem** list box don't include the make and model of your modem, log on to AOL to see if a correct modem profile is available.

Getting additional modem profiles from AOL

1. Use the keyword Modem to enter AOL's Modems & Connections area.

2. Click the **Modem Profile Library** under **Modem Information** (at the upper right), and then click the listing for Windows modem files to bring up the list shown in Figure 4.4.

3. When you have selected the correct file, click the **Download Now** option, which brings up a dialog box showing the download path on top of the Directories scroll box. Double-click the folder that represents your America Online directory (America Online 4.0 is being used for this example).

4. When the list of directories appears beneath the America Online directory, double-click the modems folder as your destination for the file you're about to download (see Figure 4.5).

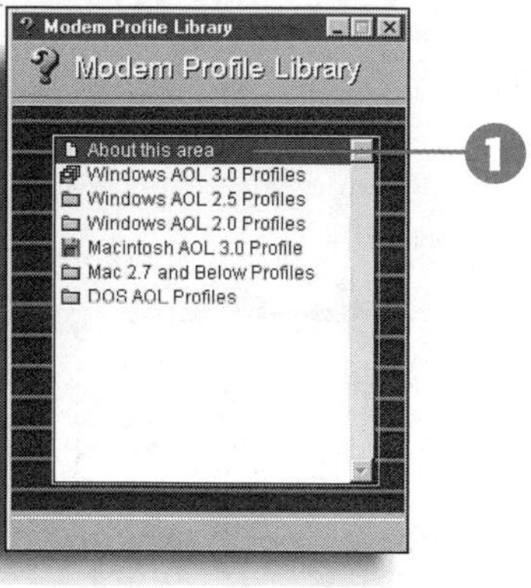

FIGURE 4.4

Connection files for many popular modems are free from AOL.

1 Double-click the library that applies to your AOL software version.

FIGURE 4.5

AOL Windows modem files are stored in the modems folder, which is located inside your America Online directory.

1 Click the **Save** button to start the file transfer.

5. Click **Save** to confirm the destination of your download.

6. When the transfer of the new file is complete, **OK** that message too.

The next time you log off and choose **Add Device** in your **Device Configuration Setup** box, the new modem file you downloaded will be displayed in the directory window.

Solving Connection Problems: Q & A

It's a sure thing that you usually will be able to connect to America Online without incident or trouble (busy signals excepted). Sometimes, however, you will have difficulty getting and maintaining an online connection. Some of the causes are due to your phone lines, sometimes it's your modem or the way it's set up, and sometimes it's the connection number you use to access

Where do Mac modem files go?

Macintosh modem files are to be downloaded to the Online Files folder, which is located in the same folder as your AOL program files. Otherwise, the steps you follow to get a new modem profile on your Mac is pretty much the same as in the Windows version.

America Online or even the service's own network. In this section many of the problems you are apt to confront are dealt with. If you have further difficulties, you can contact America Online customer service directly, or the manufacturer of your modem.

Question: I just bought a new V.34 modem, and it still connects at 2,400bps. Why?

Answer: Getting a high-speed modem is half the battle. To log on to AOL at high speed, you need an access number that supports that speed. You also need to make sure the speed you select when you set up your AOL software's Location profile matches or exceeds that speed. Read Chapter 3 for information on how to locate additional access phone numbers. You might also want to review the rest of this chapter for advice on having AOL's software help you automate the process of getting a new access number.

Question: How do I know I'm connecting at high speed?

Answer: Just look at your AOL software window when logging on. Step 3 shows the speed at which you're connecting.

Question: Why am I being disconnected constantly from AOL?

Answer: Getting bumped or disconnected from America Online shouldn't happen often, but it does occur occasionally. The following list gives you some advice on why it happens and what you can do about it:

- *Noise on your phone line.* This could be a problem with your local telephone service, but before you contact the repair center, try another access number. You can locate AOL access numbers using the tips described in this chapter.

- *For Windows 95 users: Check memory-resident programs.* Such programs as memory managers, device drivers, and terminate-and-stay-resident (TSR) programs can cause your modem to disconnect. You can try to diagnose the cause of this problem by removing these programs, and then restoring them, one at a time, until the problem returns.

Print your access number listing

Keep a printed list of the access numbers available in your area. That way, if you choose the wrong network option with your AOL software, you can refer to the original list to fix it quickly.

Some modems warn you of trouble

Some external modems (such as the U.S. Robotics Courier series) have an ARQ or error connection light on their front panels. If the light flashes on and off, it indicates that data is being retransmitted. Frequent flashing of this light may indicate a possible symptom of a connection or phone line problem.

- *Hardware problems.* Check your telephone lines, your modem, your connection cables, and your personal computer to see whether they are all working normally.

- *Other telephone equipment.* Additional telephones on your line, an answering machine, a fax machine, or even a cordless telephone can create additional noise that causes your modem connection to fail. You can diagnose this problem by disconnecting those devices and then restoring them, one by one, until the problem returns.

- *Call waiting.* If you're using call waiting, be sure it's disabled (if that's possible) by using the appropriate check box in your AOL Connection Locations setup box.

Question: *My connection hangs at step 4, Requesting Network Attention. Why?*

Answer: This might happen if the AOL access network selected in the Location setup is not correct. Because you cannot get online to fix this problem, take the following steps to adjust your phone number setting.

Finding new AOL access numbers

1. While offline, click the **Setup** button and then click **Search Numbers**.

2. Enter the area code to bring up the list of available numbers.

3. Choose the local access numbers you want; the correct access network is set automatically (see Chapter 3).

Question: *I'm getting a busy signal. What do I do?*

Answer: Just as you get a busy signal when you try to call someone who is already using the phone, the number you use to access America Online might be occupied too. If this happens, log off and try again. If your AOL software is set up with extra access numbers, after a few seconds, the next number you selected will be automatically dialed. You can also configure a number for automatic redialing by opening the Locations setup box, double-clicking the number, and then entering the number of times the number is to be redialed. Each number can be redialed up to nine times.

If you continue to get constant busy signals, use the **Add Number** button in the Connection Locations setup box to locate other access numbers to try.

Question: Help. My modem won't dial AOL.

Answer: If you've been able to connect to AOL before, something might have changed in your setup. Because they differ slightly from the Mac to Windows, the differences that apply to one computing platform or the other have been marked throughout this listing. Check the following possible setup remedies:

- Switch off your modem and turn it back on again. Sometimes the modem's firmware freezes due to a software defect or a previous connection problem. When you turn the modem on again, it's the equivalent of restarting your computer, and often has the same result. If you have an internal model, restarting your computer should bring the same result.

- Try another telecommunications program. Windows users can try Terminal or HyperTerminal. Mac users can use Microphone, White Knight, Zterm, or a similar program. If another telecommunications program can successfully make your modem dial out, the problem is definitely related to the way your AOL software is set up.

- Make sure the dial prefix or string is correct.

  - *For Windows users:* Click the **Setup** button, then click the **Connection Devices** tab. See if the proper make and model of modem is selected. If not, review the section titled "Adapting AOL's Software to Your New Modem" earlier in this chapter for information on how to configure the software.

  - *For Macintosh Users:* Click the **Setup** box while logged off. Then click the **Expert Setup** button. In the next screen, double-click a **Location** name in the **Locations Setup** box, and see whether the correct make and model of modem is selected from the **Connect Using** drop-down menu.

Getting up-to-date modem drivers

For a complete list of up-to-date modem driver files, use the keyword **Access** to access an online area where you can download the latest driver for your modem. If a modem file isn't there, contact the manufacturer.

- *For Windows 95 Users:* Check your Windows 95 Modems Control Panel and see if it's properly configured for your new modem. If not, run the Install New Modem Wizard to customize it to your make and model. Most popular modems will be readily recognized during this process.

Solving Typical Modem Problems: Q & A

Troubleshooting your modem connection on a personal computer is a fairly straightforward process. When trying to figure out where your modem problems lie, you need to look at several factors. The first place you should look is the modem itself. If the modem is okay, make sure your PC is configured properly and your software is set up correctly. By verifying that all three particulars are correct, you should be able to solve more than 90 percent of your modem problems.

If you continue to have problems getting your modem to work properly, consider the following:

- Whenever you are having problems with your modem, make sure it is hooked up properly. If you have an external modem, check to see that it is plugged in and turned on. Although this might sound simple, the number of people whose sole problem was an unplugged modem is amazing (sometimes the plug is pulled out when your home or office is being cleaned, and not reinserted). If your modem is plugged in and turned on, the next thing you should check is the serial and phone cable.

- Most external modems have two phone jacks. One is designed to connect directly to your phone line. The other jack is designed to connect to your telephone. Be sure the cables are properly connected to the correct places.

- Test the serial cable by watching the modem when AOL tries to initialize it. If you see the modem lights going on and off or hear the modem attempting to dial, the cable is likely good. If the cable seems to be okay but still has problems connecting at high speeds, you might have a non-hardware handshaking modem cable. The simplest way to

Power strips are useful accessories

Use a power strip for your personal computer and peripherals. Some models not only provide protection against voltage surges, but you also can use the on/off switch on the power strip to turn on your computer's peripherals before starting your computer. That way, you always know that your modem is on.

test cable type is to try to connect to a 2,400bps access number and see whether it connects properly. If you get a connection at 2,400bps but not at 9,600bps, it is possible that you have a non-hardware handshaking modem cable. The best solution in cases like this is to go out and spend a few dollars to buy a brand-new hardware handshaking modem cable from your local computer store.

- If the serial cable is okay, you should turn your attention to the phone line itself. The first and most obvious test is to plug the modem's phone cable into a phone and check for a dial tone. If you hear a dial tone, the other item you should check is the type of phone system you are connected to. Some office buildings, hotels, and apartment buildings use digital phone systems that are not compatible with high-speed modems. Aside from actually examining the telephone junction box itself, one of the easiest ways to tell whether you have a digital phone system is to try connecting to AOL at 1,200 or 2,400bps and then at 9,600bps (you can do this easily enough enough by lowering the connection port speed in our AOL Setup box). If the modem connects at the lower speed but not at the higher, it is possible that you are using a digital phone system. If this is the case, you need to contact someone in authority who can arrange for you to get an analog line specifically for your modem.

If you have an internal modem, you can't do too much to test your modem, aside from listening for the modem's dialing attempt on your computer's speaker.

Question: *I have call waiting, and my online connections are always interrupted when someone tries to call me. What do I do?*

Answer: Although call waiting is convenient for people (because it enables one phone line to act as two lines), modems don't deal with it well. Most modems, when confronted with the tone that announces an incoming call, spend several seconds getting back in sync with the connection. In many cases, the call-waiting click or tone causes a connection to drop.

Check for line noise

Even if the cables are perfectly fine and the phone lines are analog, line noise itself may be a big contributor to the inability to connect at high speeds. In this case, a call to the phone company is the next step. It should come as no surprise to realize most phone companies are primarily concerned with good voice connections, not fax and modem performance. You may have to go through several support people to locate someone who is able to help.

Watch out for digital systems

Many modems, especially PC-card and notebook-based models, can be damaged by connecting to a digital phone system. So if you are suspicious of the phone system you are connecting to, don't attempt a connection until you have confirmation that the system is compatible with your modem. See Chapter 3 for more advice on dealing with this situation.

When logging on to America Online from a line with the call-waiting service, be sure to disable call waiting within your software dialing string. When you configure your AOL software to work with the modem, you can also set it up to disable call waiting when you log on. The command for touch tone phones is generally *70. If you have a rotary phone in your area, the setting is 1170. These settings vary from phone system to phone system, so if you're in doubt, look inside your phone book. You might have to call your phone company and ask for help, because you might have to activate the capability to disable call waiting with a separate work order (and a modest monthly charge). If you're lucky enough to have a separate line for your modem, don't bother having call waiting installed on it.

AOL's Help Resource

If the solutions described here don't help you get a reliable hookup to AOL, AOL's own help forum may be the answer. To reach that service, use the keyword Members (or from the **Help** menu choose **Member Services**), which takes you to AOL's Help forum (see Figure 4.6).

FIGURE 4.6

Get free help here from America Online.

① Double-click the topic that matches your problem.

AOL's Member Services area is a full-service support center, and live help from an AOL representative is part of the package. If you want to enter the live support section, you have to go through several steps, however. First is to examine the help texts to see if they can help you answer your question or solve the problem (see Figure 4.7). Live help is only available as an option after you go through all the help texts.

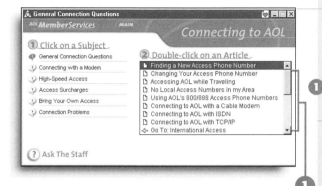

FIGURE 4.7
Click the appropriate topic to get step-by-step help from AOL.

① Scroll through the list to see more articles.

SEE ALSO

➤ *Learns how to stay connected to AOL while you are at the office or on the road, see page 47*

➤ *Learn how to set up your AOL software, see page 509*

CHAPTER 5

Exploring AOL

Why does the online artwork look different?

Hey, what's wrong with my computer? When I connect to AOL I see a totally different screen from the one you show in your book. Is it me or is it you?

It's both. The screen artwork I'm showing here requires versions 3 and 4 of AOL's Mac or Windows software to display as illustrated. The oldest versions of AOL software offer only 14 channels and a different Welcome screen format.

To see exactly what I see when I log on to AOL, you'll want to upgrade to the latest and greatest version of the software. To do that, just use the AOL keyword **Upgrade** to access the download area.

Touring AOL's Channels

This chapter assumes that you've established your AOL membership, and you've at least had a chance to log on for an online session or two. You might even be an experienced AOL user. But I'll tell you one thing: Even after several years of membership, I wasn't prepared for the sheer depth of features AOL offered until I sat down to write the *Using America Online* books. Whether you're a beginner or an experienced online traveler, you'll discover that there's a vast world of entertainment and information just waiting to be discovered on America Online.

Find the AOL Channels that Interest You

Finding the right place to visit on AOL is similar to selecting a channel on your TV, except you click an icon rather than push a button. After you've signed on to AOL and learned how to get the most out of its highly flexible software, you'll want to do more than just get your feet wet.

Every time you log on to America Online, you'll see the Welcome screen (see Figure 5.1). This screen shows you the major highlights of the service and informs you if you have email waiting.

FIGURE 5.1

See the highlights and check your new mail when you first log on to America Online.

    The arrival of email is announced here.

2   List of AOL highlights

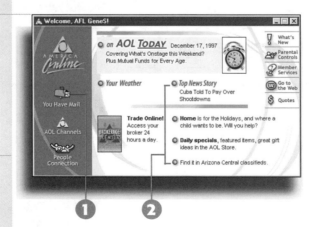

This chapter goes a bit deeper, beneath the Welcome window, actually, to the Channels screen and more, where you'll explore the various virtual neighborhoods, known as *channels*, of America Online (see Figure 5.2). The Channels screen is located just beneath the Welcome window when you first log on to America Online. The fastest way to bring it up front is to click the shaded **AOL Channels** icon at the left side of your Welcome screen.

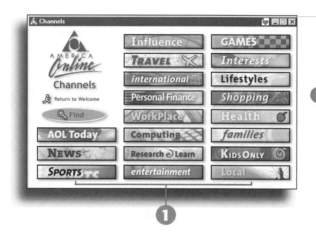

FIGURE 5.2

AOL's virtual city is divided into channels, reflecting different areas of the online experience.

1 Click a channel icon to visit online forums devoted to specific areas.

Each of the online channels or departments shown in Figure 5.2 is identified by a major topic of interest. A channel contains a number of forums, folders, services, and other areas related (sometimes loosely) to that topic. You'll learn more about those areas in Part II, "Communicating Online." For now, we'll just scratch the surface.

Find...

AOL provides a handy search tool to help you find exactly the kind of information or service you want (see Figure 5.3). You can search for AOL forums, Internet information, people, or events or you can examine AOL's huge software libraries. Just click the topic you want to learn more about.

Keyword power

Almost every area of America Online can be reached by pressing Ctrl+K (or ⌘-K for Mac users) and typing a simple keyword. Ten popular keywords are at the end of this chapter. More can be found in Appendix C, "AOL's Most Popular Keywords."

Finding that channel again

If you've closed the **Channel** menu during your online session, you can call it up again by using the keyword Channels.

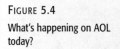
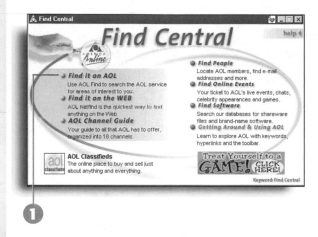

AOL Today Channel

Keyword: Today

The AOL Today directory highlights major AOL features and the top news of the day (see Figure 5.4). It's updated several times a day, with a listing of "essentials" for you to check further.

News Channel

Keyword: News

It's hard to imagine what the world was like only 100 or so years ago, when almost any news of the world, or even the country, took days or weeks to reach the eyes and ears of those who were

around then. Even 15 years ago, we still waited for the morning
newspapers to get more than just a headline service about current events. In this age of the so-called Information Superhighway, we need not wait even that long (see Figure 5.5).

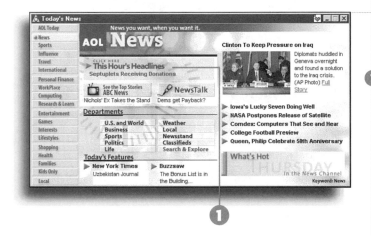

FIGURE 5.5

The corner newsstand was
never quite like this.

1 Read the latest news before
your daily paper can print it.

America Online's News channel offers a vast amount of information about the world today that is as current as it gets. You'll be
able to read the latest stories from the major wire services, or
consult the contents of the major daily newspapers, such as *The
New York Times*.

SEE ALSO

➤ *To learn more about AOL's News channel, see page 401*

Sports Channel

Keyword: Sports

When America's national pastime, baseball, disappeared in the
summer of 1994 due to a players' strike, the importance of
sports in our lives didn't diminish one iota. We talked about the
football season instead. America Online's Sports channel, shown
in Figure 5.6, covers the world of sports. It's a repository of the
latest sports news, including discussion groups and regular conferences on your favorite sports. Sometimes you'll be able to
converse, through cyberspace, with some of your favorite sports
figures too.

Customizing your AOL toolbar

If you really like a certain
online area, you can add it to
your AOL toolbar by dragging
the Favorite Places heart to the
right end of the top row of the
toolbar where you want it to be.
You'll see an acknowledgment
window in which you choose
an icon and title for the area,
and when you click OK, it'll
become part of the toolbar. To
remove it, just hold down the
Alt (Option for Mac users) key
and drag the new icon off the
toolbar with your mouse.

FIGURE 5.6

If you open your newspaper to
the sports section first, you'll
want to make a regular stop to
this online area.

 AOL's online sports pages

SEE ALSO

➤ *To learn more about the Sports channel, see page 367*

Influence Channel

Keyword: Influence

No one doubts that information makes the world go around.
The Influence channel (see Figure 5.7) is devoted to the stories
behind the stories, the gossip and intrigue behind world events
and happenings in the world of fashion and show business. Your
participation here doesn't have to be passive. You'll have every
chance to express yourself in AOL's popular message boards and
chat rooms.

FIGURE 5.7

AOL's Influence channel takes
you to the world of arts and
entertainment and gossip
about all sorts of subjects.

 AOL's forums for opinion
and gossip

SEE ALSO

➤ *To learn more about AOL's Influence channel, see page 357*

Travel Channel

Keyword: Travel

As the name implies, travelers gain gratification in the areas that comprise this channel (see Figure 5.8). One of the principal services of AOL's Travel channel is travel reservations. You can book flights on any major airline, reserve rental cars and hotel rooms, or just check schedules and prices during your visit to the Travel channel. You'll also learn about the best places to visit and where to eat (and which places to avoid).

SEE ALSO

➤ *To learn more about AOL's Travel channel, see page 471*

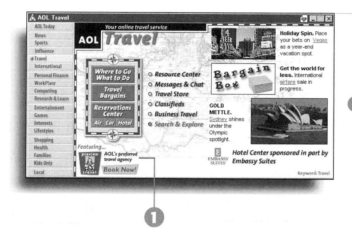

FIGURE 5.8

Book a flight or learn about your favorite tourist spot in America Online's Travel channel.

1 Use AOL's online travel agents to plan your trip.

International Channel

Keyword: International

The time has long since passed when America Online was restricted to just "America." Through partnerships with a number of international media companies, AOL has expanded into Canada, Europe, Japan, and other major world centers. AOL's International channel (see Figure 5.9) enables you to quickly access some of AOL's worldwide features.

FIGURE 5.9

AOL's International channel
shows you how AOL has
rapidly joined the world
community.

 Click a country's name to
discover more of AOL's international features.

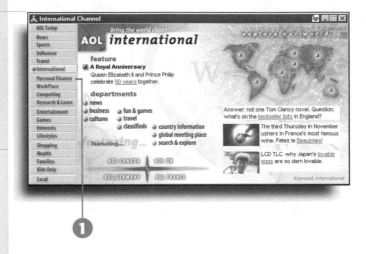

SEE ALSO

➤ *To learn more about AOL's International channel, see page 375*

Personal Finance Channel

Keyword: Finance

This department can be considered an extension of Today's
News (see Figure 5.10). The Personal Finance channel lets you
delve more deeply into all aspects of handling your personal
finances—from reviewing the day's business news (and how it
might affect your income and investment strategies) to seeking
out the profile of a company you might want to add to your
stock portfolio.

FIGURE 5.10

America Online's Personal
Finance channel has a vast
storehouse of business news
and advice.

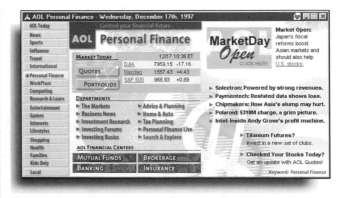

SEE ALSO
➤ *To learn more about AOL's Personal Finance channel, see page 452*

WorkPlace Channel

Keyword: WorkPlace

AOL created the WorkPlace channel (see Figure 5.11) for everyone who wants to get more value out of their job. Whether you work in a home office (as many writers like me do) or run a large business, you'll find a wealth of information and special services to consult. AOL also offers a highly flexible Web hosting service, *PrimeHost*, to give your business a presence on the World Wide Web.

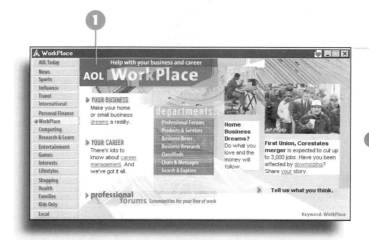

FIGURE 5.11
AOL's WorkPlace channel provides information to help you with your career and your business.

1 One of AOL's popular business-oriented channels

SEE ALSO
➤ *To learn more about AOL's WorkPlace channel, see page 461*

Computing Channel

Keyword: Computing

Welcome to one of my favorite areas on America Online. Because people use their personal computers to connect to America Online, the Computing channel is clearly one of the most popular places to visit on America Online (see Figure 5.12).

Whether you use a Mac OS computer or a PC running Windows, DOS, or OS/2, you'll find information, help, and extensive libraries of software for you to download in this area. In addition, many of the major hardware and software manufacturers have fully staffed support areas on America Online, where you can get quick solutions to problems with a specific product, or even advice on how to use that product more effectively.

FIGURE 5.12

America Online's Computing area is one of the service's frequently visited online channels.

1 Learn how to make your PC run better.

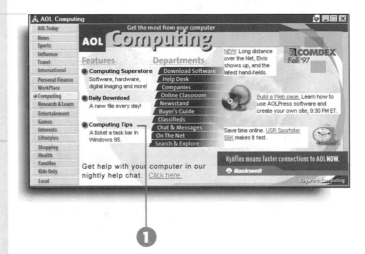

SEE ALSO
➤ *To learn more about AOL's Computing channel, see page 417*

Research & Learn Channel

Keywords: Research, Learn

Do you need help with a homework assignment, or do you want to take some special courses on a particular topic of interest? You can do that and more in America Online's active Research & Learn channel, shown in Figure 5.13. You can pay a virtual visit to the Library of Congress or the Smithsonian, sign up for a correspondence course, or get information about the next round of college board examinations.

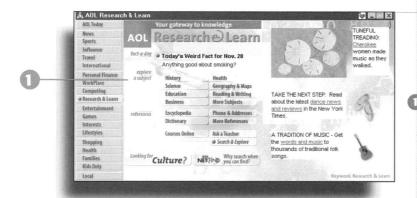

FIGURE 5.13

Sign up for a special course or visit a museum during your visit to America Online's Research & Learn channel.

1 Find facts or take an online course.

SEE ALSO

➤ *To learn more about AOL's Research & Learn channel, see page 390*

Entertainment Channel

Keyword: Entertainment

Movies, television, books, political and humorous cartoons, *Disney Adventures Magazine*, Music, the Trivia Forum, and LaPub are just a few of the Entertainment channel features that draw huge numbers of members on a regular basis. Almost no other department online has the continuous drawing power of the Entertainment channel. Both children and adults frequent Entertainment for its culturally diverse content. Be sure to stop by during your travels across America Online (see Figure 5.14).

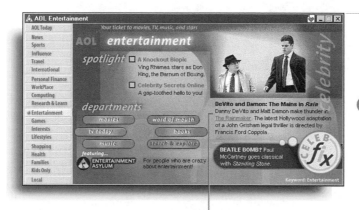

FIGURE 5.14

This screen gives you a quick glimpse of just some of the services offered in AOL's Entertainment channel.

1 Check out the goings on in the show business world.

SEE ALSO
➤ *To learn more about AOL's Entertainment channel, see page 348*

Games Channel

Keyword: Games

Members visit the Games channel for many reasons: It may be the latest CD-ROM game, a video game, one of the thousands of files available for download on AOL, or it may be advice on how to solve those clues in your favorite computer game. Whatever the reason, AOL's Games channel (see Figure 5.15) is a place you'll want to visit often for fun and exciting online adventures.

FIGURE 5.15

AOL's Games channel offers information, software, and even the chance to participate in interactive games online.

1 Join an online game, or learn about your favorite games here.

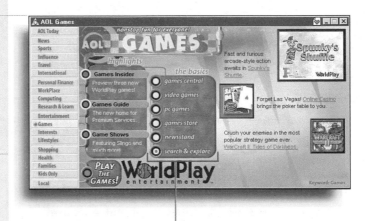

SEE ALSO
➤ *To learn more about AOL's Games channel, see page 353*

Interests Channel

Keyword: Interests

Want to join an online club, access an online health guide, learn tips about home improvement, learn how to fix that old car, or learn to cook an omelette? AOL's Interests channel provides a great repertoire of information (see Figure 5.16). You can also join an astronomy or photography club or share information about better health and exercise—all this and more in one convenient online channel.

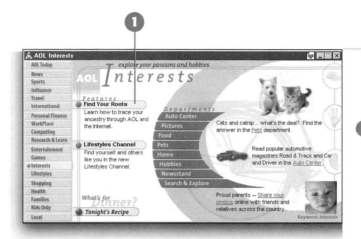

FIGURE 5.16

A large range of subjects form the forums that make up AOL's Interests channel.

1 Visit online forums catering to your hobby or special interest.

Lifestyles Channel

Keyword: Lifestyles

Are you looking to give up that nasty smoking habit, learn more about physical fitness, or find a perfect mate? You'll find information about all this and more in AOL's Lifestyles channel (see Figure 5.17). You'll also find special areas devoted to religion and beliefs, and special online communities.

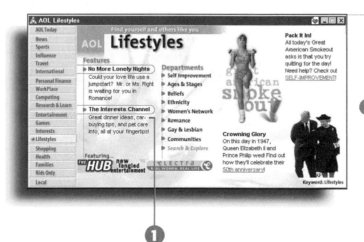

FIGURE 5.17

Join online communities, explore religion, or find ways to improve your health in AOL's Lifestyles channel.

1 Join special online communities here.

Shopping Channel

Keyword: `Shopping`

The Shopping channel is AOL's interactive shopping mall. Whether you are looking for America Online goodies, such as T-shirts and coffee mugs, wanting to buy or sell a car, or looking for computer training aids, AOL's online shopping center offers you these things and more (see Figure 5.18).

FIGURE 5.18
Time to go shopping and save some cash right on America Online.

Health Channel

Keyword: `Health`

Are you concerned with your health, or whether exercise would be of benefit? Well we are, and AOL's Health channel (see Figure 5.19) is a place you'll want to visit. You'll read news of the latest developments in medical research and get informed advice on how to live better and longer.

Families Channel

Keyword: `Families`

AOL has worked hard to make the service "kid safe." You'll want to visit the Families channel (see Figure 5.20) to discover news about effective parenting and learn about AOL's special features for kids and teens. You'll also read about AOL's Neighborhood Watch and Parental Controls features, which let you customize the online experience for younger family members. I'll cover this subject further in Chapter 7, "Parental Issues and Internet Access."

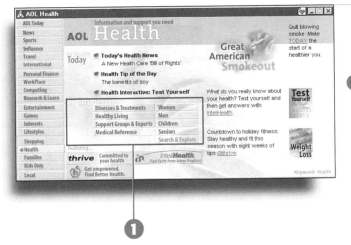

FIGURE 5.19

The Health channel provides advice, news, and a wide range of common sense information.

1 Discuss issues related to your health in these forums.

FIGURE 5.20

The AOL Families channel also offers advice on parenting, and also provides information for teens and kids.

1 AOL provides a friendly, safe environment for your family.

Kids Only Channel

Keyword: Kids

I really haven't discussed special places for kids yet on America Online, but I'll remedy that right now. As shown in Figure 5.21, young people have lots of special and friendly places to visit on America Online. *Disney Adventures Magazine* is on-hand with a special forum. Kids Chats (online conferences) are available, and you'll also find special Kids Only versions of America Online's most popular clubs, such as the Astronomy club and the *Star Trek* club.

FIGURE 5.21

Kids have a special area to call
their own on America Online.

FIGURE 5.21

Kids have a special area to call
their own on America Online.

Local Channel

AOL is for families

You can customize your child's
online experience via AOL's Parental
Controls feature (keyword:
Parental Controls). This
feature enables you to restrict your
child's access to certain online areas
and Internet sources.

Keywords: Local or Digital City

This channel is AOL's online travelogue (see Figure 5.22). By
clicking the map that identifies a particular region of the United
States, you can bring up a list of the many forums that relate to
that area. You'll find, for example, that many of the major cities
or their newspapers have set up their own AOL forums to help
travelers or even residents learn about the news and lifestyle
information you want. You can use the search tool to focus on a
specific city or state or even a number of the major foreign cities
(now that AOL is fast becoming a worldwide online service).

①

FIGURE 5.22

Take an online vacation to
many spots in the United States
and around the world with
AOL's Digital City channel.

① Visit your favorite city in
AOL's Digital City channel.

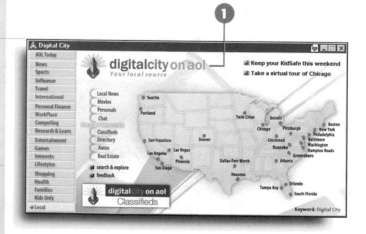

All America Online channels are described in-depth in the remaining chapters; but for now, look around and become comfortable with their general layout. When the time comes to explore your chosen areas of particular interest, the later chapters will guide you through.

SEE ALSO

➤ *To learn more about AOL's International channel, see page 375*

Making Email Work for You

We've been hearing for a few years about the Information Superhighway. A major chunk of this roadway has already been paved by such services as America Online and is already being traveled. One of the ways to travel this road is by using *email*.

America Online's electronic mail (email) system is by far one of the most popular features the service offers (see Figure 5.23). AOL's email system is simple and efficient (at least when those widely publicized system breakdowns aren't happening); it can easily be scheduled to pick up mail waiting for you and deliver your outgoing mail without any intervention from you. You don't even have to lick a stamp or address an envelope.

AOL's international look

If you access Digital City from an international version of AOL's software, or via the International channel (see "International Channel" earlier in this chapter), you'll see a list of cities in other parts of the world.

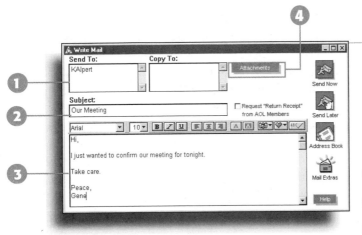

FIGURE 5.23

The America Online email form also can be used to format your message with your favorite typeface. You can also spell check your email before you send it, insert pictures, and attach files.

1. Address your email here.

2. Give it a subject.

3. Write your message here.

4. Send a file with your email.

You can send email at any time, day or night, and also include *attachments*—files from your computer's hard disk connected to your outgoing email to be delivered to another AOL member, or even a member of another online service. To send email, enter the recipient's screen name in the **To** box, type a heading in the **Subject** line, and type or paste your message in the large message box.

The people to whom you are sending your email can read your message and retrieve any files you might have attached at their leisure. You and your recipient need not be online at the same time, which saves you the aggravation and effort it would take to prearrange a time when both of you would connect your modems to complete a communication session. In fact, the recipient of your email doesn't even have to be an AOL member, because AOL's email can be sent to members of other services too.

SEE ALSO

➤ *To learn more about AOL's online email, see page 157*

Using Instant Messages for Interactive Meetings

Instant messages, or IMs for short, differ from email in several ways and have distinct advantages and disadvantages. When using regular email, you only need to know the screen names of your correspondents to be able to send a message to them, and they only need to click a **Reply** button to respond to you. The messages you exchange in this fashion do not require any knowledge on your part of the other person's activities or presence online. You can pick up mail sent to you at any time, up to a month after it was issued. Exchanging instant messages, however, requires that both you and the other party be online at the same time (see Figure 5.24).

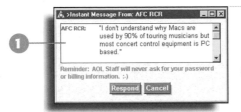

FIGURE 5.24

AOL's instant message window shows a two-way mini-chat.

1 Have a one-on-one chat with an online friend.

One big advantage to using instant messages is that both sides of the conversation take place in *real time* (while you and the recipient are online), and the topic is more easily followed without the time delays of email.

Another major difference between the two types of messages is that when using email you can include as many screen names in the addressing box as you desire, hundreds even! On the other hand, using an instant message is just between two people, and no more. IMs are as private as AOL's email and are a good way to carry on an online conversation to get to know someone better.

Secrets of Getting Files from America Online

Let's clear the air about a couple of online terms before going on. *Downloading* is the transfer of programs and files from the host computer to your computer's hard drive or floppy disk. *Uploading* is the opposite; you send files from your own hard drive to AOL.

Sooner or later you are going to find yourself downloading files (probably sooner). Most of you joined America Online in the first place to be able to download files. While exploring the various AOL channels, you probably ran across some file libraries, and, perhaps, have already dabbled in downloading.

You can download files from three sources while on America Online:

Personal online conversations

Instant messaging is the ideal way to have a one-on-one communication with an AOL member. All that's required is to have your online friend logged on at the same time as you. Your friend doesn't even have to be an AOL member. AOL has a feature called Instant Messenger that lets subscribers to other Internet access services communicate with you by this technique.

Buddy Lists

To find out whether an online friend or colleague has logged on, refer to AOL's Buddy List screen (keyword Buddy View).

- *Online forums.* You can find tens of thousands of files representing the latest shareware and free updates to popular programs.

- *Email attachments.* (Although I urge you to only accept email attachments from someone you know.) The way you set up a download session is slightly different between the two, but after it's begun, both use the same file transfer method.

- *The Internet.* You can access the Internet either by AOL's Web browser or its FTP feature. I'll cover this in more detail in the section titled "Traversing the Superhighway" later in this chapter.

Starting the process of uploading is distinctly different, however. Uploading a file via email is the most straightforward method; click the **Attach** button on your email window and select the file or files you want to send to someone else.

In the Computing channel forums, and other America Online libraries, you need to first complete a form that requests information about the file you plan to send. You'll learn more about uploading in Chapter 26, "Tips and Tricks on Finding Software."

America Online Forums: Where the Action Is

Be careful about files attached to email!

It's a sad fact that some folks have written little programs to steal your password and personal information, and they will send you such programs by email. They'll claim the program is really an instruction book or helpful document or even a screen saver. The watchwords are: *Don't download files received via email unless you know the source.* For more information on handling such issues, please consult AOL's Terms of Service area (keyword **TOS**) or go to the Notify AOL area at keyword **Notify AOL**.

The central meeting points on America Online are called *forums.* A forum, according to Webster, is a place for discussion of public matters or current issues, or an opportunity for open discussion. This could be no truer anywhere else than America Online. Forums on America Online cover numerous topics, computer-related and otherwise. More than a dozen forums are available, for example, in the Windows side of AOL's Computing channel (see Chapter 25, "Visiting the Computing Channel") and a similar complement of Macintosh forums, many dealing with comparable topics.

One good way to get used to a computing forum is to visit the Computing Help Desk (keywords `PC Help` or `Mac Help`) shown in Figure 5.25. You'll find helpful information on using your PC with AOL, and on the sort of features you'll find in the other computing forums.

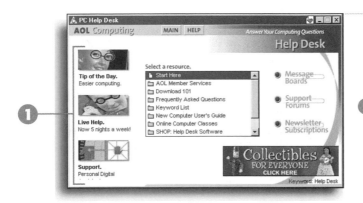

FIGURE 5.25

The America Online PC Help forum (and the Mac equivalent) shows newcomers the ropes.

1   The Help Desk can make life easier for you and your PC.

Although the basic setup is different from one forum to another, certain features appear in just about every AOL forum, and a few are specific to certain forums. For example, the PC Animation & Video Forum is shown in Figure 5.26 and can be accessed by using the keywords MM or A&V.

Each computing forum has a similar look and structure. Special features are highlighted with colorful icons on the right side of the screen, each available by a single mouse click. The forum's list box, at the left, includes the remaining features available; you can access any of them by double-clicking.

It's easy to cross computer platforms on AOL

Macintosh forums are available to users of the Windows version of AOL software, and PC and Windows forums are available to Macintosh users. You'll often find handy gateways in the individual forums themselves.

FIGURE 5.26

The PC Animation & Video Forum provides helpful guidance on harnessing the multimedia features of your PC.

1   AOL Computing channel forums provide help and hints.

What's a forum's purpose?

The first time you visit a forum, read its "About" information, which is usually at the top of the forum's list box. You'll learn the mission and goals of the forum, take a tour of its most popular features, and meet the AOL community leaders (forum volunteers) who run the place.

Help from computer companies

If you need assistance with a problem that is not handled within a particular computing and software forum, you should visit the regular companies area instead (keyword Company), where you can visit all the firms on AOL who have products devoted to the computing platform you use.

I'll explain more about how online forums are set up in Chapter 25, "Visiting the Computing Channel."

Joining an Online Conference

Keyword: AOL Live

Conferences are hosted not only by forums, but also by other AOL channels. Different area's conferences have different flavors—some conference hosts use a formal protocol to determine who speaks at what time; some hosts hold contests where everyone speaks (actually, *types*) at almost the same time. Each area's conference room usually has posted rules of conduct for members to read before entering, and you should do just that so you will act according to local customs. To use a cliché, when in Rome, do as the Romans do.

SEE ALSO

➤ *To learn more about conference room information, see page 90*

Traversing the Superhighway

Keyword: Internet

When you log on to America Online, you are not just accessing a single online service. Through AOL's Internet Connection (see Figure 5.27), you also have access to a huge, sprawling network encompassing other services throughout the world. No doubt you've read about the Internet in your daily newspaper, or you've heard or seen stories about it on the broadcast media.

FIGURE 5.27

AOL's Internet Connection is the entranceway to the global Information Superhighway.

1 Explore AOL's Internet services.

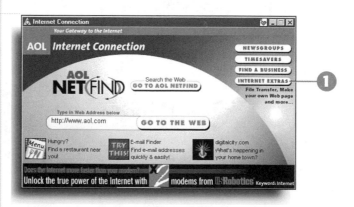

AOL was one of the first major online services to offer a huge set of Internet-related features. Some of them are summarized here. If your curiosity has been piqued, go right to Part III, "AOL as an Internet Service Provider," for a full description of AOL's Internet features. Among the Internet features AOL offers are

- *TCP/IP access.* If you have direct network access to the Internet, you can log on to AOL at ultra-high speed from anywhere in the world. If you choose to do this exclusively, you're also eligible for a lower AOL rate via its "bring your own access" plan.

- *Internet email.* You can send email directly to other online services and individual Internet subscribers.

- *Internet mailing lists.* Join any of thousands of popular mailing lists on the Internet. These mailing lists are devoted to just about everything from computers to cooking.

- *Gopher.* America Online lets you do a comprehensive database search for information and files on any subject throughout the Internet.

- *Internet newsgroups.* Join exciting, informative discussion groups on your favorite subjects. You can choose from thousands of active newsgroups.

- *File Transfer Protocol (FTP). Directly from AOL,* You can download software directly from the major software and hardware manufacturers, such as Apple and Microsoft, and access a huge storehouse of shareware and other useful files located on computers and services across the world.

- *World Wide Web.* Much of the content of the Internet is in text form, but it's easy to navigate through America Online's friendly, helpful interface. The World Wide Web is the popular Internet feature that combines text, pictures, and even sound into a single, unified presentation. Using hypertext links, you are able to click a topic and jump right to the material related to that subject. (Macintosh users familiar with HyperCard have already had somewhat of a sample of what the World Wide Web looks like.)

- *Internet chatting.* Using third-party Internet Relay Chat (IRC) software, you can have a chat with millions of Internet users across the world, whether they are AOL members or not.

In the coming years, America Online will be exploring other Internet services. You can be assured that these services will be tightly integrated into AOL's friendly, easy-to-use software, so you won't have to learn a complex new interface to take advantage of the newest features. A good indicator of what is to come can be found in the monthly letter from the service's outspoken CEO, Steve Case, in which he offers you his vision for the service and acquaints you with upcoming new services. His status reports are always available via the keyword SteveCase.

The Top Ten AOL Keywords

Is the screen moving too fast for you?

How do I stop a text window from scrolling on my screen? The Esc key on your Windows PC or Command-period on your Mac usually halts the display of text in a text window or a directory listing in a directory window (including the listing of mail you've read or sent). It takes a few seconds for AOL's host computer to get the message, however, and sometimes, if you have a high-speed modem connection, the text or directory information will finish displaying before the display process can be stopped.

As I have said in a number of places in this book, a keyword is your shortcut to get to hundreds, even thousands of places on AOL. Using AOL's own customer support department as a guidepost, I've assembled the ten most popular AOL keywords. Some provide speedier access to an online area or feature, others provide a way to reach a customer support center. No doubt you'll develop your own Top 10 as you continue to explore the service. The following list includes the keywords and a short description:

- QuickStart. This keyword is a great starting point if you're new to AOL (see Figure 5.28). You can take a fast tour around the service, learn how to customize your software, and read about new features.

- Members' Choice. Use this keyword to learn about the most popular areas to visit on AOL (see Figure 5.29). A single click on an icon, or a double-click on an item in the list box takes you to one of the places most often visited on AOL. I'll cover the entire list (as of the time this book was prepared) in Appendix D, "AOL's Members' Choice."

FIGURE 5.28

QuickStart guides you through the ins and outs of AOL.

1 A fast-paced online tutorial to the AOL service

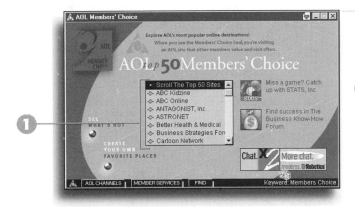

FIGURE 5.29

Learn what your fellow AOL members consider to be the most popular online haunts.

1 Members have picked AOL's most popular forums.

- Keyword. Nope, that's not a typo. This keyword lets you not only view a full list of all the AOL keywords, but it also gives you the Keyword of the Day, where you can visit a special, popular online area. You'll see more popular AOL keywords in Appendix C, "AOL's Most Popular Keywords."

- Random. Try out AOL's roulette wheel for size. You'll be presented with a random selection of popular AOL areas to visit.

- Parental Controls. You can customize the AOL online experience, so your child will have a safe visit to AOL (see Figure 5.30). To use Parental Controls, just log on using your master account name—that's the screen name you chose when you first signed up with AOL. You also can use this area to set custom mail controls so that you aren't inundated with unwanted email solicitations.

FIGURE 5.30

Create a special, safe online environment for your child with this feature.

1 Make AOL safer for your family.

■ Billing. Check your AOL billing status, or change your billing method here.

■ Member Directory. Find other AOL members, or create a profile for yourself so that you'll be a part of this online yellow pages (see Figure 5.31).

FIGURE 5.31

Make yourself known to AOL members by making your own online profile to be included as part of the Member Directory.

1 Find AOL members here.

■ Access. Visit this area to check on a new access number for your city or a city you want to visit. You'll also find advice on getting the best possible connections to AOL.

■ My AOL. Make your AOL software run the way you want, easily. This area (shown in Figure 5.32) guides you through each step of setting preferences, showing you what is changed when you click the **OK** button.

FIGURE 5.32
Configure your AOL software so that it runs the way you want.

1 Adjust software settings here.

- +Top Tips. AOL members and support staff regularly come up with cool, new ways to get the most out of your online visit. Drop in to this area regularly for updates.

SEE ALSO

➤ *To learn more about communicating online, see page 136*
➤ *To learn how to find software online, see page 435*
➤ *For more information about planning a trip, see page 471*

How to Use AOL's Online Help Forums

How to get help on AOL's time

Where to get help from other members

How to talk with AOL online

AOL's Help Options

You should expect that most of your online visits will run smoothly. But there's always the chance that something will go wrong, and you'll need some assistance to solve the problem. When trouble arises, you'll want to consult the various troubleshooting sections of this book. But I don't pretend to be able to cover all possible combinations of software and hardware issues, so there will be times you'll want to consult AOL's online help resources directly.

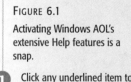

Printing Help text is easy

You can save and print any text item in the **Help** menu for later reference. Just click the text item you want to print first.

Mac AOL supports Apple Guide

The Mac version of AOL's software offers full support for Apple Guide, Apple Computer's interactive help system. Whether you need to know how to use the Download Manager or are connecting to America Online for the first time, this area most likely has the answer you need. For information about AOL's software features, see Appendix B.

The AOL Help Menu (Windows 95 Style)

AOL's **Help** menu in Windows looks pretty much like the ones you find in any other Windows program. If you need basic instructions on doing common AOL tasks, the **Help** menu provides a good amount of useful information. For more details about AOL's Windows software features, see Appendix B, "Setting Up AOL's Software."

If you are signing on to America Online for the first time, take a moment and open the **Help** menu from your AOL program's menu bar (see Figure 6.1).

FIGURE 6.1

Activating Windows AOL's extensive Help features is a snap.

1 Click any underlined item to get help on that subject.

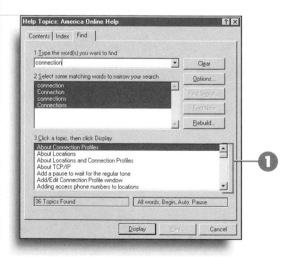

Using Online Troubleshooting Forums

As you wander around the virtual world of AOL and make use of its services, questions may arise that are not covered in the offline Help features. You also may want to find out more about your own online status. America Online offers an extensive online forum dedicated to providing you with information about its services and your account. If you are still paying for your AOL account on an hourly basis, no problem. You won't be charged for the time you spend in this support area.

Accessing AOL's Help forums

1. Select **Member Services** from the **Help** menu or use the keyword Help from anywhere online while you are connected to the service (you can also use the keyword Hotline).

2. You'll see the comprehensive online help forum, which includes live technical support (see Figure 6.2).

In the next few pages, I'll summarize some of the help services AOL offers.

FIGURE 6.2

America Online's Member Services area offers a plate of convenient information to answer many of your questions about the service.

1 Choose help topics from this list.

Help with Downloading

America Online's software makes downloading files to your hard drive a simple task; but at one time or another, you might have questions about downloading. Perhaps your downloads are taking longer than their time estimates, or you are being disconnected during file transfers. If so, getting to the right place for assistance is a task involving several steps (although it takes less time to get from here to there than to describe it). First, use the keyword Help to reach the Member Services area. Then click the **Tutorials** button and, finally, double-click **Downloading Files & Attachments** from the list of help topics at the left (see Figure 6.3).

FIGURE 6.3

AOL will guide you, step-by-step, through the file download process.

1 Follow these directions to download files from AOL.

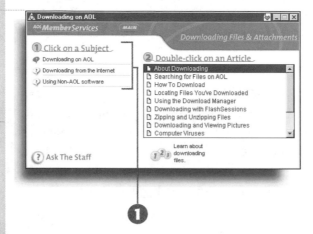

1

How to find a help topic

If you're not able to locate a help topic at first glance in the Member Services area, no problem. Click the **Find It Now** button at the bottom right of the forum screen, and enter the topic you want to explore further.

Is your Mac file a big zero?

If a Macintosh file you've downloaded has a "zero" file size, it's probably corrupt. Download it again. If you pay for your AOL service by the hour, you can request credit for the time lost as a result of the bad download. Just bring up the keyword window, type the keyword Credit, and enter your request in the information screen.

In AOL's Member Services area, you also can find help with email, help in working with the Internet gateway, modem and connect help, help with getting around on AOL, and more. (For more extensive information on AOL's Internet services, see the chapters that make up Part III, "AOL as an Internet Service Provider.")

If you are having difficulties with any of these subjects, you'll want to explore AOL's help areas for possible solutions before writing to or calling the AOL staff for answers. A full 95 percent of members' questions to AOL's support staff can be answered by reading this section of AOL, without placing a call or waiting for an email answer.

How to Resume a File Download

After you've been disconnected during a file download, all is not lost. You can usually reconnect to AOL and resume the file download at the point where you were disconnected.

To do this, first check your Download Manager to verify that the file is still listed there. Click the **My Files** toolbar icon and select the **Download Manager** option from the drop-down menu (see Figure 6.4).

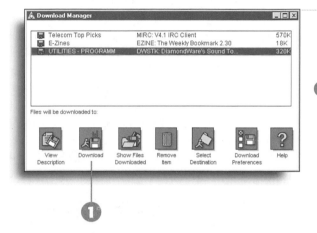

FIGURE 6.4

The AOL Download Manager can be used to resume the download process.

1 Click the **Download** button to resume file transfers.

If the partially downloaded file is present, reconnect to America Online, perhaps using a different access number. Select the file in the Download Manager window, and click the **Download** icon. The file should resume transferring in a few seconds.

To resume a download successfully, you must not throw away or move the file that represents your partially completed download. This file is usually located in the C:\America Online 4.0\download directory for Windows users, or the Online Downloads folder for Mac users. This partial file has the same name as the file you are downloading, and its icon may show a torn or jagged edge to indicate that it's incomplete.

If you intentionally or inadvertently discarded this file, the partially completed download is still listed in the Download Manager, but you won't be able to resume the download using the Download Manager. Select the item in the Download Manager listing, and then click the **Remove** icon to remove the entry from the Download Manager's list of files.

Members Helping Members

Keyword: MHM

Another handy help resource on AOL is run by your fellow members. It's called Members Helping Members (see Figure 6.5), and it consists of a series of message boards where you can ask your question or state your problem. Whether you're having trouble with your AOL software or navigating through the service, you'll find that a lot of knowledgeable online visitors frequent this message board to answer questions. As you become more knowledgeable about handling routine online problems, you might want to help out others who seek advice from this message area. I used to participate in this area often before I began writing books about AOL, and it provided me with lots of valuable information about the service.

FIGURE 6.5

Your fellow AOL members can help you solve a problem with this service.

1 Get help from other AOL members in this forum.

Member Help Interactive

When text files don't give you the assistance you need, you can interact with a live AOL representative about your problem. The Member Help Interactive Auditorium (sometimes known as Tech Live) is open from 7 a.m. to 2:45 a.m. eastern time, seven days a week (and fortunately no single person needs to staff it for that long a period). You can get live help from AOL's experienced Customer Relations staff in the free Member Services area of America Online.

Getting to the Member Help Interactive area is a little complex, because it's offered as a last resort.

Where do you get online help with your new AOL software?

If you're using a new version of AOL software, you can get help from members and forum staff in the Upgrade forum (keyword Upgrade). You'll always find convenient help texts about the new software version, and an active message area.

How to reach AOL's Member Help Interactive area

1. Open any of the Member Services Help topics as I've done in Figure 6.6.

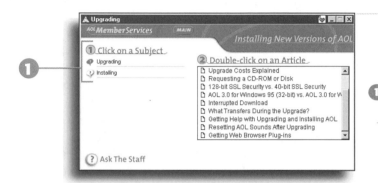

FIGURE 6.6

Use AOL's online assistance to get help with your questions about the service.

1 Choose your help topic from this screen.

2. Click the **Ask The Staff** button, which brings up information on how to get further assistance.

3. The third option includes a direct link to AOL's Tech Live Auditorium. Click that link to bring up the screen shown in Figure 6.7.

FIGURE 6.7

At last, the entranceway to AOL's one-on-one assistance area.

1 Receive live support from AOL in this area.

Checking Your Online Bill

Keyword: `Billing`

An important way to keep up-to-date on your accumulated online charges (without having to have a calculator at hand) is to review your bill on a regular basis. The keyword `Billing` takes you to AOL's account center, where you can double-click the item labeled Current Month's Billing Summary to see the charges you've run up.

Connect to AOL Through Another Online Service to Save Money

On AOL 800 and 888 numbers aren't free

Although you may have unlimited or flat-rate access to AOL, you can still run up hourly charges. If you use AOL's 800 or 888 numbers, or access the service from another country, the counter ticks and charges accumulate for every minute of your online time. Check AOL's modem access area at keyword **Access** for a list of hourly charges that may apply to certain phone numbers.

Connecting to AOL via an ISP has limits

When you sign up for AOL's "Bring Your Own Access Plan," you'll pay an extra hourly charge whenever you access AOL through its own dial-up network.

If you're a member of another Internet service, such as AT&T WorldNet, EarthLink, or Netcom, you can qualify for reduced charges to AOL. All you need to do is agree to connect to AOL exclusively through the other service. After you do that, you'll be able to sign up for AOL's "Bring Your Own Access" plan. The billing area includes information on various AOL pricing options. Be sure to read Chapter 12, "Using AOL's Internet Services," for information on how you can quickly connect to AOL after logging on to another Internet service.

AOL's BBS

Another little known help resource is AOL's own Technical Support BBS, which you can call with any of the numerous terminal programs or telecommunications packages available for your computer. The America Online BBS supports modem speeds of up to 28,800bps and is available 24 hours a day. You can find local access numbers, modem strings, and other connecting and troubleshooting information. The BBS number is toll-free: 1-800-827-5808.

The Technical Support BBS is not a part of the America Online service, so you won't need your screen name(s) or other account information when calling. The information on this BBS is provided to help you only with problems connecting to America Online and using the AOL software.

Getting Modem Help

If you can get onto the America Online service, you can also get detailed modem assistance from the Modem Help forum, available via the keyword Modem. Much of the information found here is the same as on the AOL BBS—modem setting strings, connecting tips, and some basic troubleshooting tips (see Figure 6.8).

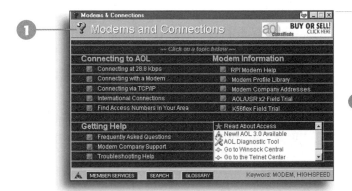

FIGURE 6.8
AOL offers convenient advice on solving common modem setup and connection problems.

1 Use this forum to get help with your modem.

If you have a modem that isn't listed in the Setup box of your America Online software, you may find a driver for your modem available for download in this area. At the least, you'll find advice on how to customize the existing profiles to work better with your modem.

Dealing with System Busy Problems

This is an all-too-common situation:

Question: *Why am I getting a message that a request to the host has taken too long or the system is busy when I try to access an online area?*

Answer: Your AOL connection to the host computer is a continuing process of communication. You make a request with your software, such as opening a window or accessing another area, and the host computer respond by delivering what you request. If the delay is more than a minute or two, you'll get a message that the system is busy (see Figure 6.9).

When you encounter this symptom, try the following:

1. Log off AOL and immediately log on again. Sometimes that's all it takes to improve system response.

2. Sometimes AOL response is slow during the peak evening hours (equivalent to prime time on network TV), from 8 to 11p.m. eastern time. If quickly logging off and on doesn't help, choose an hour when network traffic is lower.

Is AOL off the air?

America Online usually shuts down the service once or twice a month for two to four early morning hours to install system upgrades or to conduct routine maintenance and repair work on the host computer system. Usually when logging on during this period, you'll get a message screen announcing that the service is temporarily shut down, along with the approximate time the service is expected to be restored. Sometimes you won't. If you can't get past the Connecting to America Online screen when logging on, the best thing to do is wait an hour or two and try again. You can check the list of upcoming maintenance operations via the keyword **AOLInsider**.

3. Try another access number. Use the keyword Access to get the list of the numbers in your city.

4. Check your modem settings. For hints and tips on how to get the best connections, read Chapter 4, "Secrets of High-Speed Access on AOL."

If you still experience host or system response problems, read the next section, "Using the System Response Support Area," for information on how to report the problem to America Online.

FIGURE 6.9

AOL's dialog box informs you that the message isn't getting through.

 This screen shows AOL has "timed out."

Using the System Response Support Area

Keyword: System Response

On most occasions, your connections to AOL should be fast, and your performance good. Sometimes, due to a number of factors, (some related, some not) you'll have problems getting online or maintaining good response during your online visit. You may experience a failure of the host to respond or see a message that the system has too many requests to handle. You may have difficulty getting connected, or experience problems with staying online.

Refer to Chapter 4, where many of the common connection problems you're apt to encounter are explained as well as how to configure your modem for the best possible performance.

The troubleshooting item mentioned earlier describes common host-related symptoms.

If none of the steps described in the troubleshooting section of Chapter 4 get you any closer to reliable AOL performance, you'll want to check out the System Response Report Area (see Figure 6.10).

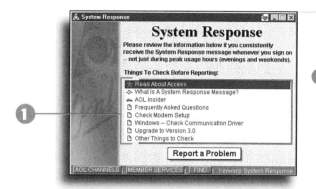

FIGURE 6.10

Report frequent AOL performance problems here.

1. Learn how to deal with AOL system problems here.

The System Response area has a number of text items for you to read, covering the most common connection problems and their causes. You can save or print these text articles for later review. If none of these articles or the steps I've described in this chapter (or in Chapter 4, which has extensive troubleshooting advice on dealing with modem-related problems) bring you closer to a solution to your problem, you'll want to file a report with AOL's technical staff, by clicking the **Report a Problem** button.

You'll have a choice of reports you can send, depending on the kind of problem you have. AOL's technicians will investigate your problem and respond to you via email in a day or two.

How to Handle a System Crash on Your PC

Although the two top computing platforms differ in many ways, both have a few things in common: a system crash. In this section, you'll find some advice on how you, as a user of Microsoft Windows, can deal with common system problems. If you cross computing platforms from time to time, you'll see some of the advice offered here is similar to the advice presented in the next section, where I discuss dealing with problems on a Mac.

The first thing to do if you experience a system error while connected to America Online is to turn off your modem. This disconnects you from America Online before a large amount of bad data is sent to AOL, which can happen during some types of crashes. A data storm, or random data, sent in AOL's direction might confuse the host into not recognizing that you have left and prevent you from signing on again after you have restarted your computer. This doesn't happen often, but it can be annoying to see a message stating that you can't sign on because you are already using AOL. If a simple application error occurred, and if that application was not AOL, you may be able to return to AOL long enough to log off; then reboot your computer.

If your America Online Windows software crashes with a General Protection Fault error, try to exit the AOL application, exit any other active applications after saving any documents that are being worked on, and then attempt to restart Windows. If you cannot restart Windows, or if attempts to resume working in Windows after restarting does not succeed, turn off your computer, and then turn it on again.

If you experience a total system lockup, sometimes you can exit a crashing application by pressing Ctrl+Alt+Delete (all at the same time). After you've restarted, you may see a directory alerting you to continue to boot Windows 95 in a Safe Mode, and you should start your computer in this manner to make sure nothing has gone wrong with your operating system software.

Reinstalling America Online for Windows

What happens if you experience repeated and confusing problems, such as constant system error messages, or the modem lights up like the Fourth of July but never dials or gives an error message? If this is happening to you, it's possible something in your AOL files that stores your individual data has become corrupted, especially if you had a recent bout with system crashes.

If you suspect that your America Online software is corrupt, you should reinstall your AOL software. Doing this is a fairly simple task. You can either perform a clean installation, where you start your AOL connection from scratch, or perform an update installation, where your previous settings are copied from your previously installed copy. I recommend the clean installation as the best and easiest method of isolating intermittent problems with the AOL software.

Doing a clean install of AOL's software

1. Choose **Settings**, **Control Panel** from your Windows 95 **Start** menu.

2. Double-click the **Add/Remove Programs** icon.

3. Select **America Online** from the Install/Uninstall window.

4. Click the **Add/Remove** button at the bottom of the screen and follow the onscreen prompts to remove your AOL software.

5. Insert your first AOL program disk or CD in your PC's drive.

6. Use the Add/Remove utility to locate and launch your AOL software installer or just double-click the **Setup** icon.

7. You will see a message asking whether you want to install a new copy or upgrade from an existing one. Choose the option to install a new copy.

8. Follow the onscreen prompts to continue with your AOL software installation.

To perform a clean installation with Windows 3.1, delete your existing AOL program folder (after transferring your downloaded files to another directory) and then run the program setup in the normal way, just as I describe in Appendix A, "The First Steps to Get Online." By re-installing your AOL software in this manner, none of the settings or downloaded artwork from the previous version will be copied to your newly installed program, thus reducing the risk of further problems.

Signing on After Re-installation

After your AOL software has been re-installed, launch the program and then start the sign-on process just as I described it in Appendix A. When you see the sign-on screen, choose the option to sign on as an existing member. From here, enter any of your AOL screen names and accompanying passwords. Your connection is then established, and all your account information is transferred to the new software.

Getting rid of your old AOL directory under Windows 3.1

If you're still using Windows 3.1, you can manually delete the AOL program directory. Just don't forget to remove downloaded files from the download directory.

Don't lose those important AOL files!

Removal of your AOL software also removes the contents of your Address Book, Personal Filing Cabinet, and Favorite Places directory. You may prefer to do an upgrade installation, where this information is transferred to the new copy of AOL. After that, you can easily delete the original AOL program directory.

If the problems that caused you to re-install your software in the first place do not recur, you can continue setting your preferences and options in your freshly installed software. For setting all the information about configuring your AOL software to your taste, see Appendix B, "Setting Up AOL's Software."

If the system crashes continue, it may well be that you have other problems in your operating system or computer to deal with instead. You may want to consider re-installing Windows 95, or consulting your manuals for further advice on troubleshooting these problems. For some really helpful insights, I suggest you get a copy of my own favorite Windows 95 reference, Que's *Using Windows 95* by Ed Bott.

How to Handle a System Crash on Your Mac

No doubt, the most annoying thing to happen to your computer is a system crash. Although they come in a variety of flavors, most system crashes taste bad. If you encounter such a problem, the following are some procedures you can follow to get up and running again:

- If you experience a system error while connected to America Online, turn off your modem. This will disconnect you from America Online before a sizable amount of bad data can be sent to AOL, which can happen during some types of crashes. A data storm, or random data, sent in AOL's direction might confuse the host into not recognizing that you have left and prevent you from signing on again after you have restarted your computer. This does not happen often, but it can be annoying to see a message stating that you can't sign on because you are already using AOL. If a simple application error occurred, and if that application was not AOL, you may be able to return to AOL long enough to log off; then restart your Macintosh.

- If the error was with the AOL application or occurred while AOL was the frontmost application, chances are you can't resume or save any work that may have been in progress. In this case, you should select the **Restart** button in the error

No sound

Help, my AOL sounds are gone. When I see a new mail announcement, I hear silence. What happened? AOL's software uses standard system capabilities to generate these sounds. If the sounds disappear, the first thing to do is see if your other system sounds are working.

For Windows Users: If your computer has stopped producing sounds, make sure your soundcard and drivers are set up properly. If you're using an add-on speaker system, you'll want to check to be certain it's switched on and plugged in (loose plugs are not uncommon). If other sounds on your PC work okay, open your Sounds Control Panel and check AOL's sounds from the scrolling list. You may have to relink (associate) these sounds to get them to work after a new installation of AOL's software.

For Mac Users: Open the Sounds or Monitors & Sound Control Panel and make sure the volume settings are high enough for sounds to be audible. If you're using an add-on speaker system, check the cables and AC plug to be sure everything is set up properly (and that the speakers are on).

message. After you've restarted your computer, look in your Trash for a Rescued Items folder when your machine restarts. If any of your open applications were using temporary files, you may be able to recover some or all the data you lost from this folder.

- If you can't get the **Restart** button in the bomb window to work, try a force quit, holding down the ⌘-Option-Escape keys. If that doesn't free the frozen application, read your Macintosh manual for instructions on activating the reset switch (on some models it's done via keyboard command) to get your Mac to reboot as painlessly as possible.

Re-installing America Online for the Mac OS

If you suspect that your America Online software is corrupt, you should re-install your AOL software. Doing this is a fairly simple task. You can either perform a clean installation, where you start your AOL connection from scratch, or perform an update installation, where you upgrade from your previous copy of AOL software. I recommend the clean installation as the best and easiest method of isolating intermittent problems with the AOL software.

Performing a clean install of your Mac OS AOL software

1. Restart your Mac OS computer with Extensions off (Shift key held down at startup).

2. Rename your America Online software folder so that the installer doesn't select it by accident.

3. Go to your System Folder and check the Extensions folder for files labeled AOL Link, AOL Link Enhanced, AOL Scanner (the latter two are not always installed), and Open OT (only appears on Macs running system versions prior to Mac OS 8). Trash them all.

4. Open the Preferences folder inside the System Folder and look for a folder labeled America Online. Trash it.

New Mac system versions are much more stable

Changes in Mac OS 7.6 and 8.0 have reduced the severity of many system crashes. For most users, the net result of a crash is an application quitting, rather than freezing. This gives you a chance to safely restart your computer without further difficulty. If your Mac is compatible with either system, I recommend the upgrade.

You should save some of those old AOL files

If you want to keep your AOL Address Book, Personal Filing Cabinet, and Favorite Places, be sure to save the Address Book and Filing Cabinet files from the Data folder inside your America Online Preferences folder. Otherwise, you'll lose your Favorite Places, stored email and messages, and your Address Book. Also, you'll want to move all downloaded files from the Downloads folder to any other available folder outside of the old AOL program folder so that you don't accidentally delete them when you remove your old AOL software.

5. Insert your first AOL software disk or CD into your Mac's drive and double-click the installer icon on the disk.

6. Proceed with the new installation precisely as described in Appendix A.

7. When the installation is complete, click the **Restart** button that appears to restart your computer.

Signing on After Re-installation

After your Mac AOL software has been re-installed, launch the newly installed program and begin the sign-on process as described in Appendix A. When you see the sign-on screen, choose the option to sign on as an existing member. From here, enter any of your AOL screen names and accompanying passwords. Your connection is then established, and all your account information is transferred to the new software.

If the problems that caused you to reinstall your software in the first place do not recur, you can continue setting your preferences and options in your freshly installed software. For all the information about configuring your AOL software to your taste, see Appendix B.

If the original symptoms persist, however, the problem probably isn't caused by corrupt AOL software. You can discard the new software and resume using the original software. To be safe, however, you may prefer to just continue working with the new copy of your AOL software and trash the older version.

After all this, if you can't get your AOL software to work, give AOL's customer service people a call at 800-827-3338 (in Virginia 703-448-8700), or contact the manufacturer of your computer for additional assistance.

SEE ALSO

➤ *Using AOL software, see page 510*

➤ *Exploring AOL, see page 72*

Parental Issues and Internet Access

AOL is for Families

America Online has become the world's largest online service for many reasons. Savvy promotion is surely one factor; the friendly, accessible interface is another. And AOL's family approach is an important consideration.

AOL is basically a warm, friendly place that you might think of as your hometown in cyberspace. But like your hometown, there are some folks who don't always use common sense and courtesy toward others. When you, as a parent, allow your kids to enter the online universe, you want to be sure their visits are always friendly, fun, and educational.

Children Online—Understanding the Risks

The online experience should be friendly and fun, and it is just that for most AOL members. As with other parts of our society, however, a few people do not have the best interests of you and your children in mind. Throughout this chapter, the methods to help protect your children are outlined. You'll want to read and discuss them with your children before they begin to explore AOL's online community.

Although problems seldom occur, a few things you and your child should watch out for during your travels on AOL are listed here:

- *Inappropriate material.* As explained later in this chapter, nude or explicit photos and related text material are not allowed on AOL. That doesn't stop some people from exchanging such files, however. You should instruct your child to bring information about such files directly to your attention so that the proper parties at America Online can be alerted.

- *Face-to-face meetings.* You should instruct your child never to give out personal information, such as your home address or telephone number to another AOL member (however friendly that member may seem) without your approval (even if the person online claims to be the same age as your child). Any personal meetings between your child and another AOL member should be done under your supervision at a public location.

- *Online harassment.* If your child receives instant messages or email that is threatening, intimidating, or contains objectionable content, have your child bring the material directly to your attention so that you can file a complaint against the member who sends such material.

- *Internet access.* The Internet is largely unregulated and not subject to Parental Controls or America Online's Terms of Service. As a result, you'll want to instruct your child carefully about both the benefits and potential downsides of accessing such Internet features as Internet Relay Chats, Usenet, and the World Wide Web before your child begins to explore.

In the next few pages, you learn how to set restrictions on areas your child may visit, and how to deal with problems if they occur.

Introducing AOL's Neighborhood Watch

Keyword: Neighborhood Watch

To help inform you of AOL's programs for a safer online community, AOL has established a feature called Neighborhood Watch (see Figure 7.1). It's an area where you learn how to set Parental Controls (I'll describe that in the next section of this chapter), how to keep from being bombarded with junk email, how to protect yourself against computer viruses, and ways to contact AOL in case of a problem.

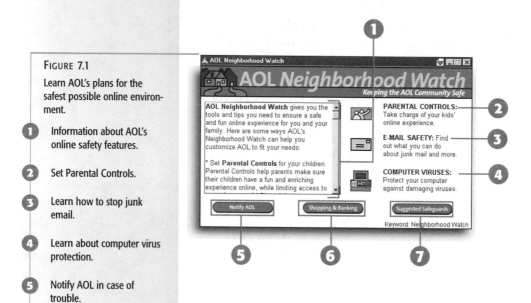

FIGURE 7.1

Learn AOL's plans for the safest possible online environment.

1 Information about AOL's online safety features.

2 Set Parental Controls.

3 Learn how to stop junk email.

4 Learn about computer virus protection.

5 Notify AOL in case of trouble.

6 Shop and bank online in safety.

7 Additional suggestions for online safety.

In the following sections, I'll describe some of these features in more detail.

Teach Yourself: How to Set Parental Controls

Keyword: Parental Controls

As with any concerned parent, you will probably want to restrict your child's access to certain areas of America Online. That's the purpose of Parental Controls. This feature permits the original account holder (the screen name you created when you first established your AOL account—the one at the top of the list—which AOL calls *Master Screen Name*) to block or restrict access by users of other screen names on your AOL account from certain areas and features on America Online (see Figure 7.2). Setting these limits can help protect your child against possible exposure to objectionable material or online harassment in some areas of the service.

FIGURE 7.2

Learn how to set Parental Controls here.

① After reading the information here, click **Set Parental Controls Now**.

After you examine the information text in Figure 7.2, you'll want to establish those settings. In the Parental Controls dialog box click **Set Parental Controls Now** to bring up the setup screen shown in Figure 7.3.

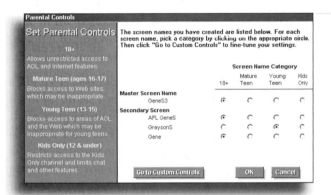

FIGURE 7.3

The Parental Controls dialog box is used to direct your child's access to AOL.

Parental Controls can be activated with the keyword `Parental Controls`, or by choosing that command from the My AOL toolbar's drop-down menu while you're logged on with your master screen name (the one you created when you first joined AOL). It's also available by clicking the icon that appears to the left of most chat room windows.

Don't tell anyone your password

Your account password and billing information are confidential. You will never be asked by an AOL employee online to give out this information. If you ever receive such a request (even from someone who claims to work for AOL), report it in AOL's Terms of Service area immediately via the keywords TOS or Notify AOL.

Give your kids their own screen name

Before you set up special controls for your kids, you'll want to create a screen name for them. You can access that feature via keyword Names. You can learn how to do this in Chapter 8, "AOL's People Connection."

Web sites are rated as family safe

Microsystems Software, Inc., of Framingham, Massachusetts uses a team of parents and teachers to examine Internet resources and determine whether they are suitable for a specific age group. In addition, AOL members can, via AOL's Custom Parental Controls (see the next section), report additional sites for the company to check out.

You can establish controls for just one or all screen names on your account. After Parental Controls are set for a particular screen name, it is in force every time that screen name logs on. Changes to Parental Control settings can be made by the master account holder at any time.

The easiest thing to do is to choose AOL's preset Parental Controls, which customizes accounts in three categories:

- **18+.** This is the default setting. It gives you full access to all regular AOL and Internet-based areas.

- **Mature Teen.** This is the account recommended for those 16 to 17. Only one main set of restrictions exist to this account, and that is Internet access. Teens will only be able to access sites approved for AOL by Microsystems Software, Inc. as appropriate for this age group. In addition, your teen will not be able to access Internet newsgroups that allow file attachments (these are ripe sources for inappropriate material).

- **Young Teen.** This setting applies to children ages 13 through 15. The primary restriction is to Web sites that do not pass muster as being safe for early teens after review by Microsystems Software, Inc.

- **Kids Only.** This account provides a controlled online experience for those 12 years or under. Your child can only access the Kids Only channel and World Wide Web sites approved for AOL by Microsystems Software, Inc. In addition, your child won't be able to send or receive instant messages (the one-on-one message system I described in Chapter 10, "Chatting Online"), or send or receive email with attached files.

Teach Yourself: How to Set Parental Mail Controls

Each element of your child's access can be customized by clicking the **Custom Controls** option (see Figure 7.4). You can set custom access for Chat, Instant Messages, Downloading, Newsgroups, Mail, and the Web. Because the range of controls is modified by AOL from time to time, you'll want to click the specific title to bring up a screen showing the current options.

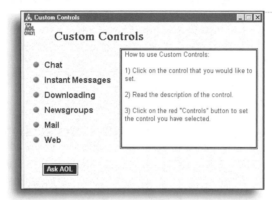

FIGURE 7.4

AOL's Custom Controls feature lets you customize access in six different categories.

One possible source of objectionable material is email. It is, unfortunately, common for folks to send out mass mailings of material without regard to whether the material is appropriate to the person receiving the information.

To customize a child's email, click the button to the left of the **Mail** option in the Custom Controls screen shown in Figure 7.4. Then click the **Mail Controls** button that appears at the bottom of the next screen to bring up the list of screen names. After you select a screen name, click **Edit** to bring up the setup panel shown in Figure 7.5.

The Mail Control features let you allow your child to receive email or block all email. You may also restrict email to certain addresses, such as family members or friends known to you.

FIGURE 7.5

This screen lets you customize your child's ability to receive email on AOL.

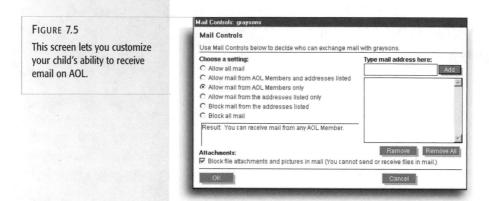

Setting AOL's email controls

1. You can designate the screen names you approve in the email address list at the right of the screen shown in Figure 7.5. First click the button to allow the email addresses, enter the name in the **Type mail address here** text box, and click the **Add** button to add the name to the list.

2. To block addresses, click the option to block mail from the addresses listed, type the name in the **Type mail address here** text box, then click the **Add** button to include the name.

3. To eliminate an email address in your list, just select the name in the email address list, and click the **Remove** button.

4. Your final option (one that is an automatic part of the Kids Only option I described in the previous section on Parental Controls) is the capability to block email with attached files.

5. After you've customized your Mail Controls for a specific screen name, click **OK** to put them in effect. If you change your mind, just click the **Cancel** button and the changes you made won't be applied.

Email Isn't Always Welcome

One time, long ago, email was just something to exchange personal messages with your friends and business associates. The Internet has become extremely commercial and the amount of unsolicited email on the Internet has become a problem.

It's no secret that every day you log on to AOL (or any online service or Internet provider for that matter), you'll see email containing ads for all sorts of promotions, ranging from work at home schemes, to sources for x-rated material. It's the online equivalent of the junk mail that fills your mailbox.

AOL has taken steps to prevent major sources of *spam email* (mass mailings of unsolicited material) from reaching the mailboxes of AOL members. They've filed lawsuits against the most blatant offenders, and they've expanded the Mail Controls feature to block entire Internet sites from sending email to you.

The firms who create this junk email sometimes get around this by forging the return address so that it appears to come from a source different from the actual point of origin. You have two methods to combat this sort of material.

First, use Mail Controls to reduce the clutter in your online mailbox. Second, use the Forward feature of your AOL email to send the unsolicited email directly to the screen name **TOSSpam**. AOL's email wizards go over this junk email on a regular basis, and take steps to stop it where possible.

None of these steps eliminate email clutter completely, any more than the junk mail you receive from the post office will ever disappear. The combination of AOL's Mail Controls feature and their online review of such email, however, definitely helps reduce the quantity of this material.

Reviewing America Online's Terms of Service

Keyword: TOS

Throughout this book, I've compared America Online to a large, sprawling city, with lots of friendly neighborhoods and friendly neighbors. To take this comparison one step further, let's realize that some people choose not to follow the common-sense guidelines of good online conduct, which is to respect your fellow AOL members and treat them with kindness.

When you first sign up with America Online, you agree to accept the *Terms of Service*, which is the set of rules and regulations under which it operates. Consider these rules somewhat equivalent to the body of laws that govern the conduct of people who live in any community.

The Terms of Service (see Figure 7.6) covers not only your contract with America Online, but a set of rules for online conduct. As in your hometown, the parents of the children who visit America Online are fully responsible for the way they behave. If your child consistently misbehaves online, you run the risk of losing your AOL membership, so these rules should be taken seriously.

FIGURE 7.6

This special information area is devoted to AOL's Terms of Service.

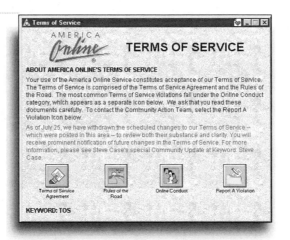

The Terms of Service Summarized

AOL's Terms of Service available for you to read at any time during your online visits. You also can save and print the text material you see there for later review. You may want to make a copy and discuss the contents with your children before they make their online visits.

The online rules I'm briefly describing here are based on the ones in effect when this book was written. The rules are modified from time to time, so you'll want to check the TOS area for the current set and the exact language.

Some of the important features of AOL's Terms of Service are described here. You can examine the full text (and it may differ somewhat from what you see here) during your AOL session via the keyword TOS:

- *Offensive communication.* Don't use vulgar, abusive, or hateful language in your communications with others online. If the conduct is reported to AOL, you may receive a warning on your account, or if the offense is blatant enough, you may lose your AOL membership.

- *Harassment.* Don't harass other members or engage in conduct that may make them feel uncomfortable. When you discuss an issue in a chat room or a message board, feel free to disagree with one's ideas, but no personal attacks, please.

- *Graphic files.* Don't transfer or attempt to post images that are sexually explicit or offensive.

- *Scrolling.* If you type nonsense text in a chat room screen, causing line after line of text to appear in the chat room window, you're disrupting the chat. You could be ejected from the chat room by an AOL Guide or chat host, or be subject to action against your account by AOL's Community Action Team (the folks who handle TOS issues). *Scrolling* means repeatedly causing the screen text to move or scroll faster than members are able to type to it. It is caused by a user entering a set of random characters or by repeatedly entering a carriage return or any such action to a similar disruptive effect. Scrolling is an expressly prohibited form of disruption.

- *Impersonation.* Don't impersonate another member or AOL staff member. If you're caught pretending to be an AOL staffer (even if only as a joke), you could have your account revoked immediately.

- *Room disruption.* In addition to "scrolling," as described previously, you should not engage in conduct that disrupts a chat room in any way. You could be ejected from the room by an AOL Guide or get a bad mark on your account record (which, if repeated often enough can result in the loss of your AOL membership).

- *Chain letters and pyramid schemes*. The post office prohibits chain letters and so does AOL. If you get such a communication, use the **Notify AOL** feature (available from the **Members** menu) to report the problem.

- *Advertising and solicitation*. Don't make commercial offerings except in areas designed for those purposes, such as AOL's Classifieds area (at keyword Classifieds).

If You See a Violation

If you see anyone violating the Terms of Service online, be a good online citizen and report the offensive conduct to AOL's online police department, the Community Action Team.

To report a problem, click the **Report A Violation** button in the Terms of Service (TOS) area or use the keyword Notify AOL to bring up the area where you can report an online problem. Either step brings up the screen shown in Figure 7.7.

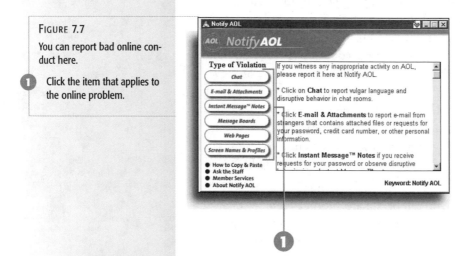

Click the item that applies to the problem you want to report. For example, if you see a violation in a chat room area, click the **Chat** icon; the Chat Area Violations window appears (see Figure 7.8). Enter the information about the problem in the clearly labeled text entry fields.

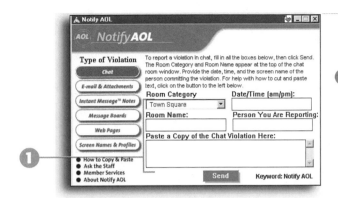

FIGURE 7.8

Use this form to report a chat room violation.

1   Use the Tab key to step through the text entry windows.

The kind of violations described in this section don't happen often. I've been an America Online member since 1989 and a Forum Leader since 1994, and I've only witnessed a handful of violations myself, despite spending thousands and thousands of hours online. The vast majority of online visitors never see these problems, but it's better to be aware of the possibility and act accordingly.

Special Forums for Parents

It's a complex world, which makes the task of bringing up children more and more difficult. America Online has set up several areas where parents can learn more about coping with the problems of daily living and how to deal with the problems and concerns of their children.

Visiting AOL Families

Keyword: AOL Families, Parents

The AOL Families channel offers a fully integrated collection of forums dedicated to parental interests and concerns (see Figure 7.9). A number of special areas that you'll want to consult from time to time are available in this forum; this section discusses just a few of them.

A shortcut for kids

A fast way for your kids to call up the report form is the keyword KO Help, which brings up the Notify AOL screen shown earlier in Figure 7.7.

You are responsible for what others do on your account

The master screen name will always be notified if a violation of Terms of Service is committed under any screen name on that account. If your child commits repeated violations, your account may be closed without notice, and it will require telephone contact with AOL's customer service department to restore the account (with no guarantees if the violations are severe enough). If the account is closed, all you'll see on the screen when you try to connect to AOL is a message that the account name is invalid, that you must call AOL for further assistance.

FIGURE 7.9

Pay a visit to the AOL Families channel to learn more about dealing with the complex parental issues of today.

① Click a button to access more features.

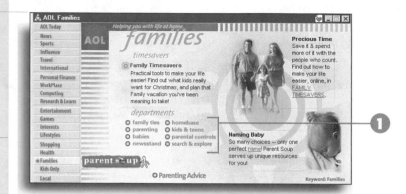

AOL emphasizes color

Most of the photos you see online are in full color. To view them that way, you need a computer that not only supports color, but a color monitor on which to view the photo.

When you first visit the Families area, click the **Parent Soup** button to see a special feature being emphasized for regular visitors. One example is shown in Figure 7.10.

In the example shown here, you'll find additional features listed in a drop-down menu.

FIGURE 7.10

The AOL Families Parent Soup area emphasizes special features and online conferences you'll want to explore further.

① The drop-down menu shows more features.

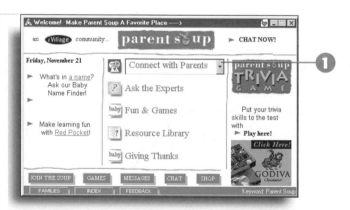

Using the National Parenting Center

Keyword: TNPC

AOL's National Parenting Center forum is designed to provide parents with useful information to make their jobs easier (see Figure 7.11). The center was founded in 1989, and the online area provides a large library of helpful information that deals with common problems and concerns of modern parenting.

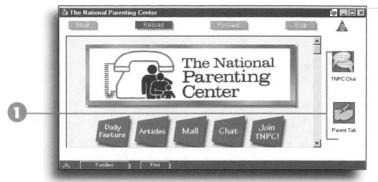

FIGURE 7.11

The National Parenting Center offers comprehensive advice for parents.

1 Click an icon to see more features.

When you visit this area, you'll want to read the online articles and participate in the Parent Forum message area. The Mall offers a selection of informative literature for purchase. Conferences are also regularly scheduled in the TNPC Chat area (shown at the right of the forum's main screen).

After reading about the activities of the National Parenting Center, you might want to consider becoming a member. Full membership information is provided in this online support area; AOL members are offered a special membership rate.

Parental Controls for the Internet

You may decide it's better for your child not to have access to certain Internet-based features. AOL has established a set of Parental Controls for this area, too, activated in much the same way as the regular Parental Controls described earlier in this chapter.

To turn on Parental Controls for the Internet, use the keyword Newsgroups, and click the **Parental Controls** button at the main Newsgroups screen (see Figure 7.12). You may also activate Internet Parental Controls from the regular Parental Controls area.

After clicking the button at the left of the screen name for which you want to establish Parental Controls, click the **Edit** button to get the Blocking Criteria screen shown in Figure 7.13.

Use your master screen name

As with AOL's regular Parental Controls, you can't activate the controls in the Newsgroups area unless you have logged on using your master AOL screen name.

FIGURE 7.12

Parental Controls settings are available from the main Newsgroup screen.

1 Click the **Parental Controls** button.

FIGURE 7.13

Select from the choices available via Internet Parental Controls.

1 Enter the names of the newsgroups you want to exclude.

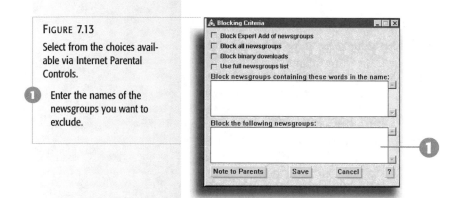

You can click the options shown to control access of other members on your account to specific Internet newsgroup features. Each option can apply to any screen name you select:

- **Block Expert Add of newsgroups.** This feature is used to prevent adding newsgroups that are not a part of AOL's standard listing.

- **Block all newsgroups.** For the ultimate level of protection, you may choose this option so that your child has no access to this feature.

- **Block binary downloads.** This feature is used to prevent a member from downloading encoded files in an Internet newsgroup. Such files are a possible source of objectionable graphic files.

- **Use full newsgroups list.** This feature affords full access to all newsgroups features, but you can selectively change their availability by selecting one or both of the next two items.

- **Block newsgroups containing these words in the name.** You can use this feature to specify certain words, such as "sex" or "erotica," which may represent newsgroups that will offer unsuitable material for your child.

- **Block the following newsgroups.** You can use this feature to specify the names of the newsgroups you want to block for a specific AOL screen name. *You need to enter the newsgroup name exactly to block it.*

- **Note to Parents.** Click this button to get an overview of Internet newsgroups and the best ways to participate in this exciting Internet feature.

By using one or more of these Parental Controls, you can allow your child limited access to the Internet within the guidelines you set, and help provide a safe online experience. Remember, however, that these changes can be made only when you've logged on using your master account name (the first screen name shown when you click the pop-up list of names in your AOL software).

SEE ALSO

➤ *Discover how your child can improve performance at school with a little assistance from AOL's educational forums, see page 390*

➤ *Learn how to get software help from AOL, see page 100*

Communicating Online

AOL's People Connection

Create a profile

Learn about other members

Find your friends

Proper online conduct

Anyone out there—find other members with similar interests

AOL's most popular hangouts

Making Friends Online

Through much of this book, I discussed AOL's channels and forums and areas accessible via the Internet. AOL is not just about forums, libraries, and message boards. For many, the most enjoyable aspect of becoming an America Online member is the ability to meet others with similar interests, whether computer-related or not.

If that's your interest, you'll find that AOL's People Connection is where it's at.

People Connection offers a number of resources to help you meet other online members. You find out about these resources in the following paragraphs. First, you probably want to learn how to introduce yourself to others.

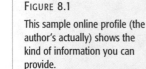

Why have another screen name?

Having another screen name can be useful to help you separate your business and personal life. If you have family members who want to visit AOL, you'll want to consider a separate screen name for each. This gives each family member their own privacy.

Teach Yourself: How to Create and Update Your Online Profile

Every member of America Online has at least one screen name. You can create as many as five screen names to use when the mood strikes you or for use by other members of your family. Every member also can create an online profile for each of those online names, for other members to view (see Figure 8.1). Your first step toward meeting people is complete when you fill out your own online profile.

FIGURE 8.1

This sample online profile (the author's actually) shows the kind of information you can provide.

1 Only the entries you type may show up here.

Besides the expected information such as your real name, screen name, and location, you can enter personal information about yourself to indicate your interests to others. Hobbies, favorite quotes, your occupation, and the kind of computers you use are some of the entries you might want to provide for your profile. To create or change your profile, open the **Members** menu of your America Online software and choose **Member Directory**. Then click the **My Profile** button at the upper right of the Member Directory screen. Figure 8.2 shows a complete list of the data you can enter.

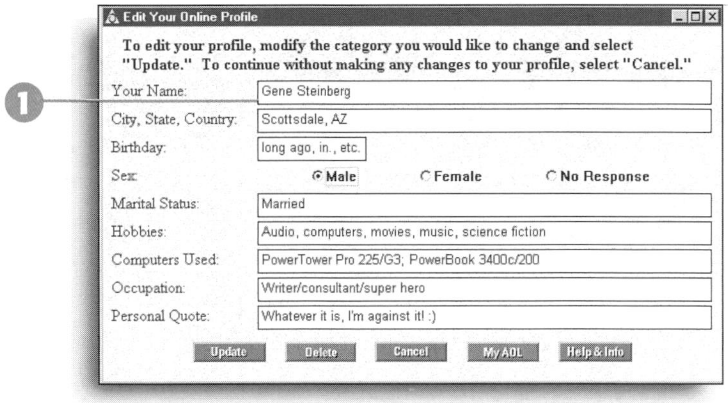

FIGURE 8.2

The data-entry screen for your personal online profile.

1 Type the requested information in the text boxes.

As you look at the Edit Your Online Profile screen, make a note to yourself about which of the entries you want other people to be able to see when they look up your profile. You might or might not want to reveal certain information, such as your gender, real name, marital status, and so on. Fill in only the information you would not mind telling a stranger. In Figure 8.2, for example, my profile states my City and State, but you may prefer to identify a region of the country (say southwest or northeast) rather than provide more specific information about your residence.

The remaining four text boxes give you the chance to tell other people about yourself as a person, instead of just listing statistics. You can begin by reciting your hobbies, then describe the kind of computer or computers you have, then add the line of work you're in, and finally quote a saying or motto that appeals to you (or use the opportunity to create one of your own).

Your name is there by default

The first time you create a profile, it defaults to include your full name. For reasons of privacy, you may prefer to delete this information and identify yourself online under only your screen name.

You don't have to respond

If you do not want to reveal your gender, be sure to click the **No Response** button on that line. Also click **No Response** for your marital status if you want that information to remain undisclosed.

Spell check your profile

After completing your online profile, review it for spelling accuracy. This step might seem fairly obvious, but after you look at a few profiles, you'll know why I mention it.

Watch your language

Your online profile is subject to America Online's Terms of Service. It is also a reflection of the face you want to put forth to the public. You are expected to refrain from using vulgar language as part of your profile description.

Choose your password carefully

The password you choose for your new screen name doesn't have to be the same as that used for your other accounts. The rule of thumb is to make it difficult enough not to be picked out at random (a collection of letters and numbers is best), and write it down, in case you forget it. If you set up a screen name for your child, be sure both you and your child have a copy.

After you've reviewed your completed profile and are satisfied with it, click the **Update** button to finish off the job, and move on to more exciting online activities.

If you aren't sure about your entries or have second thoughts about revealing some facts about yourself at this moment in time, you might prefer not to complete your online profile. In this case, click the **Cancel** button. Your profile is not saved, and the information you typed vanishes into cyberspace. If you want more information about the Edit Your Online Profile screen, click the **Help & Info** button.

Teach Yourself: How to Add and Delete Screen Names

When you join AOL, you create a special name to identify yourself, known as your screen name (or log-in name). Although you can't change that name without actually deleting your account, you can add up to four additional names to your account.

You can use these names to create another online persona (perhaps to separate your business life from your personal life), or for other members of your family.

To add or remove a screen name, you must first sign on with your master account name. This is the name you created for yourself when you joined AOL; it's the first one listed on the **Select Screen Name** drop-down menu on your AOL Setup and Sign-on screen.

After you connect with your master screen name, use the keyword Names to bring up the screen shown in Figure 8.3.

The next step is simple. Double-click the **Create a Screen Name** entry in the **Screen Names** list box, and enter the screen name you want to create. If the name is already being used, you'll be asked to make another selection. After you select a name that is not duplicated on the service, you'll be asked to create a password.

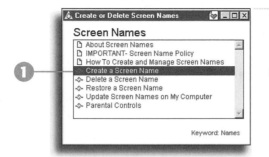

After your new screen name and password are chosen, you accept the choices you made. After you log off AOL, you'll find that your new screen name is now a part of the **Select Screen Name** drop-down menu.

To remove a screen name, choose **Delete a Screen Name** from the **Screen Names** list box.

Secrets of Meeting Other America Online Members

Meeting people on America Online has had some interesting outcomes over the years since the online community was launched. A few years back, the syndicated television talk show, *The Jerry Springer Show* even spotlighted a number of AOLers who had met and married. America Online users often inhabit the various People Connection rooms, such as the Flirt's Nook and Romance Connection, in search of friendship, camaraderie, and, yes, even love.

After you look around at the dozens of areas where other people congregate, you'll have a hard time tearing yourself away from America Online and the friends you will soon meet. (Of course, if you pay for AOL by the hour, you'll want to watch your online time too, because you can easily forget how long you've been logged on, and how much of a bill you're creating for yourself.)

Are you ready to dive in? Saying hello to people you meet on America Online is certainly a lot easier than opening a conversation with a stranger, because on America Online, with millions

Update the names on all your copies of AOL software

If you have other copies of America Online software installed on your computer or another PC, you need to update the screen name list on those computers too (it's not an automatic process). To accomplish that, log on to AOL while using the other copy of AOL software, open the Create or Delete Screen Names screen and double-click **Update Screen Names on My Computer**. After you accept this option, the Select Screen Name list on the copy of AOL software you're using will reflect the changed setup.

New rooms are created automatically

If the first Town Square is full when you enter, the room expands to additional rooms, and the room name has a number after it, such as Town Square Lobby 24.

of members, you'll find that many have things in common with you, so remaining alone is difficult.

How to Locate Other America Online Members

To begin, choose **Chat Now** from the **People** drop-down menu on your AOL program toolbar. You are immediately transported to the foyer of America Online's People Connection, as shown in Figure 8.4. These windows represent rooms in which as many as 23 people can gather and get to know one another by exchanging chat.

The mechanics of chatting involve typing what you want others to see in the small box in the lower portion of the chat window and sending it by clicking the **Send** button or by pressing Enter on your keyboard.

If you're like a lot of folks who are new to the online world, don't worry about starting a conversation right away; just hang around the Town Square chat room (online regulars call it *lurking*) and watch what other members type to each other. While you're lurking, chances are that someone will say hello to you. Don't worry about sending a reply if you aren't comfortable; no one will mind. You will, of course, want to be aware of proper online etiquette.

FIGURE 8.4

America Online's Town Square chat rooms in the People Connection area are popular places to meet fellow members.

1 Enter your chat text here, then click **Send**.

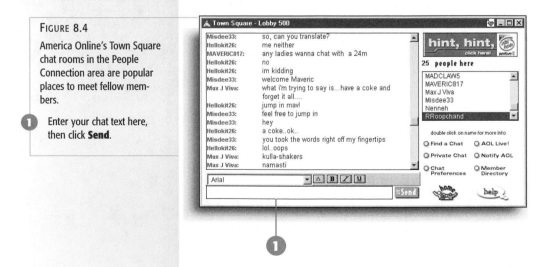

Secrets of Meeting Other America Online Members

Look at Figure 8.4 again. This window contains some items of interest apart from the text you type and the text other people have typed. For one thing, now that you've located some people online, you can find out a little more about them.

Viewing Other Members' Profiles

If you want to view another member's profile, you need to know the member's screen name or be in the same chat room with that member. The Town Square is as good a place as any to start.

Members' screen names are shown at the start of each line as it is displayed in the chat room window. If you want to know when a member enters the room or leaves, bring up your Chat preferences from your Preferences window (click the **My AOL** icon on the toolbar to access them). Then click the check boxes to be notified of a member's arrival and departure (it'll show up as an entry in the chat room window).

To see who is present, just take a gander at the **People here** listing at the right side of the window. You may have to use the scrollbars to see the entire list. The list is updated as people enter and leave so that you can watch it to observe their comings and goings.

Now, you can find out about someone. Double-click a member's name in the **People here** list box, which brings up the window shown in Figure 8.5. Then, click the **Get Profile** button. If the person you selected filled out an online profile, you see it in just a few seconds. If that member has not filled out a profile, you receive a message indicating that There is no profile available for that name or That profile is not available. In that case, try using some of the other names in the list until you find someone who has provided profile information. Depending on how much information the selected person provided, you see one or more lines of information in the Profile window.

The **Send Message** option (see Figure 8.5) brings up AOL's Instant Message window. You'll learn more about that feature in Chapter 9, "Using AOL's Email."

Just hang out at the beginning...

When visiting People Connection rooms for the first few times, you might get a better feel for the rooms' atmospheres by just watching for a few minutes or more.

Fast access to AOL's member listing

You can quickly check AOL's membership roster in the People Connection chat room by clicking the **Member Directory** icon at the bottom right of the screen.

FIGURE 8.5

You can choose to check a member's profile or send an instant message from this window.

1 Click a button to access that feature.

If you don't want to be disturbed…

If you feel a member is becoming a little obnoxious in the chat room, no problem. Click the **Ignore Member** check box in the screen shown in Figure 8.5, and you won't see that member's chat text anymore.

Annoying messages

Help! I get annoying messages from someone online whenever I enter a chat room. What do I do? You are entitled to enjoy your online visits in comfort and safety, free of annoyance from such people. The fastest way to deal with this problem is to click the **Notify AOL** button at the bottom of the chat room screen. It brings up instructions to help you inform AOL's Community Action Team about the problem.

How to Find a Member Online

As you become more comfortable using the conference rooms and People Connection rooms of America Online, you will probably begin to recognize some of the regulars. Perhaps you also know someone who uses America Online and want to find out if that person is signed on at the same time you are.

America Online provides some easy methods to locate people using the service. One method is to select the **People** icon on the AOL toolbar and select **Locate an AOL Member Online** from the drop-down menu, or press Ctrl+L (⌘-L for Mac users), and type the screen name of the person you want to locate (see Figure 8.6).

If a person you seek is online when you attempt to find him or her, the America Online host computer tells you one of two things: either that the person you want to find is Online, but not in a chat area, or the name of the chat or conference room where the person is currently. If the person is not online, America Online tells you exactly that.

FIGURE 8.6

Enter the member's name in this Locate Member Online window.

1 It takes just seconds to see if your friend is online.

Teach Yourself: Using the Member Directory

Keyword: Members

AOL's member directory (shown in Figure 8.7) is AOL's answer to your telephone book. Just choose **Search AOL Member Directory** from the People toolbar icon's drop-down menu or use the keyword Members to bring up the directory screen.

FIGURE 8.7

AOL's online yellow pages lets you find fellow members fast.

1 Enter search text in the appropriate text box.

To find a member, you can start with the person's real name, if you know it. You can also include the screen name or location in the optional text boxes.

You can also seek out members whose profile fits into a particular category, such as a specific interest, profession, or type of computer. To expand your search criteria, choose the **Advanced Search** tab on the Member Directory screen, which brings up the screen shown in Figure 8.8.

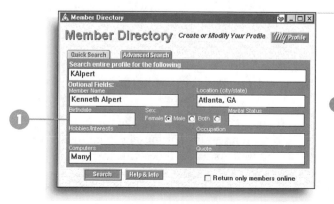

FIGURE 8.8

You can refine your search for members who meet certain criteria in the Advanced Search screen.

1 The more information you provide, the more accurate the result.

After you enter the information to help you locate the member you want, you can add one more option, shown by the **Return only members online** check box. That'll help you get in touch with a specific member right away, using AOL's instant message feature (which I explain in more detail in Chapter 9).

Click the **Search** button. If a member is found whose name or profile matches the search information you entered, you'll see the result in a directory such as the one shown in Figure 8.9.

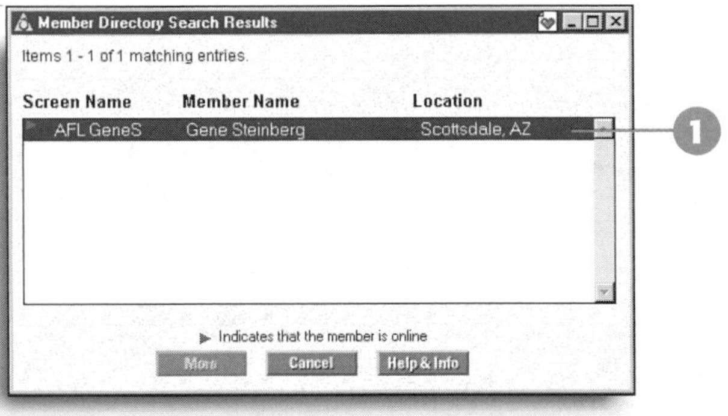

FIGURE 8.9

Success! I found myself online. An arrow is shown next to the screen names of the members who are online when the search results appear.

1 Double-click the member's name to see the profile.

Not everyone is in the Member Directory

Help! I know the member exists—I just got email from that person, but I can't find the member's name in the Member Directory. What's wrong? AOL members are entitled to their privacy. If you don't create a profile for yourself, or delete the one you have, your name won't show up in the Member Directory.

To learn more about the members you locate, double-click their names in the Member Directory Search Results screen to bring up their profiles. If a match cannot be found, you'll see an onscreen message to that effect.

Teach Yourself: How to Use AOL's Buddy List

Wouldn't it be nice if you could be notified when a friend or business acquaintance of yours is online? It would be like an online beeping or paging service.

AOL offers just such a feature. AOL's *Buddy List* (see Figure 8.10) automatically notifies you whenever someone you know is online, and lets them know you're online too.

If you want to send a message to your friend, click the **IM** button to open up an instant message window. Write your message and send it on its way. I'll describe instant messages in more detail in Chapter 9. For now, just consider this feature your way to have a private, one-on-one online conversation with a friend, virtually in real time, as they're online. It's a feature you'll probably want to use often.

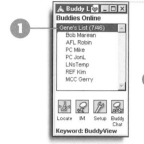

FIGURE 8.10

When you log on, AOL's Buddy List greets you with a list of friends who are online.

1 The screen names of friends who are online

Of course, before AOL's handy paging service does its stuff, you've got to set it up. To do that, type the keyword Buddy to bring up the setup window (see Figure 8.11).

FIGURE 8.11

It takes just a few minutes to create or change your own personal Buddy List.

1 Click a button to configure your Buddy List.

To create your own Buddy List, click the **Create** button, and enter the screen names of your friends in the setup window (see Figure 8.12).

You can create a separate listing from different groups of AOL members, and establish a different set of Buddy List preferences for each of those groups or individuals. After your custom Buddy List is set up, it appears the next time you log on to AOL. The same Buddy List is not available to all screen names on your account, so you need to create a separate Buddy List for each of your AOL screen names.

Protecting your privacy is easy

You do not, of course, have to allow others to know you're online. If you'd rather not notify some people when you're online—or you don't want anyone to add you to their Buddy List—click the **Privacy Preferences** icon, and choose who can include you on their Buddy List or contact you via an instant message.

FIGURE 8.12

Enter the names of your online friends so that AOL can notify you of their presence.

1 Type the screen name (not real name) here.

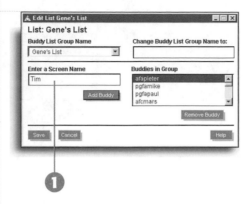

Connecting with another screen name is a snap

You can switch to another screen name on your account without logging off. From the **Sign off** menu choose **Switch Screen Name**, then select the screen name you want to use. If you haven't stored your password in your AOL software, you'll have to enter it in a text box before you connect under another name.

Gathering your friends together

If you want to invite your online friends to a conference or other online event, click the **Buddy Chat** icon at the bottom right of your Buddy List screen. Then enter the location where you want your friends to be in the **Location** text box and click **Send**. When your friends receive the message, they just have to click the **Go** button to enter that online spot.

A Neighborhood in Cyberspace

Of all the online areas where people congregate, the People Connection's Town Square is far and away the place you find most of the people who want to talk. On a busy evening, you can easily find hundreds of people in the various chat rooms in the People Connection.

Entering the Town Square

You might be saying to yourself, "Hey, wait a minute—didn't you say earlier that only 23 people can gather in a room at one time?" Well, yes, that's correct as far as it goes. What happens after the 23rd person enters the Town Square is that a new room is automatically created to hold the 24th person and all the other people soon to follow. That room is called *Town Square - Lobby 2*, and after it reaches 23 people, other rooms follow it with names like *Town Square - Lobby 3*, *Town Square - Lobby 4*, and so on.

The People Connection chat rooms are usually bustling, crowded areas. Think Grand Central Station here; people are constantly coming and going. Often they are leaving for other People Connection rooms with specific themes or going to Computing & Software conference rooms to discuss the latest industry news. Private rooms are also available. This is discussed later in this chapter.

Entering the LaPub Entertainment Connection Room

When you enter the People Connection, you go right to an open chat room in the Town Square. As you'll see after a few visits, these rooms are busy places indeed. America Online's staff saw the need for regular visitors to have a place online where they could sit back, relax, and enjoy ongoing, pleasant conversation—and have some fun while there. With this idea, LaPub was born (see Figure 8.13). To get to LaPub, type the keyword LaPub.

The bar was constructed, the refreshments were ordered and stocked, and the cheerful, highly capable Pub Tenders were rigorously trained. All this preparation for the sake of creating one of the liveliest of the People Connection areas ever seen online anywhere. The best part is that you don't have to drive anywhere; just sit in your most comfortable chair with the one-eyed monitor of your favorite computer in front of your face. Most likely, you will have at least one free online beverage of your choice offered on your first visit. Accept it, and enjoy!

While visiting the LaPub area, be sure to check for upcoming events and contests in LaPub's schedule. You don't want to miss out on their unique happenings!

Why is your Buddy List missing?

If your Buddy List doesn't appear when you sign onto AOL, or you close it by mistake or to save screen space, no problem. Just use the keyword BuddyView or click the **My AOL** icon on the toolbar and choose **View Buddy List** from the drop-down menu to bring it up again. I should mention, however, that sometimes the Buddy List is down for maintenance, so don't be surprised if it just doesn't work occasionally.

Where did those extra people come from?

At times you might actually see 24 or 25 people listed in one of these public chat rooms. The additional folks are AOL community leaders who are around to make sure everyone behaves themselves.

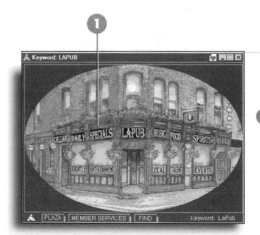

FIGURE 8.13

The LaPub is a pleasant gathering place.

1 Click a labeled icon to see more of LaPub.

A Few Notes about AOL's Terms of Service (TOS)

As with most public areas in real life, the People Connection rooms have their own etiquette and rules of conduct. First and foremost is *TOS*, or *Terms of Service*. TOS is America Online's equivalent of real-life laws. You should take some time during your first few sessions to acquaint yourself with the TOS. Use the keyword TOS to look over the Terms of Service, which is displayed in separate text files according to category. Spend at least a few minutes reviewing the contents of this area. By making this effort now, you can feel more comfortable the first time you visit the public area rooms, and you'll have a greater understanding of how things work in general on America Online. The contents of each Terms of Service topic can be saved or printed, using the appropriate commands from the **File** menu of your AOL software.

Briefly, the most important parts of TOS state that you are expected to be a good citizen when you visit America Online. You are expected to refrain from using vulgar language and to respect others in the same way you expect them to respect you. For more information about proper online behavior, read Chapter 7, "Parental Issues and Internet Access" and Chapter 10, "Chatting Online."

Visiting Private Chat Rooms

If you are like many of the People Connection's regular visitors, you'll eventually meet someone online with whom you want to communicate further. You want more privacy than the public People Connection rooms are able to offer, while still maintaining the capability to communicate with more than one person in real time. (Instant messages and email are discussed in more detail in Chapter 9.)

Private rooms look and feel exactly like any public chat room, such as a Town Square or forum conference rooms. The only difference between a public chat room and a private one is that the name of the room does not appear in any of the People Connection room lists. To join another member already in a private room, you must first know the exact name of that room.

The first step to creating this private area is to enter the People Connection Town Square. Then, click the **Private Chat** button at the bottom right of the chat room window.

To enter the room you want, or to create a new one, type it in the window shown in Figure 8.14. Remember this room name so that you can send it in an instant message or email to those members you want to join you.

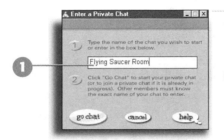

FIGURE 8.14

You create or enter a private room by using this screen.

1 Enter the name of your Private Room.

Some Additional People Connection Chat Room Features

In addition to the features mentioned earlier, a few more People Connection features are worthy of mention here:

- *Find a Chat*. Clicking this icon brings up a list of active rooms, any one of which you can enter by double-clicking the title.
- *People Connection*. This is the hub of the channel (see Figure 8.15). You'll be able to access all the features from this screen, and get some online instructions on finding and participating in chats. You can also reach this area via the keyword People.

A few chat basics

Two types of chat rooms exist on America Online. The first is a small area where you can have an interactive discussion with a group of fellow AOL members, and all the things you say are shown in the chat window.

The other kind of chat room enables hundreds, even thousands of members to gather and attend a meeting that usually involves a special guest, such as a popular show business personality. It's not a place where a large group exchanges comments with one another, however. The area is known as an AOL Live! auditorium, or Center Stage, and the rooms are set up as virtual auditoriums, where you sit in a row and can chat only with the others who are sitting in that row. You actually interact with the guests on stage by sending them messages or questions.

■ *AOL Live*. Clicking this icon in the Plaza screen (or using
the keyword AOL Live) brings up a listing of online conferences you'll want to check out.

SEE ALSO

➤ *Learn more about conferences, see page 191*

FIGURE 8.15

This is the People Connection's
central meeting point, where
you can explore all its features.

1 Click an icon to access more
People Connection services.

Entering the AOL Portrait Gallery

Keyword: Gallery

When you meet someone online, do you ever wonder what the
other person really looks like? Well, you can find out. Many
members of America Online have made disk copies of photos of
themselves and their families, and can send them to you via
email. You can also embed a picture in your email (I explain
more of this in the next chapter). Another resource for photos of
AOL members is a forum devoted strictly to the service's own
photo album—The Gallery.

The Gallery (or sometimes the AOL Portrait Gallery) might
turn out to be one of your favorite places online because you get
to place faces with screen names (see Figure 8.16).

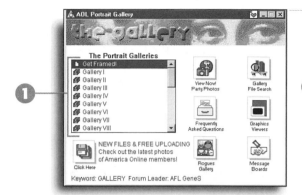

FIGURE 8.16
The AOL Portrait Gallery is one of the most popular forums on AOL.

①   The member portrait libraries are listed at the left.

The Gallery is a library that contains photos put in computer-readable form and uploaded for all to see. Thousands of America Online members have already uploaded their portraits or sent their photos to the Gallery's staff to digitize for free. As you get to know some of the regulars online, chances are good that you'll be tempted to find out what they look like, and the Gallery is the place where you might find their photo.

A separate library is also included in the Gallery for family-album types of pictures. You can gather your own clan's photos and send them to the Gallery. You can upload the files directly to the Gallery's New Files and Free Uploading library, or submit your photo to be scanned and uploaded by the Gallery's staff. The address to which you should send your photos for scanning is listed in the library information texts.

To make viewing these photos easy for all America Online users, regardless of the type of computer, the Gallery photos are currently provided in *GIF* and *JPEG* formats. These two formats offer high-quality images with a small file size. The small size keeps your download time short and makes it more convenient if you want to see photos of a number of your fellow members. Of the two formats, JPEG gets you a slightly smaller size and better quality, but the Gallery accepts digitized photos in either format.

America Online's software enables you to actually see a photo gradually appear on your screen while it's being downloaded to your computer, as shown in Figure 8.17. To view the photo files after they are downloaded, from the **File** menu, choose **Open** and then select the file you want to see. After the file is opened (or has appeared on your computer's screen right after the download process is over), you'll be able to print it just the same as any other document.

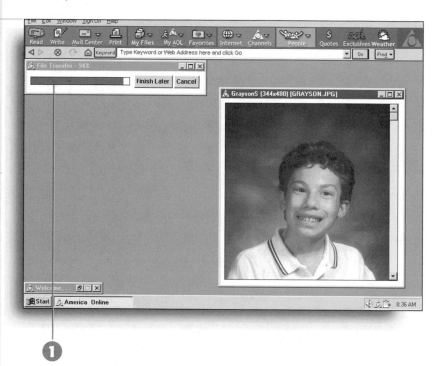

The handsome young man shown in Figure 8.17 is, by the way, my son Grayson, who was just shy of 12 when the photo was taken. If you want to know more about placing your photos in the Gallery, look at the directory window in the Gallery, and double-click the item labeled **Get Framed!** (see Figure 8.18).

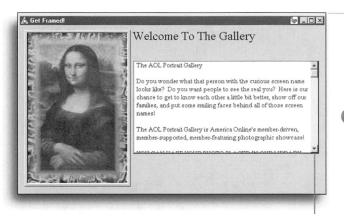

FIGURE 8.18

Read the text here for instructions on submitting a photo to the Gallery; you'll have to scroll through the text window to read it all.

1 Scroll through the text window to learn all about the Gallery.

The Get Framed text at the right of the information window can be saved and printed using the appropriate commands from the **File** menu of your AOL software. It covers the type of photos accepted, the maximum acceptable size of the photo (640 pixels wide by 480 pixels deep), and file-naming conventions. Because photos must be viewable by both Mac and PC users (including many who have yet to upgrade to Windows 95), they should adhere to the standard PC naming convention, consisting of eight letters for the filename, followed by a period and the GIF or JPG extension depending on which file format the photo is saved in (for example: Thephoto.gif or Thephoto.jpg). The information text screen also includes instructions about AOL's free scanning service that is provided to members who cannot get their own photos scanned.

Finding an Online Pen Pal

Keyword: Pen Pal

When I was a kid, I had some pen pals. In those days there were no online services (yes, there were cars, more or less). Anyway, I remember when a girl from another part of the country found my name in a directory and started writing to me. I wrote to her for several years, and we ended up getting married. (It didn't work out so well, but we remain friends after all these years.)

Looking for a relationship?

The Portrait Gallery is not the only online area on AOL where you can post your photo. If you're looking for romance, AOL's Romance channel (keyword **Romance**) is a great place to check for a member's picture. You'll also find member photo libraries in AOL's Digital City channel (keyword **Digital City**).

In any case, whether you just want to write to someone, or you're looking for a lifelong friend, AOL's Pen Pals feature can help you out (see Figure 8.19).

You can contact Pen Pals from AOL's Digital City's channel, or from around the world through its International Pen Pals service. Just to show you how it works, click the **Digital City Pen Pals** icon (see Figure 8.20).

FIGURE 8.19

Meet new friends through AOL's Pen Pals service.

1 Click an icon to access online Pen Pals.

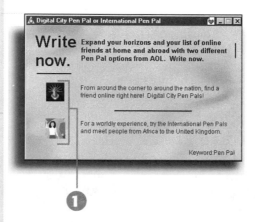

FIGURE 8.20

Look for a pen pal or insert your own here.

1 Scroll through the list to learn more about this area.

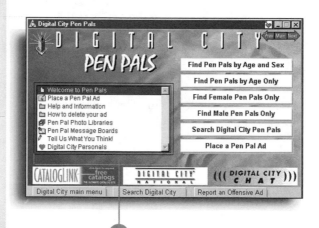

When you look for an online pen pal, you have a choice to search by age and/or gender, or by another criteria, such as geographic location, hobbies, and so on. To place your own ad for a pen pal, click the **Place a Pen Pal Ad** button, which brings up the information screen shown in Figure 8.21.

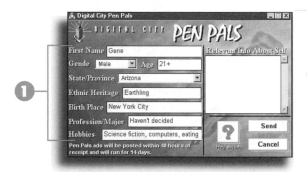

FIGURE 8.21

Write something about yourself here to place a pen pals ad.

1 Use the tab key to move from text box to text box.

After you've entered your information, double check the text to be sure it's correct. Then click the **Send** button to have it posted. The Pen Pals staff, at the time this book was written, posted ads within 48 hours after they received them, and the ads remained on display for two weeks.

Online Abbreviations

When you chat online, the other person cannot, of course, see whether you are smiling, or crying, or frowning. So a nifty shorthand language has been devised in cyberspace so you can communicate your feelings and reactions to what other online visitors say. Some of these letters and symbols are downright obscure, others are almost always fairly obvious when you see the shortcut, such as LOL, which stands for Laughing Out Loud.

In Chapter 10, "Chatting Online," I've gathered together a set of these shortcuts for you to keep on hand as you become accustomed to the online universe. Some of them are quite obscure, and seldom-used (although you encounter them occasionally). Many will soon become familiar to you and, I'm sure, second nature as you begin to experience the rewarding experience of meeting fellow travelers of the online universe.

SEE ALSO

➤ *Learn how to participate in chats, conferences, and one-on-one communication with fellow members, see page 191*

➤ *Learn how to locate messages and how to find responses to your messages, see page 206*

➤ *Learn where to seek support and information about all your computer-related problems, see page 418*

➤ *For a hands-on tutorial that will help you master your software, see page 509*

Using AOL's Email

AOL's email and instant messages

The email Formatting toolbar

Automate your visits with Automatic AOL

Internet email

For AOL Members, Email Often Comes First

When I ask a fellow member why they joined AOL, email is often at the very top of their list of things to do. In the previous chapter, "America Online's People Connection," I described it as a place where you can meet your online neighbors in small and large groups. On any given evening, it is not uncommon to find thousands of members in the various chat rooms of People Connection, Computing channel conference rooms, and other online gathering places. As for email, although you don't see it, millions of pieces of it fly across cyberspace at all hours of the day and night.

In this chapter, you learn how to use email and instant messages for online communication, not only with the text you write, but with pictures too.

Getting Started with Electronic Mail

Writing email begins with a single, simple step: clicking the **Write** icon from the toolbar. Keyboard enthusiasts may press ⌘-M (Ctrl+M for Window users) to begin a new mail message. The resulting form is the jumping off point for all your original email (see Figure 9.1 for the Mac version and Figure 9.2 for the Windows edition). Later in this chapter you learn how to reply to email without using a new mail form.

America Online is insistent about a few things regarding its email system.

Start your email your way

Although most folks begin their email by addressing it, you can write the subject or body of the message first. Just use the Tab key to move from text field to text field.

- You must include at least one address, a subject, and a message. It does make sense. After all, receiving a blank message is like picking up the telephone and finding no one on the other end.

- The address fields of the email window can contain literally hundreds of electronic mailing addressees. If you use AOL's Windows software to send a message to more than one person, each person's screen name must be separated by a comma or a return. (On a Mac, be sure to press Return, not Enter; hitting Enter sends the message.) When you use the Return key to separate multiple names, the window list is easier to read than when the names are separated by commas.

FIGURE 9.1

America Online's Mac email form looks a little different from the Windows version, but the functions are essentially the same.

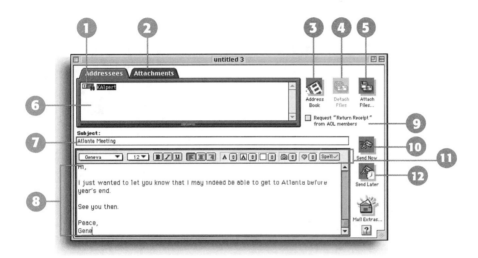

1. Click the pop-up menu to choose the recipient type

2. Click this tab to see the list of attached files

3. Access your AOL Address Book

4. Detach the files

5. Attach files to your email

6. Enter the recipient's email address here

7. Subject of your message

8. Body copy of your message is entered here

9. Get a return receipt when your message is read

10. Send your email now

11. Format your text, attach pictures, and spell check

12. Send it later, via an Automatic AOL session

FIGURE 9.2

America Online's Windows email form puts the same functions in a different position.

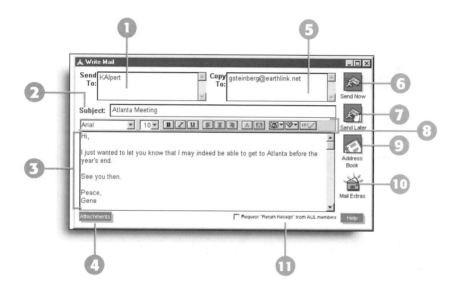

1. Enter the recipient's email address here. When you first conjure up a new email window, the cursor is automatically positioned within the **To** field of the form.

2. Subject of your message

3. Body copy of your message is entered here

4. Attach or detach files to your email

5. Send a carbon or courtesy copy of your email

6. Send your email now

7. Send it later, via an Automatic AOL session

8. Format your text, attach pictures, and spell check

9. Access your AOL Address Book

10. Call out special email features while online

11. Get a return receipt when your message is read

- If you want to send a carbon copy of your email to another recipient, enter that name in the CC: field at the right.

- Be sure the email address of the recipient is accurate. Even one incorrect letter or space could send it to the wrong person.

Now that you've decided who's getting the message, move to the **Subject** field and let the recipient know what your message is about without making them read it to find out. This step is both convenient and considered normal email etiquette. After the subject, move the cursor to the message body and compose your message.

Formatting Email Text is Easy

A unique feature of America Online email is that you may style your message by using a different type of size, style, and color. The Formatting toolbar displays the attributes that you may change within the email message (see Figure 9.3).

As you see from Figure 9.3, your AOL Formatting toolbar is similar to the one you see with your word-processing program.

Mac addressing options

In the Mac version of AOL's email form, each email addressing option is selected from a pop-up menu at the left of the recipient's name.

AOL's Address Book comes in handy

If you've entered any addresses in your AOL Address Book, you can also click the Address Book icon to select names for the email addresses. See the section "Teach Yourself: How to Use AOL's Address Book," later in this chapter.

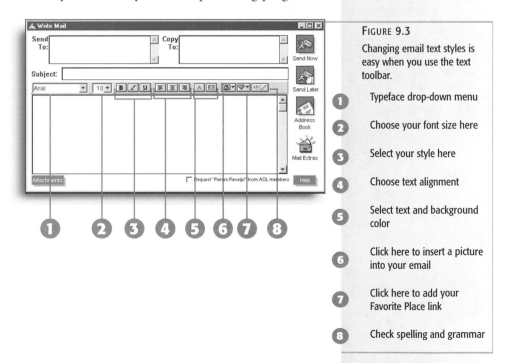

FIGURE 9.3

Changing email text styles is easy when you use the text toolbar.

1. Typeface drop-down menu

2. Choose your font size here

3. Select your style here

4. Choose text alignment

5. Select text and background color

6. Click here to insert a picture into your email

7. Click here to add your Favorite Place link

8. Check spelling and grammar

Email formatting has its limits

Your formatted email can really look great if you take a little care with it, but it all goes to waste if the recipient of your email is a member of another service. That's because the formatting is lost when it leaves the boundaries of AOL's email system.

More cool AOL email features

A cool AOL email feature is the capability to insert a hyperlink into your message. This embeds a clickable path to an AOL forum or Internet source. It's a terrific way to take your friends directly to an online place you want them to see. The option appears as a Favorite Place heart on the formatting toolbar. Or just drag the hyperlink reference from your Favorite Places folder or the actual forum or Web site window and drop it directly in your email message.

Be careful with that file you want to upload

When you attach a file to your email message, do not delete or move the file until the email has been sent. Otherwise, the attachment won't be sent to the recipient. You may also abort an automatic AOL session this way.

How to Send Email

After you compose your email, you can send it in a number of ways. When you're logged on to AOL, the fastest way to send your email is to click the **Send Now** icon on the right side of the email window. The mail is sent immediately, along with any attachments. See "Attaching Files to Email for Other AOL Members," later in this chapter.

If you compose your outgoing email when you're not connected to AOL or sign off before composing it, you can choose to use the Send Later feature that saves the outgoing mail on your hard drive. You find it in the Mail Waiting to Be Sent folder when you open the Read Offline Mail screen from the drop-down menu on the Mail Center toolbar.

You can send your saved mail manually on your next online visit or automatically during your next automated mail session (see "Scheduling Automatic AOL Sessions Using Walk-Through" later in this chapter).

Sending email over the Internet (or in other words, sending it to non-AOL members) works the same as sending normal America Online email to other members. You just type the Internet address of your intended recipient rather than the America Online screen name you normally use to send mail to other AOL members. Addressing Internet mail is that simple.

You must, however, follow a couple of rules. After you've read these rules, which follow, you'll be sending worldwide email with ease.

- An Internet address never contains blank spaces. If someone's mail address has blank spaces, replace them with underscores (_) in the Internet Address. For example, you might see `john[_]smith@veryhugecorp.com`, in which the space between the user's first and last name is replaced with an underscore character.

- Also, every Internet address must have the username and domain (location) specified. For our purposes, the username is everything before the @ symbol, and the domain is everything after the @ symbol. In the domain, a company name is followed by a suffix that describes what type of organization it is. A business, for instance, uses the suffix *com;* educational institutions use *edu;* military sites use *mil;* a nonprofit organization, such as a computer user group, uses *org;* and government offices use *gov.* (You can also find business Internet addresses in *New Riders' Internet Yellow Pages*, available at your favorite bookstore).

How to Receive Email

This is the easy part. All you have to do is log on to AOL and, if you have mail, the happy guy that lives inside the AOL program tells you, "You have mail!" (Assuming, that is, that you have your Mail Sounds activated in the Member Preference settings, and if you're a Windows user, you also need a computer with a sound card). A special **You Have Mail** icon is also displayed on the Welcome screen (see Figure 9.4).

You can click the **You Have Mail** icon on the Welcome screen, or you can press ⌘-R (Ctrl+R for Windows users) to view a list of new mail (see Figure 9.5). You can then double-click to open each piece of mail. You may also click the **Next arrow** icon on the mail form to advance to the next message (see Figure 9.6). The **Previous** arrow enables you to move backward through the mail. The left and right arrow keys are equivalent to clicking the Next and Previous arrows.

As you read each piece of mail, a check mark is placed in front of the item as it appears in the New Mail window. If you do not read all your mail in one session, the pieces that have the check mark do not show up when you next open the New Mail window. Only those items that you have not previously read appear there.

To receive mail from the Internet, you need to know your own Internet address, just as you need to know a recipient's. Your address is simply your America Online screen name, with any word spaces removed, plus @aol.com. If your screen name is JohnUser, for example, your Internet address is `johnuser@aol.com`.

Put pictures in your email

In addition to fancy text-styling, you can add pictures to your AOL email. All you have to do is click the camera icon on the email form's formatting toolbar. This step will open an Open Image dialog box, where you can select the file that you want to include in your email. It'll appear right where the cursor is positioned on the email form in the message field.

Other services handle email differently

Each online service has its own requirements and limitations. AOL's Internet Connection contains help text that helps you to address your email to other services. As other services change their Internet offerings, these help texts are revised.

FIGURE 9.4

The Welcome screen indicating that you have mail waiting to be read.

1 Click here to see your incoming mail.

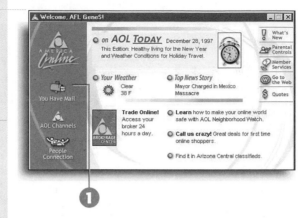

FIGURE 9.5

A list of email waiting to be read.

1 **New Mail**

2 **Old Mail** (previously read)

3 **Sent Mail**

4 Read the selected email

5 Status of email you've sent

6 Mark email as new, even if you've read it

7 Delete email from list

8 Email Help menu

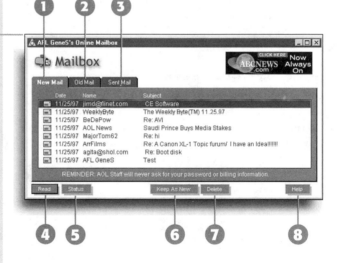

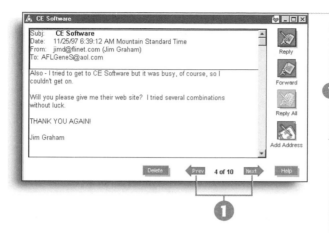

FIGURE 9.6

The Read Email form. Note the navigating arrows in the lower corners.

1 Click the arrows to move to the next or previous message.

The following is a rundown of the remaining **New Mail** features:

- **Status.** Check to see if any other members who are receiving this message have read it yet.
- **Keep as New.** This option keeps the message in your list of waiting mail even after you've read the message. It's useful if you want to use that message as a reminder of an upcoming event or if it contains a specific bit of information that you want to review the next time you visit America Online. You can also use this option for messages in your Old Mail list.
- **Delete.** This option removes the message from your list of incoming mail, unread. Of course, the person who sends you email will know, by checking the message status, that you have deleted the message.
- **Help icon.** Need further assistance in using your AOL email? Click this button for more assistance.

Responding to Email

When you respond to email, it's customary to quote a portion of the message you're answering. This way, the recipient, especially if that person sends lots of messages, knows precisely what you are talking about. When replying to a message, select the material

---

Be careful about the address

If you do not address your Internet mail in the correct format, the mail is returned marked unknown. If this happens to you, verify the original recipient's correct email address (even an error involving one letter or number is enough to bounce the letter). Internet email can travel through an email over long, circuitous path on its way from AOL's mail server to its destination. Sometimes errors can occur during transmission, and sometimes correctly addressed mail is returned. The best solution (after verifying that the address is correct) is to send the letter again.

Mac mail notification

When email is waiting to be read, Mac users see a flashing mailbox icon at the upper left of the menu bar while online. This icon shows even if you've switched to another program during your AOL session.

you want to quote and click the **Reply** icon on the email message you received (or **Reply All** if your answering email addressed to a number of recipients and want them all to see your response). The quoted text automatically appears at the top of your email message. As with message board and newsgroup postings, it's a good idea just to quote the important parts of the message (or just enough for the response to make sense), not all of it.

Two ways to format quoted text in a message are the AOL way and the Internet way (the preferred method). The choice can be set with your Mail preferences (accessed by choosing **Preferences** from the **My AOL** toolbar icon). I'll cover these options in more detail in Appendix B, "Setting Up AOL's Software."

Attaching Files to Email for other AOL Members

America Online's email system enables you to attach files from your computer (files on your hard drive or from a disk placed in your computer's floppy drive or any other attached drive) to a piece of email. When you send your email, you also send the files that you attached to it.

To attach a file when composing email, simply click the Attach icon, and use the accompanying dialog box to select the file that you want to attach (see Figures 9.7 and 9.8).

The file you attach must be on a disk drive connected to your computer or a drive that you mounted from your network, and you must attach the file before you send the email. The recipient sees two extra buttons in the received email window, **Download File** and **Download Later**. Clicking the **Download File** button transfers the file from America Online's host to the recipient's computer. Clicking **Download Later** marks the file for the Download Manager for transfer at a later time (see Figure 9.9). (For additional information on the Download Manager, see Chapter 26, "Tips and Tricks on Finding Software," and Appendix B.

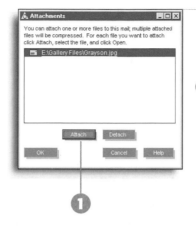

FIGURE 9.7

To include a file with your email, you need to use the Attach function.

1 Click the **Attach** button to select another file.

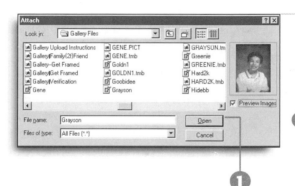

FIGURE 9.8

Selecting files to attach is easy in this dialog box, which is no different from the regular Open dialog box you see in other software.

1 Click **Open** to attach the selected file.

If you believe other AOL members could make use of a file you have, consider posting the file to a forum library instead of sending it on email. By posting the file to a forum, you are not charged for the connect time spent sending (uploading) the file to AOL's host (if you're still on the hourly billing plan). (See Chapter 26 for more information about uploading files to an AOL software library.)

Make sure the files aren't too big

If you pay for AOL by the hour, you are charged only for the time needed to send your message and the attachments to the AOL mail processing area. Similarly, the recipient of the attached file is charged for the time needed to transfer the file from AOL's host to his or her computer. If you or your recipient have this sort of billing plan, you may want to limit the size of the email attachments that you send.

FIGURE 9.9

The Download Now and Download Later icons in the email window indicate an attached file.

1 Clicking **Delete** removes the email from your list so that you can't call it up again.

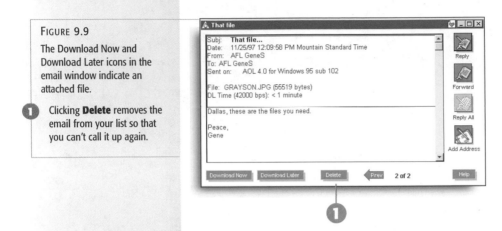

Watch out for unsolicited files

It's an unfortunate fact of the online world that some folks can send virus infected files or files designed to extract your personal information from your AOL software or other programs. Virus software cannot detect these files! *It is a good idea not to download files from someone you don't know.* For more information on handling email with such unknown attachments, use the keyword **TOS** to access AOL's Terms of Service area.

Don't compress picture files

If you are transferring a GIF or JPEG image file to another AOL member, compression is probably not going to provide much benefit. These formats are already compacted internally and rarely benefit from additional compression. Besides, you probably want both Mac and Windows users to be able to download these files with similar ease, and the compression technique that works on a Mac may not work if a Windows computer

Attaching Files for Non-AOL Mail Recipients

If the recipient of your email is a member of another service, you can still attach files to your email in most cases. You should not have to do anything special to the file or your email. AOL's email system converts the files to a format that can be read via most Internet-based services. If you are unsure whether the process works or not, send a small file attachment to the member of the other service as a test or have that person contact the service for information about whether they support files attached to AOL email.

Here's some further considerations about Internet email:

- Text and picture formatting is not retained when you send your email to another service via the Internet.

- As of the time this book was written, AOL file attachments for Internet email were limited to 2MB in size. If you want to send a larger file, you'll want to explore other options, such as using any available FTP site on the other service. Email sent to another AOL member can include a file as large as 16MB.

- In the event that you decide not to send the attached file but you still want to send the original email message, you can click the **Attachments** button and then detach the file on the screen that appears to break the link between the unsent email and the files. At this point, you can still attach a different file to your letter before it's sent.

- Files attached to your Internet email are automatically converted to *MIME* format. In order to read those files, the recipient may need a separate program, but that's something that the recipient may have to check with the other service. One example of a good decoder utility is UUCODE by Sabasoft for Windows users. Mac users will want to check out Decoder, a program I've often used. A quick check of a shareware software library yields many treasures of this sort. In addition, the latest version of StuffIt Deluxe, a commercial program from Aladdin Systems (4.5.1 as this book was written), works just fine with MIME files.

  By the way, MIME isn't something that refers to an actor performing without speaking. It stands for *Multipurpose Internet Mail Extensions*. It's a technique used to convert the file to text form so that it can be read on different kinds of computers.

- If someone sends you a long text message (containing more than 27,000 characters), it is converted to an attached file. You see the first 2,000 characters in the body of the email message, and the full, original message is attached as a file.

- Tell the person who is sending you files by the Internet not to attach more than one file to the message. Otherwise, you have to use another software program (a MIME converter) to change it back to its normal form. Instead, suggest to that person that they make the files into a single compressed archive, using one of the standard Mac or PC compression programs. (I recommend StuffIt or ZIP because AOL's software automatically decodes files in either format.) You can find a MIME converter in AOL's software libraries using the File Search feature (choose Software from the Find toolbar button's drop-down menu). Again, Mac users want to consider StuffIt Deluxe.

You can't put a novel in your email

America Online's email form can contain up to 27,000 characters, or a few hundred words, of text. If your message is larger than that, you want to save your message as a separate file, attach it to your email, and then send it on its way.

AOL's software libraries have the files you want

If you ever need a program that converts MIME files, check AOL's software libraries (using the File Search technique I describe in Chapter 26).

AOL's family atmosphere doesn't extend to the Internet

Graphic files on the Internet do not have to follow America Online's Terms of Service regarding nude or sexually explicit content. Be sure to examine the article's header or look at the title and purpose of a newsgroup before transferring material from that area to your computer.

Saving Your Email

After reading each piece of your email, you have a few options. The first is to simply click the close box of the window, which moves your access to the mail to the **Old Mail** tab in your online mailbox form. You can always find and read mail you've previously viewed by clicking the **Old Mail** tab.

You have the option of copying individual mail to your Personal Filing Cabinet, a file AOL's software puts on your hard drive that can hold tons of saved email, message board and newsgroup posts, information about downloaded files, and other online information. To save an open email message to the Personal Filing Cabinet, simply choose that command from the **File** menu. You can retrieve this email item at any time, even if you are offline. Your stored email can also be accessed through your Incoming Saved Mail drawer (accessible from the Mail Center toolbox icon's drop-down menu).

You can also save your email as an individual file. America Online has two special file types for email—one is the standard email format, the other straight text (see Figure 9.10). By opening the **File** menu and choosing **Save As**, you can choose to save your email as one of these types of files or as plain text. Saving your mail as plain text enables you to view or change the contents of the email in any text processor, such as your favorite word-processing program.

FIGURE 9.10

Your handy file **Save** options for your AOL email.

1 Click **Save** to store the file on your PC's drive.

To print a hard copy of your email, open the **File** menu and choose **Print**. This works the same way as in almost every other application that supports printing. Remember, however, that if you changed printers since the last time you printed anything from AOL, you first have to choose **Print Setup** (it's **Page Setup** for Mac users) to verify your printing options.

Secrets of Getting AOL Email Without AOL Software

Unlike the email you send with a regular Internet provider, such as EarthLink, your AOL email usually can't be accessed unless you connect with AOL software. That's because AOL's email software isn't compatible with standard Internet email protocols; however, you can overcome this limitation.

One way to access your email without using the regular AOL software is to use AOL's NetMail feature, which is being developed at the time of this writing. This feature enables you to read, write, and sent AOL email. while logged on to a regular Internet provider. To do it, you need the Windows 95 version of Microsoft's Internet Explorer Web browser (version 3 or 4 is okay). After the feature is installed, you'll find information on how to use the feature (and whether it'll be expanded to other operating systems) in AOL's Mail Center (at keyword Mail Center).

Another way to access your AOL email without using AOL's software is a nifty program from Apple Computer's Claris division, Emailer. You can use this program to run automatic email sessions on all your AOL screen names and send and receive files from each of them. What's more, if you have accounts on CompuServe, or many Internet-based services, you can run your sessions from these services as well, all with Emailer. Because I have a number of online accounts, I have found this program to be an invaluable way to keep tabs on all the email I have to manage. Because various Claris software products have returned to the parent company, Apple Computer, it's not certain whether the Emailer will continue to be developed or whether a promised Windows version will ever appear.

Mac users: Select your printer first

If you are using a Macintosh and do not have a printer selected in the Chooser after you start your AOL program, you are likely unable to print a text window; you just see a little flicker from the **File** menu when you choose the **Print** or **Page Setup** functions. Should this happen to you, log off America Online, selecting the Quit rather than Sign Off option. Select your printer in the Chooser, launch America Online's software, and then log on again. You should then be able to print normally.

AOL is extending email compatibility to other areas too. For the future, it plans to use Microsoft Outlet Express technology to enable you to access your AOL email, and Qualcomm's popular email software, Eudora, is also expected to be updated to support AOL.

Teach Yourself: How to Use AOL's Address Book

You can use your America Online Address Book to store mail addresses that you use regularly so that they are available at the click of a mouse.

Suppose that you have an online friend named Grayson Steinberg, and you exchange mail with him often. His screen name on America Online might be Rockoid (this is not a real screen name, folks!). You'll probably find it more convenient to store his name in your Address Book rather than to type it manually each time you compose mail. To add the name to the Address Book follow these steps:

Configuring your AOL Address Book is easy

1. Open the Mail Center toolbar icon's drop-down menu and choose Address Book, which brings up the Address Book window (see Figure 9.11).

FIGURE 9.11

Create and edit your Address Book entries here.

1 Click **New Person** to add an entry.

2. To add an individual to your Address Book, click **New Person**. A blank New Person entry form appears onscreen (see Figure 9.12).

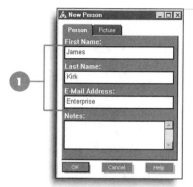

FIGURE 9.12

Enter the information about your online friend in this form.

1 Use the Tab key to go to the next text field.

3. Type the first name of your friend in the appropriate field; for example, Grayson.

4. Type the last name of your friend in the appropriate field; for example, Steinberg.

5. Type the screen name of your friend in the **Email Address** field; for example, Rockoid.

6. Add other identifying information, such as a person's phone number, occupation, or other material in the **Notes** field. It won't become part of the email that you address.

7. Click the **OK** button to save your additions or changes.

Now, the next time you want to send a piece of mail to Grayson, or any other person, simply open a new mail window, click the **Address Book** icon on the right side of the email form, and double-click the name of the person to whom you are sending email.

I mentioned earlier in this chapter that you can enter groups of people in the mail window if you want to send a single email to a number of recipients. Well, you can also include group addresses in your AOL Address Book. As an example, suppose you have a group of online associates with whom you correspond regularly, perhaps your staff at work or your favorite Forum Leaders on

Update your Address Book regularly

As you meet new friends and associates online, be sure to add their names to your Address Book. That way, you won't lose track of your online contacts.

You can add photos too

Click the **Picture** tab of your Address Book form (as shown in Figure 9.12) if you want to insert a photo of your online friend. When you do that, a **Select Picture** button at the bottom of the screen can be used to select the photo.

Special email tip

You can automatically open a pre-addressed email form simply by double-clicking the appropriate name entry in the Address Book.

Address it correctly

When you address your email or create an entry in your Address Book file, remember that the email address is the sign-on or screen name of the member. *This name may be totally different from the person's real name.* A member named John, may call himself Bear online or something totally different. I cannot tell you how many times I've received email addressed to someone named Gene, one of my AOL screen names, only to find that the person was looking for another Gene, with a totally different email address. When making this all-too-common mistake, folks have shared their life histories with me—a stranger—their financial information, even their confidential work files and personal phone numbers. So, before you send your email, *be sure it's addressed correctly.*

America Online. To create a group of addresses in your Address Book follow these steps:

Adding a group to your Address Book

1. Open the **Mail** menu and choose **Edit Address Book**.

2. Click the **New Group** button, which brings up the **Edit New Group** form (shown in Figure 9.13).

3. Type a name for your group in the **Group Name** field—for example, My Staff.

4. Type the screen names of all the people that you want in that address group into the Addresses field—for example, Gene, PGFA AlexP, AFC RCR.

5. Click the OK button to save your additions or changes.

Congratulations! You set up a group address and, when you double-click **My Staff** from your Address Book, all the names you entered for that group appear on the email address field on your Mail form.

FIGURE 9.13

Send email to all the people on a list with one action using this handy form.

1 Just press the Return key after each entry.

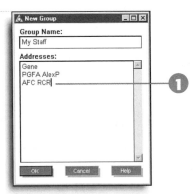

Teach Yourself: Using Automatic AOL to Send and Receive Messages—Windows Version

Automatic AOL is a marvelous way to have your AOL software run your sessions at the times you set. You can use these sessions to send and receive email, download attached files and those in your Download Manager queue. And you can use it to receive and post messages in AOL's message boards and in Internet newsgroups.

To set your Automatic AOL preferences, select **Setup Automatic AOL** from the **Mail** menu. The first time you choose this option, America Online guides you through the process of scheduling your automated session, using a special feature called Walk-Through (see Figure 9.14).

Scheduling Automatic AOL Sessions Using Walk-Through

The center button at the bottom of your first Walk-Through window gives the option of an Expert Setup. If you are familiar with setting up Automatic AOL sessions in the Mac OS version of America Online's software or you've done it before in the Windows version, you may prefer to use the Expert Setup.

If you'd rather go through the process in a more leisurely fashion, click the **Continue** button to begin your Walk-Through, which opens the screen shown in Figure 9.15. This screen gives you the option of retrieving unread mail during your Automatic AOL sessions.

Large mailing list tip

If you have a long list of email addresses you want to add to a group, you can easily copy and paste them into the Address Book group.

Changing it to CC instead

If you want to use a different recipient type (other than Send To) for a person or group selected from your Address Book, simply click the entry once to select it, and then click either the **Copy To** or **Blind Copy** buttons at the right edge of the Select Address window.

Mac and Windows Automatic AOL setups are different

The next two sections of this chapter have separate sets of instructions about using the Automatic AOL feature in both AOL's Macintosh and Windows software. Because the techniques and end results are similar, some of the text is the same. Unless you're using both platforms, you have no need to read both.

FIGURE 9.14

An Automatic AOL Walk-Through guides you step-by-step through the process of activating automatic email sessions.

① Click **Continue** to enable AOL to show you how to use this feature.

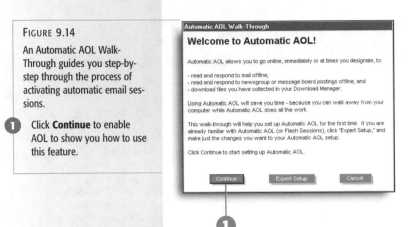

FIGURE 9.15

Your first decision in preparing an Automatic AOL session is whether you want to receive your unread mail during these automatic logons.

① Click **Yes** to get your email automatically.

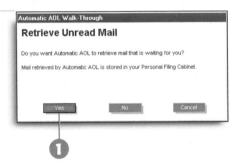

The next screen (shown in Figure 9.16) only appears if you decide to retrieve incoming mail. You are then presented with another choice, whether to download files attached to your email. If you don't accept this option, you are instructing the AOL software not to download files that are attached to incoming email. If you are paying for AOL by the hour or calling AOL long distance, it's probably a good idea to leave this option off.

If you click **No**, you have the capability, for up to seven days after you read the email, to download its attached files manually. Even easier, you can select the **Forward** icon on the email that you receive with the attachment and send it to yourself. Turn on the **Automatically Download Attached Files** option before the next connection, and the file is downloaded at that time.

FIGURE 9.16

Here you decide whether to automatically download files attached to your email during an Automatic AOL session.

1 Click **Yes** to receive automatic file transfers, but use this one with caution.

The next email option (shown in Figure 9.17) is whether to send your outgoing mail automatically. This choice is very useful. It enables you to compose all your email while offline, so you don't incur online charges to your account if you still pay for AOL by its hourly plan. When you complete your email, simply click the **Send Later** icon, and it is added to your queue of Outgoing Mail. The only disadvantage is that you cannot select which mail to send during a particular Automatic AOL session. It's all or nothing, but you probably want to click the **Yes** button for this option.

AOL doesn't store email for very long

AOL only stores unread email for about seven days or until the mailbox hits its maximum of 550 pieces (in which case the older email is discarded). This means that if files are attached to that mail, they may become inaccessible. So, you want to try to retrieve your email via Automatic AOL at shorter intervals, or just tell those who send you email with file attachments when you expect to be available to receive it.

FIGURE 9.17

Here you decide whether to automatically send your outgoing email during your automatic session.

1 Click **Yes** to send email automatically.

Download Manager Preferences

The Download Manager stores a list of files that you've selected using the **Download Later** option. This feature enables you to transfer all the files you want in a single session. The option shown in Figure 9.18 enables you to retrieve all your selected files in the Download Manager when Automatic AOL is running. Because you cannot selectively download a single file this way, you may want to think a bit about this option before giving it the okay.

FIGURE 9.18

If you click **Yes**, you're able to retrieve all the files selected via AOL's Download Manager during your Automatic AOL session.

❶ Click **Yes** to download waiting files.

Message Board and Internet Newsgroup Options

You can also receive and send messages from AOL's message boards Internet newsgroups as part of your Automatic AOL session. You have separate options to receive messages and send them. In order for this feature to work, however, you need to actually select message boards and newsgroups for offline reading.

SEE ALSO
➤ For more information about message boards, page 205
➤ For more information about newsgroups, page 295

Saving Passwords

When you get past the message boards option, you see another screen (shown in Figure 9.19) that enables you and your family members to enter passwords for your screen names. This step is necessary so that you do not have to be present for scheduled sessions. Otherwise, you have to enter your password manually each time you log on to AOL. Remember that if you store your passwords, be sure that no unauthorized persons have access to your machine. As you enter your password, what you type is entered as asterisks, so someone looking over your shoulder won't see what your password is.

FIGURE 9.19

To log on automatically during
an Automatic AOL session, you
need to enter your password
for each account in this window for which you want to
schedule your session.

1 You can enter a password
only while using that screen
name.

Scheduling Automatic AOL Sessions

Up until now, you've decided what you want to do when you run
an auto AOL session. Now it's time to decide when to run those
sessions. You can run your sessions two ways. One is simply to
open the **Mail** menu and choose **Activate Automatic AOL**, and
then click the **Begin** button. The Automatic AOL session begins
on the spot, using the preferences you've selected.

The second way is to run an unattended Automatic AOL session
at regularly scheduled intervals. The next few screens of your
Automatic AOL Walk-Through enable you to plan your sessions
in advance. You can change your settings at any time, as your
needs change. The first screen (shown in Figure 9.20) gives you
the option of scheduling your sessions. If you opt to run the sessions manually, click the **No** button; otherwise, click the **Yes**
button to continue. You then have three sets of selections to
make.

Scheduling your Automatic AOL sessions

1. The first option (shown in Figure 9.21) is used to establish
    when want your Automatic AOL sessions to take place.

2. Your next choice (shown in Figure 9.22) is how often you
    want to schedule the session, ranging from every half hour
    up to just once per day.

**Others may be able to use your
account**

When you save a stored password with your America Online
software, anyone who has
access to your computer can log
on to the service with your
account. Before using this
option, be certain your computer is not easily accessible to others without your permission.
You may want to consider using
a security program to prevent
unauthorized access to your
computer.

FIGURE 9.20

If you want to automate your AOL sessions, click the **Yes** button. If you want to decide later on or run the sessions manually, click **No**.

 You can click **Cancel** at any time to stop the setup process.

FIGURE 9.21

Click the boxes corresponding to the days of the week that you want to schedule your Auto AOL sessions.

 Check the days on which your sessions are run.

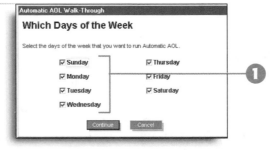

FIGURE 9.22

Click the boxes corresponding to the frequency of your sessions.

 Click the frequency of the sessions.

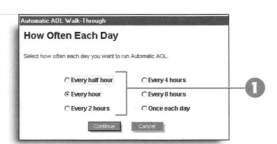

3. Finally, you want to decide what time your automated session should begin, as I've done in Figure 9.23. If your computer is not on during a scheduled session, you receive no warning message that the session did not run.

America Online's internal login calendar is now working and connects to the service at the times you scheduled. To deactivate automatic connections, select **Setup Automatic AOL** from the **Mail** menu, click the **Schedule Automatic AOL** icon, deselect the **Starting At** check box, and click **OK**.

FIGURE 9.23

Indicate the starting time for your first Automatic AOL session for each day you've selected.

Click the up or down arrows to choose the hours and minutes.

Teach Yourself: Using Automatic AOL to Send and Receive Messages—Macintosh Version

You can set a schedule for your America Online Macintosh software to log in automatically when you're too busy or nowhere near your computer. You can even schedule these sessions for any one or all the screen names on your account.

To set up a schedule, choose **Set Up Automatic AOL** from your AOL Mail Center toolbar's drop-down menu, which brings up the screen shown in Figure 9.24.

The following list is the options that you can select for your schedule. Just click the appropriate check box to activate that task during your session. The email and files that you receive will also be displayed in your Incoming/Saved Mail Drawer, which is accessed by clicking the icon for the drop-down menu on the Mail Center toolbar.

- **Using the Following Screen Names.** Click the appropriate check box to select the screen names for which you want to run an automated AOL session.

- **Perform the Following Tasks.** Choose whether to send and receive your AOL email and whether to receive files attached to your email.

- **Message Board Tasks.** You can send and receive messages from your selected AOL message boards and Internet newsgroups. To activate this function, though, you must activate offline reading for your favorite message boards and Internet newsgroups.

Don't lose those partial files

If an Automatic AOL session that includes attached files for downloading is interrupted for any reason, the status of the download process is reflected in the Download Manager. The next time you log on to AOL, either for a regular session or an Automatic AOL session, you're able to resume the download precisely where it left off. Do not delete the partial file created during the original download or move it to a different directory or folder; if you do, you're unable to resume the download where it left off, and you have to start the process from the beginning. If your file *upload* is interrupted for any reason, however, you always have to start from scratch. Remember that your PC must be on for the Automatic AOL session to run.

Avoid unwanted files

If you don't receive a lot of files from your online acquaintances, you may want to deselect the option to download files. This way, you don't risk downloading files that you don't want.

- **Download Manager Tasks.** The checkbox at the bottom of Figure 9.25 needs to be checked to automatically receive file downloads during your Automatic AOL session.

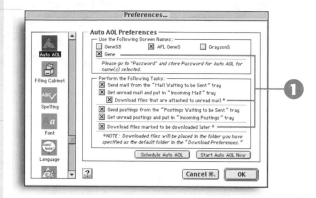

FIGURE 9.24

The Mac version of Auto AOL preferences are used to decide what tasks AOL will perform.

❶ Click the check box to activate that feature.

Don't lose that email

AOL only stores unread email for about seven days (or until 550 messages are received, at which time older email is discarded). This means that if files are attached to that mail, they may become inaccessible. So, you want to try to retrieve your email via Automatic AOL sessions at shorter intervals, or just tell those who send you email with file attachments when you expect to be available to receive them.

SEE ALSO

➤ *For information on how to use message boards, see page 205*

➤ *For information on Internet newsgroups, see page 295*

Scheduling Automatic AOL Sessions

If you want to have your AOL visits run on automatic pilot, you are almost there. You've selected the Automatic AOL options in the previous section, and all that remains is to schedule your automatic logins and enter the passwords for the screen names used during these sessions.

The next step involves calling up the Auto AOL Scheduler Preferences (see Figure 9.25) by clicking the Scheduler icon at the left of the Preferences window.

Now you need to follow these steps to select your preferences for the Scheduler.

Scheduling your mac AOL Automatic sessions

1. Click the **Perform scheduled Auto AOL sessions** check box to activate this feature.

2. Click the pop-up menu to the right of the **Sign On** option to determine how often your sessions are to be run (it ranges from every half-hour to once per day).

FIGURE 9.25

Use the Auto AOL scheduling
window to decide when your
automated logons are to occur.

1 Click the check box to activate that feature.

3. Under **On the following days**, click the check box to the
left of the days of the week that you want the sessions to
run.

4. Click **OK** to close this window and to store the settings that
you made.

Storing Your Passwords

This feature enables you and your family to enter passwords for
your screen names. This is necessary so that you do not have to
be present for scheduled Auto AOL Sessions. Otherwise, you
have to enter your password manually each time you log on to
AOL.

Storing passwords

1. Click the **Passwords** icon in AOL's Preferences window.

2. Enter your passwords in the fields next to the screen names
shown. Notice as you enter your password that bullets (small
round circles) appear, rather than the characters you type.
This feature prevents others from looking over your shoulder and seeing your password onscreen.

3. Click the **Valid for Auto AOL** check box if you want to
store the passwords strictly for automated sessions on AOL.

4. Click **OK** to save your settings.

America Online's internal login calendar is now working and
connects to the service at the times you scheduled. To turn off

---

Stored passwords

When you save a stored password with your America Online
software, anyone who has
access to your computer can log
on to the service with your
account and use online time
that is charged to your monthly
bill (if you pay by the hour for
the service or for long-distance
telephone access). Before using
this option, be certain your
computer is not easily accessible
to others without your permission. You may want to consider,
for example, using a security
program to prevent unauthorized access to your computer.

automatic connections, select Set Up Automatic AOL from the mail menu, click the Schedule icon, deselect the Perform scheduled Auto AOL sessions check box, and click OK.

Managing your Incoming and Outgoing Mailboxes with Automatic AOL Sessions

Each piece of email that you create for an Automatic AOL session is stored in your Personal Filing Cabinet and accessed from the **Read Incoming/Saved Mail** command in the Mail Center toolbar icon's drop-down menu (see Figure 9.26). Before a message is actually sent, you can open and read it to review or edit the contents. You can even delete a message, should you not want to send it. After all your outgoing letters have been sent, the messages are moved to the Mail You've Sent folder.

FIGURE 9.26

The directories of mail sent and received via Automatic AOL sessions.

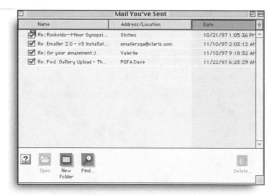

Downloading software

The best time to schedule Auto AOL sessions to download software is early in the morning or late at night. That's when traffic on AOL is lowest, and download times are speedier.

While online, you can also view your Online Mailbox simply by clicking the **Mail Center** icon on the toolbar, and choosing **Read Mail** from the drop-down menu. Your Online Mailbox (see Figure 9.27) not only lists the mail waiting to be read, but the messages you've read (Old Mail) and the ones you've mailed (Sent Mail).

FIGURE 9.27
The Online Mailbox stores
recent sent and received email.

Mail Status Reports

When you send your email to another AOL member, you can click the **Request Return Receipt** option (which applies strictly to AOL-directed email) at the bottom of the email form and get a notice when the recipient has read your message. You can also check the status of your email at any time by selecting your email from the Online Mailbox, and clicking the **Status** button (see Figure 9.28).

This handy feature, however, doesn't register when Internet-based email is read.

Online Mailbox

Your Online Mailbox stores up to 550 pieces of received mail before the older messages are deleted. Old Mail, the email you've received, remains accessible online for up to 7 days. Sent Mail remains accessible for up to 30 days, but if you email very often, the time frame is apt to be less. If you want to keep a record of everything you've sent and received, set your Personal Filing Cabinet preferences—accessible from the My AOL toolbar icon's drop-down menu—to store everything (you can always delete it later on).

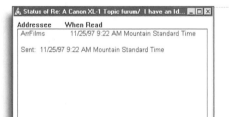

FIGURE 9.28
As you see, this message has already been read.

The Lowdown on Instant Messaging

You're not being ignored

If you send an instant message and don't get a response immediately, it doesn't mean that the other member is being rude or ignoring you. Sometimes a person is online but not present in front of his or her computer, such as during an Automatic AOL session. At other times, the member may be in the middle of uploading a file and cannot respond to you. If you don't receive an answer, try sending another instant message after a few minutes, or just use email instead.

The first part of this chapter described how to use email to communicate with other AOL members. Although email messages are sent almost instantaneously to other AOL members, and with only some delay through the Internet, the only way they can be read is for the recipient or recipients to log on to the service and open the messages (or to run an Automatic AOL session). This section describes the technique used to communicate with fellow AOL neighbors one-on-one, while both of you are online, using instant messages.

To send an instant message while online, select instant message from the drop-down menu on the People toolbar or press ⌘-I (Ctrl+I for Windows users). You see a new window in which to address and compose your message (see Figure 9.29).

If you receive an instant message, click the **Respond** button, which brings up a brand new two-pane reply window. Enter your reply in the lower portion of the Instant Message window, and click the **Send** button (see Figure 9.30).

FIGURE 9.29

The originator's Instant Message window.

1 Change text styles with the Formatting bar.

FIGURE 9.30

The recipient's Instant Message window.

1 Scroll through the message to see all the text.

You can have a two-way conversation with any AOL member by leaving the Instant Message window open after you send a response. When a new message arrives from your friend, it appears in that window. (If your online sounds are activated, the arrival of the message follows a pleasant musical tone.) The actual conversation appears in the upper text field, while the responses you type appear in the lower portion of the window. You can hold numerous instant message conversations simultaneously.

As with other types of text windows in AOL, you can print or save the Instant Message window's contents by opening the **File** menu and choosing **Print** or **Save**.

A Look at AOL's Instant Messenger

Keyword: Instant Messenger

AOL's Instant Messenger feature extends AOL's instant messages to the Internet. It enables you to have a one-on-one meeting with your friends and business acquaintances who have a regular Internet account. In order to set up this feature, just call up AOL's Instant Messenger invitation service (shown in Figure 9.31).

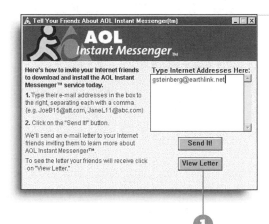

Instant message keyboard shortcut

If you are using a Macintosh, you can press the Enter key on the numeric keypad rather than click the **Send** button to send your instant message. You can't use the Return key to send your message because this key starts a new line in your message text. If your keyboard does not have an Enter key, use ⌘-Return. If you are using America Online for Windows, you can press Ctrl+Enter rather than click the **Send** button.

The message doesn't always get through

If you send an instant message to someone just when they log off, or they are disconnected from AOL for some reason, the message appears to go through, but you soon see a message on your screen that the message didn't reach its recipient

FIGURE 9.31

You can use Instant Messenger to communicate with friends who are members of other services with Internet access.

1 Click here to send that invitation to your Internet friend.

Don't give out your password or credit card number

This warning appears on your Online Mailbox and your Instant Message window, but I cannot repeat it often enough. *AOL staff will never ask you for password or billing information.* If someone claims to be a staff member of AOL and asks for this information, just ignore the message. Then use the keyword `Notify AOL` to open a form to report the offender. You'll also find a Notify form in Instant Message windows and People Connection chat rooms.

Troubleshooting

Help! My desktop is cluttered with instant message windows. When I hear that little noise about their arrival, I just don't know what to select.

Welcome to the club. We've all had that problem. What I try to do is close the instant message windows for conversations I'm no longer involved in. Then I group the rest of the windows in a neat pile at one corner of the screen. On your Windows PC you can minimize the windows. You can do the same with Mac OS 8, by clicking the little square at the upper right of a document window's title bar. These steps help keep my desktop relatively free of scattered instant messages (most of the time anyway).

All you have to do to invite friends to use AOL's Instant Messenger is to send the addresses of your friends and business associates on other services to AOL. In response, they receive an email invitation and information on how to download special software from AOL's Web site to activate this feature. When they install the software, they are able to exchange instant messages with you nearly as easily as you can send such messages on AOL, and their names also appear in your Buddy List when they're logged onto their Internet account with the special Instant Messenger software.

SEE ALSO

➤ *For more information on the Buddy List, see page 144*

➤ *For more information about email and Instant Messages, see page 87*

➤ *Learn more about the AOL Computing channel, see page 418*

➤ *For information on how to seek out and participate in message boards, see page 205*

Chatting Online

People Are Talking on AOL

They come from the world of show business, the political world, from the book best-seller charts. And they have one thing in common, participating in an online conference. Over the past few years I've attended conferences from such diverse personalities as author Tom Clancy, *Tonight Show* host Jay Leno, David Letterman, former L.A. cop and O.J. Simpson case investigator Mark Fuhrman, and even Paul McCartney.

The best part is, I didn't have to leave my home or office, brave rush-hour traffic and long lines at a ticket counter, or fight the teaming crowds for a good seat. I was able to attend every one of these meetings while seated in front of my desktop or laptop computer, by logging on to America Online.

Every night on America Online, literally dozens of virtual rooms and auditoriums are open and active. In them, you'll find thousands of members engaged in online chats or sitting in the audience of huge online auditoriums. In those auditoriums you'll have a chance to meet famous movie stars, TV stars, and book authors.

The Differences Between Chats and Conferences

You can think of a chat room as the equivalent of a small classroom or meeting room. Capacity is limited to 23 folks in the People Connection before another room is opened automatically. In a forum chat room, the capacity is 48; then, as in People Connection, a new chat room is automatically created. Chapter 8, "AOL's People Connection" covers this area in more detail.

Because forum conferences are designed to be held in just one room, however, the second room created for an overflow crowd is best suited for hanging out until someone leaves the main room again. It's like waiting for an available seat in a restaurant. The setup is informal. Often, you can just make a comment on the proceedings (so long as you don't interrupt the chat) without having to get anyone's attention.

Watch out for protocol!

When a special guest is present, some forums invoke something called *chat protocol*. If you've been an AOL member for awhile, you know that some famous personalities have been invited to participate in online conferences. Some of these personalities, especially the world-famous rock stars who visit America Online, can draw crowds sometimes numbering in the thousands. A regular chat room won't cut it for handling that kind of crowd; having hundreds of AOL members vying for the guest's attention by posting questions and comments in a chat window would be chaotic.

AOL Live!—Where the Action Is

Keywords: Live, AOL Live

The AOL Auditorium (see Figure 10.1) is a special kind of online environment that's designed to handle such highly attended events more sensibly. AOL and People Connection came up with this unique interactive concept that's structured in such a way that folks have a chance to interact with the special guest, but not at the expense of having hundreds of questions asked all at once. You can compare this conference area to a regular auditorium, complete with rows for the audience and a stage for the guests. Several auditoriums are available at any one time, all of which you can reach through the keyword AOL Live.

The AOL Live! auditoriums are America Online's largest gathering places, capable of accommodating thousands of members spread over several separate auditoriums for fun-filled game shows and special events. You'll learn just how conferences are conducted a little later in this chapter.

Where to find help in an AOL auditorium

If you're still unsure of the setup in a particular conference room, click the **Help** icon at the bottom right of the auditorium screen.

FIGURE 10.1

AOL Live! is a gathering place where you can meet well-known figures on AOL.

1 Check schedules for online conferences.

Teach Yourself: Join and Participate in Online Chats

Before you go to a chat or conference, you'll want to find out which one you should attend. Forum chats and conferences are sometimes promoted via the AOL Today feature in AOL's

Many AOL conferences are logged

In case you miss a conference, don't worry. The AOL Live! staff logs most every event, and the logs are always posted in the area's software libraries, available when you click the Intermission icon. Because the logs consist of straight, unformatted text (which you can usually open with your AOL software or any word processor), the file sizes are small; you can generally download a log in just a minute or two.

Welcome window, which you see when you first sign on to the service (see Figure 10.2).

In addition, the Computing channel of AOL (see Figure 10.3) has its own custom announcement display for online meetings called Computing Live (accessed via the keyword CompLive). To return to the regular Computing channel window, click the Main button at the top middle of the screen.

Online conferences are also advertised in the AOL Live! window (refer to Figure 10.1), which you can access via the keyword Live. The day's conferences are listed when you click the **Today's Live Events** icon. The **Coming Attractions** icon offers a list of upcoming events (see Figure 10.4).

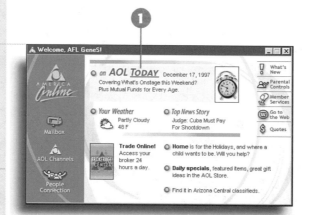

FIGURE 10.2

AOL Today, in the Welcome window, is one place where you'll find news about online conferences.

1 The schedule for upcoming online conferences.

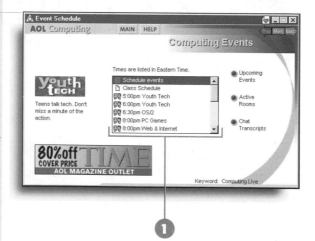

FIGURE 10.3

The Computing channel's Computing Live section advertises upcoming chats and special events.

1 Check out listings for computer-related chats.

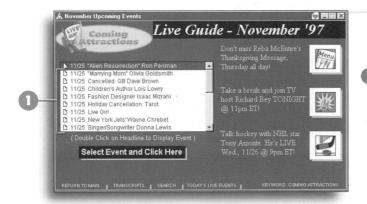

Participating in Online Chats

After you know what chat or conference you want to attend, the
next step is to enter the conference hall by clicking the appropriate icon in a forum, or AOL Live! (refer to Figure 10.1).

When you first enter an AOL Live! auditorium (see Figure
10.5), the service (euphemistically referred to as Online Host)
reminds you that only those in the same row as yours can see the
text you type to the screen. You can talk by entering text in the
conference room window, and then clicking the **Send** button (or
pressing the Return or Enter key).

If you find that the conversation of members in the same row is
distracting from your concentration on the main event (somewhat like being disturbed by folks around you in a movie theater), you can turn off the chat feature. Just click the **Who's in
My Row** icon shown in the conference room window; then click
the **Turn Chat Off** button in the window that appears (see
Figure 10.6). When the Chat feature is turned off, you can enjoy
the event while seeing only text that appears from the stage—
text from your hosts, guests, and contestants.

FIGURE 10.5

This AOL Live! conference is already in progress.

1 Conference text.

2 Enter your chat row text here.

3 Interact with the conference host or guests.

4 Another source of online conferences.

5 Learn about the people in your chat row.

6 Notify AOL in the event of a problem with another member.

7 List of people on stage.

8 Click this icon to check on AOL Live! events.

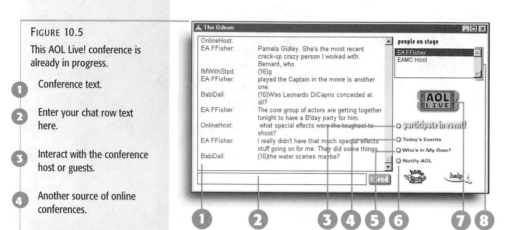

From this window, you also can look for other members who might be online (so that you can tell them what a great time you're having at the online conference), list people in your chat row or any other row, and create a new chat row. If you want to move to another seat, click the **Other Rows** button, select the row you want to enter, and click the **Switch Rows** button. Because chat rows are each limited to eight members (16 members in some larger conference rooms), you won't be able to enter a row that's already filled.

FIGURE 10.6

More chat controls for the AOL Live! Auditorium are found in the Chat Rows window.

1 Choose whether you want to see what the people in your row have to say.

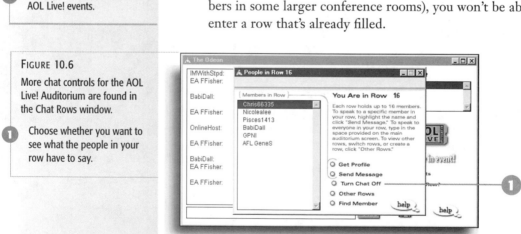

The best part of attending an online conference is to ask a question of the special guest and have it answered. To pose your question, click the **Participate in Event** icon in the main conference room window (see Figure 10.7), enter your question, and then indicate, by clicking the appropriate button, whether it's meant to be a question or a comment. The **Vote** and **Bid** buttons are meant for special online contests.

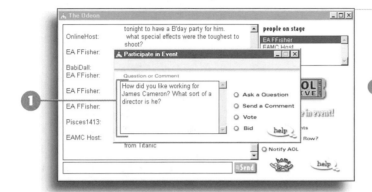

FIGURE 10.7

Enter your question for the conference guest here, then send it.

❶ Ask a conference guest a question or make a comment.

Chat Text Styles—Keep It Simple

An online chat is fun and a great way to relax after a hard day at the office. In addition, you can be creative in a regular chat room, using AOL's convenient text styling features (see Figure 10.8 for an example of some basic online creativity). Remember not to get too carried away with the manner in which you style text. You want your chat text to be easily read by other members.

Instant Messages and Online Chatting—Some Cautions

Instant messaging on AOL, as described in previous chapters, is a great way to have a one-on-one conversation with a fellow AOL member. During a forum chat, it's also a way to get information about the subjects dealt with in a chat or to elicit further information from a guest or a forum staff.

If you see someone involved in a chat whom you'd like to know better, you can send an instant message to that person. If you have a problem or a question about a subject other than that being discussed, you can send an instant message about it.

Why wasn't your question answered?

Online conferences might be attended by hundreds or thousands of AOL members, so there probably isn't enough time to answer all the questions. The conference moderator tries to use a representative sample of the questions submitted, but do not expect that your question, however important it is to you, can always get a response. Sometimes, however, guests respond to unanswered messages via email. It depends on the conference. Show business personalities, for example, often appear using temporary online accounts and will probably not respond to email after the conference is over.

Chat text styles have their limits

The text styling feature is designed to work in a regular chat room, not the large conference auditoriums.

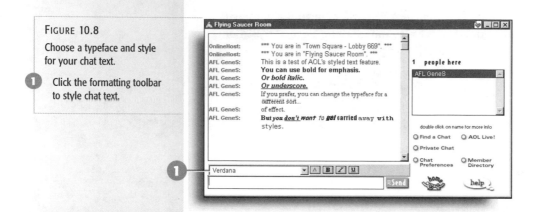

Welcome to an online chat

When you first enter a chat room, often you'll receive an instant message from a forum staff member that offers information about the night's chat, and, sometimes, a message as to whether chat protocol is in effect. (You learn what chat protocol is all about in the next section.) If you get a message of this sort, try not to engage that staff member in an extended instant message chat, because the staff member is probably busy greeting other visitors.

Consider the following before you send an instant message:

- Try not to send an instant message to a special guest in a chat. Often that guest will be busy answering questions and won't have time to engage in personal chit-chat with you. It might be better to wait until the chat is over or send the person email.

- Participants in an online conference in one of AOL's auditoriums are usually *unable* to receive instant messages while on stage. Don't be disappointed if you don't get a response. Use email instead (assuming, of course, that the guest isn't using a temporary account).

Some Insights into Proper Online Behavior

As with other online areas, AOL's chat and conference rooms have their own conventions of online etiquette. Beyond normal considerations of courtesy and good taste, you should be aware of a few things when attending an online chat.

The Rules of the Road

Chapter 7, "Parental Issues and Internet Access," describes important parts of America Online's Terms of Service, the list of regulations that you are expected to follow during your online visits. You should apply those standards when you attend a chat room also. Keep these things in mind:

- *Watch your language.* Sometimes chats can become exciting; no doubt you'll find yourself reacting emotionally at times to what someone is saying. Remember, vulgar language in a chat is just as inappropriate as it is in your email, instant messages, and message board discussions.

- *Don't interrupt.* It's hard to know sometimes when you engage in a regular conversation when to add a remark of your own. It's even more difficult in cyberspace, because you don't always know when others have stopped talking. Look out for the following when reading a chat window or when conversing yourself:

  1. Use of an ellipses (…) to signify that the statement is not yet finished, and more text is to be added.

  2. Use of the words "go ahead" or the initials GA to indicate that the member's statement is finished and others can now begin to talk.

- *Avoid irrelevant topics.* Unless the chat is an open session, in which no particular subject is up for discussion, try to confine your conversation to the subject or subjects at hand. If you need to contact the forum staff about another subject, send an instant message to see whether email would be a better way to raise a subject.

A chat is meant to be fun and informative. If you pay attention to the ground rules, you can sit back, relax, and enjoy the session, and even participate at the right time.

Using Chat Protocol

When a forum has a large crowd and a special guest, chat protocol is often put into effect. This is not meant to restrict the flow of conversation, but to give everyone a chance to participate without filling the screen with lots of unconnected comments. The rules of chat protocol are simple:

Don't be afraid to ask!

If you're unsure about the topic or setup of a particular chat, and you haven't gotten a notice about it, don't hesitate to send an instant message to the forum staff about it (they generally have an AFL, PC, or a similar designation in front of their screen names).

Don't disrupt a chat

Deliberately and repeatedly interfering with the flow of dialogue in a chat room, even if meant as a joke, can be considered a violation of AOL's Terms of Service. Take the time to watch the flow of conversation in a chat room to see what topics are being discussed.

- Type **?** in the chat window if you have a question.

- Type **!** in the chat window if you have a comment about the topic being discussed.

- Don't ask your question or make your comment until you are called upon by name by the chat host (even if your name shows up at the beginning of a list of waiting questioners that appears in the chat window).

Often at the tail end of a chat, protocol will end to give visitors a chance to hang out and talk informally about whatever is on their minds. You'll usually see a message about free chat time or a similar announcement when the formal part of the session is over. (A free chat *doesn't* mean you're online time is free [if you pay for AOL by the hour], only that the formal structuring of the meeting is over.)

Chatting and Internet Relay Chats—Is There a Difference?

The chats and conferences I described in this chapter occur on AOL, and are controlled by the rules of the service. Internet Relay Chat is yet another kind of chat you can join. You'll read more about it in Chapter 14, "Internet Chats." Those chats are shared events, held across the Internet. The rules and regulations are different and AOL's Terms of Service do not apply (except for your personal behavior).

Sometimes the chat monitor (or channel operator) runs the session within the bounds of good taste. Sometimes they'll run them with no taste whatever, and sometimes they'll be arbitrary about whom they admit into a chat. If they don't like your name, or your point of view, you're ejected. In any case, if you encounter an Internet Relay Chat of this sort in your wanderings, just go to another where your presence is welcomed.

What did I miss?

If you miss a chat or arrive late, don't worry. Most of the time, the forum or conference staff posts a log of the chat in a few days (just as is done with AOL Live! events). Just watch the software libraries for it.

Using Abbreviations and Shorthand Symbols

Chatting online is, obviously, different from talking to a person whom you can see. For one thing, you have no way to convey emotions in the usual manner, by voice inflection or by body language. All your conversation is conducted via keyboard with the words that you write, and sometimes it's not obvious what emotions might be attached to a specific statement. You might mean for something to be serious, sarcastic, or humorous, but the words themselves can sometimes be subject to several meanings. As a result, a series of keyboard abbreviations, called *smileys* or *emoticons*, has been created over the years to convey emotions online.

This section offers a listing of many of the abbreviations and shorthand symbols you might see while online in AOL's People Connection, in chat rooms, or on message boards. They are a result of the need to show what cannot be shown when online—facial expressions and body language.

Online Abbreviations

Often when chatting, America Online members shorten long phrases into a few letters so that they can be typed quickly. Some of the more common online abbreviations are

Abbreviation	Stands For...
LOL	Laughing Out Loud
ROFL or ROTFL	Rolling On The Floor Laughing
AFK	Away From Keyboard
BAK	Back At Keyboard
BRB	Be Right Back
OIC	Oh, I See
IMO	In My Opinion

continues…

...continued

IMHO	In My Humble Opinion or In My Honest Opinion
TTFN	Ta-Ta For Now
TTYL	Talk To You Later
GMTA	Great Minds Think Alike
IHTBHWYG	It's Hard To Be Humble When You're Great
<g>	Grin
GA	Go Ahead

Online Shorthand

Learning online shorthand might take a bit of time, because of the many possibilities in the list that follows. You'll find, however, after you gain online experience, that only a relative few are in common use, and some are encountered infrequently at best (a few I've never encountered in years of online visits). In putting this list together, I've collected a number of sometimes brilliant examples of online shorthand—keyboard symbols that convey human expression. Tilting your head toward the left will help you to see most of the symbols; for example, the characters :) form a sideways smiley face. The following are some common examples:

Shorthand	Symbolizes
[ ]	A hug, repeated as needed for degrees of enthusiasm, such as [[[[[[[[ ]]]]]]]]
:)	Basic smile
:(	Frown
:/	Ho-hum smile
;)	Winking smile
:D	Smile with a big grin
:*	Kiss
8)	Wide-eyed smile

Shorthand	Symbolizes
B-)	Wearing sunglasses
[:|]	Robot
:>)	Big nose
:<|	From an Ivy League school
:%)%	Acne
=:-)	Hosehead
:-)8	Well-dressed
8:-)	Little girl
%-)	Cross-eyed
#-)	Partied all night
:-*	Just ate a sour pickle
:-'|	Has a cold
:-R	Has the flu
:-)'	Tends to drool
':-)	Accidentally shaved off an eyebrow
0-)	Wearing a scuba mask
P-)	Getting fresh
|-)	Falling asleep
.-)	Has one eye
:=)	Has two noses
:-D	Talks too much
O:-)	Smiley face with halo; very innocent
:-{}	Has mustache
:-)}	Has goatee/beard
:-d~ and :-p~	Smokes heavily
Q:-)	New graduate
(-:	Australian
M:-)	Saluting (symbol of respect)
8:]	Gorilla

continues…

…continued

Shorthand	Symbolizes
8)	Frog
B)	Frog wearing sunglasses
I)	Salamander
:8)	Pig
3:-o	Cow
pp#	Cow
:3-<	Dog
pq'#'	Bull
}.'\	Elephant
+O:-)	The Pope
C=:-)	Galloping Gourmet
=):-)	Uncle Sam
=I:-)	Abe Lincoln
4:-)	George Washington
5:-)	Elvis Presley
7:-)	Fred Flintstone
:/7)	Cyrano de Bergerac
>:*)	Bozo the Clown
#:o+=	Betty Boop
>>-O->	General Custer
8(:-)	Walt Disney
>:^(	A headhunter
-=#:-)	Has wizard status
(: (=I	Going to be a ghost for Halloween
=:-H	Plays for NFL
(V)=I	A Pac-Man champion
M-):X):-M	See no evil, hear no evil, speak no evil

Shorthand	Symbolizes
C):-O C):-O C):-O C):-O	A barbershop quartet
>:-(	Sick and tired of reading this nonsense
|-O	Bored
*-)	Shot for the last posting
~~\8-O	Needs to fix frayed cord on terminal
8-O	Took too many No Doz to work on thesis
L:-)	Just graduated
$-)	Just won the lottery
:-@	Extremely angry
:-o	Shocked
B-)-[<	Wearing sunglasses and swimming trunks
:-#	Punched in the mouth
R-)	Broken glasses
:-7	Talks out of the side of the mouth
%')	Finished off a fifth for lunch
:-(O)	Yelling
. .	Lying down
|:-)	Heavy eyebrows
{:-)	New hair style
{:-{)}	New hair style, mustache, and beard
(:-)	No hair
:~)	Ugly nose (needs a nose job)
:-E	Major dental problems
C:-)	Large brain capacity
|:-|	Excessively rigid
:-)))	Very overweight

continues…

...continued

Shorthand	Symbolizes
:-G-	Smokes cigarettes
\:-)	Wears a French hat
]:-)	Devil
8=:-)	Chef
0-)	Cyclops

Where can I learn more about online shorthand?

If you're interested in learning more about smileys, you'll find AOL has an entire area set up to explore online shorthand. The keyword to access this feature is `Smileys`.

SEE ALSO

➤ *Learn more about email and instant messages, see page 157*

➤ *For more information about using AOL's chat rooms and auditoriums, see page 148*

➤ *Learn more about AOL's Computing forums and forum conferences, see page 417*

How to Use AOL's Message Boards

AOL's message boards

Finding the messages you want

Expressing yourself online

Online etiquette

The Differences Between Message Boards and Email

AOL can be experienced the way you want. Your online visits can be either passive or active.

The passive technique involves seeking out and reading information on a topic that might interest you, such as the news of the day, or methods to solve common problems with your favorite software. This technique is passive because you are not actually communicating with anyone else during your online visit.

In Chapters 8 and 9, you learned several ways to actually talk to fellow members, such as sending email, participating in chats, attending conferences (more of which is covered in Chapter 10, "Chatting Online"), and exchanging instant messages with another member. These last items can be considered active. They are especially enjoyable because you get an instant response from your fellow member, and it's surely a terrific way to build a lasting friendship. This chapter deals with a more permanent form of online expression—the use of forum message boards.

How to Find the Right Message Area

Message boards (sometimes called *discussion boards*) and email are similar, with one major exception. Email contains a message that is designed for a single recipient or a group of recipients. A message board is, pure and simple, a public statement, put on display in an area where any other member of America Online can read and respond to it (sort of the online equivalent of a neighborhood bulletin board). A message board in a particular forum is generally devoted to one subject. For example, in the Computing channel forums, messages might be devoted to one aspect of your computing experience, such as handling problems with your computer's operating system, or finding the right multimedia software with which to make a presentation. In a cooking forum, messages might be devoted to the best ways to use a wok for preparing vegetables, or how to make a particular kind of omelette.

One advantage of message boards on America Online is that you don't have to communicate only with members who are online at the same time you are. When you leave a message, you can wait several minutes, hours, or even days before checking back to look for responses. You can also respond to a message placed there (or posted) by someone else.

Chapter 5, "Exploring AOL," presents a capsule summary of many of AOL's channels, the sections devoted to different aspects of your online experience, such as the Computing channel, the Entertainment channel, and so on.

Throughout the book are chapters that detail the workings of each of those channels and the forums they include. You can use these chapters as a guide to help you choose the forums that seem to match the topics that interest you during your online visits.

Before posting anything in a forum's message boards, you should take some time to learn about a particular forum and its specific topics of interest. To do this, you need to explore and get a feel for the material discussed. You'll want to read older messages (you learn how to limit your search a bit later in this chapter), so you can see if the comment you want to make has already been voiced by another member, or if the question you want to ask has already been answered. Most forums have a weekly update text that you can read online to find out what's new and what's happening in that forum.

For an example, take a look at the forum information from the Mac Animation & Video forum (see Figure 11.1); the keyword is MMM. (Of course, because this is my book, I figured I may as well show a forum I used to manage.)

Read older messages first

The best thing to keep in mind when getting accustomed to AOL's message boards is to look and read before you post. Be sure your message is appropriate to a particular board, and please don't post the same message over and over again.

FIGURE 11.1

This is the Mac Animation & Video forum, part of AOL's Computing channel.

① Click the Message Boards icon to see the latest postings.

AOL Message Board Features

AOL's message boards include features that provide for easy navigation and offline reading. Some of the capabilities of this flexible system include

- *Threaded.* Many of the message boards are set up to group messages by topic so you that can easily follow a discussion.

- *Viewing preferences.* The capability to sort your messages the way you prefer, oldest, newest, or alphabetically.

- *Send an email copy.* You can automatically send a copy of your message direct to the author of the message to which you're replying.

- *Offline reading/posting.* Read and respond to messages via AOL's handy Automatic AOL feature (see Chapter 9, "Using AOL's Email" for the specifics).

Many message board options are available

This section describes the various descriptive buttons and labels you find on AOL message boards, and I'm showing a few of them as they'll appear during your AOL visits. Depending on which icon you click, you'll bring up a different range of options to see the messages you want to read. After you know what the options mean, the sequence in which they appear doesn't make a big difference.

How to Navigate Through a Message Area

After you find forums you want to explore further, and after reading the forum update information, look over the message boards to find discussions in which you want to get involved.

To find messages in a forum that might interest you, click the Message Boards icon, which generally appears on the forum's main screen. This brings up the window shown in Figure 11.2, or one similar to it. The general subject matter of the forum is described briefly at the top of the Message Boards window.

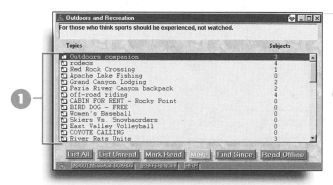

The illustration shown in Figure 11.2 usually represents the top level of a message board (sometimes you'll see the second level, or subject level, described later in this chapter).

You'll notice six buttons at the bottom of this window, five of which take you further along the road to finding messages you want to read. I'll describe them first, then we'll set message board preferences and browse through a typical board to see how it's organized. The buttons and their descriptions are

- **List All.** As the title states, click this button to see the subjects of all the messages in that message board (at least as far back as you specify in your message board preferences).

- **List Unread.** Click this button to bring up the listing of unread subjects in the selected topic folder.

   If you are visiting a forum for the first time, choosing this button can produce literally dozens of topic folders and hundreds of messages. You might be better off using the next option, Find Since (I'll get to that one shortly).

- **Mark Read.** Whether or not you actually intend to read these messages, clicking the **Mark Read** button tells AOL's host computer to assume you have and not display them again (unless you choose List All of course).

These options apply to message board topics

The buttons described here always work on topic folders you select in the message board window; they don't apply to all the listed topics at the same time. You have to apply the actions one topic folder at a time.

- **More.** This button is grayed out in Figure 11.2, but if there are lots of boards in a specific area, click the **More** button to bring up additional entries.

- **Find Since.** This button lets you choose the time frame for display of messages (see Figure 11.3). The first time you visit a message area, no doubt you'll want to choose no more than 15 to 30 days so that you're not inundated with hundreds of messages to explore.

FIGURE 11.3

How far back do you want to search for messages? Indicate your choice here.

1 Click the search option you want.

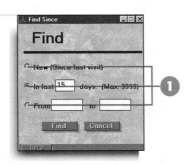

A tale of changing icons

When a message board, or topic folder is set up for Offline Reading, the Message Board icon at the left of the topic title appears with a little clock icon when you reopen that message area after changing the setting. Clicking the **Read Offline** option again turns off the capability to download messages and (when you visit the board again), the regular message board icon returns. You can see all the message boards you designated for offline reading in a single listing via the keyword My Boards.

- **Read Offline.** Click this button and the selected topic folder is marked for offline reading. The unread messages can now be downloaded to your computer as part of an Automatic AOL session. Read Chapter 9, "Using AOL's Email," for more information on how the Automatic AOL feature is used.

Setting Message Board Preferences

You can start reading your messages without any preference changes at all. After you navigate through them for awhile, you'll want to customize the way they appear, and maybe include a signature to insert into the message automatically. So let's start our message board viewing by clicking the **Preferences** button at the bottom of a message board window (see Figure 11.4).

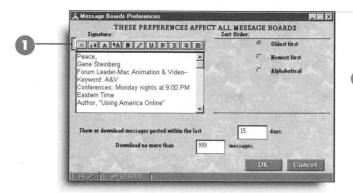

FIGURE 11.4

Set your message board preferences here.

1 Use the formatting toolbar to style your signature.

The choices you make here apply to all AOL message boards. The message board options you can set are

- **Signature.** Enter your online signature in the text box (up to 256 characters) and it'll appear automatically in all the messages you send (that is if the option to include your signature is checked). You can use the formatting toolbar to give color and style to your signature.

- **Sort Order.** By default, the oldest message appears first, but you have two more options to try. The second is **Newest first**, which puts the messages in reverse order (somewhat akin to reading the end of a book before the beginning). The final choice is **Alphabetical**.

- **Show or download messages posted within the last xx days.** What's the maximum number of days for which you want to see messages? You can set up to 999 days, but 14–28 days is usually enough to keep from being overwhelmed with messages to read when you first check out an area.

- **Download no more than xx messages.** Decide the maximum number of messages you want to download during an Automatic AOL session. Two hundred or 300 is probably enough to start with, unless you select a big number of message boards for offline reading. The maximum setting is 999 messages.

Teach Yourself: Your First Message Board Visit

Now you're ready to visit a message board and check and read the latest postings from your fellow AOL members. Because this is a new board, you'll probably want to restrict your search so that you don't have to read too many messages the first time.

Your first step, then, is to click the **Find Since** button and enter 14 in the **In last *xx* days** box, and click **Find**. A list of discussion topics posted in the last two weeks appears, as shown in Figure 11.5.

FIGURE 11.5

Forum messages are subdivided by topic.

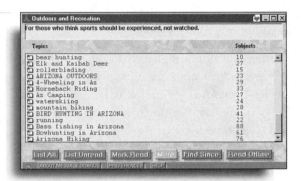

Each forum divides its message boards by titles, which represent a group of general topics that relate to the forum's field of interest.

To get to the next step in your message-reading process—the actual subjects (or message threads) for which messages are posted—double-click one of these general topics. You'll see a list of subjects much like the one shown in Figure 11.6.

FIGURE 11.6

The subjects discussed in this board appear when you double-click a topic title.

1 This type of screen appears when you click a topic.

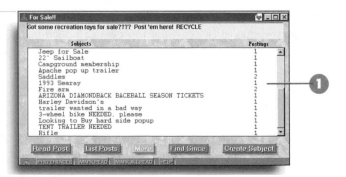

The five buttons at the bottom of the window include the following:

- **Read Post.** Click this icon to bring up the first message in the thread or subject you've selected.
- **List Posts.** This option brings up a list of unread messages on the selected subject. From there you can choose individual messages to read.
- **More.** With more than 50 items available, this icon won't be grayed out, and you'll click it to bring up more entries.
- **Find Since.** This is the same option I described previously (refer to Figure 11.4), but the search option only applies to the topic folder that's open.
- **Create Subject.** If you find no subjects that appeal to you, you can use this option to create one yourself. It'll bring up the screen shown in Figure 11.7.

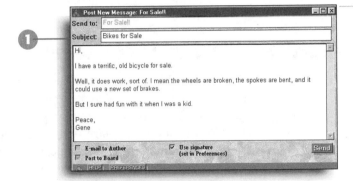

FIGURE 11.7

Create a brand new subject for a topic folder, and write your first message here. Just be sure it's relevant to the subject matter dealt with in that message board.

1 Use the Tab key to move from the **Subject** text box to the body of the message.

To begin reading a new message, select a subject by clicking its title, and then click the **Read Post** button to bring up the first message. You'll see a screen much like the one shown in Figure 11.8.

FIGURE 11.8

A typical message is shown here. Note the navigation buttons at the bottom.

1 The navigation buttons are grayed out if no more messages are available.

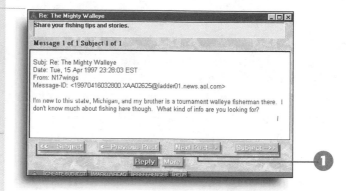

Message board keyboard shortcuts

After you open the first message, use the arrow keys on your keyboard to move to the next or previous posting. You can move from one subject to the next by holding down both the Control and arrow keys at the same time (next or previous).

If no new messages are there…

If no unread messages are in a topic or subject folder when you click the **Read Post** button to bring up the list, you'll see an onscreen message to that effect. It'll give you the option to list all the articles, by clicking the **OK** button, or to just **Cancel** the process.

Can't create a new subject?

If the capability to create a subject is grayed out in a message board, it means the staff who runs that forum has decided to only make new folders via direct request to them.

Is your question already answered?

Before you respond to a message, read the other responses first. It's possible that the message has already been answered or your question has already been dealt with by another member.

To read the next message, click the **Next Post** button. If it's grayed out, you're at the end of the message thread (or subject). Click the **Subject** icon at the right of the screen to see the next message thread.

When the next **Subject** button is grayed out, it means no more new messages are available in that topic folder.

Before You Post Your Messages

After you've found a suitable message board in which to post your message, you'll want to prepare your message and then add it to that message board. Before doing so, however, it's a good idea to think carefully about what you're about to say. Although writing a message seems similar to writing an email letter, there's an important difference. With email, you are usually creating a personal message designed for one recipient or a group of recipients, often someone you already know. Your language can be conversational and personal in nature. When you get involved in a message board discussion, you have to think about a wider audience.

America Online has millions of members; at the least, thousands of those members might read your message while it's available. This means you have to consider your comments much more carefully than you might when just communicating among friends. Consider the following when preparing your message:

- Check your message carefully for spelling errors and poor grammar. Remember, the message reflects on you, and spelling mistakes detract from what you are trying to say.

- Do not include personal information, such as your address, telephone, or credit card number. Remember, you are revealing this information to a potential audience numbering in the thousands (or millions). If you are writing a message in an area run by a software publisher, do not include the serial number of your software (which might reveal it to a software pirate). If the publisher wants it, they'll contact you via private email.

- Be sure the topic your message covers is relevant to a forum's message boards. You wouldn't want to discuss your favorite Windows software in a Macintosh forum, or vice versa (unless it's devoted to debates about one computing platform versus the other), or discuss cooking in a forum devoted to home audio systems.

Teach Yourself: Posting Your First Message

Posting a message after you write it is a one-click process not unlike sending email.

When you want to respond to a message, click the **Reply** button at the bottom of the message board window (refer to Figure 11.8).

You'll see a Post Response window, such as the one shown in Figure 11.9. The Subject line will be filled in with the subject of the message you're answering.

Did you check your spelling?

AOL's handy spell checker lets you check for spelling errors before you post your message (just as you can with your AOL email).

Where'd those messages go?

After a period of time, America Online forum staff members often remove outdated messages or archive them to software libraries. If your message suddenly disappears, this might be the reason. If the message is not considered appropriate to the forum, however, you'll usually get a message from the forum staff about it. Some boards are designed so that older messages are automatically scrolled off (removed) after a given amount of time, usually 30 to 60 days. If you've just posted a new message, you'll need to close the subject window and open it again to bring up your new message or any other postings made since you last checked this message board. And don't forget it may take a few minutes or longer for the message you just posted to actually show up.

Watch the subject

If you change the Subject information, your message appears in a brand new thread or subject listing. Consider that before you alter the text here.

FIGURE 11.9

Enter your new message here and click Send to add it to the message thread.

❶ Click **Send** to post your new message.

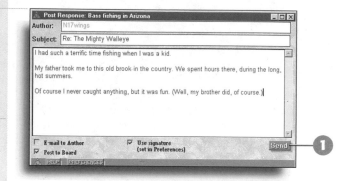

FIGURE 11.9

Enter your new message here and click Send to add it to the message thread.

❶ Click **Send** to post your new message.

Sign your message before you send it

As with regular email, it's considered good online etiquette to sign the messages you post in a message board.

Your new message may not appear right away

After you send your message, you'll get an acknowledgment on your screen right away that it has been sent, but it may take several minutes before the message actually appears on the board (especially if it encounters a lot of online traffic). Also, to see the newest postings, you have to close a subject window and then open it again from the topic window. It doesn't automatically update for you.

Don't post over and over again

Posting a message more than once in a single forum is considered bad online etiquette. Some AOL members might even get upset about having to read the same message over and over again on billable time. When you have something to say, take a moment to choose the topic folder or directory that closely matches what you want to write about. In many forums, you can create your own topic to begin a discussion.

After you have written your message and spell checked it, you have three options to consider before your message is sent.

- **E-mail to Author.** When you send your message, a copy is emailed to the author of the message to which you're replying.

- **Post to Board.** This option is the default. The message you send is added to the ones already in that subject folder, or in a new subject folder if you create one.

- **Use signature (set in Preferences).** When this is checked, your message will contain the signature you've entered as a message board preference (refer to Figure 11.4).

After you write your message, you'll probably want to read it carefully in case you want to make changes. After you're sure it's what you want, click the **Send** button to add it to the message board.

Common Sense Advice on Online Etiquette

So far in this chapter, I've discussed how to locate and use message boards, and the mechanics of writing your message. Over the years, a set of unofficial online traditions has been established that cover the organization of messages and good online behavior. In Chapter 7, "Parental Issues and Internet Access," I outlined America Online's Terms of Service, which cover, to some extent, proper use of language in message boards. This section describes some of the rules of the road. They are similar to what is called netiquette, which is one of the topics discussed in Chapter 17, "How to Join and Participate in Internet Newsgroups and Mailing Lists." The following are a few tips based on my experiences over the years on America Online and other services:

- *Read before you post.* Be sure your message is appropriate to a forum, and also review past messages just to be sure your questions or comments haven't already been covered.

- *Consider your audience.* When you respond to a message, consider that you are not just posting a response to a single person, but to an audience that could number in the millions. If you decide you want to restrict your audience to a single person, send that person email instead.

- *Show respect and be polite when you post a message.* If you disagree with someone's statement, try to stick to the issues, and refrain from personal attack. Such attacks are regarded as *flaming*, and although they might be entertaining on some television talk shows, they are not considered good taste in an America Online message board. In addition, a personal attack can be considered a violation of AOL's Terms of Service.

- *When responding, quote often.* When responding to someone else's message, quote the relevant portions of that message at the beginning of your response, or before each part of your response that refers to that message. Don't quote the entire message (it wastes a lot of space). The usual convention is to place a forward sign (>), to signify a quotation mark, at the beginning of each line, as shown in the following example. Just remember that this message is just meant as a sample; I happen to have enjoyed just about every Tom Hanks movie I've ever seen:

  > I really don't understand what the big fuss
  > over the new Tom Hanks movie is all about.
  > I thought Philadelphia was a much better
  > flick.

- *Be brief.* Cover the points you want to bring up, or ask your question in a clear and direct manner. Although you might be tempted to add a literary flourish if you like to write, remember that some AOL members who read your message are still paying for their online time by the hour. They prefer that you get right to the point.

- *Keep an eye on the Subject line.* When you click the **Reply** button in a typical America Online message board, the topic of the previous message will automatically be inserted into the Subject line, preceded by the abbreviation Re: (see Figure 11.10). If your comments are not intended as a response to the previous message, be sure to change the Subject line to one that's appropriate for your own message.

FIGURE 11.10

If the subject of your reply doesn't relate to original message, it's best to clear the Subject line and start over.

1 Replace the text in the Subject line if your message isn't relevant.

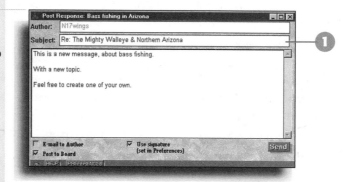

Be careful about creating new message threads

When you change the material in the Subject line you are, in effect, generating a new message thread, which may not be your intent. So consider this step before you actually alter the Subject text.

- *Express emotions and humor with care.* When you speak with someone in person, often body language and the inflection of your voice reveals whether you are serious, or whether you are angry or happy about something. Your words alone must be the mirror of your feelings on America Online. Experienced online users express emotions with smileys: :). See Chapter 10 for a list of common smileys and emoticons, and a few that aren't so common.

- *Watch your language.* Four-letter words and other vulgar epithets might be a part of many books and movies (and perhaps the conversational demeanor of many people), but they have no place on America Online, which is a family-oriented service. Also remember that using such language might result in having your message removed by the forum staff, or a having a Terms of Service complaint lodged against you by another member.

- *Pay attention to copyrights.* Do not post copyrighted material without the permission of the copyright holder. You can, of course, quote brief portions of a copyrighted work when commenting on that material. That is considered "fair use," but try to limit your quotations to no more than a few sentences at most.

- *Do not cross-post.* Choose the forum in which you want to post your message, and then select the message topic that seems most appropriate or, if possible, create a topic of your own. Don't post the same message over and over again. Internet surfers call this *spamming*, and I call it bad manners, because it's not polite to expect fellow members to read the same thing over and over again.

Looking for a Response

After you've posted your message, no doubt you will be anxious to read an answer of some sort (if you posted a question), or see if anyone else has commented about your message. Posting a message does not guarantee that someone will respond; this is a hard fact, but one that's generally true. A forum with a well-stocked message board tends to get a large number of visitors, however, so it is likely other AOL members will, in time, get to read your message. Some might have a response. If you've asked a question directed to specific people, such as the manufacturer's technical support representatives in a company support area, it might take a little while to see a reply—especially if you post on a weekend, when support people are not generally online.

The best thing to do is be patient. The next time you visit America Online, return to the forum's message area, and use the **List Unread** feature in the forum's message window to see the messages posted since the last time you logged on.

Recording those messages for posterity...

If you want to keep a text record of the contents of a message board folder, turn on the Log Manager (click the **My Files** icon on the toolbar and select it from the drop-down menu) and create a System Log. Then, open subject folders that interest you and navigate the messages. When you're done, just close the log, or use the **Read Offline** feature.

Be patient when looking for an answer

If you don't see an immediate response to a question you've posted, you might be tempted to post the same message again, perhaps in a different topic. My advice is don't. Other AOL members who see the latest messages will just end up seeing both messages, and might become annoyed rather than informed when they read the same thing a second time.

Message boards can be Favorite Places too

If you want to continue to visit a message board, just add the topic window to your Favorite Places by clicking the heart-shaped icon at the right of the screen. You can add an entire message board, a single topic, or even a subject for a later revisit. You'll probably want to make a Favorite Place of a message board where you post a message, so that you can get back there again quickly.

No threading?

Help! Every time I move from message to message, or post a message, it's in a new subject. Where's the threading feature? Not all AOL message boards are threaded. In some cases, the staff of a forum has opted not to have this feature. In this case, the messages appear in chronological order (or whatever order you selected in your message board preferences) without regard to subject.

If you don't see a response to your message or question after a few days, look over AOL's channels and see if there's another forum that might be related to the subject of your message. For example, if you have a problem with a modem, you might seek out the Mac or PC Telecommunications Forums, or the Mac or PC Hardware Forums. Posting one message in a different forum isn't against good online practice; in fact, it might be a good idea, because you can reach an additional audience. Not everyone will necessarily visit both forums.

SEE ALSO

➤ *For more informaiton about email and instant messages, see page 157*

➤ *For more information about AOL's Computing channel and forum conferences, see page 418*

➤ *For more information on message threading and using AOL's Internet Connection, see page 295*

AOL as an Internet Service Provider

Using AOL's Internet Services

What the Internet is

America Online and the Internet

Just the beginning—using the Internet

Calling up AOL via the Internet

AOL's Expanding Internet Services

Stories about it are in your newspaper or on TV and the radio just about every day. Even our business cards mention it.

Everyone is talking about the Internet—that huge, amorphous, global computer network that is the centerpiece of the Information Superhighway. The reports are filled with such buzzwords as World Wide Web, Usenet, IRC, Gopher, Archie, Veronica, and a host of other expressions that seem obscure and mysterious (when they don't mean furry animals or comic book characters, of course).

The Internet has even become fodder for political debate in the halls of Congress and other government bodies. The most recent examples include the controversy over a measure to ban pornographic material on the Internet or efforts by local phone companies to hike access fees. Because the major online services, such as America Online, provide a growing stable of resources to the worldwide Internet community, such debates have provided a source for much discussion on message boards and on talk shows.

By providing Internet access, America Online has brought you into an exciting new universe. You are already a member of not only America Online, but also a part of the exciting Internet, your gateway to communicate with tens of millions of fellow computer users from across the globe. America Online's Internet Connection provides information and access into some of the Internet's most popular features. These include email, Internet chatting, database searching, mailing lists, newsgroups, File Transfer Protocol (FTP), and the colorful World Wide Web.

Over time, America Online will be providing you with instant access to even more features of the Internet. The best news is that the new features won't require you to learn about a whole new environment. America Online provides virtually seamless Internet access, with new areas made to look and feel very similar to the forums and message boards you're already familiar with on the service.

Indeed, the Internet can seem like a magical, mystical place— one that is almost a separate world unto itself. In the next few chapters, I'm going to begin to take some of the mystery out of the Internet. More importantly, I'll tell you how many of the same techniques that you've used so far to travel across America Online's own friendly neighborhood can be used to access a whole world of fascinating information and services.

The Internet—History, Features, and the Future

At first, like so many endeavors that ended up in the hands of civilians, the Internet began in the late 1960s as a government project, under the protection of the U.S. Advanced Research Projects Agency. It was known then as ARPANET, and it was an experiment to learn the best methods to exchange data among remote computers. At first, the new computer network was installed at four educational institutions located in California and Utah.

As it was designed and developed over the years, the Internet has had the unique distinction of having no hubs or central control points, and was set up with the assumption that the rest of the network was totally unreliable. In the 1970s, methods were established to build a networking technique to enable computers of all shapes, sizes, and operating systems to communicate with each other seamlessly.

Because it began as a government-supported project, network traffic in the early stages of the Internet consisted of civilian and military information. The burgeoning network became popular with scientists and other researchers who used it to send information files and to engage in correspondence, known as *electronic mail* (*email*), with their colleagues. Central computers or sites were established in which to store files, using *File Transfer Protocol* (FTP), which I'll discuss later in this chapter and in more detail in Chapter 15, "Using File Transfer Protocol."

Individual email exchanges also blossomed into mailing lists, in which information was sent to a large number of users, in the

The Web is where it's at

The World Wide Web is the focal point of today's Internet. From its graphical point-and-click interface, you can access information, shop for everything from RAM for your PC to a new car, and see clips from the latest movies opening at your neighborhood theaters. You'll discover more about it in the section entitled "Accessing the World Wide Web," later in this chapter and also in the next chapter.

form of collections of correspondence, articles, and reports. Internet users with special interests created *Usenet* (users' network) discussion groups in which messages were posted about their favorite topics and responded to by other users. You'll find complete coverage of both in Chapter 17, "How to Join and Participate in Internet Newsgroups and Mailing Lists."

By 1983, the rapidly growing network was split into two parts—one was dedicated to military use and the other was dedicated to civilian use. The method used to transfer data along the network is called *Transmission Control Protocol/Internet Protocol* (or TCP/IP).

Today, the Internet stretches beyond the borders of any single country. It has no central authority or governing body. It knows no limitations in terms of the type of computer or the operating system it uses. So the user of a Power Macintosh running Mac OS 8.1 can easily communicate with another user who has a mainframe computer or even a Compaq Pentium running Windows 95, to name just a few examples. Ancient boundaries of gender and race are also less relevant on the Internet, which truly has become a global community.

Accessing the Internet

At one time, getting Internet access was difficult. You had to work at a place where access was available, or be able to log on to a network at a local educational institution, or even set up your own computer as an Internet server. It wasn't always a terribly cost-effective proposition either. Times have changed. Beginning several years ago, the powers that be at America Online realized the incredible potential of the Internet and began to introduce access to the global network to its membership. As described later in this chapter, AOL has created an information center, the Internet Connection (use the keyword Internet or just click the **Internet** icon on AOL's handy toolbar and choose **Internet Connection** from the drop-down menu), to offer advice to help newcomers and even experienced Net surfers learn the best, most efficient ways to use Internet services.

Another way to connect to AOL

A growing number of America Online members use TCP/IP capabilities to access the service at extremely high speeds. As a side benefit to this method, you pay a lower rate if you "bring your own access," as AOL refers to it. You learn how to do that later in this chapter.

The Internet has worldwide influence

Those who first established the Internet probably never realized how much it would impact our present-day society. One of the major uses for the network originally was to enable scientists at widely separate institutions to share their research with each other, which meant only a small number of people were involved.

In this chapter, I want to help you get started with your Internet access on America Online. It would take a large book to cover the length and breadth of the information and services the Internet offers. At the end of this chapter, I'll recommend an excellent source for further reading.

For now, get ready to travel across the Internet from the comfort of your own home or work area, and your own personal computer.

AOL's Internet Services

Keyword: `Internet`

America Online's Internet Connection is the solution you need to overcome the confusing interfaces and other obstacles presented by the Internet network (see Figure 12.1). Every America Online member has easy access to the Internet. You are able to travel the length and breadth of the Internet just like you use any other part of America Online.In the following sections,

I'll cover some of those Internet access features currently offered on AOL.

<table>
<tr><td style="border:1px solid #000; padding:8px;">Caution: It's a jungle out there!

The Internet is still an open, largely unregulated frontier, despite government thoughts to enact some regulations. As a result, you are apt to encounter files and discussions that contain subject matter and language that is against America Online's Terms of Service. You should carefully monitor the access of children to AOL's Internet services.</td></tr>
</table>

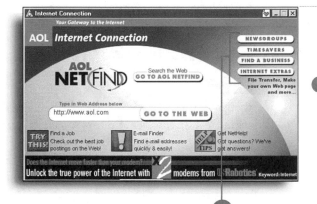

FIGURE 12.1

America Online has a special area devoted strictly to Internet access.

1 Choose the Internet service you want to try.

Using the Mail Gateway

Keyword: `Mail Gateway`

Your email doesn't have to stop at the frontiers of the AOL service network. Through AOL's Internet mail features (see Figure 12.2), you can send email to friends and businesses on other online services, and on local BBSs with Internet access. You can also send email to universities, businesses, and government agencies with direct Internet connections. The process is not much more complicated than sending email on AOL. For more information, see Chapter 9, "Using AOL's Email."

FIGURE 12.2

AOL's Internet email center is a repository of advice on how to send email to members of other services.

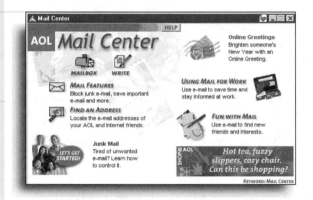

Sending Internet email is easy

You don't have to be in AOL's Mail Gateway or Internet Connection to compose Internet-destined email. All you have to do is open a blank mail form, address it accordingly, compose the message, and send it. You can even write your message while offline and send it via an Automatic AOL session (see Chapter 9 for more information on Automatic AOL sessions).

Accessing the World Wide Web

Keyword: `WWW`

At the start, Internet services were text-based. You ended up seeing countless directories and text windows during your Net journey (or *surfing*, as it's generally known). The World Wide Web is a different animal, however. Although the technique of creating this information is text-based (using a special text-entry format called *Hypertext Markup Language*, or *HTML*), the interface you'll see is decidedly graphical, filled with colorful pictures (animated too), text, and sometimes sounds. The sample shown in Figure 12.3 is what you see when you click the globe-shaped **Internet** icon on the toolbar of your AOL program and choose **Go to the Web** from the drop-down menu. You'll find equally fancy Web facilities from all the major computer manufacturers, and many commercial concerns and private institutions. Read all about Web sites in Chapter 13, "Using the World Wide Web." You'll also find Web sites mentioned in many other chapters.

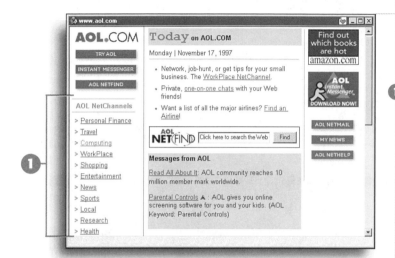

FIGURE 12.3

Direct from AOL's Web browser, here's the home page for America Online.

① Scroll through the screen for more choices.

Internet File Transfer

Keyword: FTP

Thousands of files are available through the Internet. They come from such commercial sources as Apple, Corel, Microsoft, and many private repositories of freeware and shareware. Internet files are sent via file transfer protocol (FTP), and AOL offers a special area where you can access these huge libraries (see Figure 12.4). Getting these files is not altogether different from downloading files in AOL's own libraries, but you'll want to know a few extra ground rules first (and take some additional precautions), which are described in Chapter 15.

FIGURE 12.4

Huge software libraries can be tapped on the Internet via FTP.

 Click **Go To FTP** to see AOL's Favorite Sites.

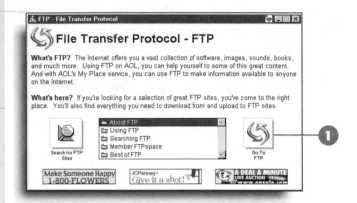

Seeking Information Resources on the Internet

Keyword: Gopher

Placing hundreds of encyclopedias end upon end still wouldn't add up to the amount of information you can get from the Internet. The only trick is to find it all. Using AOL's extensive collection of Internet search tools (see Figure 12.5), you can seek out many of these information resources, without ever leaving your home. See Chapter 16, "How to Search for Information on the Net," for more information.

FIGURE 12.5

AOL's database search tools let you tap into a wide range of information resources.

Click an icon to access that feature.

Joining Internet Newsgroups

Keyword: Newsgroups

The closest thing to a message board on the Internet is Usenet (see Figure 12.6), also known as newsgroups. Usenet offers thousands of discussion boards where you can discuss almost anything under the sun, and in some cases (the ones devoted to such subjects as psychic phenomena and UFOs), even beyond the sun. Before you get involved in a newsgroup discussion, see Chapter 17.

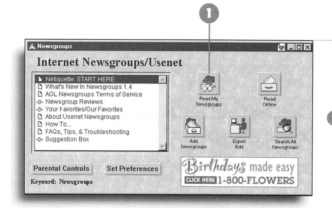

FIGURE 12.6
You can participate in thousands of newsgroup discussions on AOL.

1. Click **Read My Newsgroups** to see the latest messages.

Joining Mailing Lists

Keyword: Mailing Lists

AOL lets you join any of thousands of mailing lists and receive information on anything from recipes to car racing. You can search for lists to subscribe to through AOL's Internet Mailing List Directory area (see Figure 12.7), and soon your mailbox will be filled with exciting information (but don't overdo it). You'll find more information, along with a directory of popular mailing lists, in Chapter 17.

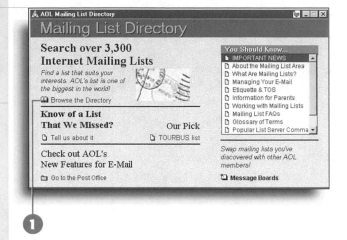

SEE ALSO

➤ *Joining an Internet mailing list, see page 295*

Caution: Don't overdo it!

You should exercise care in subscribing to an Internet mailing list, because any single list can result in filling your mailbox with dozens of new messages each day. If you find your mailbox is becoming overwhelmed with new messages, you may want to consider canceling your subscription to lists that produce messages you don't intend to read right away. I can tell you a few stories about the time a computer hacker put my name and that of others (including the President and Vice President) on over 2,000 mailing lists; that story even earned coverage in *Time* magazine's science column.

Connecting to AOL from an Internet Connection

Computers that hook up directly to the Internet speak a language called *TCP/IP*, short for *Transmission Control Protocol/Internet Protocol*. A number of computer networks (perhaps at your office) have direct Internet connections via this protocol (they don't come cheap, but they are capable of really fast performance).

If you opt to connect to AOL strictly via a separate Internet service, you get a bonus. You can qualify for a lower price for your AOL membership using AOL's "bring your own access plan." You get the lower price because you're not using AOL's own dial-up network.

For information about current pricing, use the keyword Billing.

If your computer network is hooked up to the Internet, TCP/IP is a convenient way to experience America Online without going through the usual local-access phone numbers. Both the Windows and Mac OS versions of America Online's software offer a TCP/IP connection tool. To use it, you need to change your modem setup.

To access America Online through TCP/IP, you need version 1.5 or later of the Windows AOL software and version 2.5 or later of the Mac AOL software. Both software packages install the proper TCP/IP tools on your personal computer. If you're using other TCP/IP tools to browse the Internet, such as Netscape, your access to AOL through TCP/IP won't affect the use of these programs. In fact, you can also access them through your AOL account, as explained in Chapter 13. Of course, with AOL's own integrated Web browser available, you may find yourself using those tools less and less.

You can find ads for dedicated Internet providers in computer magazines, local user group magazines, or even a local newspaper. AOL also offers a list of these services, but, of course, doesn't recommend any specific provider. You can locate this list using AOL's File Search feature. Just enter PDIAL in the list field.

Teach Yourself: Setting Up AOL Software to Use TCP/IP

Connecting to AOL via TCP/IP

1. First click **Setup** on your AOL software's opening screen, which brings up the Connection Setup screen (see Figure 12.8).

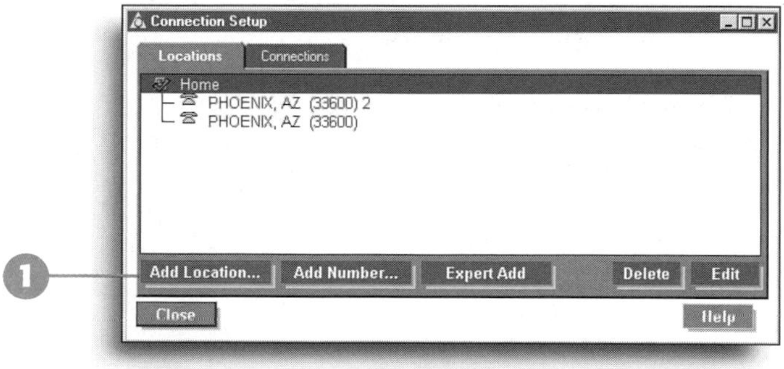

> **Caution: Be careful about choosing an ISP**
>
> After you change your billing plan, however, going back even for a one-time connection to AOL's dial-up network can cost. Expect to have to pay an hourly charge for the time you spend on AOL if your Internet provider becomes unavailable, so choose your provider with care. AOL has made arrangements for low-cost access via AT&T WorldNet and other national services.

> **You may need a software upgrade to use TCP/IP with AOL**
>
> If you have an older version of AOL software that doesn't support TCP/IP access, use the keyword Upgrade to visit an area where you can download the latest versions of both the Mac and Windows AOL software. If a pre-release version is available, you'll find it with the keyword Preview.

FIGURE 12.8
You can create and edit your setup profiles from this convenient dialog box.

1 Click the **Add Location** button.

2. From here, click the **Add Location** button to bring up the Setup box shown in Figure 12.9.

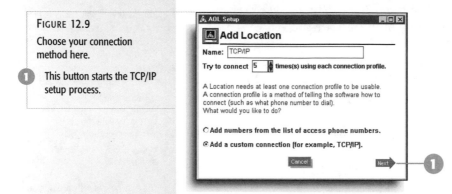

3. In the Add Location dialog box give your setup a name (TCP/IP or Via ISP would be most informative). Then choose the option labeled **Add a custom connection (for example, TCP/IP)** and then click the **Next** arrow at the right. You'll then see the screen shown in Figure 12.10.

4. We're close to the finish line. Now just name your profile as you see fit. If you're using a regular Internet provider and not doing a special connection through an office network, leave the default setting, **Automatic Connection Script: Direct TCP/IP Connection**, selected. Click the **OK** button to put your settings in effect. If you need a special setting, you may want to contact your network administrator for further assistance.

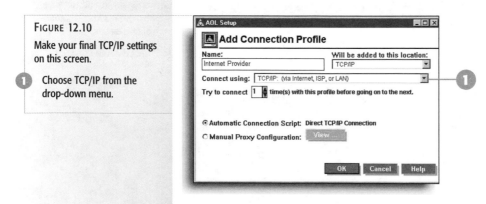

5. To activate your TCP settings, choose that option from the **Select Location** drop-down menu on your AOL software's Setup and Sign-on Screen. I covered setting up AOL for modem and TCP/IP connections in Chapter 3, "Connecting to AOL," and Appendix B, "Setting Up AOL's Software."

When you log onto AOL using TCP/IP, performance is limited only by the speed of your network or Internet service. It can be much faster than your present telephone connection (especially if you use one of those new cable modems). If you have direct TCP/IP access, give it a try and see.

Using AOL Windows with TCP/IP

After you've secured your TCP/IP capability, logging on through AOL is easy.

You need the following to access AOL's TCP/IP capability:

- Windows 3.1 or Windows 95
- TCP/IP Winsock 1.5 or later
- America Online for Windows 1.5 or later

After you've met the minimum requirements, complete the steps in the following section.

Signing on to AOL via TCP/IP

1. Set up your AOL software to use TCP/IP access, as described in the first portion of "Secrets of TCP/IP Access," earlier in this chapter.
2. Make your SLIP or PPP connection.
3. Click the **Sign On** button to connect to AOL.

In some Internet setups, you can access your Internet connection by signing on to AOL directly. After you click **Sign On**, you automatically connect to your TCP/IP service, and then you log on to AOL in the usual way.

Your TCP/IP setups may already be there

In some versions of AOL software, a TCP/IP connection is already set up for you. Just choose it from the **Select Location** drop-down menu on your AOL sign-on screen.

Has something gone wrong?

If you can't switch to TCP/IP via the steps described previously, recheck your network or Internet provider settings to be sure they are correct before proceeding further. If you run into difficulties, contact your network administrator or Internet service provider for further help.

What Mac users need for TCP/IP access

Macintosh users need Apple's MacTCP software to take advantage of AOL's TCP/IP capability. MacTCP is automatically available when you install the latest Mac AOL software. If you're using System 7.5.2 or later and have Apple's Open Transport networking software installed (it's standard for System 7.6 or later), you'll make your Internet settings in the TCP/IP Control Panel.

Using AOL Macintosh with TCP/IP

Watch out for those Winsock files!

If you can't get a satisfactory connection to AOL, make sure you don't have multiple copies of Winsock.dll on your hard drive. The best way to test for this is to open the Windows Explorer program and then do a search on your hard drive(s) for the Winsock.dll file. If you find more than one copy on your hard drive(s), you should remove all copies except for the one located in your C:\Windows\System directory (unless you keep a second copy in another directory as a spare, of course).

After you've secured your TCP/IP capability, logging on through AOL on your Macintosh is hardly more complex than making a regular AOL hookup. Just remember that you need the MacTCP or TCP/IP Control Panels properly installed in your System Folder.

The requirements to access AOL's TCP/IP capability on a Mac include the following:

- System 7 or System 6.0.5 with Communications Toolbox installed
- MacTCP 2.0.6 or later or TCP/IP (when using Apple's Open Transport)
- America Online for Macintosh 2.5 or later

After you've met the minimum requirements, complete the steps in the following section.

Connecting to AOL via TCP/IP on your Mac

1. Open your AOL Macintosh software.
2. Make your SLIP or PPP connection as designated by your network administrator or Internet provider.
3. Select **TCP** from the **Select Location** drop-down menu on the Sign On screen.
4. Sign on to America Online normally.

Diagnosing Some Common TCP/IP Connection Programs

If you find that you're having trouble connecting to AOL via TCP/IP, check that your access to your Internet provider is working. Try the following to check your access:

- To test whether you have a working TCP/IP connection with your Internet provider, log on normally, and run an Internet program, such as Microsoft Internet Explorer or Netscape. If your connection is working, you should be able to access any active Web site, and you should be able to log on to AOL normally, so long as you are using the proper TCP settings in your AOL software.

- A common cause of TCP/IP connection difficulties is having your TCP/IP software set to the wrong IP address, broadcast address, or subnet mask. If any of these settings are not entered correctly, your connection will fail.

- If you dial in to the Internet with either a SLIP or PPP connection, it is also important to make sure that your login ID and password are set correctly, along with all your modem and communications port settings.

- If you check all the settings and the connections still fail, you should consider attempting to remove and then reinstall your TCP/IP software.

- If you are still unable to get connected, contact your network administrator or Internet provider to make sure that your connection to the Internet is working and that your settings are correct. Because these settings vary a great deal from service to service, I won't attempt to suggest the proper configuration here.

- If you are able to connect to another computer on the Internet, but still cannot connect to AOL, contact AOL customer support for further assistance. If you can access AOL via the regular dial-up connection, you may want to contact AOL through their Tech Live area, where you can chat online with a support representative about your connection problem. You can access that area from AOL's Member Services area (keyword Help).

For Further Reading

The Internet is a huge, complex, and exciting place to visit. America Online has purchased Internet access companies and has created an entire division with which to provide Internet services for various businesses. After you get your feet wet, maybe you'll want to review some background information about the Internet. At the least, the information provides a greater understanding of the whys and wherefores of this global network, and makes your visits all the more enjoyable.

Special Edition Using the Internet, 4th Edition, published by Que Corporation, contains historic information about the Internet, and I recommend it to you highly. This massive work (over 1,200 pages) includes a CD-ROM that provides over 100 Internet tools for Microsoft Windows. Even if you have a Macintosh and can't use those tools (although they probably will work with SoftWindows or a DOS card on your Mac), you'll find the material in the book works with both computing platforms. It's well written and highly recommended. (Note the name of the fellow who wrote the chapter covering Internet access by online services.)

In addition, Que's *Windows 95 Communications Handbook* will help guide you through the hurdles of setting up your PC and Windows 95 for the most efficient telecommunications possible. Some additional titles you'll want to check out at your bookstore include Que's *Using Your Modem* and *Special Edition Using the Internet with the Mac*.

SEE ALSO

➤ *For information on locating files on AOL and the Internet, see page 435*

➤ *For more information on tapping AOL's huge resources of educational and reference information, see page 390*

Using the World Wide Web

The World Wide Web Makes the Internet Colorful

Many of the features of the global Information Superhighway are text-based. Even many of the graphic files you find on the Internet are in text form, unless you download them using AOL's handy decoder feature. But the Internet can have color and excitement too, depending on which features you try.

The World Wide Web is a case in point, which is why Web access is becoming one of the fastest growing Internet services. It adds full-color pictures, and sometimes sound and video, to the otherwise somewhat drab interface the Internet puts forward. The Web is not only a constant source of information about a huge range of subjects, but also an area where you can observe the creative efforts of a growing number of computer artists who have generated the fancy artwork you see.

What Is the Web?

As with the origins of the global Internet, the *World Wide Web* began as a development in a scientific laboratory. It was the outgrowth of experiments conducted in the latter part of the 1980s by *CERN (European Laboratory for Particle Physics)*. The original intention was to develop a communications protocol that would enable scientists and researchers to have fast access to data they wanted to share. The traditional Internet-based search tools could be cumbersome at times. You had to do a separate search for each item you wanted. Because there wasn't an integrated Internet access tool, such as AOL's own software, you often had to launch separate programs for each step of your Internet travels.

By 1990, the work of CERN had resulted in a technique that integrated text and graphics into a single, easily accessible document that could be retrieved from anywhere in the world using a single program, known as a *browser*. The browser is an application that can locate documents on what is now known as the *World Wide Web* (it's often referred to as *the Web* or *WWW*).

These documents, which are known as *pages*, are retrieved by the browser program, which then translates them to a form that displays both pictures and text on your screen.

By 1993, browser programs were available for most popular computing platforms, including Macs and PCs. Some of these programs were provided in the form of fully integrated Internet access tools. In addition to being able to locate and open Web pages, you could do Gopher database searches, access files through FTP, and send and receive email.

The Elements of a Web Page

Because the Internet is text-based, the CERN researchers developed a way to format a text document so it could be read fully formatted on any computer by using the browser program to translate the format into a readable form.

If you're into desktop publishing and familiar with such programs as QuarkXPress and Ventura Publisher, no doubt you've seen how a page is *tagged*, or marked with commands that describe the way the document is to be formatted. Such tags may designate a particular type style, or the overall elements of a paragraph or table format. A closer example to the technique used for the World Wide Web is Adobe's *PostScript language*, which translates all the elements of the printed page into a set of text commands.

Web pages are formatted in a language known as *HTML* (short for *Hypertext Markup Language*), a series of commands that are inserted adjacent to text items in a Web document that identify how the page is formatted and where graphic images are included. Like PostScript, it isn't really necessary to know the nuts and bolts of how the Web page is constructed to use it effectively.

It's even possible to make such a page yourself (of course, you need access to a firm that can put your page on the Internet; AOL gives you limited WWW storage space unless you sign up for its extra cost PrimeHost service). You can locate a number of HTML translation programs on AOL that automatically take your word processing or publishing document and insert the

AOL uses Microsoft's browser

To make Web access easy, AOL has teamed up with Microsoft to integrate the Internet Explorer browser into AOL's simple program interface. You can also use the other major browser, Netscape, as part of your AOL session (you'll learn how later in this chapter).

You don't need an HTML program to create HTML

If you'd rather not learn a new program to create HTML documents, no problem. The major word-processing programs, such as Word 97 and WordPerfect, are all able to convert your regular documents into HTML format.

correct HTML codes in it. To locate these files, use the keyword `File Search` to bring up AOL's software library search screen, and enter `HTML` in the text box.

Hypertext: The Web Method of Turning Pages

With the page of a regular printed book, you turn the page to read further. With your publishing or word-processing document, you have a **Go To** command of some sort that enables you to select the page you want to see. In America Online, you type a keyword to get to a specific forum or channel, double-click an item in a directory, or click an icon to access another area.

The closest match to the Web technique of moving among pages is the **Help** menu provided on many Mac and Windows programs (see Figure 13.1).

To access another part of your Help document, click the underlined text that describes the topic of the item you want to see. In a Web page, it's called *hypertext*, which is the name for text that has a built-in link to other text. Figure 13.2 shows a typical Web page with hypertext links.

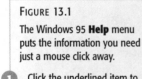

AOL gives you free space online

As an AOL member, you get 2MB of storage space for each of your screen names. You can use that space to set up an FTP site, build a WWW page, or both. For information on how to make your own simple WWW page with AOL's software, use the keyword `Personal Publisher`. You'll learn more about all this (and AOL's sophisticated HTML editor, AOLPress) in Chapter 18, "Become a Web Publisher on AOL."

FIGURE 13.1

The Windows 95 **Help** menu puts the information you need just a mouse click away.

1 Click the underlined item to access that information.

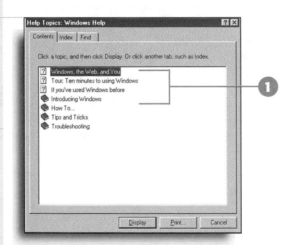

When you click those underlined items, you are telling your Web browser program to find and access the page that's identified by that link. The chosen page appears on your computer in a few moments. Just to give you an idea of how those links—or more properly, hyperlinks—work, refer to the WWW site shown in Figure 13.2.

FIGURE 13.2

A typical Web site contains plenty of hyperlinks.

1   Each underlined item accesses more information.

A fancier form of Web page navigation is activated in Web pages that use *hypermedia*, which are documents that include not only text but also graphics, sound, and sometimes even animation. A typical hypermedia Web page contains not only text-based links to other documents or Web sites, but also icon links (just like AOL's own forum windows). You just click the icon or photo rather than the text, to get to the identified area.

How to Call Up a Web Site

Everything has to have a beginning, and before you can use the handy links among Web pages and Web sites, you need to get from here to there. As Chapter 12, "Using AOL's Internet Services," described, before you can visit any Internet site, you need to know its address. The same technique is only partly true for a Web site. After you access one area, often clicking the

HTML takes you there

One really powerful feature of the World Wide Web is the fact that clicking a hypertext or hypermedia link can automatically take you to another page at the same Web site, or transport you to another Web site located across the world.

Caution: Be exact

Be sure to enter the exact URL information shown to visit one of these sites. Even a single incorrect character will result in failure to access these locations (the URL is not case sensitive, however). The author and publisher are not responsible for errors, however, so if you cannot find a particular site using the information provided in this and the next chapter, you can contact that source directly for additional assistance, or use one of the search tools described in this chapter for up-to-date information.

AOL's browser can fill in the blanks

AOL's browser is clever enough not to need the http:// prefix in a URL as long as it has a "www" or other identifying command, such as "ftp." It'll be converted automatically. You have to enter the URL, however, in the **Go** text box on the bottom row of AOL's program toolbar. It won't work as a keyword.

hypertext or graphical link is sufficient to transport you to another site; the route of travel and the locations to which you travel are determined by what links you click.

To get to a particular site from scratch, however, you need to know its address, known as its *URL* (short for *Uniform Resource Locator*). The URL information you enter contains information that references the location of the site. The following is the format of a typical URL:

```
http://www.aol.com
```

The letters http stand for *Hypertext Transfer Protocol*, which is the technique developed by the architects of the World Wide Web to locate and access Web sites. The colon (:) and the two slashes (//) inform the software that the information that follows is the actual Internet address of the site being accessed (www stands for World Wide Web). The last extension added to this particular Web site, com, identifies this particular location as a commercial enterprise. If the extension is edu, it refers to an educational institution.

In addition, a URL can get you a lot more than just a WWW site. The prefixes ftp:// will take you to an FTP site, Gopher:// to a Gopher site, and news:// to a Usenet newsgroup.

What's a Home Page (and Can You Really Go Home Again?)

When you access a Web site, you normally go to its *home page*, which is Web talk for the opening window or introductory screen of a particular site. It's similar to a book or magazine's cover page or even AOL's own Welcome screen. The home page usually offers information on how a particular site is set up and briefly lists its contents (see Figure 13.3).

From the home page, you can easily navigate to other pages by clicking an icon or underlined text. You need not know the URL for that additional page to get to its precise location. That's the beauty of hypertext and graphical links.

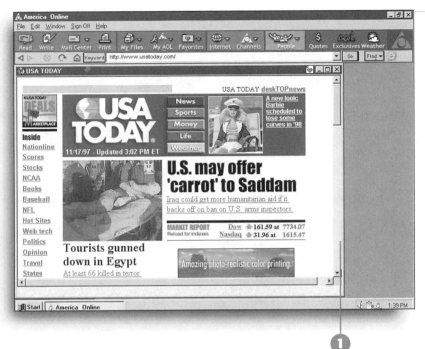

FIGURE 13.3

A typical Web home page tells you about the site and lets you access other features of that site.

1   Scroll through the page to see more.

For information on how to create your own home page, see Chapter 18.

Using AOL's WWW Browser

Keyword: WWW

Using the World Wide Web from your AOL software is no different from accessing other Internet-based services on AOL. Use the keyword WWW, or just click the **Internet** icon on the AOL toolbar and choose **Go to Web** from the drop-down menu. When you enter this area, AOL's home page appears on your screen in a new document window (see Figure 13.4).

Troubleshooting: If you get disconnected

I was browsing away and suddenly my Web access stopped. What's wrong?

To connect to a Web site, you need to be logged onto AOL. If you log off, you're disconnected, or AOL's Internet access has briefly become interrupted; you then receive a message about it in the browser window or a sign-off screen.

If you're still online, try accessing the site again. Sometimes a network problem is cleared up in a few minutes. If you've been disconnected, just log onto AOL and make another attempt. If the problem continues, you might want to try using the World Wide Web at a later time.

FIGURE 13.4

AOL's home page is your first WWW gateway.

1 Scroll through the page to see more.

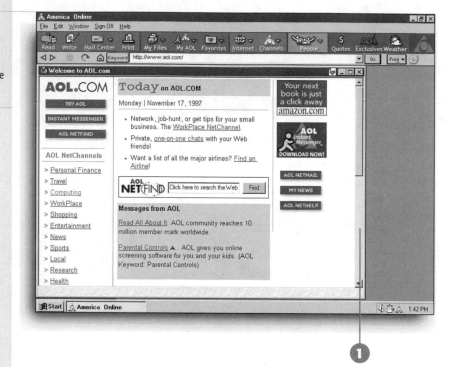

Troubleshooting: Slow images

Why does it take so long for Web images to appear on my computer's screen, especially compared to the images I see on AOL?

The images retrieved by AOL's Web browser are sent from a remote computer and the transmission process is not as efficient as it would be on AOL's host computers. Also, the speed at which you connect to AOL is a major factor in how long it takes for a Web page's image to appear. At the least, you need a 14,400bps modem and 14,400bps AOL connection to get adequate speed on the World Wide Web.

Easy to print or save

Just like any document window you access via AOL, the pages you retrieve by the World Wide Web can be printed by clicking the **File** menu and choosing **Print**.

If you want to visit another Web site, enter the URL or site address in the text box in the bottom row of the AOL toolbar (as I said before the "http://" prefix isn't really needed if a "www" is in the URL). Then press the Enter key or click the **Go** button at the right of the text box to call up the remote site you want to reach.

After AOL's home page has appeared on your screen, you can use the five control icons at the bottom left of the AOL toolbar to control the display of WWW pages. The icons are:

- **Back.** Returns to the previous selected Web page or AOL area.

- **Forward.** Switches to the next Web page, or AOL area if one has previously been accessed.

- **Stop.** If you decide you'd rather not load the current Web page, you can use this button to stop the process.

- **Reload.** Reloads the WWW page currently being displayed. It's an option you want to use if a transmission problem prevents clear display of the original page or if you want to retrieve a newer version of a page that's already displayed on your screen.
- **Home.** The house icon takes you to AOL's home page (or in fact, any home page you specify when you set up the WWW preferences for your AOL software).

Using AOL with Other Browsers

Although AOL's regular WWW browser, based on Microsoft Internet Explorer, can meet most of your needs, you may have already become accustomed to using another browser on another service.

If you'd rather use another browser anyway, that's no problem. Just log on to AOL, and then launch the other Internet program. You'll find more information about this simple technique in Chapter 14, "Internet Chats."

Using AOL with Netscape

Right now, perhaps the most popular browser on the planet is Netscape (see Figure 13.5). Making it a part of your AOL connection is simple. Just log on to AOL first, then launch Netscape. The version I'm displaying for this book is Macintosh version 4.0, dubbed *Communicator*. It includes email and newsgroup tools, and an HTML editor.

Netscape is expandable, and you can add to its functions with plug-in modules (somewhat like the components you'd add to such programs as Adobe Illustrator and Adobe Photoshop to enhance their capabilities).

Web access via a keyword

You can also use AOL's Keyword feature (Ctrl+K for Windows, ⌘+K for Macs) to directly access a WWW site. Enter the URL address in the Keyword screen (it *must* include the full URL, even the "http://" prefix), then click the **Go** button to access that site.

Caution: Some files are stored on your PC's drive

A WWW browser *caches* (or stores) a copy of each graphic it accesses on your hard drive. If the cached files become corrupted, you may experience poor performance or even see your AOL software freeze. Although cached files are automatically removed when the cache directory is filled (the older ones first), you may want to use the option in your Web browser to empty the cache folder if performance problems continue. To delete the cache, choose Preferences from the My AOL toolbar icon. Click the WWW icon, and then the **Advanced** tab and finally the **Settings** button to see the option to empty the trash folder (for Mac users it's at the bottom of the WWW Preference panel screen).

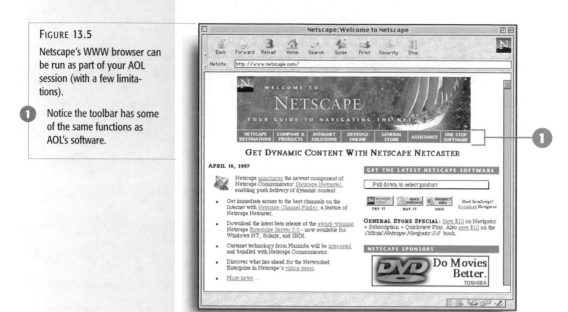

How to Speed Up Web Access

Under any circumstances, the World Wide Web can tax the fastest computer's CPU with its vast array of photos, sounds, and animation. As convenient and as useful as WWW access is, don't expect speedy performance. Sometimes, heavy network traffic slows image displays to a crawl, and all you can do about it is try to log on to AOL at a different time, or use a different access number. You can, however, make AOL's Web software perform better. Consider the following:

- *Get a faster modem.* Chapter 4, "Secrets of High-Speed Access to AOL," provides information on the modem options available to you, and how to configure your modem for the best possible performance.

- *Find a faster access number.* Chapter 3, "Connecting to AOL," describes the steps to take to locate other access numbers on America Online. Because AOL's own AOLNet network with 33,600bps and 56K access is expanding, check occasionally for newer phone connection choices.

- *Get a faster computer.* It goes without saying that Macs and PCs are getting faster and cheaper. If you have an older PC, it might be time to look at a new model equipped with an Intel Pentium or PowerPC microprocessor. These new models can outperform older models by a huge factor.

- *If you use a Mac, give a program more RAM.* Quit your AOL Mac software if it's running, and then select the **Program** icon. From there you can use the **Finder's Get Info** command (see Figure 13.6). You then enter a higher preferred memory setting, usually in increments of 500KB or higher.

- *Try Connectix Surf Express.* A new PowerPC Mac and Windows 95 program from Connectix, Surf Express, can really speed up retrieval of frequently accessed Web pages (it can seem almost instantaneous at times). It only works with separate browsers; as this book was being written, the program did not support the browser used for the Mac version of AOL's software.

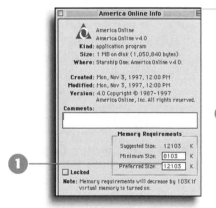

FIGURE 13.6

Enter a higher memory setting in the America Online Get Info window. In this example, using Mac OS 8.1, change the setting in the **Preferred Size** text box.

1. Type the memory setting in the **Preferred Size** text box.

- *Give your AOL browser a bigger cache.* Choose the **Members** menu and click **AOL Preferences**. Then click the **WWW** icon, and click the **Advanced Settings** tab. From there, just click the **Settings** button which brings up the screen shown in Figure 13.7. You can easily enlarge your browser cache from here, or just empty the entire folder. Mac users will find a similar option by choosing **WWW** from the **Preferences** window.

FIGURE 13.7

You can set aside more disk space to store cached WWW artwork.

1 Click the up arrow and move it to the right.

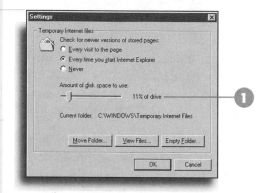

Searching for the Information You Want on the WWW

When visiting AOL's home page, you'll be able to take advantage of its popular NetFind feature, which quickly lets you find the information you want on the Internet. I cover that search tool in more detail in Chapter 16, "How to Search for Information on the Net." To begin this section, let's briefly review some popular sites you'll want to begin to explore.

Internet Underground Music Archive

`http://www.iuma.com/`

If your musical tastes are eclectic, visit the Internet Underground Music Archive, which, at the least, has one of the most interesting selections of artwork you're apt to find on the World Wide Web (see Figure 13.8). This site is designed to represent the interests of hundreds of budding musical acts, and enables you to get in touch with the artists, buy their recordings, and share comments about them with fellow music lovers.

Mac users: Make sure you have enough memory

To give your Mac AOL software a greater dose of RAM, you need to have enough free memory to accomplish this task. If your computer has less than 16MB of RAM, it might be time to consider a memory upgrade.

Use Favorite Places to return there quickly

You can add your favorite sites to your list of Favorite Places for fast retrieval. Just click the heart-shaped icon at the upper-right corner of the screen to begin the process.

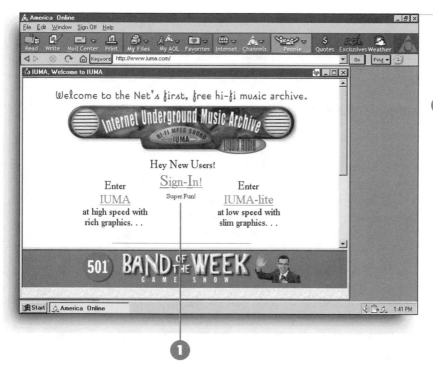

FIGURE 13.8

The Underground Music Archive is a popular resource for music information on the WWW.

1 Click **Sign-In** the first time you visit this site.

National Public Radio

http://www.npr.org/mosaic.html

When shock jocks and loud music become a little too much to bear, many of you probably URL to National Public Radio for a less frenetic look at the world around you. Their Web page has a simple design, so it loads onto your computer quickly, but it covers a wide range of subject matter. This site offers information about current programming, lists stations in your area carrying this network, and includes special areas set up for regular listeners of some of their shows.

Wines on the Internet

http://www.wines.com/

If you're into gourmet cooking or just having a glass of superior wine with dinner, you'll want to check out the wines on this

Internet site. When you visit this site, you'll take a virtual tour of a winery, and consult a list of featured products. You'll find lots of useful information that will help you make a better selection for your home or at a restaurant.

Buena Vista MoviePlex

`http://www.movies.com`

The Buena Vista MoviePlex is dedicated to movies produced by Walt Disney Pictures and its related companies, Hollywood Pictures and Touchstone (see Figure 13.9). From this screen, you can learn about current releases and some that were due for future release when this book went to press. This is a place where you can download movie trailers from these flicks and learn more about the stars of these productions. As you explore the Web, you'll find that all the major motion picture companies set aside special WWW sites for nearly all their new releases.

FIGURE 13.9

Information about the newest flicks released by Buena Vista can be accessed here (the film you see here disappeared so fast you may not have seen it, except, perhaps, on your VCR).

1 Click the movie's title to learn more about it.

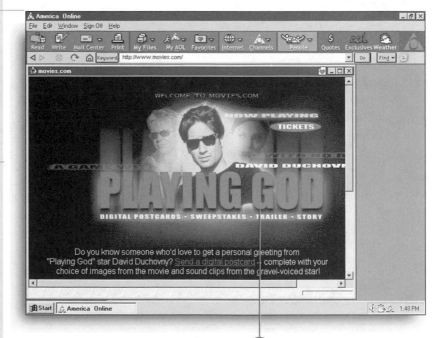

Locating Other WWW Sites

The previous selections are but a few of thousands of Web sites that can be found across the world. The question, then, is how do you find a particular site, or find out if a particular business or educational concern has a Web site.

Fortunately, this is becoming easier to do because more and more representatives of such firms include their URL on their business cards and stationery. You also find WWW listings in popular magazines and newspapers. Press releases announcing new products or services will also mention the Web site address somewhere in the text.

I'll cover some of AOL's convenient Web site search tools shortly. For now, you can use this fast and dirty technique to find out if a company has a Web site.

Let's say, for example, that you want to look for a site run by Now Software (a division of Qualcomm, the publisher's of Eudora), who provides time management software for the Mac and Windows platforms. Having read this far, you know that all Web sites have the same prefix, `http://www`. You also know that a business will have a `com` suffix on its URL, so now you just need to fill in the blanks.

First, you can try `http://www.now.com` and see what happens (see Figure 13.10).

Because the first attempt didn't work, let's try an abbreviation for that company's name instead: `http://www.nowsoft.com`. You'll be pleased to discover that this is a not just a valid WWW address, but that it takes you to the correct location (see Figure 13.11).

Troubleshooting: If you get a fatal error

Why am I getting a `Fatal error` *message when I try to access a WWW page?*

Most of the time, you get that error when the page you are trying to reach isn't available, or you've entered the URL information incorrectly. When you get this message, recheck the URL and make sure that every character is accurately entered (whether caps or lowercase doesn't matter). Remember no word spaces, for example, are allowed in a URL. If you've confirmed that the URL is correct, you might want to recheck the source from which you got that site location to make sure the address hasn't changed.

FIGURE 13.10

Whoops, this is an online magazine, not a software publisher.

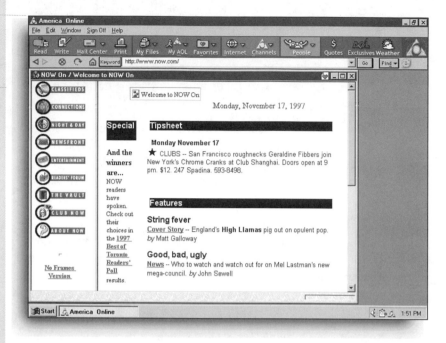

FIGURE 13.11

Success! This software publisher's Web site was quickly accessed through trial and error.

❶ Click a product's title to learn more about it.

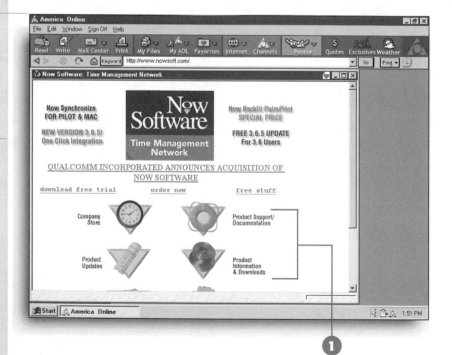

Other Search Tools

The technique described in the previous section will also easily get you to sites run by Adobe, Apple, Compaq, IBM, Intel, Microsoft, and many, many other firms. Sometimes, however, URLs are not so simply labeled, nor is their meaning as obvious. This is especially true for sites that cater to a hobby or special interest, or sites run by an educational institution.

To locate those sites, you want to have access to a site that can do the searches for you. In addition to AOL's popular NetFind search tool, based on Excite technology (see Figure 13.12), other convenient Web search tools are also available.

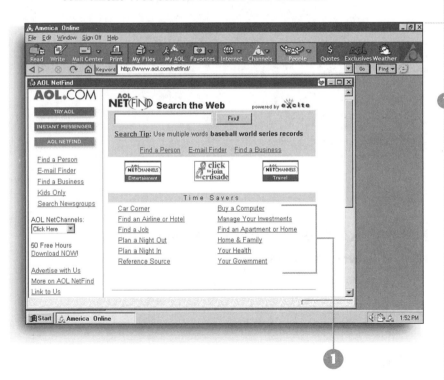

FIGURE 13.12

AOL NetFind not only helps you find a site, but reviews many of them for you.

1 Click a headline to learn more about that feature.

You'll learn more about using NetFind in Chapter 16.

Another search facility worth trying is Yahoo! (http://www.Yahoo.com), which provides extremely comprehensive Web search capabilities (see Figure 13.13). This site started life as a hobby for a pair of college students but soon blossomed into a full-time business, with many large corporate sponsors.

FIGURE 13.13

From hobby to full-fledged business, Yahoo! is a popular Web-based search facility.

①   Click a subject to see more choices.

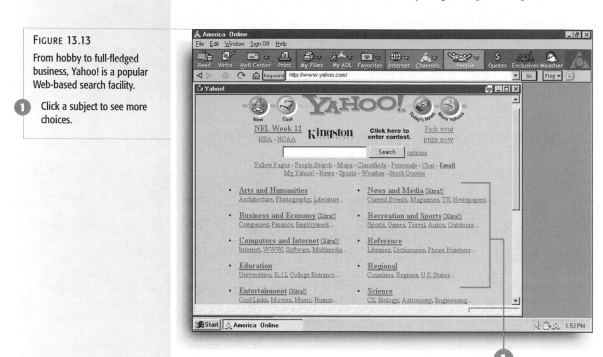

Some Quick Tips on Finding the Internet Information You Want

A huge amount of information can be accessed on the WWW. First you have to find it, however, and for that a number of handy search tools are available, some of which are briefly described in this book.

Most of these tools work essentially the same way, and if you follow these suggestions, you'll quickly find the information you want:

■ Be as specific in your request as possible. If you want to know about camcorders, don't just ask about video or consumer electronics because you'll then get a lot of matches that don't cover the subject you want to know about.

- If you want to search a phrase rather than single words, place the phrase in quotes. For example:

  `"upright vacuum cleaners"`

- To keep your screen from being cluttered with extra information, limit the number of search results you want. The default setting is usually 25, and the results are listed in descending order, with the items that come closest to your search request at the top of the list.

- If your search request isn't calling up enough information, go the reverse route. Broaden the subject. In this case, if "camcorders" doesn't cut it, you may indeed want to try "video" or "consumer electronics" as well.

- If you want your search to include more than one word, place AND between them. Example:

  `"cars" AND "V-8s"`

- If you want your search to include either of the words or both, put the word OR between them. Example:

  `"Buick" OR "cars"`

- If you want to exclude the second word in a search request, place the word NOT between the two. Example:

  `"Apple" NOT "fruit"`

And be sure to use all caps, as I've done, in defining the conditions of your search. I'll describe the specific elements of AOL's NetFind search tool in Chapter 16.

For Further Reading

This chapter only covered the basics of the World Wide Web, including a history of the Web and a tutorial on how to use AOL's Mac and Windows Web browsers. No doubt you'll want to read more about this fascinating subject. Perhaps you'll also want to learn more about creating your own Web page.

I can highly recommend two resources for this information: *Special Edition Using the Internet, 4th Edition*, and *Special Edition Using the World Wide Web*. Both are from Que Corporation and are available from your favorite bookseller. The first book provides a well-written introduction to the Web, and lists some popular sites you'll want to examine further (I wrote the chapter on online services, by the way). If you desire additional information, the second book provides complete background details on every imaginable Web-related subject and easy, step-by-step instructions to help you master just about every nuance of Web techniques and terminology.

SEE ALSO

➤ *For a basic overview of the history of the Internet and AOL's Internet features, see page 225*

➤ *For information on how to send email across the Internet, see page 163*

➤ *For information on getting involved in Internet newsgroups, see page 308*

➤ *To discover how to have a one-on-one chat with fellow Net surfers, see page 263*

➤ *To download softeware from Internet FTP sites, see page 277*

Internet Chats

Chat on the Internet

How they differ from regular AOL chats

Don't just jump in

Introducing Internet Relay Chats

In Chapter 10, "Chatting Online," I discussed the information and excitement you can discover when you visit an online conference. You learned about instant messages, AOL's one-on-one method of interactive chatting with your online friends.

One sort of messaging system I discussed was AOL's Instant Messenger, which lets folks who aren't members of AOL, but who have Internet access, communicate with AOL members. This technique is for one-on-one communication, and one of the participants has to be on AOL.

In this chapter, you learn about another type of online chatting; but this kind of chat is not confined to one network or one online service. It is a conference that can be shared by computers worldwide—the Internet Relay Chat (IRC).

AOL's Chat Feature and IRC—What's the Difference?

You need extra software

Participating in an IRC requires installing a client program that is able to communicate with the Internet-based IRC servers that exist in various parts of the world. Such client programs range from simple freeware utilities that get you connected and little else, to full-blown programs that provide the capability to search IRC servers for the conferences in which you want to participate, add color and basic formatting to the chat text, and provide a variety of sound effects to enhance the presentation. Some programs even speak the chat text back to you in a variety of computerized voices.

It wasn't long ago that I held an Internet chat. Actually it was a simulcast, such as you might find when something is broadcast over two or more TV networks, or on both radio and TV. The chat was run in a regular AOL conference room and on the Internet. The Internet portion was done via an Internet Relay Chat, a way to hold conferences that transcend the borders of any single service.

So what's the difference between IRC and AOL chats? Well, many differences exist between the two. It's not only the location, but it's the setup and ground rules. Some of the specifics include the following:

- Because IRC chats are not limited to the confines of a single online service, you'll be able to talk online with anyone who has Internet access and a chat client (software to access the chatting feature).

- You can participate in several Internet conferences at the same time, but only attend one conference at a time on

AOL (when you switch to a second conference on AOL, you are automatically moved out of the first one).

- America Online's Terms of Service do not apply to an IRC. In an IRC, you will find discussions with content and behavior that you may consider objectionable. As an AOL member, you are expected to behave in accordance with AOL's rules of the road. In addition, those who moderate such chats can kick you out if you violate the rules, or just because they want to.

IRC's may not be kid safe

Because AOL's Terms of Service are not enforced outside of the service, and Internet conferences may sometimes contain material that is not suitable for children, you should carefully monitor your child's use of the IRC feature.

The Language of IRC

As with other Internet protocols, IRC has a language of its own. The following list briefly describes some of the most common terms; you will become acquainted with other terms during the remainder of this chapter.

- Participating in IRC is sometimes called *IRCing* (pronounced urk-ing).

- An individual IRC conference is called a *channel*. Each channel has its own discussion, its own ground rules (some of which can be quite arbitrary), and its own regular participants.

- When you join an IRC session, you give yourself a *nickname* to identify yourself to the crowd. You may use your regular AOL screen name, your real name, or another name that you feel uniquely identifies you to others. Such names are limited to nine characters.

- As participation in IRC increased, another server system was built to handle the additional traffic. It's called the *Undernet*.

Setting Up AOL for Third-Party Internet Software

Getting a third-party Internet program to work while you're hooked up to AOL is easy, because you really don't have to do anything special. Although you used to have to struggle with extra helper files (such as Winsock files for AOL Windows users), that's no longer necessary. Version 4.0 of AOL's software (both the Mac and Windows versions) automatically loads the resources necessary to run your favorite Internet software when you log on. After you are connected to AOL, launch your Internet program and you're ready to go.

Setting Up an IRC Client Program

As part of your AOL connection, you can run a number of handy Internet programs while connected to AOL. AOL's software libraries have a number of IRC clients available. Just bring up the software file search feature at keyword File Search, choose the **Shareware** icon, and enter **IRC** as your search topic. You'll probably want to try several programs and see which ones perform best.

In this chapter, I'll be setting up a popular shareware Internet program for Windows that enables you to participate in Internet chats. It's called *mIRC*, written by Khaled Mardam-Bey. Although it's not the only IRC client available, it's a good way to begin. The program doesn't take long to download, isn't too hard to install, and runs swiftly and reliably. In addition, it can be easily configured to your tastes, and has a handy toolbar for easy navigation through its most-used features.

If you like the program, you'll find the cost is modest compared to any commercial product (it was just $20 when this book was written). So, if you do like this program, please be sure to send your fee direct to the author. He's worked on developing and improving the program and deserves your support.

Take a look at these basic hints on how to get mIRC installed and running from within your AOL software:

Not all Internet software is user friendly

Although AOL's client and WWW browser are easy to use, the same can't be said for some Internet programs. So, before you attempt to install a third-party Internet program, read the installation and setup instructions carefully. AOL's Internet Connection area (keyword: Internet) offers text files and other helpful information on setting up these programs so that they work efficiently as part of your AOL session.

Great Mac IRC programs are available too

Mac users shouldn't feel left out. You'll find a good selection of Mac IRC chat client software as well from AOL and Internet-based software libraries. One popular choice is ircle. When you get past the differences in program installation, the basic steps to configure the software to recognize AOL's host computer and get started with Internet chatting are pretty much the same.

Installing your IRC software

1. Download the software to your PC's drive, following the steps I describe in the "Teach Yourself: Download Your Files Fast" section of Chapter 26, "Tips and Tricks on Finding Software." The usual directory path will be C:\American Online 4.0\download.

2. Click your Windows 95 **Start** menu and choose **Run**.

3. Enter the full path and name of the file in the **Run** text field. In a typical example it would be C:\America Online 4.0\download\mirc511t.exe.

   You can also use the **Browse** feature in your Run window to help locate the file for you.

4. Press the **Enter** key and read the onscreen instructions (see Figure 14.1).

mIRC gets regular updates

The instructions that follow apply to mIRC version 5.11. Because mIRC is updated often, you may find some of the features have changed or that new ones have been added when you check out this program.

Install it your way

A true 32-bit Windows 95 program may also be installed via the Add/Remove Programs Control Panel. Choose the method you like best.

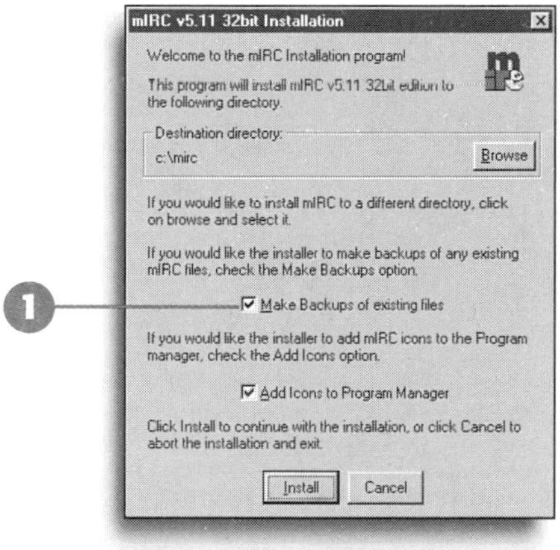

FIGURE 14.1
Just follow the simple onscreen instructions to get mIRC running.

1 A click or two installs mIRC.

Teach Yourself: How to Join an IRC Channel

The first time you open mIRC after it's installed, you see the shareware notice and then a Setup screen (see Figure 14.2). You just need to make a few simple settings, and soon you'll be chatting away on your favorite subjects. (The IRC servers setup will be discussed last.)

When your screen's a jungle

When you are running your third-party Internet program, you can reduce screen clutter by minimizing your AOL software window.

FIGURE 14.2

Set up your network and
nickname preferences in
mIRC's handy Setup window.

1 Pick a name and type it
here.

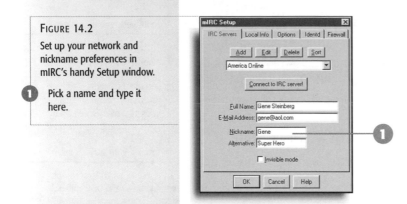

Finding active Internet chats

After you've connected to the IRC
server, you can click the **List
Channels** icon in the IRC program's toolbar (sixth from the left)
to search for active chats. I'll tell you
more later in this chapter in the section titled, "Finding a Place to Talk."

Setting up mIRC for chatting

1. Enter your **Real Name** in the appropriate box.

2. Enter your AOL Internet email address where requested.
Remember, that's your AOL screen name to which you add
@aol.com. So my email address would be entered as
gene@aol.com.

3. Choose a nickname and enter it where requested. The nickname doesn't have to be your real name or your screen
name. You could use a name your friends might have given
you (but keep it clean). As mentioned earlier in this chapter,
a nickname is limited to nine characters.

4. If you sometimes want to be known by a second nickname,
enter it in the **Alternative** information field.

Now you want to choose an IRC server to log onto. Because
you're logged onto AOL, you'll want to include AOL's IRC
servers on the list.

Choosing an IRC Network

1. Click the **Add** button, which brings up the Add Server dialog box.

2. In the first list field, give a name to your new IRC server. I
chose, to be totally unoriginal, America Online.

3. Insert irc01.irc.aol.com in the next list field.

4. If it's not already included, add 6667 as your **Port #**.

5. Add Undernet as the **Group**.

These entries produce the results shown in Figure 14.3.

6. Then click the **Add** button to include your network setting in the ARC servers listing, which returns you to the main Setup screen.

Now it's time to get your fingers ready to do the chatting. To hook up to AOL's IRC server, select it in the list field, and then click the **Connect!** button. This immediately brings up a window with the MOTD!—that's the Message of the Day!—from AOL and then the programs' default mIRC Channels Folder (see Figure 14.4).

Another AOL IRC server to try

If the AOL IRC server setting I suggested previously doesn't work for you, try this one. Enter irc02.irc.aol.com in the **Enter Server** field of the Add Server window. Use the same port setting (6667) and enter EFnet as the group.

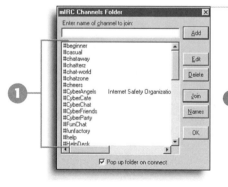

FIGURE 14.4

A few IRC channels AOL has selected to help you get started with Internet chatting are listed here.

1   You can begin Internet chats with these sessions.

Entering a chat is just a matter of clicking the name once, and then clicking the **Join** button. Within seconds, you see a message window showing the chat in progress (see Figure 14.5).

FIGURE 14.5

This channel's chat was
already going full tilt as I
joined it.

1   See the chat text on this
screen.

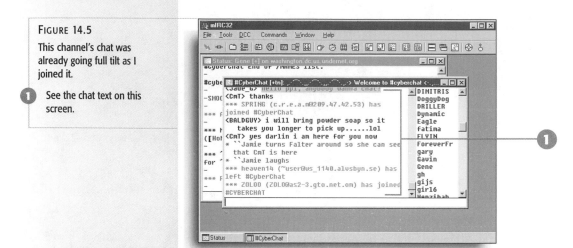

An IRC can bog down

The quality of Internet traffic is
unpredictable. Don't be surprised if
you experience a long delay
between the time a comment is
sent via IRC and the time it appears
in your document window. Don't
expect it to be nearly as fast as
AOL's own chat rooms, although
most often the happenings in an
IRC channel move along at a reasonably smooth pace.

Getting thrown out of a chat

If you don't contribute to an IRC
chat for a long while, the channel
operator might bump you from the
chat. Don't be offended, they usually just want to keep things active. A
good rule of thumb is to leave a
chat if you don't want to participate.

The IRC chat window has some of the elements of AOL's regular chat windows. At the right is the list of the folks attending
the chat, and the larger window contains the dialogue that
scrolls onto your screen (usually quite rapidly) as the meeting
progresses. If you want to participate, enter your comment in
the line at the bottom, and press the Return or Enter key to
send it out into cyberspace. As I said, the process is much like
the one you find in AOL's own chat rooms.

To leave the chat, close the window. You can, of course, leave it
open and join more chats, each of which occupies a separate
document window. The **Windows** menu of the mIRC software
lists the open windows so that you don't lose your way.

Finding a Place to Talk

Several thousand chats may be in progress at any one time, and
if you don't know the address, you'll want to search the IRC
server for discussions about topics that interest you. mIRC offers
a List Channels feature (see Figure 14.6) that enables you to
quickly (well, relatively quickly) search the topics of the chats for
those that match your search string. You can access this feature
from the program's toolbar. It's the sixth icon from the left on
the version I'm using for this book. Because it's not clear what

the icon means, you can verify the function through the ToolTips feature. Just hold the mouse cursor above a toolbar icon to see a display of what the icon is for.

After you enter your search string, click the **List!** button and the IRC server is checked for topics that match your request. Depending on the speed of your modem's connection and how much network traffic is present, it may take several minutes for the list to be consulted.

After the available channels are checked, you see the list of likely prospects (see Figure 14.7) along with the number of people already involved in the discussion. All you need to do now is select and double-click the chat that interests you.

Another way to find chats

You also can search the channels on the IRC server for active chats on subjects that interest you by typing /**list** <search string> in the bottom of the Status window.

The IRC answer to AOL's Favorite Places

You can add the name of your favorite IRC channels to the mIRC Channels Folder so that you can access them whenever you want.

FIGURE 14.6
Use the List Channels window to search for chats you may want to join.

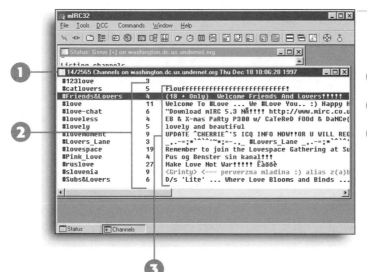

FIGURE 14.7
Your list of active channels on the subject you selected.

1 Name of chat room

2 Number of people in room

3 Location

You can find lots of good IRC software on AOL

Although I focused on some of the basic features of one software package in this chapter, your explorations of AOL's software libraries yield other Internet chatting clients. Some of them add voice features and other handy variations on the original theme.

Another method of online chatting

In addition to the Internet chat methods described here, you may want to check out a handy program from Abbott Systems, known as At Chat. This software comes in both Windows and Mac OS versions. And it works fine with your regular AOL or Internet connection. Chatting with this program provides the ultimate in privacy, because you can *only* connect to another user who has the same program installed.

Additional IRC Features

In addition to sharing conversation in the manner of AOL's own conference rooms, most IRC programs let you send direct messages to a single person, just as you do with AOL's Instant Message feature. You can also exchange files with individuals and, as a measure of self-protection if someone gets out of hand, prevent someone else from communicating with you.

SEE ALSO

➤ *To learn how to meet and stay in touch with fellow AOL members, see page 135*

➤ *To learn how to participate in chats, see page 191*

Using File Transfer Protocol

What is FTP?

How to get the most out of FTP

Get the latest software

Run your own FTP site

You Can Get Software on the Internet Too

AOL's simple, flexible software libraries are among the best you'll find. These libraries contain tens of thousands of files, ranging from text material to one of the biggest selections of Macintosh and PC software available. The libraries are easy to access and downloading can be automated, using AOL's Download Manager so that you can get the files you want when network traffic is lowest and get the fastest data throughput.

Yet another method to download files on America Online exists. The source of these files is not AOL's host computer system, but remote computer systems located throughout the world. The software is accessed on AOL through the global Internet, using File Transfer Protocol, or FTP for short.

What Is File Transfer Protocol?

The closest equivalent of an FTP site is the server on a regular computer network. You may have such a setup at your office. The *server* is a computer that is used as the repository of files, which are meant to be accessed by other users on the network, the *clients*. When you need to access a file or transfer data to the server, you log on to the server, using your networking software, and then send or retrieve the files you want.

The difference between this setup and an FTP site is that the server you are accessing is not located in the same room or in a nearby office, but perhaps in another city, another state, or even another country. The network transfer protocol may be different, too, but the underlying principle is the same.

America Online's Internet connection brings FTP access online in an easy-to-use format so that you don't have to deal with text-based commands or the other complexities that often are involved in Internet file transfers. This feature enables you to tap a huge source of software libraries containing files that may not yet be available on America Online, such as the latest system

FTP performance can vary

One other big difference in accessing an FTP site is performance. If an FTP server is overloaded, or Internet network traffic is congested, it may take much longer for that file to get to AOL and to your PC. You may want to first see if the files are available from AOL before you look elsewhere.

PART **III**

What Is File Transfer Protocol?   CHAPTER **15**   271

software updates from Apple and Microsoft. As you'll learn soon, access to these files is not much more complex than locating and downloading files from AOL's own software libraries.

Anonymous FTP

Experienced network users know the routine: When you access your server, you usually have to establish what essentially is an account with the network administrator, using your name and a password. A similar technique is used to access America Online; your screen name is given to AOL's host computer automatically when you log on, then your password (typed or stored) is presented for verification.

The usual method of hooking up to one of these remote file servers is Anonymous FTP, which means that you access these sources as a guest; you don't have to establish an account that has an Internet address and a password. The time-honored technique is to type anonymous as the username and your screen name (such as gene@aol.com) as your password. The beauty of AOL's Anonymous FTP feature is that the logon routine is done for you behind the scenes, giving you easy entry to an FTP file server.

Restricted FTP Access

Not all FTP servers allow anonymous logons, however. Some servers require you to establish an account before you can access the server. After you register your name and a password with the site administrator, you must enter that information whenever you want to access the site.

Access to an FTP site may be restricted for several reasons. A computer manufacturer, for example, may set aside certain directories or folders on its server for public (anonymous) access and establish other areas for restricted access (just as a local area network might be organized). Restricted access may be available to allow employees of a company or beta testers (those testing prerelease versions) of a hardware or software product to send and retrieve information with a reasonable measure of security.

In addition to accessing FTP servers anonymously on AOL, you can connect by providing your username and password, using AOL's FTP feature.

Finding FTP Files

Later in this chapter, in the "When You Don't Know the Address of an FTP Site" section, I'll tell you how AOL's FTP search function works. This feature enables you to look for FTP sites across the world by name or subject and then, using that information, log on to those servers to examine and retrieve files.

Although this technique enables you to locate a specific server, you don't know what's actually on those servers except in a general way, based on the information retrieved in your site search. If you need to find a particular file, you should use AOL's ultra-fast NetFind feature.

To access NetFind, click the globe-shaped **Internet** icon on your AOL toolbar and choose **AOL NetFind** from the drop-down menu. From there, you can conveniently search for files and information on a host of subjects.

SEE ALSO
➤ *Locating the files that you want, see page 435*

Using File Search

Teach Yourself: How to Transfer Files

Keyword: FTP

America Online's Anonymous FTP area (see Figure 15.1) is an important element of AOL's Internet services, offering easy access to files on remote Internet servers worldwide. You can log on as a guest using the automatic anonymous feature, or you can use an account name and password. AOL offers a list of popular FTP sites that you can download. You can connect to any of the sites by double-clicking the site's name.

When you first visit the FTP area (unless you want to connect to a specific site directly), review the Favorite Sites choices. Just click the **Go To FTP** icon at the right of the FTP screen to bring up the listing (see Figure 15.2). Depending on which platform you use to connect to AOL, you'll find a slightly different listing, and that list changes from time to time as new sites are discovered, checked, and added to the roster.

FIGURE 15.1

AOL's anonymous FTP area maintains a list of popular FTP sites for your downloading pleasure.

❶ Click **Go To FTP** to access AOL's Favorite FTP sites.

FIGURE 15.2

AOL sets aside a collection of popular FTP sites for you to examine.

❶ Scroll through the list to see all the selected sites.

If the FTP site to which you want to connect doesn't appear in the Anonymous FTP window, you can click the **Other Site** button and then enter the address of the site (see Figure 15.3). As you do with any Internet address, you have to enter the name accurately, or you won't make a connection.

FIGURE 15.3

Enter the name of the FTP site you want to access in the Site Address text box.

① Click **Connect** to access the site.

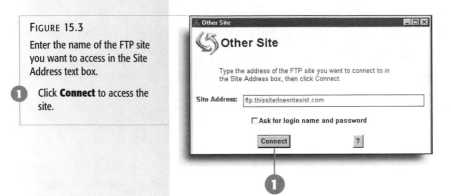

Using the Download Manager with FTP

Under normal use, AOL's FTP transfer process prevents use of the Download Later function (part of the Download Manager feature). You can get around this, however. After the file-transfer process begins, click the **Finish Later** button. The file is automatically added to your Download Manager (available from the My Files submenu), and you can complete the download whenever it's convenient for you (perhaps after you select several files this way).

SEE ALSO

➤ *Learn more about login names and passwords, see page 275*

After you connect to an FTP site, the next step is to look through the file directory to locate files you want to retrieve. Because the **Download Later** option doesn't appear (except for that little trick I mention in the sidebar), you won't be able to download these files via an Automatic AOL session. Files normally are received one at a time while you are actually logged on to the FTP site. In Figure 15.4, I have selected a file to retrieve.

FIGURE 15.4

Choose the file you want to download.

① Click **Download Now** to get the selected file.

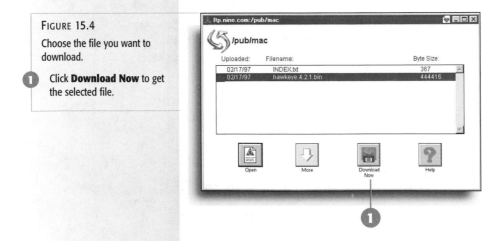

When the Other Site Isn't Anonymous

Some files are in text form

Files at FTP sites are often stored as encoded text files (especially Mac files). As I explain in the section, "How to Translate Files So You Can Use Them," later in this chapter, you need to translate these files after they are downloaded to make use of them.

Not all FTP sites are anonymous. Some sites won't grant you access to the entire site or to a special area unless you have established an account with the site administrator. If you work for a firm that has an FTP site, or you're a beta tester or registered user of a software product and need to retrieve files that are not available to the public, contact the firm involved for information on gaining access to its site.

After you set up an account, however, the process of logging on is no more difficult than beginning an AOL session. Type the site address in the **Site Address** text box on the Other Site screen (refer to Figure 15.3), and then click the **Ask for login name and password** check box. When you're connected to the remote FTP site, you are asked to enter your name and password in the Remote Sign-On dialog box (see Figure 15.5).

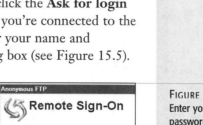

FIGURE 15.5
Enter your account name and password in the appropriate text boxes.

1 Use the Tab key to jump to the next text box.

The password that you type appears as a series of asterisks (small circles, or bullets, for Mac OS users) so that anyone who happens to look over your shoulder won't know what password you're entering. After you enter the correct information (enter it carefully, because the entry has to be exact), click the **Continue** button to go to the appropriate FTP site directory.

No connection

I entered my name and password, but I still can't connect to the FTP site. What's wrong? Sometimes, the inability to access an FTP site is caused by just a network error, but most often it's because you didn't enter the login information correctly. It's case-sensitive, meaning that you have to type uppercase and lower-case letters accurately. Whatever the cause of the problem, the Other Site dialog box reappears. You have to check the **Ask for login name and password** check box again before you click the **Connect** button to repeat the login process.

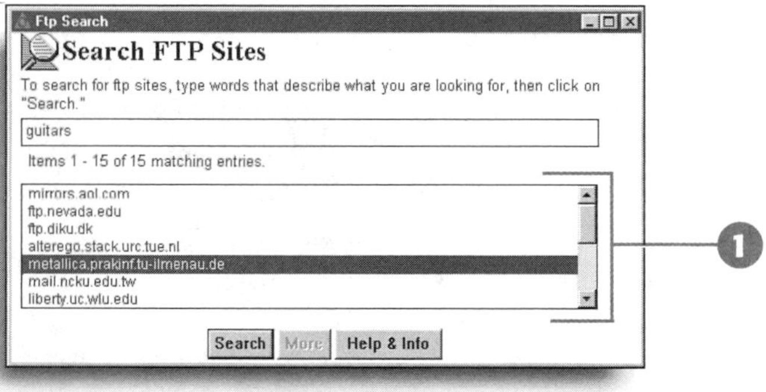

When You Don't Know the Address of an FTP Site

If you want to locate an FTP site but don't know the site's exact address, you can use the FTP Search function to get the site address. To access the search feature, click the **Search for FTP Sites** icon in the main FTP window (refer to Figure 15.1). AOL's FTP Search dialog box appears (see Figure 15.6). Type the search string in the text box and then click the **Search** button. If the search is successful, you see a list of potential matches in a few seconds.

FIGURE 15.6

To search for an FTP site, enter the name or subject of your search here.

1 The list of matching FTP sites.

When you're confronted by a list of prospects, you may want to learn more about each site before choosing the one to visit. Double-click an entry in the FTP Search dialog box; usually (but not always), you see some information about the software that the site contains (see Figure 15.7).

Don't give up

If your search doesn't yield a positive result, you may want to enter the information a little differently (maybe with a different spelling of a product or company name, for example).

Don't worry if you can't remember the address

Instead of trying to remember the complex FTP site address when you use the FTP search feature, try this: Double-click the title of the site in the search window; then select and copy the site name. Paste that address in the **Site Address** text box on the Other Site screen, and click **Connect**.

When you determine that you have the right FTP site, enter the FTP area. Click the **Other Site** button and type the name of the site. Then click the **Connect** button to initiate the anonymous login process.

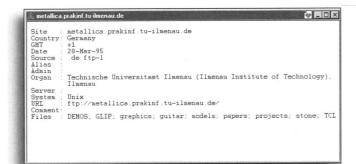

A fast way to find some FTP sites

If you're familiar with the address of a firm's WWW site, many times you can access the FTP site by substituting FTP for WWW. A common example is Microsoft's Web site, www. microsoft.com, and their FTP site, ftp.microsoft. com.

FIGURE 15.7

Clicking an entry in the FTP Search dialog box gives information about what that FTP site contains.

Downloading the Files with FTP

When you select a file to download, double-click the filename. You see a window that enables you to initiate the download process (see Figure 15.8).

The window identifies the file by name and displays the estimated download time for the modem speed at which you're connected. When you click the **Download Now** button, the following three-step process begins:

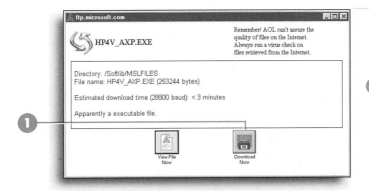

Web browsers support FTP too

AOL's Web browser can also access FTP sites. Just enter the FTP site address as a URL in the **Keyword** text box of the AOL toolbar, and AOL's clever browser does the rest. Some folks prefer to do it this way (but you can't trick your AOL software into including the file in the Download Manager via this method).

FIGURE 15.8

This screen gives information about the file you're about to download.

① Click **Download Now** to start the file transfer.

Here's How You Download Files by FTP

1. AOL's host computer network retrieves the file from its remote source (see Figure 15.9). This can take a while with large files and slow FTP servers.

FIGURE 15.9

AOL's computers retrieve a file for you.

1 The file is first transferred to AOL's network.

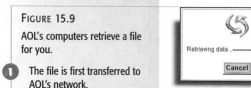

2. When the file retrieval process is complete, a dialog box appears asking you to specify the directory on your hard drive where you want to receive the file (see Figure 15.10).

FIGURE 15.10

Choose the location where you want the file stored.

1 Click **Save** to start the file transfer.

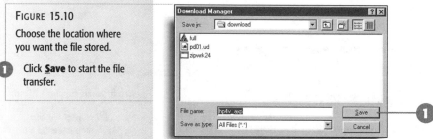

3. The file transfer begins (see Figure 15.11). If you want to stop or delay the transfer, click the **Finish Later** button (the file is now listed in the Download Manager, available from the **My Files** submenu).

FIGURE 15.11

The selected file is now being transferred to your computer.

1 Click **Finish Later** if you want to stop the transfer.

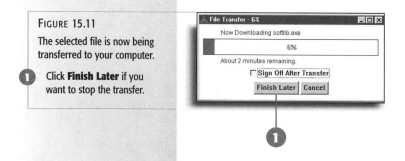

How to Translate Files So You Can Use Them

Internet-based servers may be Macs, PCs, or UNIX workstations, and they may use any of several computer operating systems. The format of the files also may vary, depending on the source from which you get the file. By looking at the file extension attached to a filename, you can determine the file's format. Following are some of the common formats that you may encounter during FTP visits:

- PC users commonly find files with .exe extensions. These represent executable files that you run with your Windows Explorer program (or by double-clicking the program icon). They are also found with .txt extensions, which represent files you can open in any word processor or text-editing program (even AOL's own software, if the files aren't too large).

- PC files with a .zip extension are saved in PKZip format. AOL's Windows software expands most of these files automatically when you log off, or you can choose the **File** menu, and select the **Open** command; then select the file that you want to expand.

- Macintosh files consist of two parts—a data fork and a resource fork. So that these files can be transferred on the Internet, they generally are saved in BinHex format, which converts the files to ASCII text. Therefore, these files have the extension .hqx.

Fortunately, the latest Mac OS version of AOL software automatically decodes .hqx files when you log off of AOL (so long as the option to decompress files is selected as a Download preference, which is the way it's set up by default).

Too many users?

Help! I tried to log on to an FTP site, and I got a message that I couldn't log on because there were too many users. What do I do? Many FTP sites consist of a single computer that handles a limited number of networked connections. Even a computer manufacturer's support sites, for example, may support fewer than 100 or 200 users at any one time. When too many folks are trying to hook up simultaneously, you get a message signifying that the server has too many anonymous users. The situation is just like a telephone busy signal; you have to try again until the server can handle your anonymous login request from AOL.

Some site administrators may set up *mirror sites*, additional servers with the same set of software, to enable more users to connect. If you get the message that too many users are connected to the site you want to bring up, look over the message for suggestions about alternate sites that may have the same files.

Small files can be viewed immediately

You can display small files that have a .txt extension on your computer's screen without transferring them to your computer. When you can read a file this way, a View File Now icon is available; double-click this icon to produce a text window that contains the contents of that file. As you can with text windows in other areas of AOL, you can save and print the text for later review.

Check for viruses

AOL displays a virus warning in the information window about a file you're about to download. The files that you get from an FTP site cannot be analyzed by AOL for the presence of computer viruses. Therefore, you should download files only from popular, well-maintained sites; you also should check all files that you download with up-to-date virus-protection software. You can get such software from AOL's libraries or you can buy a commercial virus-protection product. Examples include VirusScan from McAfee (you can get evaluation versions for both Mac and Windows users online), Dr. Solomon's Anti-Virus ToolKit, Norton Anti-Virus for Windows, Symantec Anti-Virus Utilities for Macintosh (also known as SAM), or Virex (which was in the process of being merged with Dr.Solomon's virus detection software when this book was written).

Going to another directory

A quick way to get to a particular file directory at an FTP site is to use the following UNIX-based commands after typing the site address in the Other Site window: :/<name of directory>. By linking directory names with a slash preceding them, you can easily navigate a complex directory hierarchy.

Secrets of File Compression

Your online time is valuable and Internet bandwidth may be an expensive commodity for some network users, so programmers have found a technique for making a file smaller for speedier transfer via modem and then restoring that file to its normal size after the file is transferred. This technique is called *compression*. For most AOL members, compression is seldom noticeable, because your AOL software expands files that are compressed in some common Mac and PC formats as soon as you log off the service (it's a preference option you can turn off if you prefer).

Although the programming schemes used to make files smaller are quite complex, the principle is simple. The compression software looks for redundant data and uses a shortcut of some sort to identify this redundant information. (An example is finding all the occurrences of the letter *e* in a text document.) When you expand the compressed file, the program uses its programming algorithm to identify and restore the redundant information.

PC programs generally are compressed in PKZip (.zip) and ARC (.arc) formats. For user convenience, files are often saved in self-extracting form. When you use the **Run** command in your Windows **Start** menu, these files (which have an .exe extension) are expanded automatically, sometimes in connection with a software-installation process.

Macintosh programs generally are compressed in Compact Pro (.cpt), DiskDoubler (.dd), and StuffIt (.sit) formats. The extension .sea (self-extracting archive) indicates that the file itself contains the code for extracting its contents; you begin the process by double-clicking the file. An .sea file does not require additional software to extract the contents.

Both the Mac and Windows software libraries have a large selection of compression software (some of it free) that you can use to expand files saved in formats that your regular AOL program doesn't support.

Teach Yourself: Your Own FTP Site on AOL

In addition to being able to access FTP sites across the world, AOL has set aside up to 2MB of space on its computer network for you to establish and maintain your own FTP site. The feature is called *FTPspace*. If you have more than one screen name, you'll get up to 2MB of storage space for each one. You can even upload an HTML (Hypertext Markup Language) file there and set up your own World Wide Web page.

SEE ALSO
➤ *Setting up Web pages, see page 328*

Teach Yourself: Using AOL's Personal Publisher to Make Your Home Page

How to Get to Your FTP Site

Accessing your personal FTP site is simple. Double-click **members.aol.com** from the Favorite Sites box in AOL's FTP area (refer to Figure 15.2) and your own FTP page appears (see Figure 15.12). How you use your site is up to you. You can place files there for other members to access. If you use your AOL account for business purposes, you can place promotional files and other useful information there, up to the 2MB limit imposed by AOL's host computer. You can also access your site via the keyword My Place and, in the screen that appears, click the **Go to My Place** icon.

> **AOL software can compress and expand your files**
>
> America Online's Mac and Windows software automatically expands compressed files in such formats as ARC, StuffIt, and PKZip when you log off (unless you turn off that option in your downloading preferences). Encoded .hqx files are also translated after you end your AOL session. You also can extract files by choosing the **File** menu and selecting **Open**, and then choosing the files that you want to expand.

> **Some neat uses for your FTP site**
>
> You can use your FTP site to store the files for your Web site or just document files you want your friends or business associates to use. You can also attach a link to a file in your Web page, which makes access simpler than browsing through your FTP site (which as you saw earlier, involves several steps).

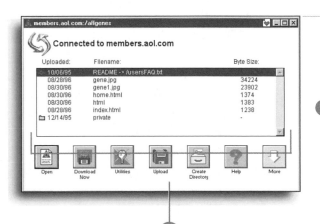

FIGURE 15.12

Your FTP site is available not only to other AOL members, but to anyone with Internet access.

1 Click the icons to manage your FTP site.

To reach someone else's FTP site, click the **Other Site** button and enter the following site address members.aol.com:/*<member-name>*.

You can organize your personal FTP site in the way that suits you best. In the example shown in Figure 15.13, I created a special directory for file uploads. At the bottom of the FTP window is a row of icons you can use for file transfers and to organize your site. The following list describes what the icons do:

FIGURE 15.13

Use the icons along the bottom of the screen to organize your FTP site.

1 Click the button to access the feature.

- **Open.** Opens a file or file directory.
- **Download Now.** Transfers files from your FTP site.
- **Utilities.** Deletes or renames a file or directory.
- **Upload.** Transfers files to your FTP site or to any other FTP site that allows file uploads, using the following process:
    1. First type the name of the file you want to send in the **Remote Filename** text box. Then select from two options—**ASCII (text documents)** or **Binary (programs and graphics)**.
    2. Click the **Continue** button.
    3. In the next window, click the **Select File** button. Then locate the file you want to send (see Figure 15.14) and click **OK**.

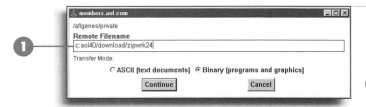

4. To begin the file transfer process, click the **Send File**
button on the screen that appears after you selected the
file.

- **Create Directory.** Use this tool to make your own directory at your FTP site.
- **Help.** If you have problems in setting up and running your
FTP site, consult this handy help text for additional information.
- **More.** If the site has more items than will fit in a single document window, click the **More** button to bring up additional
selections.

Finding Your Favorite FTP Sites

America Online's FTP area includes a list of Favorite Sites, consisting of remote file servers run by major universities and computer firms, such as Apple and Microsoft. Some of these sites are
mirrored by America Online, which means that the files themselves are duplicated on AOL's host computer network to enable
more users to access them at the same time. The procedure is
similar to using a backup of your own computer's hard drive.
Like many backups, mirroring is done on a daily basis, so you
can always get the latest software and related information from
these sites.

The advantage of providing a mirror of a remote FTP source is
speed and convenience. Having the files stored on AOL's host
computer network means that the files do not have to be
retrieved from a remote site (which may take a long time when
network traffic is high). Also, you have a much lower chance of

The popular FTP sites list changes regularly

AOL's Favorite Sites listing changes often, as new sites are set up, and older ones changed. Check the area on a regular basis to see the latest offerings.

getting a busy signal when an FTP site has more users trying to log on than it can handle.

SEE ALSO

➤ *Locating files on AOL, see page 435*

How to Search for Information on the Net

Discover AOL's special Internet searching tools

Locate the Internet-based material you want

Learn to deal with common search problems

AOL's NetFind finds information and rates sites

Searching for Information on the Internet

As I explained in Chapter 12, "Using AOL's Internet Services," the Internet is a sprawling, largely unregulated mass of information, both useful and otherwise. You can think of it as the equivalent of thousands and thousands of libraries of books, magazines, photographs, and software, and it all is there for you to access if you can acquire the catalog file.

Fortunately, America Online offers helpful database search tools that enable you to tap this huge resource of information and get exactly the material you want.

To make your searches more efficient, AOL combines the best features of the Gopher and WAIS database search systems so that you can easily find the information resources you want with as little fuss and delay as possible. Most important, the skills required to search through these databases are already known to you. To make Internet database searching as easy as possible, AOL has included it as part of its World Wide Web browser.

Teach Yourself: Using AOL's Gopher Feature

Keyword: Gopher, WAIS

The Internet contains hundreds of free databases on topics as diverse as home brewing, NASA news, recipes, congressional contact information, and the works of Shakespeare. These databases are indexed, meaning you can search them for information by using keywords and phrases. This database and search process is similar to how you would search for files on America Online using the File Search feature, which is described in Chapter 26, "Tips and Tricks on Finding Software." AOL's Gopher area (see Figure 16.1) offers you fast, easy access to these information resources.

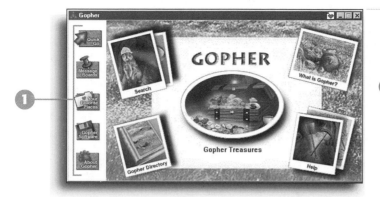

FIGURE 16.1

AOL offers a full suite of Internet database search capabilities.

① Click an icon to access that feature.

Using AOL's Gopher Database Searching

The best way to demonstrate how an Internet database search works is to conduct one for yourself. America Online's Gopher center offers a list of common topics you might want to search through its Gopher Treasures feature. If the topic you want information about isn't shown in the listing, click the **Search** icon, which brings up a special Web browser window (see Figure 16.2).

From here, enter the subject you want to learn more about in the **Search for** text field. Within seconds you'll see a list of items that match your search request, as shown in Figure 16.3 (or a message that the information you want isn't available). Click any underlined item you see to learn more about that subject.

Show me the WAIS

WAIS is short for *Wide Area Information Server* . It's an Internet search protocol that, in effect, provides the equivalent of a book's index to help you find the information you want. It was originally designed to work with supercomputers, but as personal computers became more powerful, it proved to be useful for them too.

FIGURE 16.2

AOL's Gopher search window uses AOL's Web browser.

① Type the search text here.

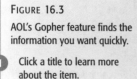

FIGURE 16.3

AOL's Gopher feature finds the information you want quickly.

1 Click a title to learn more about the item.

Trouble accessing an Internet database?

Why is it taking so long for you to open a Gopher database? Is there something wrong with your modem? Unlike accessing other parts of America Online, when you access an Internet database, you are literally logging on to another service. It might take awhile for the request to reach that computer and for AOL's host computer network to retrieve the information. This is perfectly normal.

Why does AOL says it can't retrieve?

You're getting a message that AOL can't retrieve the Gopher information you want. Why? It's important to realize that when you access any of AOL's Internet services, you are calling upon resources that extend beyond the boundaries of the service's computer network. If there's an undue delay in getting the information back to AOL, you'll get a message of this sort.

It's easy to refine your search request to provide a greater range of information or a more precise description of what you want. The following tips show you how (just be sure to use uppercase where it is noted):

- To find a resource that contains information on two or more topics, separate the topics with the word AND.

- To get information on either one topic or another topic, use the word OR.

- To specify certain items you don't want, use the word NOT.

By using any of these words in combination, you can greatly increase the flexibility and accuracy of your search requests and be assured that you will get precisely the material you need.

Secrets of Expert Access to Gopher Servers

If you already know the name of a specific Gopher server you would like to use, click the **Quick Go** icon at the top left of the main Gopher window (refer to Figure 16.1), and enter the name of that site (see Figure 16.4). You can also access a Gopher site directly from AOL's WWW window. Just enter gopher://
[*sitename*].edu in the **Enter URL** field (if you enter the WWW

window from AOL's Gopher forum, "gopher://" is already typed). The last part of the address, edu, assumes the site is sponsored by an educational institution.

AOL lets you run many Internet programs as part of your AOL connection without any special setup. If you're used to a specific Gopher browser, no problem. AOL has a selection of many of these programs in its software libraries. Click the **Gopher Software** icon (refer to Figure 16.1) and download the program shown, or click the **More** button for additional choices (see Figure 16.5).

Use AOL's Favorite Places feature for fast access

After you've located Gopher databases that provide the information you want, you can easily add them to your list of Favorite Places by clicking the little heart icon at the right side of the title bar. You'll then be able to quickly revisit those sites whenever you want.

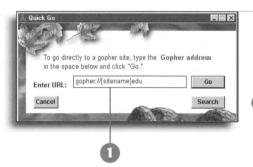

FIGURE 16.4

Enter the location of the Gopher site you want to access at the cursor in the Quick Go window.

1. Type the address in the text field.

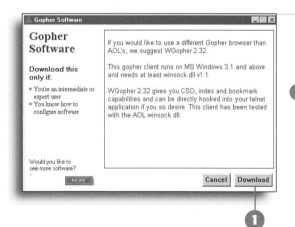

FIGURE 16.5

AOL makes it easy for you to use a different Gopher browser program, if you prefer.

1. Click **Download** to get the file.

For most users, AOL's own Gopher feature should be enough to get the job done, but that shouldn't deter you from trying out another program, if you want to experiment, or you are happy with the software you've used previously.

Don't try to remember a complex URL!

Because pointing and clicking is more accurate than entering a long Gopher site's name correctly (and host computers are notoriously picky about precise syntax), just enter the main site name as the URL at the top of the browser window, and navigate through the site's directory to the one you want by clicking the directory names in the body of the browser document.

How to Search for Information on the Web

In addition to exploring AOL's Gopher area to search for information, you can use AOL's NetFind feature to comb the Internet for the material you want. To call on NetFind, just choose AOL NetFind from the Internet toolbar icon's drop-down menu. The result is shown in Figure 16.6. The keyword NetFind brings up the same browser screen.

Harnessing AOL's NetFind search tool is simple. Just enter the word or words you want to check, click the **Find!** icon, and NetFind gets into motion to find the information you seek. Within seconds, you'll see a listing of the search results (see Figure 16.7).

FIGURE 16.6

AOL's NetFind feature gets the information you want using industry-standard search engines.

1 Click a title to learn more.

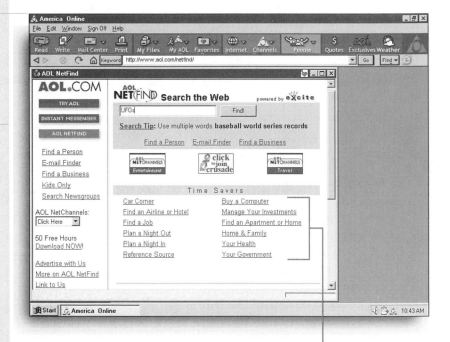

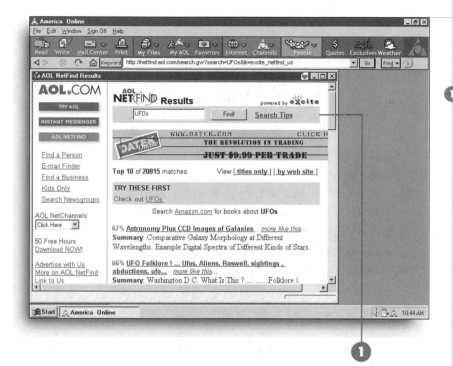

FIGURE 16.7

From *Star Trek* to cooking, NetFind combs the Internet to find what you want.

1 Enter the search text, then click **Find**.

Quick Tips for Using a WWW Search Tool

The sort of results you get when you do an Internet search are only as good as the information you enter into your search string. When you start your search, you have two choices for how the search is to be done. The first is for NetFind to search the entire Web (the little box at the left of the NetFind screen that's selected by default), and the second is to consult the AOL NetFind reviews for the information you want, by checking the second option.

To refine your search further, follow these seven tips AOL offers toward the most efficient database search:

- *Phrase it.* Instead of using just one word, try a phrase instead. Just remember to put the phrase "in quotes."

- *Be specific.* Tell the search engine exactly what you want. If, for example, you want a security program, asking for "freeware security software" is much better than just saying "PC software."

- *Check NetFind reviews.* AOL's NetFind staff reviews lots of Internet sources for high-quality information. Using the AOL NetFind Reviews option as part of your search often brings the best matches.

- *Add it up.* If you want to have NetFind locate information based on all the words in your string, use "AND" or a plus sign ("+") between the words, such as "rock AND roll."

- *Cut it out.* This is not meant as an insult, just a piece of advice. Use the words "AND NOT" or a minus sign ("–") to refine your search. An example is "computers AND NOT UNIX."

- *More Like This.* If your search string is too general, you may end up with thousands of choices. Your search screen may include a **More Like This** link at the bottom or right side of the screen that brings up advice on how to be more specific in your search request.

- *Refine your find.* At the bottom of the search screen, you'll see another **Search** field where you can refine your search request, to bring up a better, more accurate list of information.

Let NetFind do the walking

Let AOL's NetFind feature do all the work. Click the **Search Tips** icon at the right of the NetFind screen for additional tips on how to search for specific types of information.

Additional Web-Based Search Tools

AOL's NetFind feature uses the Excite search tool as its core technology, and will definitely suit most of your Internet search requirements. You may be more accustomed to other Internet search capabilities, or just want to see other options.

An overview is provided here of some other popular Internet search engines. They can all be used via AOL's seamless Internet access.

- *AltaVista (http://www.altavista.digital.com).* Digital's AltaVista search engines form the core technology for a number of other search facilities. These include (hold your breath, the list is long): Yahoo!, LôôkSmart, 100hot Websites, InfoSpace's Directories, BlueWindow, LawCrawler, PeekABoo, WorldPages, Internet Sleuth, TechWeb, Carrefour.net International, THE ANGLE, Netcreations, WhoWhere, Bigfoot, Webreference.com, Austronaut, 123Link, The Mining Company, Netway Austria, Samara Zimbabwe, YUPI: Internet en Español, and FIREBALL: die Suchmaschine.

- *HotBot (http://www.hotbot.com)*. Last time I checked, this site was boasting its winning status in a *PC* magazine search engine shoot-out. You'll find the latest news, simple tips on using the search features, and a set of popular sites in such categories as Reference, Business, Culture, SciTech (science and technology), and Politics.

- *Lycos (http://www.lycos.com)*. The operators of this site modestly refer to it as "the most complete catalog of Web site addresses available today." It provides convenient searches using its Go Get It feature, top news stories, and a special feature called Lycos Pro, which includes Java technology.

- *Yahoo! (http://www.yahoo.com)*. This is a site that grew from a hobby to a full-time commercial enterprise, complete with advertiser support. It remains a popular source of Internet searching. After trying it a few times, you may just want to add it to your Favorite Places directory.

SEE ALSO

➤ *Tapping AOL's Internet resources, see page 230*

➤ *For more information about newsgroups, see page 296*

➤ *Transfering FTP files to your personal computer, see page 272z*

How to Join and Participate in Internet Newsgroups and Mailing Lists

What Internet newsgroups are

What netiquette really means

How to find Internet newsgroups

How to participate in Internet newsgroups

A world of information in your mailbox

When the information gets too overwhelming

Introducing the World of Internet Message Boards

There are tens of thousands of messages on America Online, covering a wide range of subjects. These message boards are valuable resources for sharing information and debating topics that interest you. This chapter is devoted to other types of discussion boards. These discussion boards are similar to those you find in message boards throughout AOL, yet quite different because they are not restricted by the boundaries and requirements of a single online service—they're a part of the global Internet network.

Some of the most interesting parts of the worldwide Internet are newsgroups, also known as *Usenet newsgroups.* Newsgroups are popular and active exchanges and are the Internet counterparts of message boards on America Online. Some of these discussions also go on via Internet mailing lists, which I'll discuss later on in this chapter. These discussions cover almost any topic you can think of.

Internet Newsgroups—The Ground Rules

Before you begin to check out Internet newsgroups for yourself, you should get acquainted with the ground rules. In some respects, newsgroups are different from America Online's own message boards. First, they usually are not moderated, which means no AOL community leader is around to monitor the message boards and remove messages that contain inflammatory, irrelevant, or vulgar statements. As a result, participants in newsgroups take a free-wheeling approach to participating in these areas, and sometimes they are a little slow to welcome new visitors, or *newbies*, as beginning Internet surfers are called. This doesn't mean, however, that you should abandon considerations of good taste when posting in such areas. Some of the rules of the road, referred to as *netiquette*, will be explained later in this chapter.

Of course, a smaller number of newsgroups do have moderators. These moderators are somewhat like the forum staff on America

Online, but they exercise a greater measure of control over what appears in their message boards. Unlike the messages you post on AOL, every message you post to a moderated newsgroups is reviewed by a moderator in advance for content before it is released, and they will censor messages they don't consider relevant to the topic at hand. You'll often find the decisions of the moderators to be rather arbitrary.

America Online's Internet services provide access to literally thousands of newsgroups. Using AOL's Newsgroups area shown in Figure 17.1, you can select the newsgroups that interest you and place that list of newsgroups in a customized list. America Online keeps a database of popular newsgroups, but as explained later in this chapter, you can seek out others that interest you too.

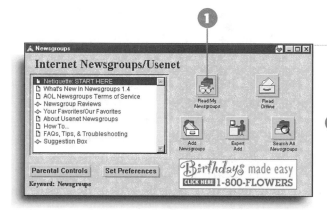

FIGURE 17.1

One of the most exciting Internet features offered by AOL is Usenet newsgroups.

1 Click **Read My Newsgroups** to check the messages.

After you've joined, or subscribed to, a list of your favorite newsgroups, you need only click the **Read My Newsgroups** icon to keep current on your favorite topics. Using this message board, you can discuss your special interests with people from all over the world.

Before you start to add newsgroups to your lists, take a few moments to review the text files displayed in the main forum directory window (refer to Figure 17.1). You can read these text files while you're online, or you can save and print them for later reference. These files contain some helpful advice on traversing the sometimes wacky world of Usenet newsgroups.

The next few pages cover the ground rules of participating in newsgroups and take you through the steps of configuring AOL's *news reader* (the AOL software component you use to view and respond to newsgroups messages). You'll find that the features of the Macintosh and Windows versions of AOL's news reader are somewhat different from those of other areas of AOL service.

What Is Netiquette All About?

No doubt when you first visit AOL's Newsgroups area, you'll want to dive right in and get involved in a discussion board yourself. Before you do so, however, you should learn something about newsgroups in general and about how to introduce yourself to a discussion group. Over the years, the Internet, although largely unregulated and unsupervised, has developed some forms and conventions you should know about first.

The following are a few tips based on hard-won experience on the net:

- You'll be tempted to get involved right away in a discussion that interests you. My advice: don't. Spend a little time reading messages or following discussions (which experienced net visitors sometimes call *lurking*). Often you'll find a set of FAQs (Frequently Asked Questions), text files that provide a list of ground rules for a specific discussion group, and responses to typical user questions. After you've developed a feel for the flavor of a particular group, it's time to consider posting a message of your own.

- There are literally thousands of newsgroups. The number of messages you are likely to encounter will be in the hundreds of thousands. You can quickly become overwhelmed by the sheer volume of information if you don't pick and choose carefully. To begin with, you should restrict yourself to only a small number of discussion groups, take time to digest the messages, and add more newsgroups only when you think you can devote the time necessary to keep up-to-date on all the information you'll receive.

- When you respond to a message, consider that you are posting a response to not just a single person, but an audience that could number in the millions. If you decide you want to restrict your audience to a single person, send that person email instead. The option to reply to just the author rather than the group is available in America Online's newsgroups reader.

- Before writing your message, carefully choose the appropriate forum. It wouldn't necessarily be a good idea to promote the use of a Macintosh in a discussion group oriented toward users of Microsoft Windows, for example, unless you want to risk generating a lot of ill will. (There are advocacy newsgroups where you can debate the merits of one computer platform over another, of course.)

- Show respect and be polite when you post a message. If you disagree with someone's statement, try to stick to the issues and refrain from personal attack. Such attacks are regarded as *flaming*, and although they might be entertaining on some television talk shows, they are not considered good taste on the Internet.

- When responding to someone else's message, quote the relevant portions of that message at the beginning of your response, or before each part of your message that refers to the other message. AOL's newsgroups reader will handle the quoting for you, if you follow a few simple steps. (It's a little more complicated than the way it's done in your email.) I'll tell you how later in this chapter, in the "How to Reply to a Newsgroup Message" section.

- It is customary to use your email address as your personal signature, but your name and affiliations can be placed there as well, as shown in Figure 17.2. Some users also include their address and phone number, but before you do this, consider how you feel about giving this information out to millions of strangers. Other users add a statement or motto that reflects some aspect of their personality. Before preparing your own signature, you might want to see how others do it first.

Don't overdo it!

When you create an online signature for yourself, try to keep it short and to the point (such as your name and, if needed, company affiliation or a short motto). Long signatures with elaborate artwork waste bandwidth and may upset users who pay large amounts for Internet access.

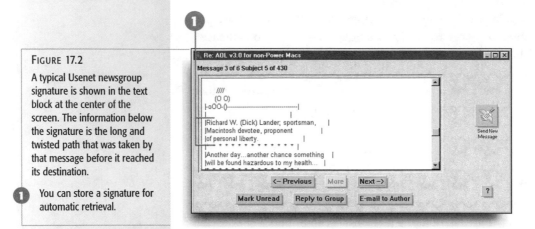

FIGURE 17.2

A typical Usenet newsgroup signature is shown in the text block at the center of the screen. The information below the signature is the long and twisted path that was taken by that message before it reached its destination.

1 You can store a signature for automatic retrieval.

- Keep your messages short and to the point. You are reaching an audience that spans the entire world here, and you don't want to waste anyone's time because some users still pay high prices for Internet access. Also, try not to cross-post, or send your message to more than one newsgroup at a time (unless you think it's really necessary).

- Choose a subject title that specifically describes the topic of your message. It is better to use "GPF crash in CorelDraw 7.0" than "System Crash" if you are seeking advice on solving a problem in a computing newsgroups. You do not, of course, have to include the title of the destination newsgroup as your subject.

- Express emotions and humor with care. When you speak with someone in person, often body language and the inflection of your voice reveal whether you are serious, angry, or happy about something. In your messages, however, your words alone must be the mirror of your feelings. Experienced online users express emotions with smileys (or "emoticons").

SEE ALSO

➤ *To learn more about using abbreviations and shorthand symbols, see page 199*

➤ *For information about proper online behavior, see page 196*

- Before you respond to a message, take the time to see whether someone else has already answered it. Time on the busy Internet is at a premium, and reading the same sort of message over and over wastes everyone's time, including your own.

Using AOL's Newsgroup Reader

Keyword: Newsgroups

If you've used a newsgroups reader on another online service, you're apt to find some differences in the news reader offered by AOL. AOL's news reader is a graphical service, and some of those other Internet services still use text-based software.

In the next few pages, I'll explain how to set up AOL's news reader for best performance. Then you'll begin to seek out and participate in some popular newsgroup discussions.

Setting Newsgroup Preferences

The opening Newsgroup window (refer to Figure 17.1) has two sets of preferences. Yet a third set of preferences exists, but you can't access that until you open a list of messages. This third set will be described later in this chapter. For now, look at the two rectangular buttons at the bottom of the Newsgroups window—**Parental Controls** and **Set Preferences**. You'll learn more about the first button, **Parental Controls**, in Chapter 7, "Parental Issues and Internet Access."

The **Set Preferences** button produces a collection of preferences you can set separately for each screen name on your AOL account (see Figure 17.3). Using these preferences, you can create a signature that automatically appears at the bottom of your newsgroup messages and dictates how those messages appear.

Three types of preferences are available, which are described in the sections that follow.

Headers

As shown in Figure 17.2 earlier in this chapter, Internet transactions go through a circuitous route, from computer to computer,

Caution: Don't advertise in the wrong group

If you want to sell or buy something, search out a newsgroup that caters to such things. (It will often have the word "marketplace" in its name.) Posting an ad in a newsgroup that's not devoted to such topics is a severe breach of etiquette, and, rather than sell anything, you'll just find your mailbox inundated with complaints if you post such a notice in the wrong place.

on their way to America Online. You can choose whether you want to see any of this header information, which displays the long, complex path your message takes. (You might want to leave it off, to keep message windows free of unwanted clutter.) The header options to choose from in the Preferences dialog box are as follows (see Figure 17.3):

- **Headers at top.** The path your message travels is included at the top of your message window.

- **Headers at bottom.** The path your message travels is included at the bottom of your message window.

- **No headers.** Ah, that's more like it. (This is the default setting.) The headers are stripped from the messages you see. The header is limited to the date and time the message was sent, the message ID information, and the Internet address of the author of the message.

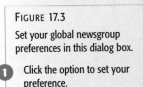

FIGURE 17.3

Set your global newsgroup preferences in this dialog box.

1 Click the option to set your preference.

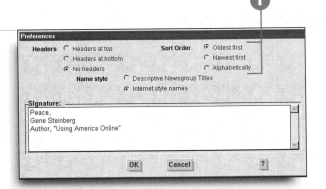

Sort Order

How would you like your messages displayed? By default, you see the oldest first, and then you move through them, in chronological order, with messages grouped by thread (topic). Your sort order choices in the Preferences dialog box are the following:

- **Oldest first.** This is the default setting, which enables you to read the messages in their normal sequence.

- **Newest first.** To some, this choice might seem like reading the end of a book before the beginning, but if you have a huge number of messages to read through, you might find it convenient to look at the latest messages first. This option makes following a message thread difficult, however, because the response comes before the question.

- **Alphabetically.** This setting groups messages by topic, in alphabetical order.

Name Style

Newsgroup names follow a specific naming convention that might seem confusing to some who are visiting the Internet for the first time. You have two options as to how the names in your newsgroups list are shown (see Figure 17.4 for an example, using the Read My Newsgroups directory that's accessed from the main Newsgroups screen).

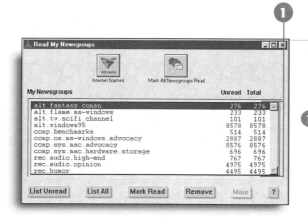

FIGURE 17.4

A list of newsgroups is shown here with their standard Internet names.

1 Scroll through the list to see more selections.

Two types of naming preferences are available:

- **Descriptive Newsgroup Titles.** For this setting, which is the default configuration, a newsgroup might be identified as Help with Newsgroups.

- **Internet style names.** When you select this option, Help with Newsgroups is shown as `aol.newsgroups.help`.

Another way to see the Internet name

If you are viewing your newsgroups with English style names, you can see the actual Internet name by clicking the **Internet Names** icon at the top of the Newsgroup message window (refer to Figure 17.4). This action brings up a window showing the Internet versions.

As you see, the Internet name, despite its odd syntax, is really not difficult to define even for the newbie, but whether to choose this option is up to you. It's okay to try both methods. You can change your preferences at any time by opening the Set Preferences window, making your alterations, and then opening your list of newsgroups again. The changes take effect immediately.

A Quick Directory of Newsgroup Names

As you have seen from other Internet chapters in this book, the net has a language all its own, replete with abbreviations and traditions. Table 17.1 is a brief list of the common newsgroups prefixes, and which category they fall into.

TABLE 17.1 Newsgroup prefixes

Name	Definition
alt	Alternative, a less formal type of newsgroup sometimes with offensive and inflammatory messages
aol	(Need I say more?)
biz	Business
comp	Computers
news	General news and topical items
rec	Recreational (hobbies and arts)
sci	Scientific
soc	Social
talk	Debate-oriented
misc	Newsgroups not easy to categorize

How to Add Newsgroups

As I explained earlier in this chapter, thousands of newsgroups exist, catering to interests of all sorts. Many newsgroups overlap in terms of content too, so you probably will want to select more than a single newsgroup that covers topics in which you're interested.

America Online maintains a listing of the most popular newsgroups in its own database. Just click the **Add Newsgroups** icon in the Newsgroups main screen (refer to Figure 17.1). You see a directory listing that displays many categories of interest (see Figure 17.5).

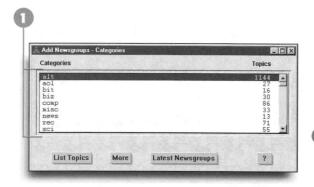

FIGURE 17.5

The first step in locating a newsgroup to join is to get a list that caters to your favorite subjects.

1 Double-click an item to see more choices.

After you've picked a subject, click the **List Topics** button to bring up a list of newsgroups that fit the description (see Figure 17.6).

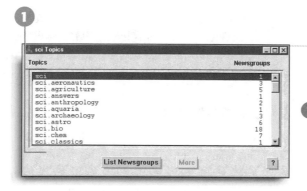

FIGURE 17.6

A list of newsgroup categories catering to one area of interest.

1 Double-click an item to see newsgroups in that category.

Now you've gotten to the heart of the matter. To see a specific newsgroup, you need only click one of the categories shown to bring up the final listing. To add a newsgroup, double-click the newsgroup's name to bring up its description, and then click the **Add** button (which appears in the description window) to include it in your listing.

Of course, you don't have to join that newsgroup yet. If you'd rather sample the flavor of a particular discussion group, just click its name and you'll see a listing of the available messages, shown in Figure 17.7. You can read those messages, but because you're just sampling the newsgroup for now, you cannot actually post a response to a message or create a topic of your own. To do that, you must actually add that newsgroup to your list. (It's also called *subscribing.*)

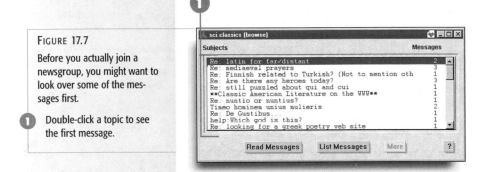

FIGURE 17.7

Before you actually join a newsgroup, you might want to look over some of the messages first.

1 Double-click a topic to see the first message.

When you've actually added a newsgroup, it appears under the Read My Newsgroups listing, which will be discussed later in this chapter, in the "Teach Yourself: How to Participate in a Newsgroup" section.

Using Expert Add

As with email addresses, the titles of newsgroups are identified by a special syntax, with words generally separated by a period. An example is `comp.sys.mac.advocacy`, which as the title suggests, is a discussion group with active debates on the subject of the Apple Macintosh versus other computing platforms. If you know the exact title of a newsgroup, you can bypass the search mechanism or America Online's own listing and join by clicking the **Expert Add** icon (which appears on the main Newsgroup screen), as shown in Figure 17.8.

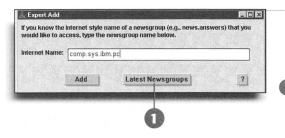

FIGURE 17.8

If you know the name of the newsgroup you want to join, enter it here.

① Click **Latest Newsgroups** to see more choices.

After you've subscribed to the newsgroups that interest you, it's time to read the messages.

How to Search All Newsgroups

If you don't find a newsgroup that interests you, you can perform a more thorough search of the available newsgroups. Click the **Search All Newsgroups** icon in the Newsgroups area to bring up a search window, as shown in Figure 17.9. Enter the subject for which you want to locate a newsgroup in the **Search Phrase** text box.

Type the address carefully

America Online's Expert Add feature is literal-minded. For it to work, you need to enter a newsgroup name using the exact spelling and punctuation. Otherwise, the newsgroup won't be located, or worse, you'll add the wrong newsgroup.

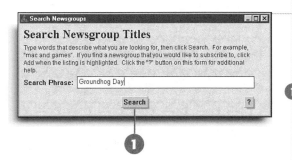

FIGURE 17.9

You can search from among thousands of newsgroups for one that piques your curiosity.

① Click **Search** to find the newsgroup.

If a newsgroup meets your search criteria (and sometimes you have to refine the phrases a bit or even try related ones), the newsgroup title appears in a window. From there, you can read a capsule description by double-clicking the newsgroup title. You'll find, however, that many newsgroups do not actually have any description other than the titles themselves. The folks who established these newsgroups feel the titles are sufficient to describe their mission (or just haven't bothered to try to define it any further).

Expand your search

If you want to search for more than a single item, you should insert the word **and** between words and phrases to separate subjects. You may expand your search with the word **or** when you want to look for one option or the other, and you can exclude an item with the word **not** to designate a subject or word you don't want to use in the search result listing.

Unlike the Add Newsgroups feature, the searching mechanism doesn't enable you to sample a newsgroup before adding it to your list. This isn't a major shortcoming, however, because you can remove a newsgroup later by the mere click of a button.

Teach Yourself: How to Participate in a Newsgroup

Now that you've subscribed to some newsgroups, it's time to get involved.

First, click the **Read My Newsgroups** icon at the main screen of the Newsgroups area. You see a listing of all the newsgroups you've subscribed to, as shown in Figure 17.10. When you enter this area for the first time, you see a list of popular newsgroups that America Online has automatically included for you, but you can remove them at any time by highlighting the name of the newsgroup and clicking the **Remove** button. The **Mark Read** button enables you to flag the messages in a selected group as read without actually opening the messages themselves (so use this feature with caution if you want to read those messages later).

FIGURE 17.10

The newsgroups you've joined are listed here.

1. Scroll through the list to see more groups.

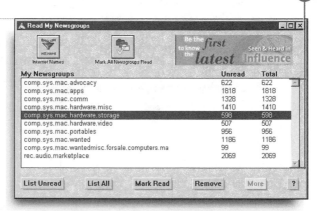

Before you begin to read the messages in your selected newsgroups, you'll want to review "What Is Netiquette All About?," earlier in this chapter. After you've done that, take some time to read the messages themselves. The first time you read the messages, you might find there are literally thousands in a single newsgroup alone. Because the messages are grouped by topic (also known as message threading), as shown in Figure 17.11, you'll be able to easily pick the messages you want to read.

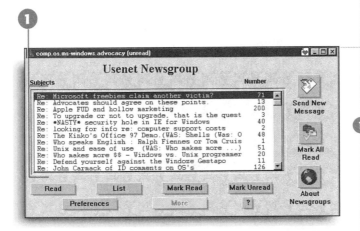

FIGURE 17.11

Newsgroups messages are threaded—grouped according to topic.

1 Double-click a selected item to see the first message.

How to Follow a Message Thread

All newsgroup messages are normally sorted by date and then by topic. You can choose to display them in a different order, using the Set Preferences feature described earlier. In this description, however, the messages will be referred to in their regular order.

The process of organizing the messages into topics is known as *threading*. It enables you to read messages and responses about a single topic without having to read through messages on other subjects. The setup is similar to AOL's own message boards, which are described in Chapter 11, "How to Use AOL's Message Boards."

After you've read all the messages in a single thread, the **Message** button will be grayed out. Just click the **Subject** button to go to a new thread. If you want to bypass that subject, just close the message window; you can then look over the directory of unread messages for another topic you want to follow.

The same topic in different places

Because messages in a single thread are often posted at widely varying times, you might actually find two or more listings for messages concerning a single topic. In addition, if you change even a single character in the title of a message thread when you reply to it, a new thread will be created.

Setting Message Preferences

Another set of newsgroup preferences covers the time frame of messages shown when you open a message window. It's similar to the Find Since feature that you use on a regular AOL message board. By clicking the **Preferences** button in a Newsgroup message window, you have options that will serve you now and in the future (see Figure 17.12).

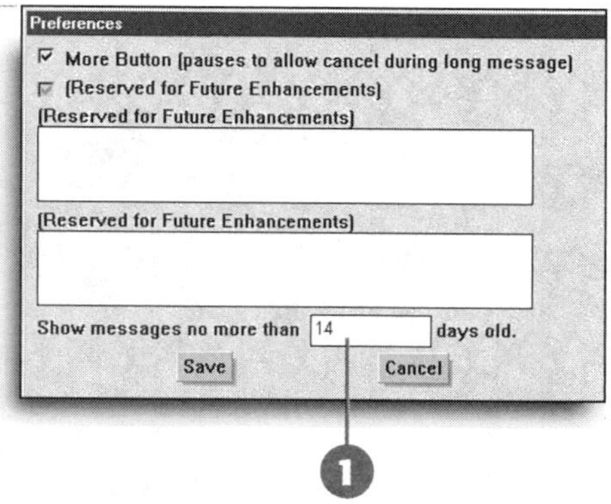

FIGURE 17.12

Choose the time frame under which messages will be displayed and other options.

1 Enter the number of days here.

As you can see by the "Reserved for Future Enhancements" notation, at the time this book was written, some of the message preferences hadn't been activated. The sole option that was available was the one at the bottom, where you can select the time frame in which messages are displayed. This option can save you the drudgery of having to pore over thousands of accumulated messages during your first visit to a newsgroup, or when visiting a newsgroup after you've been absent from AOL for a few days.

The option at the top, the **More Button**, can be ignored, because the function is now replaced by one that enables you to download a long message to your computer. In the future, you'll be able to ignore messages with certain words or phrases in them, or those sent by certain users you'd rather not read messages from.

Caution: These message board preferences are not global

The message board options you choose apply only to the individual newsgroup in which you select them. Preferences must be selected separately for every newsgroup to which you subscribe.

Troubleshooting: Too Many Messages

Help! I selected the option to show messages for no more than a day or so, yet I'm still seeing thousands of messages displayed after I click the Save button and close the Preferences window. Why?

You need to reload the message list on your computer. The following shows you how:

Reloading newsgroup message listing

1. Close the window containing the message list that displays when you select Read.

2. Open the Read My Newsgroups window (if it's not already opened), and then double-click the newsgroup you just closed.

You then see only the unread messages posted within the time frame you set on your message preferences.

Using the List All Feature

When you first open your personal newsgroup list and select a topic, double-clicking the topic name or pressing the Enter key brings up a list of unread messages. If you want to review messages you've read previously, click the **List All** button instead. This brings up a display of all messages available in that newsgroup (within the time frame you selected via the message preference window), whether you've read them or not.

How to Reply to a Newsgroup Message

After you've read the messages in your favorite newsgroup, no doubt you'll be tempted to respond to a particular message. When you bring up a message window, you can use the **Reply** button to add your message to the existing thread so others will see your response also. You can respond to a message in two ways. First, click the **Reply to Group** button, which brings up the two-paned screen shown in Figure 17.13. If you want the author of the original message to receive a reply by email, check the CC: Author box at the lower-left corner of the message window.

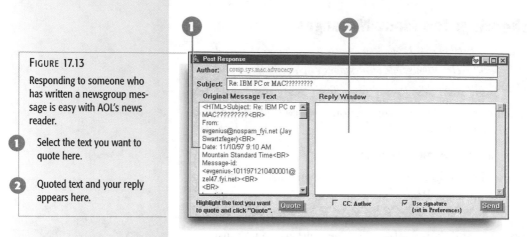

FIGURE 17.13

Responding to someone who has written a newsgroup message is easy with AOL's news reader.

① Select the text you want to quote here.

② Quoted text and your reply appears here.

The second option shown in a message window is **email to Author**, which enables you to send your response as email instead. This window (which looks similar to the one shown in Figure 17.13) gives you the choice of having the same message posted in the newsgroup, by clicking the check box.

Before actually writing your response, it's customary to first quote the relevant passages of the original message you are writing about.

Newsgroup message quoting

1. First select the text you want to quote in the Original Message Text window.

2. Click the **Quote** button.

The text you've quoted will appear in the Reply Window.

The Use signature (set in Preferences) check box automatically adds the signature you set in the newsgroup preferences box to your message (you don't have to add it). If you prefer not to use this signature, or to use a different signature, click the check box to disable this option.

Caution: Don't quote too much

When I say, "the relevant passages of the original message," I mean just that. If you quote the entire message, and intend only to respond to a small part of it, you waste everyone's time with material that has no bearing on the statement you're trying to make. If you just want to say you agree with someone's long message, just quote a short paragraph from that message that seems to summarize it reasonably well, and leave it at that, along with your statement of agreement.

Troubleshooting: Dealing with Offensive Material

Help! I'm getting offensive messages from the Internet. What do I do?

America Online's Terms of Service, of course, does not apply to members of other services (although they do govern your conduct on the Internet, so be careful). If you get objectionable or threatening material, however, you often do have a way to protect yourself. The easiest way to deal with this situation is to check the sender's return address, especially at the domain of the service that person is using (such as @<service>.com).

If you received the material as email, you can use AOL's forward feature to send the offensive message in email form directly to the folks who administer that service—in this case, it would be postmaster@<service name>. (Some services set up a special email address, abuse@<service name> to handle such problems.)

If the material was contained in a message posted in an Internet newsgroup, select the entire message, choose **Copy** from the **Edit** menu, and insert the message into the body of an email form, along with your own request that the problem be dealt with.

Most services have rules and regulations for their users, and they do not consider such conduct any more acceptable than you do. They will act against that member in accordance with the rules covering their service.

It's also true that some Internet-based services may only be concerned with whether the messages get through, not their content (unless it promotes illegal conduct). You should complain anyway if the message you received is especially offensive to you.

Cross-Posting

Although cross-posting the same message to different newsgroups is not a good practice, some of the messages to which you respond are already posted in more than one place, so your response will be too. AOL's newsgroup reader, at the time this book was written, was not able to eliminate multiple destinations from a message. You won't want to contribute to the newsgroup clutter, however, so try not post the same message in different newsgroups. Try to choose a newsgroup that seems most suitable to the kind of message you want to send.

How to Post a Newsgroup Message

If you are not responding to a message in a particular thread and you want to create a new topic, click the **Send New Message**

Troubleshooting: Slow postings

Help! The message I posted still hasn't shown up in the newsgroup I sent it to. What's wrong?

The Internet email and messages you send must pass through a number of computer networks before they make their way to your newsgroup or to the recipient of your message. Your message can sometimes get to the other side of the world in a matter of minutes, yet other times it takes a day or two to arrive. This is to be expected, and you should be patient and give the message some time. In a few cases, a message does get lost in cyberspace, but because the systems are reliable, that doesn't happen often.

icon at the top of a message window. This action brings up a blank message window, into which you can insert the topic and then the body of your message.

After you've finished reading the messages in your selected newsgroup and have responded to the ones that interest you, click the **Mark All Read** icon at the top of the directory of available messages. That way, you won't be presented with the same list of messages the next time you visit your newsgroup.

If you've read all the messages in a newsgroup and closed the message window, and then you decide you want to add a message of your own, follow these steps:

Adding a new message on a new subject

1. Double-click the directory listing for that newsgroup, which brings up a sequence of two messages, shown in Figures 17.14 and 17.15. You must click the **OK** button of the first message to see the second.

FIGURE 17.14

You're notified that no unread messages are available.

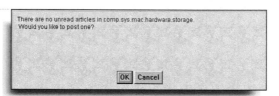

FIGURE 17.15

Decide whether you want to post a new message.

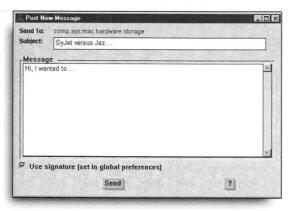

2. If you want to add a new message of your own, click the **OK** button, which brings up a standard blank Newsgroup message window.

If you decide not to add a message, click the **Cancel** button.

Offline Message Reading

You can use the same time-saving techniques you learned in Chapter 9, "Using AOL's Email," to stay abreast of your favorite newsgroups. Just schedule your Automatic AOL sessions to include newsgroup postings, and then use AOL's Offline Reading feature to include the latest messages from your favorite newsgroups as part of that session.

Choosing newsgroups for offline reading

1. Click the **Read Offline** icon in the opening Newsgroups window, which brings up the screen shown in Figure 17.16.

   The listing at the left contains all the newsgroups to which you've subscribed.

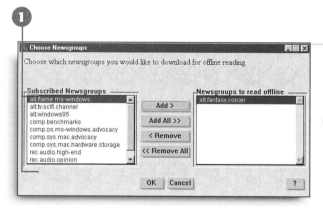

FIGURE 17.16

Add the newsgroups you select for offline reading from the list on the left.

1. This is the list of your newsgroups.

2. Click a newsgroup you want to add to highlight that selection.

3. Click the **Add** button to include your selection among the newsgroup messages to be downloaded during your Automatic AOL session.

Caution: Don't add too many

Use the Add All option with caution, otherwise you may be inundated with unread messages next time you run your Automatic AOL Session.

A better quoting option

One great advantage of replying to newsgroup messages offline is a more efficient automatic quoting feature. It works in the same fashion as your AOL email. Just select the portion of the message you want to answer, click the **Reply** button, and you see it quoted, with full Internet-style formatting, in the body of your message window. No need to mess with two side-by-side windows from which to select and quote text, as you do when you're online.

You can't turn the signature off with offline reading

The signature that you set in your newsgroup preference box is stored by AOL's host computer network. You cannot turn it off when you post a message offline. If you don't want to use a signature on every message, you may be better off not putting one in the newsgroup preference box. Instead, you may prefer to have it put in a note pad, and copy and paste it as needed into your messages.

4. To add all the newsgroups at once, click the **Add All** button.

5. To remove a newsgroup from the list specified for offline reading, click the newsgroup to select it, and then click the **Remove** button.

6. To remove all newsgroups from the offline reading list, click the **Remove All** button.

The unread messages in your selected newsgroups will be downloaded to your Personal Filing Cabinet during your Automatic AOL sessions. To find those messages, click the **My Files** icon on the AOL toolbar and choose **Offline Newsgroups** from the drop-down menu. The newsgroup messages (and regular AOL message board postings) you downloaded during your session will appear in the Incoming Postings folder.

The neat thing about this feature is that you not only can read your messages while offline, but you can respond to them as well. Your new messages will be posted in the appropriate newsgroup during your next Automatic AOL session.

To learn more about scheduling your Automatic AOL and selecting the options to transfer mail, files, and newsgroup messages, check out Chapter 9.

Decoding Newsgroup Files

In the last part of this chapter, which covers Internet mailing lists, I'll tell you how AOL's host computer can automatically decode files sent via the Internet. The process is transparent to you, so you don't have to worry about configuring your email in any special way to attach a file to it for Internet delivery.

When it comes to reading encoded newsgroup messages, you can let AOL's software do the work for you, using AOL's File Grabber feature. When you open an encoded message, or one too long for AOL's news reader to display in one piece, you get the message shown in Figure 17.17.

If you click the **Download File** or **Download Article** button, AOL's File Grabber works behind the scenes to locate all portions of the file and then retranslates the file to its original form.

You then get a dialog box (see Figure 17.18) asking where you'd like the file to be downloaded to.

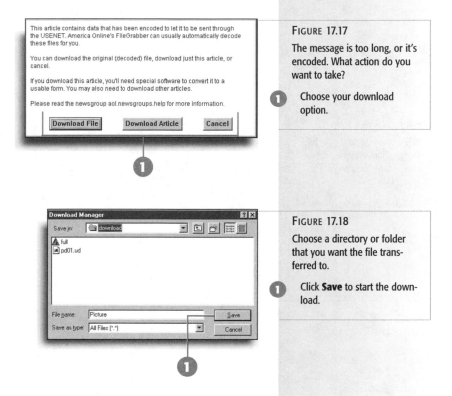

FIGURE 17.17

The message is too long, or it's encoded. What action do you want to take?

1 Choose your download option.

FIGURE 17.18

Choose a directory or folder that you want the file transferred to.

1 Click **Save** to start the download.

The remainder of the process brings up a display that's identical to the one you receive when you transfer files directly from America Online. You have the same option to Finish Later, if you'd rather not complete the download during your present session.

Updating Your Favorite Newsgroups

Literally thousands of Internet newsgroups are active at any one time. New ones are always being introduced, and others are being discontinued. When you first visit AOL's Newsgroups area, you'll find a list of several newsgroups automatically added to your list. Over time, you can choose to change or add to this listing. The Add Newsgroups icon shown on the main Newsgroups area window lists many of the popular newsgroups you'll want to add.

Because new ones are being created all the time, consult AOL's Newsgroup Reviews feature (see Figure 17.19) to get an idea which ones are best. Just click the categories that represent the subjects that interest you, and you'll find reviews of many of the most popular discussion areas.

FIGURE 17.19

AOL's own staff and your fellow members review the latest newsgroups on a regular basis.

1 Click a topic to see the list of reviews.

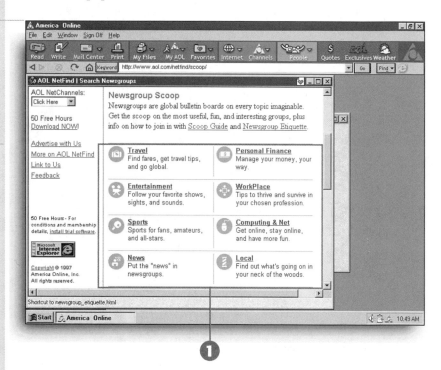

Caution: Watch out for explicit files

Graphic files on the Internet do not have to follow America Online's Terms of Service regarding nude or sexually explicit content. Be sure to examine the article's header or look at the title and purpose of a newsgroup before transferring material from that area to your computer.

How to Find Internet Mailing Lists

Keyword: Mailing Lists

So far in this chapter, I've discussed Usenet newsgroups, which are similar to AOL's own message boards. Participating is an active task. You have to log on and browse through various directories to see the messages you want. The Offline Reading feature helps somewhat, but if you're an active participant, you'll still want to check directly for new messages from time to time.

Another Internet messaging technique is also used, one that's more or less passive. This feature, *Internet mailing lists* (see Figure 17.20), consists of ongoing email discussions sent via the Internet to groups of people who share similar interests. Using regular Internet email, information is exchanged in a continuing, interactive fashion with people all around the world. The entire text of these discussions will appear regularly in your AOL mailbox. You just have to sit back and read them (but don't get carried away with subscribing to mailing lists, for reasons that will be discussed later).

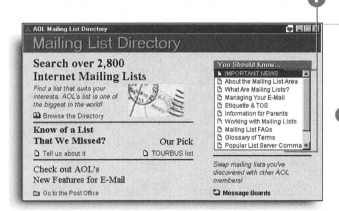

FIGURE 17.20

AOL's Internet Mailing List Directory is your introduction to a fascinating world of information and discussions.

1 Click here to find mailing lists.

Thousands of Internet mailing lists exist today, encompassing almost every topic imaginable: computer technology, American literature, philosophy, cooking, chess, motorcycling, sports, the environment, rock music, UFOs, alternative lifestyles—take your pick.

AOL's Internet Mailing List Directory has various helpful text articles containing background and instructions on using the Mailing Lists features of the Internet Connection.

To locate specific mailing lists that might appeal to your interests, click the **Browse the Directory** button. You'll access a database of mailing lists you can search by entering descriptive words (see Figure 17.21).

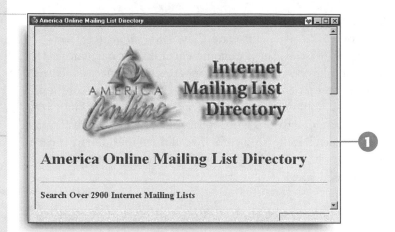

After a list of entries that matches your search description appears, click the title of the one that interests you (see Figure 17.22). You'll see a full description of the mailing list, how to subscribe, and most important, how to remove yourself from the list if you change your mind later.

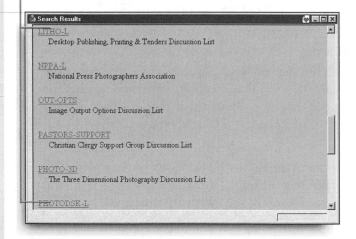

Teach Yourself: How to Join an Internet Mailing List

The description of a mailing list contains instructions on how you can subscribe to the mailing lists that interest you by using your America Online Internet email address. Follow the instructions carefully; they tend to differ slightly from list to list. Remember also to note how you can leave (or *unsubscribe* to) any lists you join, in case you change your mind later. Most of these lists generate a large amount of mail and can quickly fill your online mailbox if you don't check in regularly.

Remember, also, that these mailing lists sometimes are run not by an individual reading your request, but by a software program. The software program automates the process of establishing and maintaining these mailing lists and sending the regular mailings to subscribers. Because you are communicating with another computer and not an individual, it's important that you make your requests follow the exact directions in the mailing list subscription.

Keep these things in mind when joining a mailing list:

- Use the exact commands specified in the information about joining a mailing list to subscribe and unsubscribe (sometimes called *add* and *remove*).

- Remember that Internet email might take a couple of days to reach its destination, so be patient about getting a response. Also remember that mailings to subscribers might be sent only at infrequent intervals.

- If a mailing list is also available as a Usenet newsgroup, you might prefer to use that option. With a Usenet newsgroup, you don't have to handle unsolicited email. You can easily limit reading messages to the ones that interest you within a given time frame, and ignore messages dealing with topics you do not want to see.

You may have to confirm your subscription

It is common these days for mailing list servers to automatically generate a confirmation letter when you ask to join a specific list. You won't actually get any mailings untill you return this request. This step is being taken more and more because of occasional attempts by computer hackers to sign folks up to mailing lists they never really wanted to join. Having faced tons of unwanted email myself as a result of such annoying pranks (the wild sordid story, involving several writers and even the White House, was written up in *Time* magazine in fact), I can tell you I'd rather have the confirmation to my subscription request.

Responding to Mailing List Messages

The material you receive from a mailing list looks the same as any standard email message (see Figure 17.23). And you respond to those messages in exactly the same fashion. Generally, you will use the Reply to All feature on your mailing list email to include your comments about a particular article in a subsequent group of messages. Just using the Reply option sends your response to the individual whose message you're answering rather than to the list itself.

FIGURE 17.23

Typical email from a mailing list.

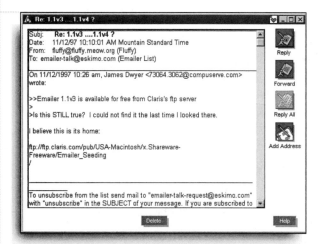

If you want to post an article to a mailing list, first consult the original instructions for that mailing list to see if any special steps are involved.

How to Leave a Mailing List

The instructions you receive when you first join a mailing list generally include online information on how to cancel, or unsubscribe to, the mailing list. If the mailing list is run by an automated list server (usually identified by the word "listserv" as part of the address), you must make your request using the exact format contained in those instructions. If the list is run by a person, you can just send a regular email request.

Caution: Change of address reminders

If you change your screen name or cancel your AOL account, be sure to unsubscribe to all your mailing lists (the mail won't be forwarded). If the list is maintained by a person, you can send whatever mail-forwarding information is appropriate. Otherwise, you'll have to resubscribe to the mailing lists from which you want to continue getting email.

What to Do if Your Mailbox Is Filled

So many fascinating mailing lists exist that you will no doubt be tempted to join a number of them. It's not uncommon to overdo it a bit, and you might find your mailbox clogged with messages still unread. Your Automatic AOL sessions can produce huge incoming mailboxes. The best advice is to be judicious about managing your mail so that you aren't overwhelmed.

Presently, your AOL online mailbox is limited to 550 items. This number includes not only the mail you have read, but also the mail you have not yet seen. The list of mail you've sent remains in your mailbox for up to 30 days; the mail you've read is deleted after up to 7 days (depending on the Mail preference you've set).

On the other hand, the mail you've received in an Automatic AOL session (or automatically saved to your Personal Filing Cabinet) remains on your computer's drive until you delete it. Mac users can also specify the amount of time before email, message board, and Usenet postings are automatically deleted as a Filing cabinet preference.

Use these common-sense tips to help you keep your mailbox down to usable proportions:

- Be sure you subscribe only to mailing lists you really want to read.

- Take note of directions on how to unsubscribe to a mailing list when you join, in case the mailing list doesn't meet your expectations or you find your mailbox getting a little too crowded.

- Check your email regularly to keep your mailbox as small as possible.

SEE ALSO

➤ *For a detailed overview of AOL's huge selection of Internet resources, see page 224*

➤ *For more information about working with AOL's own discussion boards, see page 206*

➤ *For helpful hints and tips on AOL's email feature, see page 158*

➤ *For advice on how to prepare your children for an Internet session, see page 116*

Caution: When your mailbox is filled

If the amount of unread mail exceeds 550 pieces, new email will be returned to the sender with a `Mailbox is full.` message. Consistent returned messages may result in being dropped by your favorite mailing lists. By managing your mailbox carefully, you'll avoid losing messages you might want to read.

How to find out about that mailing list again

If you've lost directions on how to subscribe or unsubscribe to a mailing list, search for it again using the search feature in AOL's Internet Mailing Lists area. The results of your search can be saved and printed for later review.

Setting Up Your Personal Web Page on AOL

18

Become a Web Publisher on AOL

Build a Web page in five minutes

Doing it via HTML

A look at AOLPress

AOL Gives You Free Online Storage Space

So far in this book, I've detailed use of AOL's Internet resources. I've shown you how to use AOL's Web browser, and how to locate sites on the World Wide Web. I've even given you a look at some of my favorite sites.

In this chapter I'll take this one step further. As an AOL member, you get 2MB of storage space in your personal FTP site for each screen name you've created for the service. You can use this space for your personal files, or to receive files from your friends and business associates. You can also use that space to become a Web publisher.

In the next section, I'll show you how AOL's Personal Publisher feature gives you a set of powerful tools to create and publish your own home page on the Web without knowing anything about HTML coding or document formatting. If you're interested in using the Web for your business, you'll also want to read Chapter 28, "AOL's WorkPlace Channel."

Teach Yourself: Using AOL's Personal Publisher to Make Your Home Page

Keywords: My Home Page or Personal Publisher

When the first Web pages were created, the folks who made those pages had to learn many commands to format the page so it would look good on your computer screen. The skill is reminiscent of what typesetters had to do in the days before desktop publishing was established on personal computers. Using a technique called *HTML* (for *Hypertext Markup Language*), commands were inserted that described the format of the page.

Although many skilled Web authors continue to use HTML to fine-tune their work, a growing number of popular programs are available that enable you to generate the pages using techniques similar to those employed in desktop publishing software. These techniques use *what-you-see-is-what-you-get* (*WYSIWYG*) methods to create your pages, without having to know a single HTML tag.

AOL's Easy Web Authoring Feature

AOL's Personal Publisher is an online Web page authoring tool that gives you a simple, but powerful tool to make your Web page on AOL (see Figure 18.1). In Chapter 8, "AOL's People Connection," I described the steps to make an online profile, which you can use to tell your fellow AOL members something about yourself. Personal Publisher takes this process one big step further. It enables you to assemble text (profile-type information and much more), pictures, and templates into a fully formatted Web page. You can then publish (make available) the page to the entire Internet, even to folks who aren't members of AOL.

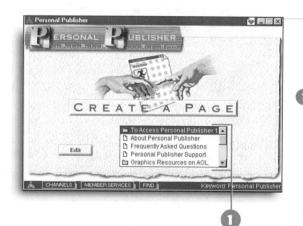

FIGURE 18.1

Create your own Web page in minutes with AOL's Personal Publisher feature.

1 Scroll through the list to see more choices.

To access Personal Publisher, click the **My AOL** icon on the toolbar and choose **Personal Publisher** from the drop-down menu. You can also use the keywords.

What Can You Get for Free?

AOL's Personal Publisher feature is a terrific starting point to becoming a Web author. All the hard stuff is under the surface.

All you have to do, as I've shown here, is fill in blanks and presto, you've got a Web page.

You do have some serious limitations, however. For one, the 2MB storage space AOL gives you can fill up rather quickly. Your basic page is text, and that doesn't take much room. When you add a few illustrations and backgrounds, however, suddenly it adds up. You can get a rough idea of how big your page will be by adding up the file size of all your added artwork, and then allow something for any templates you create with AOL's software. The actual figure is available when you visit your personal FTP site on AOL (you'll learn more on that in Chapter 15, "Using File Transfer Protocol"). As soon as you enter the site, you'll see an onscreen window showing how much space is left for you to work with.

One way to limit the size of graphics is to save them in JPEG format, with the maximum possible compression (but be aware that quality decreases as you make the file size smaller). You can also scale down the pictures, so they take less storage space, and load faster when someone accesses your page.

Past the limit of space, a limit in the look and feel exists. Personal Publisher can only go so far, giving you a picturesque member profile or the introduction to your business. If you want more sophistication, AOLPress, AOL's own no-cost Web authoring software (described later in this chapter) and a host of popular commercial products will do the job. If you want to promote your business, you may want to sign up with AOL's PrimeHost service (keyword PrimeHost).

The Basic Ingredients

You can use the information you placed in your online profile to start your Web page, but many more elements can be added. Possible elements you can add include:

- *Templates.* You can choose from AOL's basic design templates or build your page from scratch.
- *Hyperlinks.* You enter the URL of your favorite Web sites or AOL Favorite Places (or both) and they'll be added to your home page.

- *Graphics.* You can include photos and drawings (in GIF and JPEG formats). In addition to graphics you may have on hand, you can find some useful clip art by clicking the **Home Page Graphics** icon in AOL's Personal Publisher area.

- *Text.* You can write text captions for the photos and provide information about you, your family, your philosophy of life, your business, and so on. You can write about anything you think would interest AOL's members or the Internet at large, as long as you keep it in good taste (within the bounds of AOL's Terms of Service).

- *Automatic Email.* You can insert an automatic email link. When a visitor to your Web site clicks the link, it opens up an email form already addressed to you.

- *HTML Support.* If you know HTML, you can code your Web page manually and have it fully formatted. AOL's browser, at the time this was written, supported version 3.2 of the HTML command set.

Now, as promised, you'll learn how to build your first Web page in five minutes or less (probably in less time than it'll take to read the instructions in this book).

Selecting Templates

AOL's Personal Publisher area gives you some basic templates you can use to set up the basic design elements in a simple to use format (see Figure 18.2). You'll want to use the template that most describes the purpose of the page. Remember, choices you make now can easily be changed at a later time.

The following list gives a brief description of the basic templates AOL gives you. When I wrote this chapter, you had a choice of three, or no template at all. More choices will be added, however, perhaps by the time you read this book.

- **Personal.** If your Web page is designed for friends and family, this is the one to select.

- **Business.** Use this design to introduce your business to the World Wide Web.

> **Caution: Watch what you say!**
>
> You have a lot of freedom with which to make your Web site on AOL, but violating AOL's Terms of Service is not one of them. If you violate those terms (which you can view at any time via keyword **TOS**), AOL reserves the right to remove your site from public view and place a warning on your account record.

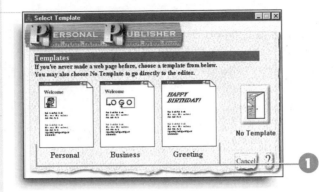

FIGURE 18.2

Choose the template design that matches your decision objective.

1 Click the template you want.

- **Greeting.** This template is useful for announcing a special event, such as a party or business meeting.
- **No Template.** This option takes you right to the editing screen (which you'll see later in this chapter), where you can construct your Web page in any order you choose.

Just double-click the template you want to get to the next editing screen.

Entering the Title and Headline

With your basic design template selected, you need to give your page a title and headline (see Figure 18.3). If you are using your Web page to sell a product or service, an eye-catching headline is important. Otherwise you can structure it in a more casual fashion.

FIGURE 18.3

Enter your title and headline, and click the Next arrow to continue.

1 Use the Tab key to go to the next text box.

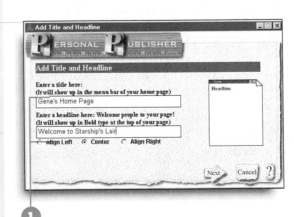

After your headline and title are chosen, you'll want to decide how the headline aligns on the page (left, center, or right), then click the **Next** button to move to the next phase.

Adding Your Background

The next design element you'll be asked to choose is the background color or texture of your page. You can choose not to have one, leave the background white and move to the next design feature, or select an image or color (see Figure 18.4). AOL gives you a choice of backgrounds, but you can also choose an art file from your computer's hard drive instead.

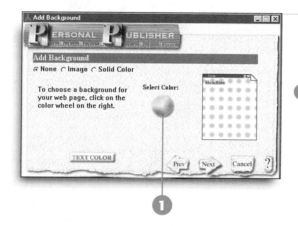

FIGURE 18.4
Double-click the background image to get a preview of how it will look on your page.

① Click the color wheel to see your choices.

Considering that the background color or artwork you select will fill the entire Web page, you'll probably want to test this a few times to see what looks best on your computer screen.

Now you can select a picture for the page itself.

Inserting Images

AOL provides a small selection of clip art to use on your Web page (see Figure 18.5). Just double-click the one you want from the scrolling list, and you'll see a preview of it in the screen in the middle.

Use the tutorial

If you reach a sticking point in your WWW page creation process, just click the **Tutorial** or **Help** icons that are sprinkled about various places of the page creation area, and you'll get additional assistance.

FIGURE 18.5

Choose some artwork from
AOL's selection, or select one
of your own.

1   Scroll through the preview
to see more of the picture.

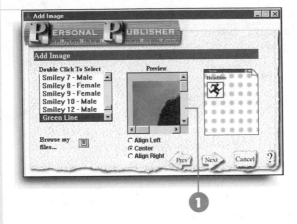

Caution: Check the copyright first

Before you include clip art from
your own collection, be sure to
examine any copyright or licensing
information that comes with it.
Double check that you can publish
that artwork on the Internet without
paying an additional fee. Otherwise,
you do not want to use it until you
get permission to do so.

If you don't like the selection offered (and it is small), no problem. You can find a huge selection of clip art in such places as
Mac or PC Graphics forums. You may even have some of your
own, already available on your computer. To add those files, just
click the **Browse My Files** icon and select the file you want to
transfer to your Web page.

Got Something to Say? Add Some Text!

You'll be ready to finish your Web page real soon now. The next
step is to enter the kind of text material you want to include (see
Figure 18.6). The options shown here serve as your introduction. More options are available (see Figure 18.7).

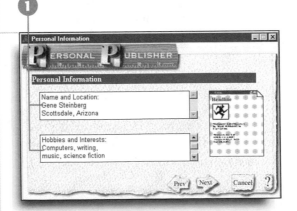

FIGURE 18.6

Your text can include
information based on your
online profile as a starting
point.

1   Use the Tab key to go to the
next text box.

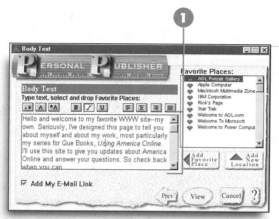

FIGURE 18.7

After your personal information is entered, you can add body text, Favorite Places links, and a link to your email address.

1 Scroll through the screen to read the entire message.

Your body text can include details about yourself, your business, your hobbies, your favorite restaurants, or even your first novel. You'll have an immense amount of freedom to customize the look and feel of this site, and the ability to change it as often as you want.

Ready to Publish?

After you've put all the pieces of your Web page together, you need to see the results of your work before you make it available to the rest of the world. Click the **View** button, to bring up the screen shown in Figure 18.8.

Scroll through each element to see if your Web page meets your expectations. If it doesn't, no problem. Just click the **Edit** button to bring up AOL's handy Editing screen (see Figure 18.9). From here you can select the design element you want to change or eliminate.

You have two ways to edit your page. The first is Add Contents, where six elements of your page can be altered. These choices include an HTML editor, where you can use true HTML codes to format your page (I'll explain this feature in more detail a little later in this chapter). In Figure 18.9, the Edit Contents section allows you to click and drag elements to refine your layout.

Check your spelling

Your Web page provides a window to your personality. To put the best face forward, spell check your text, and double-check the quality of your graphics before the page is published.

Caution: Don't make it too complicated

Just remember that the more material you have on your page, the longer it takes for it to appear on a computer screen. Large, complex backgrounds and big pictures combine to make a Web page take several minutes to appear. You may prefer to make several Web pages, and include links from one to another to reduce the time it takes for your visitors to see your home page. When you're ready, you can test your page on your PC to see how quickly it shows up.

FIGURE 18.8

This is the final step before you publish your Web page on AOL.

1 Scroll through the page to see it all.

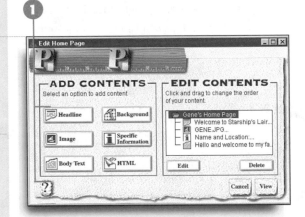

FIGURE 18.9

You can always modify your Web page here.

1 Click a label to access that function.

Check its progress

Before you publish your Web page, click the **View** icon, which appears on several screens on the Personal Publisher Edit screens, to check the progress.

When you're satisfied that your Web page meets your needs, click the **Publish** button in the viewing window. You'll see an onscreen progress bar showing the transfer of the contents of your Web page from your computer's drive to your FTP site (see Figure 18.10).

HTML—The Language of the Web

AOL's Personal Publisher and some of the newest Web authoring software hide it, but underlying all Web pages is a set of commands that identify the document's format. If you know HTML, you can enter your page's actual script instead of choosing the formatting options offered by AOL's Personal Publisher. To enter your HTML text, click the HTML icon shown earlier in the editing screen in Figure 18.9, which brings up the text entry window shown in Figure 18.11.

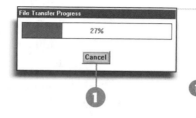

FIGURE 18.10

Your Web page is sent to AOL's servers after you click the Publish button.

1 Click **Cancel** if you change your mind.

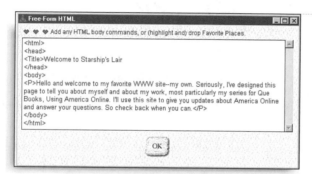

FIGURE 18.11

This is a simple Web page written in HTML.

Just as a basic example, the HTML screen consists of several basic elements that apply to all pages, a headline and body text. You'll notice that the HTML tags are entered at the beginning and end of each element of the Web page, with a slash to identify the command as the closing or end portion of that element. The meanings for the commands shown in Figure 18.10 (and some additional choices for you to consider) are

- *<html>*. This command identifies the material that follows as an HTML script.
- *<head>*. This command identifies the text that contains the title of your document.
- *<Title>*. This command identifies the actual title.
- *</head>*. This command ends the section that contains the headline text.

You can use other Web software

You don't have to use AOL's Personal Publisher feature to send a Web page to your FTP site. You can upload your own HTML-formatted document to that site and have it become accessible via AOL's Web browser.

- *<body>*. This command signifies that the text that follows contains the body text of your document.
- *<H1>*. This command identifies this text that follows as a heading. Standard HTML has six levels of heads, and the first, of course, is the largest.
- *</H1>*. This command identifies the end of the heading.
- *<P>*. This command identifies the beginning of a paragraph of body text.
- *</P>*. This command identifies the end of a paragraph of body text.
- *</body>*. This command signifies the end of the body text of your document.
- *</html>*. This command identifies the end of your document.

Some additional HTML lingo includes

- *<UL>*. An unordered list, much like the one I've used here to describe various HTML tags.
- *<LI>*. This identifies the text that follows as a bulleted list (just like this one). No end tag is needed.
- *<BLOCKQUOTE>*. This tag is used to identify quoted text.
- *<TABLE>*. This tag is used to set up a table in your HTML document.
- *<FRAMESET>*. This tag is used to set up a frame in a document. *Frames* are Web pages that consist of two or more panes (side by side), each capable of being scrolled separately, with its own scrollbars.
- *<A HREF>*. This tag is used to identify a hyperlink on your Web page.

As I said, I'm covering some basic information here just to whet your appetite. When you get the hang of it, you'll be able to extend your coding abilities to the most sophisticated types of formatting. On the other hand, with so many good Web authoring programs around to shield you of such concerns with their graphic interface, you can probably create many Web pages without ever having to confront raw HTML codes.

Check your language

Remember that the command slash is needed at the beginning of an HTML tag to close or end the format.

AOLPress: A Brief Tour of AOL's Free Web Authoring Software

Keyword: AOLPress

When you're ready to spread your wings on Web page creation, AOL has one solution already online, and it won't cost you anything (except for the time it takes to download the file). It's AOLPress, a program offered by AOL, via the keyword AOLPress (see Figure 18.12). It's a WYSIWYG editor, working in the same fashion as your word processing or desktop publishing software. You can style your Web pages via simple formatting menus without having to learn HTML. Don't attribute price to value in this case. AOLPress is a highly sophisticated program, with lots of power to do some nice things to a Web page when you get the hang of it.

FIGURE 18.12

Use AOLPress to build sophisticated Web pages in the smallest amount of time.

1 Scroll through the list to see more choices.

Getting Started with AOLPress

AOLPress is available for users of both the Mac OS and Windows 95. It installs in the same manner as your other software. After you download AOLPress, double-click the **Setup** (or installer) icon to begin the installation process. Just follow a few onscreen prompts, and the program will be ready to go in minutes.

AOL's Web hosting service

You'll notice in Figure 18.12 that AOLPress is offered by AOL's PrimeHost service. PrimeHost is a full-featured Web hosting service for businesses, which is more fully explained in Chapter 28. Read that chapter if you want to explore commercial opportunities on the Internet.

After you've installed AOLPress, double-click the program icon to get it running. You'll see a screen similar to that shown in Figure 18.13.

FIGURE 18.13

The opening screen of AOLPress gives you basic tutorial information on getting the program working for you.

1 Click a title to access that information.

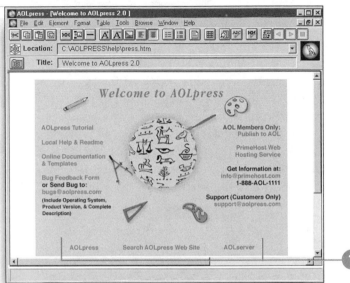

The first steps to prepare your Web page in AOLPress

1. To make your first Web page, open the **File** menu and choose **New**, and then **New Page**, which brings up a screen similar to the one shown in Figure 18.14.

2. Enter your headline. To format your headline, select it and open the **Format** menu. Choose **Heading**, and then choose **Hdg 1**.

3. Make your body text into a list. Just select it and open the **Format** menu. Choose **List**, and then **Bulleted List**. The results are shown in Figure 18.15.

4. Add Web links to your favorite sites. Then select the links, open the **Element** menu and choose **Link** to format them correctly.

5. To receive email about your Web page, add your own email link. Enter it on your page, select it, and choose **Email Link** from the **Element** menu. When a visitor to your Web page clicks the link, they'll see a blank email window already addressed to you.

6. Give your page sparkle and color by formatting it with colors and artwork. Just choose **Page Attributes** from the **Format** menu to bring up the first part of the color selection menus (see Figure 18.16).

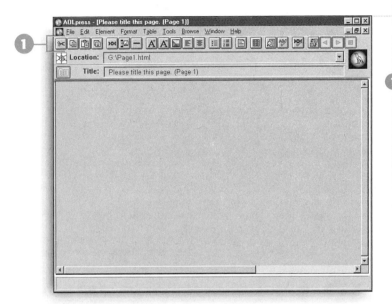

FIGURE **18.14**

A blank Web page ready to be built.

1 Access some features via the button bar.

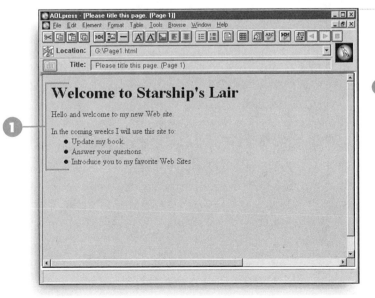

FIGURE **18.15**

AOLPress helps you make a bulleted list without knowing anything about HTML.

1 Your page is shown fully formatted.

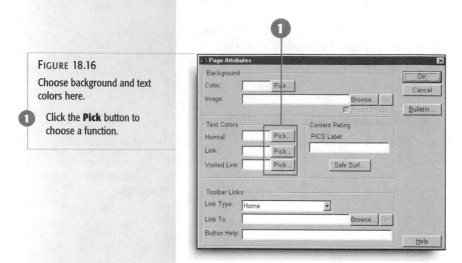

FIGURE 18.16

Choose background and text colors here.

1 Click the **Pick** button to choose a function.

Find it fast on AOL

AOL's software file search feature (keyword `File Search`) will yield many more treasures for HTML authoring. Just use the search phrase "HTML editor" and you'll see many choices. Windows users should try out such programs as HotDogPro (it's shareware, by the way).

7. Save your document. Choose **Save As** from the **File** menu to make a copy of your document. Choose a directory on your hard drive for these pages. Save frequently, so you won't lose any work in the event of a system crash.

8. Publish your page. Upload it directly to your MyPlace FTP site to make it accessible via the Internet. I explain more about using your personal FTP site in Chapter 15.

AOLPress is just one of many Web authoring programs available. These programs work by converting what looks like a regular desktop publishing or word processing document to include HTML instructions, so they can be translated into a page on the World Wide Web.

Some Web Authoring Advice

Having the right tool is only part of the equation. As you can see from the previous sections, making a Web page can take minutes, whether you use AOL's Personal Publisher feature, or a sophisticated Web authoring program, such as AOLPress.

If you want to take the plunge and get involved in more sophisticated Web page creation, consider the following:

- *Appearance*. The look is half the battle. Spend a little time seeing how other WWW pages are organized, so you can use them as a guidepost as to what looks good to you.

- *Easy navigation*. You will be tempted to put lots of graphics and URL links on your page. The best thing to do is keep it simple and label everything clearly, so the first-time visitor can see it all clearly without waiting a long time for the pictures to appear on the screen. If you must add lots of artwork, create links to other pages, and use part of your home page as a sort of table of contents to access the other pages.

- *Keep text short and sweet*. No sense writing your first novel on a WWW page. Be brief and to the point, and consider that visitors to your page will be viewing everything on a computer screen where too much text may strain the eyes. If you want to express your thoughts in a more complex and lengthy fashion, you can always attach or link a file to your WWW page, so your visitors can download the file and read it at their leisure. Don't forget to spell check your document before it's uploaded to AOL.

- *Practice, practice, practice*. Web authoring is no different from other artistic skills. Read as much as you can about the subject, and practice as much as you can to hone your skills. Don't be afraid to be a little daring, and don't expect your first effort to be a finished product. You'll probably want to change things over and over again until your project meets your satisfaction.

If you reach some sticking points in your Web authoring, don't hesitate to visit AOL's Desktop & Web Publishing forums in the Computing channel (there's a Mac and Windows version) for some assistance.

How to Find AOL Member Home Pages

To view the page you've created for yourself, or access one belonging to another member, use this URL:

```
http://members.aol.com/<screen name>.html
```

If you're not sure whether a member has such a page, use this URL: `http://members.aol.com/`. A document window appears in which you can enter the screen name of the person whose page you're trying to find.

For Further Reading

This chapter only covered the basics of the World Wide Web, including a history of the Web and a tutorial on how to use AOL's Mac and Windows browsers. No doubt you'll want to read about this facinating subject. Perhaps you'll want to learn more about creating your own Web page.

I can highly recommend three resources for this information, *Special Edition Using the Internet, 4th Edition*; *Special Edition Using the World Wide Web*; and *Creating Your Own Web Pages on America Online*. They're all from Que Corporation and available from your favorite bookseller. The first book provides a well-written introduction to the Web, and lists some popular sites you'll want to examine further (you'll also notice a chapter on online services that I wrote for the current edition). If you desire additional information, the second book provides complete background details on every imaginable Web-related subject and easy, step-by-step instructions to help you master just about every nuance of Web technique and terminology. You'll begin with basic HTML skills (extending far beyond the page or two I've devoted to the subject here) and proceed to advanced formatting to provide the best look with the latest browser software. The third book will extend the basic skills you've learned here to new heights.

SEE ALSO

➤ *For a basic overview of the history of the Internet and AOL's Internet Connection, see page 225*

➤ *To discover how to have a one-on-one chat with fellow Net surfers, see page 263*

➤ *To download software from Internet FTP sites, see page 277*

Troubleshooting: Different browsers give different looks

Help! When my friend sees my Web page on Netscape, it looks different from the way I made it. What's wrong–how do I fix this?

Web authoring is not yet as precise as traditional typesetting and printing (although the technology is getting better). Each Web browser may interpret pages differently, so what looks one way on AOL's browser, which is based on Microsoft's Internet Explorer, is apt to look somewhat different with Netscape. Also, different versions of a browser may or may not support certain HTML tags in the same way. If you're using your Web site for business or artistic reasons, view it with several browsers, so you can edit the pages for the best possible overall appearance.

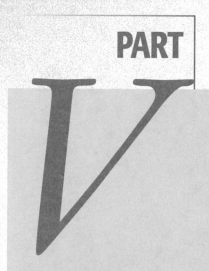

PART

V

A Wealth of Information:
AOL's Channels

AOL's Entertainment and Games Channels

AOL's popular Entertainment channel

Become a critic on America Online

AOL's Games channel

The Entertainment Channel

America Online has a large, active channel devoted strictly to entertainment, which is the focus of this chapter. First I'll describe the vast online resources for information about television, radio, and movies. Then we'll explore AOL's popular Games channel where you can learn about your favorites, or participate in AOL's own roster of exciting games. Wherever your interests lie, America Online has a place where you can find the entertainment information you seek.

Exploring the Entertainment Channel

Keyword: Entertainment

To begin the search for entertainment-related information, look at America Online's Entertainment area. To access this area, use the keyword Entertainment or click the handy icon in AOL's Main Menu. The directory window shows just a few of the areas you visit in this chapter (see Figure 19.1). During your online visits, you will discover many more locations that provide not only information but also an opportunity to participate in discussions on a host of related subjects; you can even post your own TV and movie reviews.

You'll learn about many features in the Entertainment channel throughout this chapter. Because the under construction sign is normal at AOL, expect new features to be added regularly to America Online's resource roster and expect the feature set to change often. Take a look at some of the features.

- **Entertainment Spotlight.** Each day, AOL's Entertainment channel offers the latest entertainment news headlines and spotlights movies, TV shows, and your favorite stars.

- **Departments.** Each show business category gets its own forum. The Books category that is shown in Figure 19.2, includes features on the best-sellers list—I'll be looking for this book to appear there—plus features on your favorite authors.

The fastest route from here to there

A quick shortcut to your favorite area is a keyword. Just press Ctrl+K (or ⌘-K for Macs), enter the name of the area you want to visit (the keyword), and click OK. Then you're on your way. The keywords you need to find the features described in this chapter are indicated at the beginning of each section.

Printing AOL text is easy

As explained in Appendix B, "Setting Up AOL's Software," you can save and print any text document you see on America Online, using the appropriate commands from the **File** menu.

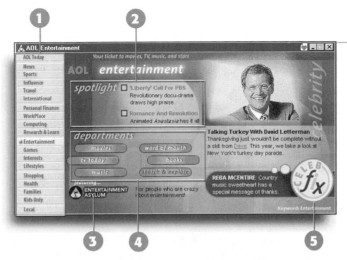

FIGURE 19.1

The Entertainment channel is America Online's gateway to many information resources for TV, radio, music, and the movies.

1 Click here to call up another channel.

2 Daily entertainment spotlight

3 Explore the Entertainment Asylum

4 Entertainment channel departments

5 Your daily Celeb Fix

- **Entertainment Asylum.** Each day, AOL's Entertainment channel gathers a set of feature stories and links to popular online features. It's unpredictable and lots of fun to check out, which is why it's called an Asylum (see Figure 19.3).

FIGURE 19.2

One of the most popular areas of AOL's Entertainment channel.

1 Learn about all the new books here.

- **Celebrity Fix.** You can learn the latest gossip about your favorite stars here (see Figure 19.4). You'll be able to consult AOL's news sources, and some of your favorite entertainment magazines and Web sites.

FIGURE 19.3

If you can't stay away from the hottest show-biz news, check this area.

1 Some entertainment news is really, really unusual.

FIGURE 19.4

Learn the latest about your favorite entertainers.

1 Learn what the stars are doing.

Teach Yourself: Finding Entertainment Resources

In the next few pages, I'll cover a broad section of online forums devoted to entertainment. Virtually all of them are available direct from the Entertainment channel, but many have their own keywords. If you want to return to any of the forums discussed in the following sections, you should add them to your Favorite Places roster. You may do so by clicking the little heart-shaped icon on the AOL toolbar.

Online Music Resources

Keyword: Music

AOL's Music department is typical of the way many AOL forums are organized; it represents a gateway to other forums with music-related information (see Figure 19.5). You'll be able to access areas run by *Entertainment Weekly* magazine, MTV, *Spin* magazine, and more.

FIGURE 19.5

Many of America Online's music forums can be reached courtesy of this part of AOL's Entertainment channel.

1 Music-related news is always current on AOL.

Visiting TV Today

Keyword: TV

AOL's TV Today information area provides a quick link with many of the popular TV networks, and information about upcoming programs (see Figure 19.6). Before you decide what you want to watch or tape, America Online gives you a chance to preview what's coming up on the tube.

Find more with those handy drop-down menus

Many AOL forums, such as the Movies, Music, and TV Today departments, have a drop-down menu that gives you quick access to additional features.

FIGURE 19.6

You'll want to visit AOL's TV forums often.

1 Find online forums devoted to your favorite television programs.

Getting all your files at once

You can use your AOL software's Download Manager to queue up files you want to download from various libraries throughout AOL. First, select the files you want using the Download Later feature. When you log off, you can download all the files in one continuous operation.

Because additional networks are always being added to AOL's roster, the directory window you see in this book is apt to change from time to time, with more and more broadcast entertainment forums being added as months go by. If you prefer to listen rather than watch, no problem. AOL has a radio forum too, at keyword Radio.

Visiting the Movies Forums

Keyword: Movies

One of my favorite parts of AOL's Entertainment channel is the Movies section. You can access it via the keyword Movies, or by choosing Movies on the left side of the Entertainment channel screen. Either action brings up the screen shown in Figure 19.7; it changes on occasion as new areas are added to AOL's sprawling online city.

FIGURE 19.7

Just some of the forums featured in AOL's Movies department.

1 The newest flicks get special forums on AOL.

What the Critics Have to Say

Keyword: Critics

Like most of you, before I buy a book, see a movie, or even rent a videotape, I want to know what the reviewers have to say about it. America Online's Critics Inc. is a compendium of thousands of reviews and discussions about the entire spectrum of the world of entertainment (see Figure 19.8).

FIGURE 19.8

FIGURE 19.8
The Critics' Choice area is where you can read what the critics say, and become one yourself if it suits you.

1 Post your own book and movie reviews.

You can find reviews of your favorite movies, concerts, television shows, books, and even video games in the Critic's Choice area.

Playing Online Games

Keyword: Games

You can really get involved in this online channel. AOL has a number of games-related forums you can access through the Games channel. Rather than discussing these in detail, the illustration in Figure 19.9 serves as a brief guide.

Take a look at some of the Games channel features in more detail. You'll find lots more during your online visits.

- **Games Insider.** Learn about featured games and special offers in this area.

- **Games Guide.** Check the bill of fare here. You'll discover the games you can play on AOL, and the difference between free games and premium ones (other than the price).

- **Game Shows Online.** Discover online sources for some of your favorite interactive games (see Figure 19.10). They start with Trivial Pursuit and continue on to many other fun-filled selections.

What's that icon stand for?

If you don't know what an AOL forum icon (or toolbar icon) means, just hold the mouse cursor above it. In a second or two, you'll see a label on the screen showing what the icon represents (this is mostly a Windows feature).

FIGURE 19.9

Many of America Online's popular games-related forums can be accessed via the AOL Games channel.

1 Click here to bring up another AOL channel.

2 Check out the Games Insider.

3 Learn the basics about your favorite games.

4 AOL's Games Guide

5 Join Game Shows online.

6 WorldPlay, AOL's premium games area

- **Games Central.** Learn the secrets about your favorite games, the little hints and tricks that you don't find in the manual.

- **Video Games.** Learn more about all your favorite games (see Figure 19.11), from Diddy Kong Racing to the classic games you've played for years.

FIGURE 19.10

Lots of online gaming areas can be found here.

1 Join in on an online game.

- **Computer Games.** Mac or PC? You'll find information about the popular computer games here. You can also download demos and shareware programs.

- **Games Store.** AOL has a well-stocked online store containing your favorites at competitive prices. You'll learn more about online shopping in Chapter 30, "Secrets of AOL's Shopping Channel."

FIGURE 19.11

Check out your favorite video game systems here—Nintendo, Sega Genesis, Sony PlayStation, and more.

❶ Find the secret clues to master your favorite video game.

- **Newsstand.** Your favorite magazines can be found on AOL, or by clicking a link to the World Wide Web.

- **Search & Explore.** If you can't find the feature you want among the offers you've seen so far, you can probably seek them out using AOL's powerful search engines.

SEE ALSO

➤ *To learn how to participate in virtual sporting events, see page 368*

➤ *To learn how to find your favorite magazines online, see page 402*

Caution: Not all online games are free

Some of AOL's online games are part of its Premium Games service. If you participate in one of those games, you'll pay an hourly surcharge for your AOL service (it was $1.99 per hour when this book was written). Although you should see an onscreen prompt if you enter an area where extra cost services are involved, it's easy to dismiss a warning prompt by mistake if you're in a hurry. You can find out more about these special services by using the keyword Premium.

AOL's Influence, Interests, Lifestyles, and Health Channels

AOL's channels devoted to lifestyles and special interests

Finding members who share your interests

AOL's news and entertainment discussion areas

Entertainment on AOL

What would you like to do on AOL? Get the real skinny about world events or the doings of your favorite entertainers? Explore the stars, upgrade your stereo, look up your family history, or debate with other AOL members about everything from computing platforms to the news of the day? Or join a community that shares your religious beliefs? Well, America Online offers all these opportunities and much more in the online channels I'll cover in this chapter.

When I sat down to write this chapter, I spent many, many hours exploring all the areas on America Online that cover lifestyles, hobbies, and special interests. Some of these places were discussed in Chapter 19, "AOL's Entertainment and Games Channels." You learn even more in this chapter, and you'll finish your tour of lifestyle information resources in Chapter 24, "Visiting the News Channel."

I soon realized that my survey could only scratch the surface. There were hundreds of resources to check, and many more are being added to AOL each week. This chapter just touches on the highlights.

AOL keywords get you there fast

If you can't find the specific forum that interests you on America Online, try locating it with a keyword. Most keywords either contain the name of an area or its subject, so if you don't know which keyword is correct, don't hesitate to try a few out. Suppose, for example, that you want to learn more about upgrading your stereo. Type the keyword **Stereo** and guess what? It takes you directly to the *Stereo Review* magazine forum on America Online. For a choice selection of popular AOL keywords, read Appendix C, "AOL's Most Popular Keywords."

The Influence Channel

Keyword: Influence

To say there's an information explosion is an understatement. Even the explosion seems to be exploding. So much information exists, you hardly know where to start. Do you want to learn the real story behind the headlines? Do you want to explore the latest trends in show business and fashion? Just what are your favorite stars *really* up to? You can discover information about this and lots more in AOL's Influence channel (see Figure 20.1).

Let's explore some of the Influence channel's departments in more detail.

- **Seen & Heard.** Do you want to know the truth behind all that gossip? The Seen & Heard forums give you the inside scoop (see Figure 20.2).

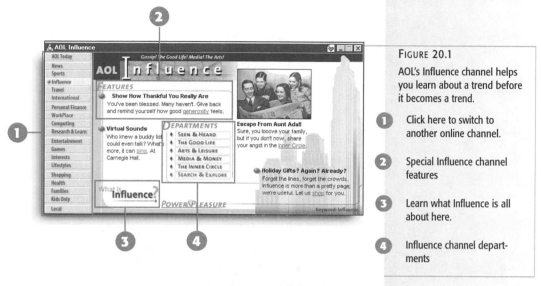

FIGURE 20.1

AOL's Influence channel helps you learn about a trend before it becomes a trend.

1. Click here to switch to another online channel.

2. Special Influence channel features

3. Learn what Influence is all about here.

4. Influence channel departments

FIGURE 20.2

Check out the latest inside reports from columnists such as Liz Smith and others.

1. Click the drop-down menu to bring up an additional list of online columns.

- **The Good Life.** Learn about fine dining, fashion, traveling to the "in" spots around the globe, and more.

- **Arts & Leisure.** Learn about the newest Broadway play and other cultural events, best-selling books, museum exhibits, and other interesting happenings.

- **Media & Money.** Learn what the movers and shakers of the media are doing. Explore such popular online financial forums as the Motley Fool and *Business Week* magazine.

- **The Inner Circle.** This is your place to shine. Express your views in message boards and in online chats. Don't forget to subscribe to the channel's popular newsletter. Just click the

Some forums are in more than one channel

As you learn your way around AOL, you'll discover that some forums are found in more than one channel. For example, you'll locate the Motley Fool area not only in AOL's Influence channel but in the Personal Finance channel too. Others turn up in such places as the Entertainment and News channels.

Send button onscreen announcing the newsletter and it'll turn up in your AOL email box regularly.

- **Search & Explore.** You'll find this feature in just about every AOL channel. It brings up AOL's powerful database search engine, where you can quickly locate the features or information you need.

AOL's Lifestyles Channel

Keyword: Lifestyles

Figure 20.3 introduces you to the Lifestyles main window, which you can find by typing the keyword Lifestyles, or by clicking the icon in the Main Menu. As you can see, the features you can call up from this point are numerous, diverse, and intriguing.

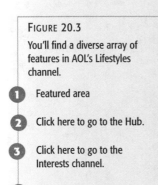

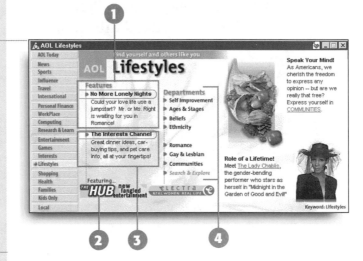

FIGURE 20.3

You'll find a diverse array of features in AOL's Lifestyles channel.

1. Featured area

2. Click here to go to the Hub.

3. Click here to go to the Interests channel.

4. Lifestyles channel departments

Touring the Channel

All your Lifestyles channel resources are as easily accessed as other online spots. A few of the areas you'll want to explore further are described in the following list.

- **Self Improvement.** You can learn how to better cope with personal problems or deal with issues that help you live a better life.

- **Ages & Stages.** Visit special forums catering to your age group, from kids and teens to seniors.

- **Beliefs.** Whatever your religious conviction, AOL probably has an area devoted to it.

- **Ethnicity.** Explore AOL forums that cater to specific ethnic categories or multicultural communities.

- **Women's Network.** Whether you work at home or at an office, or try to juggle both, you'll find valuable information here (see Figure 20.4). Special sections are devoted to relationships, family issues, home computing, and more.

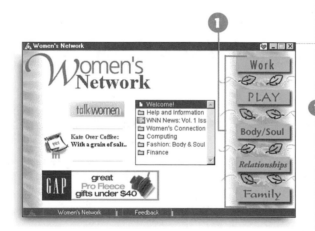

FIGURE 20.4

Women's issues are the focus of this online area.

1   Click one of the fancy icons to bring up more selections.

- **Romance.** Learn more about finding the right mate for you. You can visit such areas as AOL's Astromates, Love@AOL, and Romance forums.

- **Gay & Lesbian.** AOL's Gay & Lesbian forums are among the most popular on the service. A number of forums are covered in this area.

- **People & Communities.** AOL members have set up their own online communities to interact with other online visitors who share similar interests (see Figure 20.5). You'll find forums devoted to specific beliefs, senior citizens, baby boomers, and more.

FIGURE 20.5

AOL members have formed their own special online communities. Come and join the one that matches your interest.

1 Click the drop-down menu to see more features.

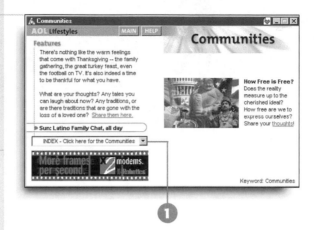

Scroll down for more

The directories shown in many forum listings can be scrolled; they generally contain many more features than those shown in the illustrations included in this book. Also, new forums are regularly added to the roster.

Exploring AOL's Interests Channel

Keyword: Interests

Your interests may be recreational or professional, but it doesn't make a difference on AOL, where you'll definitely find a hobby or club forum to interest you. Type the AOL keyword Interests (or just choose this channel from AOL's Main Menu) and see what's available (see Figure 20.6).

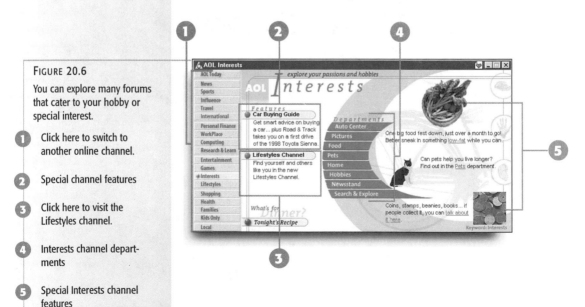

FIGURE 20.6

You can explore many forums that cater to your hobby or special interest.

1 Click here to switch to another online channel.

2 Special channel features

3 Click here to visit the Lifestyles channel.

4 Interests channel departments

5 Special Interests channel features

Examine some of the popular Interests channel features:

- **Auto Center.** Discover ways to make your car run better or get a good deal on your next vehicle. You'll also visit AOL forums run by the editors of *Car & Driver* and *Road & Track* magazines.

- **Pictures.** AOL's photography forums help you take better pictures, either with film or with the new generation of digital cameras. You'll also find a quick link to the AOL Portrait Gallery.

- **Pets.** Learn the secrets about proper pet care here. That includes getting that cute little puppy to sit on command (well at least you can try).

- **Home.** Well, it's really not all that hard to replace the washer on your faucet. At least you'll learn how in one of AOL's home-related forums. Sections are also devoted to gardening, crafts, and home improvement issues.

- **Hobbies.** Are you interested in exploring the stars, buying antiques, bird watching, cooking, scuba diving, photography, writing? You'll find forums covering these interests and more in AOL's Hobby Central (see Figure 20.7)

FIGURE 20.7

AOL's Hobby Central runs the gamut from amateur radio to sewing and knitting.

1 Scroll through the list box to see the full list of hobby-related forums.

- **Newsstand.** AOL's popular newsstand area features links to many of your favorite publications. You'll even be able to check out the latest edition before it hits your corner stand.

SEE ALSO
➤ *To learn more about AOL's People Connection, see page 135*
➤ *To learn more about the News Channel, see page 402*

Visiting the Health Channel

Keyword: Health

Whether you are a health-care professional or are just seeking the route to better health and a longer, more productive life, the Health channel is a place you might want to visit often.

As you can see in Figure 20.8, this channel is a gateway to a huge amount of information on all sorts of health-related issues. It's not intended to replace a regular visit to your family physician; it's designed to give you a better range of knowledge about the issues that are most important to you.

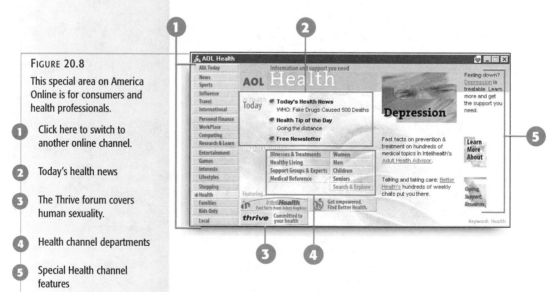

FIGURE 20.8

This special area on America Online is for consumers and health professionals.

1. Click here to switch to another online channel.

2. Today's health news

3. The Thrive forum covers human sexuality.

4. Health channel departments

5. Special Health channel features

You'll find many handy health-related resources in this area. Daily updates are given on research not only on common illnesses, but on such life-threatening ailments as AIDS. The information you receive when you search this area will help you interact in a more precise manner with your doctor. The forum is also a great resource for information on the latest findings in various health-related fields.

Let's take a brief look at some of the Health channel's departments:

- **Illnesses & Treatments.** Although not meant to replace your doctor, this area gives you up-to-date information on common and not-so-common conditions and treatments.

- **Healthy Living.** Discover how the right combination of diet and exercise can make your life more fun. You'll also find areas here devoted to weight control, parenting, relationships, and other important subjects.

- **Support Groups & Experts.** If you have a specific medical condition or emotional problem to consider, you'll be pleased to know AOL has many support groups online to help you through a crisis, or refer you to local help when necessary (see Figure 20.9).

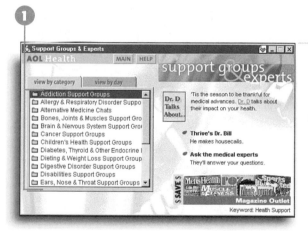

FIGURE 20.9
Some of the online support groups on hand to help you when the need arises are listed.

1 Get a helping hand online when you need to deal with a crisis.

- **Medical Reference.** AOL can sometimes be thought of as one huge information library. Access to many reference works and links to a number of health-related organizations are available.

- **Women, Men, Children, Seniors.** These areas cover health issues related to specific age and gender categories and how to deal with them.

SEE ALSO
➤ *To learn more about the Research & Learn Channel, see page 390*

AOL's Sports Channel

AOL's Sports channel has the latest from the world of sports

Behind the scenes information

Play games online

Sports News

Sports news isn't just confined to that section in the middle of the daily newspaper that many of us read first.

When an athlete gets into legal trouble (such as a certain ex-football star we all know about) or an entire league goes on strike, you can bet it'll be front page news. Let's not forget the impact of the Super Bowl or a world championship boxing match.

For the sake of this chapter, however, let's consider sports as less of a serious news item and more of something to enjoy—or something in which you might want to participate.

Visiting AOL's Sports Channel

Keyword: Sports

If you played Little League sports when you were a child, have children interested in sporting activities, watch sports events regularly on television, or have been known to attend a game or two, you might want to visit America Online's virtual sports page. To do so, choose the Sports channel icon from AOL's Main Menu window to display the Sports screen shown in Figure 21.1.

Take a closer look at the AOL Sports channel and see what's available:

- **Scoreboard.** Learn how your teams and athletes fared, and see all the stats so that you can compare their performance.

- **Top Stories.** What's happening in the world of sports. Check the details from the major wire services, TV networks, and sports magazines here.

- **The Grandstand.** Discuss sports with your online friends or participate in AOL's fantasy leagues. You can assemble your own team and pit them against other online teams, all without leaving the comfort of your home or office and your PC. I'll discuss this feature in more detail later in this chapter.

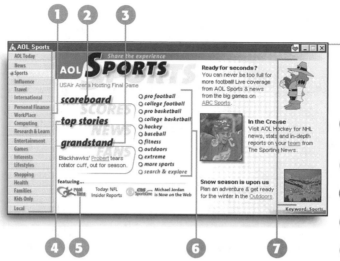

FIGURE 21.1

Whatever your favorite sport, you'll find information about it on America Online.

1   Click here to go to another AOL channel.

2   AOL's scoreboard.

3   Visit AOL's Grandstand.

4   The latest news and scores

5   Explore AOL's Real Fans forums.

6   Choose your favorite sport from this list.

7   Special featured attractions.

- **AOL's Real Fans.** If you're truly dedicated to sports, you'll find lots of inside information in this special forum (see Figure 21.2). You'll get the latest scoop, and you'll be able to share information with fellow members in this forum's chat and message area.

FIGURE 21.2

The Real Fans Sports Network gives you the top news and inside information that you can't find elsewhere.

1   Click the **Go** button to learn more about this forum.

- **Choose a Sport.** AOL's Sports channel supports all the popular sporting activities. You see virtually a complete forum for each.

- **Extreme.** This forum (see Figure 21.3) is devoted to activities in which you can participate, such as mountain biking, skiing, and scuba diving. You'll discover where to buy the gear you need, and learn how to perform better at any of these exciting activities.

FIGURE 21.3

Where the action is hot and heavy—AOL's Extreme sports forum.

1 Click the drop-down menu for more features.

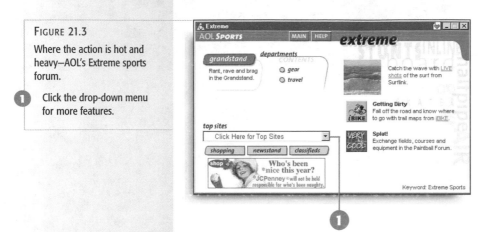

- **Search & Explore.** If you can't find a specific forum devoted to your favorite sports activity, check this area and call on AOL's powerful database search tools to locate the information you want.

Visiting AOL Sports Internet Center

Keyword: Sports IC

When you take the giant leap from AOL's own Sports channel to the worldwide Internet, you'll find that AOL reaches out to the Internet behind the scenes, so you only have to be concerned with the sort of information source for which you're looking. The roster of Internet-based sporting information resources is huge and growing daily. Click the **Internet** button to get to the Internet Center as shown in Figure 21.4.

The AOL Sports Internet Center is not only a collection of popular Web sites, it's a whole lot more:

- **Top Web Sites.** Click this icon for an ever-changing selection of sports-related Internet sites.

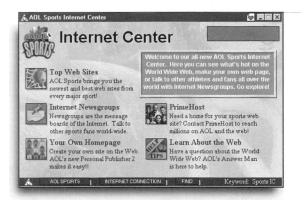

FIGURE 21.4
Sporting information from
Internet-based resources is just
a click away from America
Online's friendly interface.

- **Internet Newsgroups.** It's wild and wacky, and it's hot and heavy. Discuss sports with folks from all over the world in a newsgroup.

- **Your Own Homepage.** You can create your own personal Web site on AOL in just five minutes.

- **PrimeHost.** AOL can help you set up your own commercial Web site. You'll find out how when you click the PrimeHost icon located in various forums on AOL.

- **Learn About the Web.** First, you'll want to read Part III of this book, "AOL as an Internet Service Provider," of course, and if you have further questions, just call on AOL's Answer Man.

SEE ALSO

➤ *Joining newsgroups and mailing lists, see page 295*
➤ *Publishing on the Web, see page 328*

Taking a Seat in the Grandstand

Keyword: Grandstand

The Grandstand (see Figure 21.5) is where all you sports lovers can discuss the latest news about your favorite games, report on how your favorite teams fared the night before, and participate in online conferences with other fans. It is the entrance to America Online's sports stadium. The biggest attraction of this forum, however, is the participation of sports fans, a place where you can get involved and post your own messages about the happenings on or off the field, or the court, or the rink, and so on.

FIGURE 21.5

Take your seat in the Grandstand to enjoy your favorite sport.

1 Scroll through the list box to see more features.

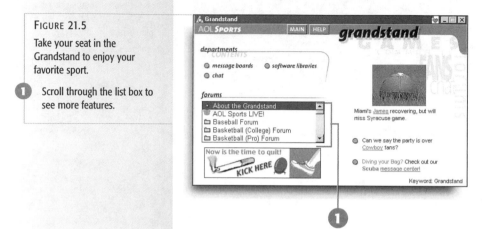

Teach Yourself: Play Fantasy Sports Online

Keyword: GFBase

If you've ever watched a sporting event and felt you could manage a team better than the pros, here's your chance to prove it. Check out one of AOL's Fantasy Leagues.

Fantasy Leagues are what the title implies. You can participate in your own sports league in cyberspace. To give you an idea of how it works, let's explore Grandstand Fantasy Baseball. You'll find this area (shown in Figure 21.6) by clicking the reference in the Grandstand list box or via the keyword GFBase. A league exists for many of your favorite sports. You can have a wrestling match without ever breaking a sweat and participate in an auto race without ever getting in a car.

Let's see how you can participate in your own Fantasy sports events:

- **Sign up to Play.** Click this icon in the Fantasy Baseball window to bring up the screen shown in Figure 21.7. To start, click a few screens and enter the information about

Caution: It's not free!

Participation in the Grandstand's Fantasy Leagues area is an extra-cost item. For information on the modest charges and how to participate, please check the information text in the various Fantasy Leagues forum areas.

your new team. Because there's an extra charge for this service, you'll also have to give the proper billing information.

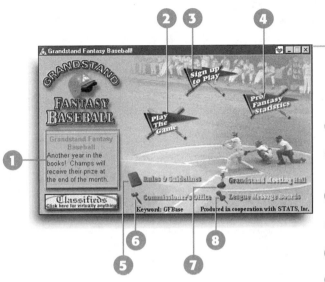

FIGURE 21.6

From baseball to auto racing, let your imagination be your guide.

1. Click here to learn more.

2. Play the game by clicking here.

3. Sign up to play here.

4. Pro/Fantasy Statistics.

5. Learn the rules here.

6. Get help from the Commissioner's Office

7. Meet other team owners here.

8. Talk about league matters here.

- **Play The Game.** Click this icon in the Fantasy Baseball
  window and the screen shown in Figure 21.8 appears. You
  can set up your team, trade players with other teams, and
  keep tabs on how your team is doing. You can choose players
  from a roster of real-life athletes, and the results you see
  with your team will be based on the performance of these
  players in real life.

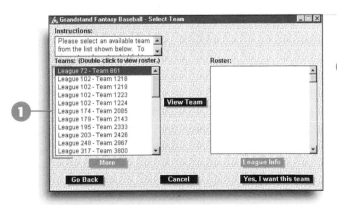

FIGURE 21.7

Set up your fantasy team here.

1. Click a team to see the players list.

FIGURE 21.8

Now it's time to pit your skills against other AOL team owners.

1 You get additional help and advice when you click the **Message Boards** icon.

- **Pro/Fantasy Statistics.** How does your team stack up in the fantasy league? Learn how the teams are performing by clicking here.

- **Rules & Guidelines.** As with professional sports, a set of rules and regulations exists that you need to follow to play in this league. Learn about them here.

- **Grandstand Meeting Hall.** Have an online conference with your fellow team owners. Share thoughts, debate the issues, and have a good time.

- **Commissioner's Office.** Well, someone has to be in charge, and here you can consult with league management about your needs and resolve problems with your players and other teams.

- **League Message Boards.** Share information with fellow team owners and other interested folks.

Are you ready to run your own team? After checking out this online area, you just might be. It's a favorite of thousands of AOL members. Even if you just want to keep tabs on how your fellow members are doing with their teams, it'll be a fascinating experience.

SEE ALSO

➤ *To learn how to visit new channels, see page 402*

AOL's International Channel

AOL Spreads Its Wings

When I first joined America Online, it was strictly a U.S.-only service. Hence the first word, *America*. Although users around the world could log on via local access numbers, the service was strictly U.S. oriented. This is a situation that has rapidly changed, because the online world knows no boundaries of city, state, or country. Anyone, anywhere in the world with access to a computer and a modem can stay in touch.

America Online formed partnerships with a number of communications companies around the world to forge the building blocks for a worldwide service. The next few pages take a brief look at AOL from the viewpoint of its growing roster of overseas members, and you learn how you can communicate with your fellow AOL members around the world.

It All Starts with the International Channel

Keyword: International

AOL's International channel (see Figure 22.1) brings together the folks who have joined AOL's new services in Canada, France, Germany, Japan, the United Kingdom, and elsewhere. You can share lifestyle information, news, entertainment, sports, and financial reports from the major world capitals, from a single location. You also can search AOL's International channel for travel information, so that you can learn about the sites and local customs of the areas you'll be visiting.

AOL has special software for members in other parts of the world, and I'll show you the U.K. version later in this chapter. For now, let's explore the International channel, element by element:

- **Feature.** Explore special features of AOL around the world. You'll also see news about live events and featured stories.

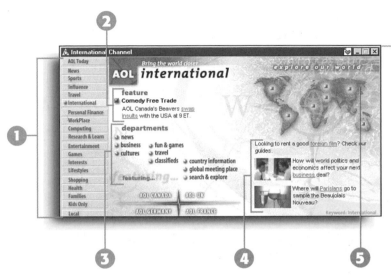

FIGURE 22.1

From Bonn to Tokyo, AOL is now a worldwide service, and the International channel brings members from around the globe together in one valuable community that you'll want to visit often.

1 Click here to go to another channel.

2 Special online feature

3 International channel departments

4 These special features change daily.

5 AOL around the world

- **Explore our World.** Click one of the buttons on the map to access one of these areas (see Figure 22.2). You'll get a bird's-eye view of the service as seen by your neighbors in other countries, and learn more about local culture, weather, politics, and entertainment. You'll be able to download international versions of AOL software to experience the full content of AOL's international services.

FIGURE 22.2

In this example, I'm showing AOL's South America information center.

1 Scroll through the list to see more countries.

- **News.** The latest events around the world brought to you via AOL's special hookups to the major wire services and news networks.

- **Finance.** Special information from the major financial centers around the globe (see Figure 22.3).

FIGURE 22.3

Learn all about transacting your business in another country.

1 Scroll through the list to see more choices.

- **Cultures.** Whether you're an international traveler or you just want information about local customs, you'll find lots of useful information in this area.

- **Fun & Games.** From Liverpool to Monaco, learn what your favorite international stars are doing and about their latest appearances. How did the people of Argentina react to Madonna's starring in *Evita?* You'll find information about that and similar topics here.

- **Travel.** Planning a trip, or are you just trying to learn a little more about your favorite cities? You'll find the information you seek here.

- **Classifieds.** Check AOL for thousands of buy and sell announcements. Place an ad of your own if you would like.

- **Country Information.** Bring up a database search screen, where you can search for the information you need about a specific locale.

- **Global Meeting Place.** The most popular AOL features, worldwide, are chats and message boards. This area offers both for your online pleasure (see Figure 22.4).

FIGURE 22.4

A list of live chats and message boards divided by region and topic.

1 Scroll through the list to see more chats.

AOL in Canada

Each AOL service is localized to offer the content tailored to what members in a certain country prefer. So, for example, when you sign on to AOL in Canada (see Figure 22.5), you see many of the same online channels you are familiar with in the United States, but their look is different, and many of the forums you reach are different, too.

FIGURE 22.5

AOL Canada's service has a totally different look.

1 Click an icon to access that channel.

On the Finance channel (see Figure 22.6), you'll find financial information from the United States because it's the world's financial center. You'll also find resources tailored to the specific needs of your home country. Notice the **Stocks & Investing** list box in this channel has handy icons to indicate U.S. and world-wide resources.

FIGURE 22.6

U.S. financial news is only a small portion of what AOL Canada offers.

① Scroll through the list to see more choices.

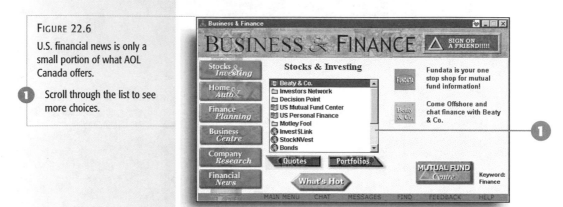

AOL in Europe

AOL has partners in France, Germany, and the United Kingdom. Each has set up a custom online service that not only offers the features you are accustomed to in the United States, but a wide range of other resources. Here, for example, is the Main Menu (or **Channels** menu) for the German branch of AOL (see Figure 22.7).

FIGURE 22.7

When members of AOL's German affiliate log on, they see this screen.

① Click the icon to bring up that channel.

Teach Yourself: Using AOL U.K.

When you join AOL in Great Britain, you'll see many of the same sites you're familiar with in the U.S. version, but the look and feel is decidedly British. When you open the program, for example (see Figure 22.8), you'll find the Setup and Sign On screens reversed (mirroring, perhaps, the reversal of the position of a car's steering wheel in the United Kingdom).

When you click **Sign On**, your login process goes through the same steps as you see in your U.S. AOL experience. The difference is that you'll be greeted by another person when you're logged in, a woman who intones the **"Welcome"** message (see Figure 22.9), followed by—if you have email—an announcement that **"You Have Post"**.

You need the International version

To see the entire AOL U.K. interface as pictured here, or any other AOL service designed for a specific country, you need to acquire the version of the software designed for that country, which is available in that country (or sometimes via the World of AOL area in the International channel). If you log on using the U.S. version of AOL, regardless of where you're connecting from, you'll see the same service that you see from the United States. The major exception is the International channel, where you can experience some of the look and feel of the overseas versions of AOL software.

FIGURE 22.8

The Mac version of AOL U.K.'s software puts the **Sign On** button on the left.

1   Click here to connect.

FIGURE 22.9

AOL's U.K. Welcome window arrives with news that there is "post" waiting to be read. Arizona information is shown because I connected from the United States.

1 Click any icon for more information.

AOL U.K.'s Channels

The U.K.'s **Channels** menu doesn't list as many options as the U.S. edition (see Figure 22.10), but many of the same features are available. Just click the icon that interests you to see more.

FIGURE 22.10

Not only does the Main Menu have a different look from AOL in the United Kingdom, but also things such as typefaces and forum artwork are different.

1 Click the icon to access that channel.

AOL U.K.'s Life Channel

In the United States, the Lifestyles channel presents most of its services on the main screen. The U.K. version (called Life as shown in Figure 22.11) only shows the highlights. Click the **Contents** icon at the upper-right side of the screen to see the rest.

FIGURE 22.11
The Life channel features the highlights on the main screen.

1 Click a title for more choices.

SEE ALSO

➤ *Learn more about the Influence, Interests, Lifestyles, and Health channels, see page 357*

Member Help in the United Kingdom

When you have a problem using your AOL U.K. software, or need another access number, use the keyword Help to access the Member Services area (see Figure 22.12). Every month you can read the latest service updates from AOL U.K.'s Managing Director.

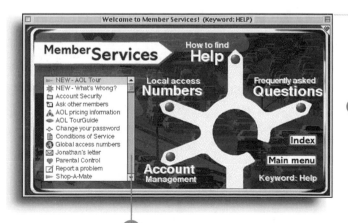

FIGURE 22.12
AOL U.K. members receive assistance for online problems or retrieving billing information.

1 Scroll through the list to see more choices.

Teach Yourself: Visit the Major Cities via the Digital City Channel

Keyword: `Digital City`

When it comes to visiting another city, nothing compares to being there in person. If you're planning a trip, or you just want to learn more about a specific city, however, you'll want to visit AOL's Digital City channel (also available from the **Channels** menu as `Local`) as shown in Figure 22.13.

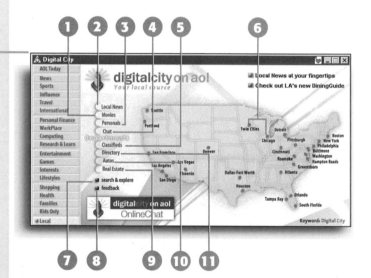

FIGURE 22.13

You'll find major cities around the world by way of AOL's Digital City channel.

❶ Movie information

❷ Local News from many cities

❸ Personal ads

❹ Chats and messages

❺ Classified ads

❻ Click a labeled button for fast access to many cities.

❼ Search AOL's database for more information.

❽ Tell AOL what you think about Digital City.

❾ Real Estate offerings

❿ Automobile ads and information

⓫ Directory of Digital City services

The version you're looking at is the national or U.S. version of AOL's Digital City channel. If you're a member of one of the foreign AOL affiliates, you'll see a different screen, such as the U.K. version shown in Figure 22.14. Here you have fast access to AOL forums devoted to different parts of the United Kingdom.

FIGURE 22.14
The U.K. version of AOL's
Digital City channel.

Find It in a Digital City

The best way to see how the Digital City database feature works is to try it on for size. You can choose a general geographic region from the U.S. map display on the channel's opening screen, or you can use the Search & Explore feature (refer to Figure 22.13) to zero in on the significant information in a particular locale. To begin your search, click the **Search & Explore** button, which brings up the screen shown in Figure 22.15, and enter the location you want to examine.

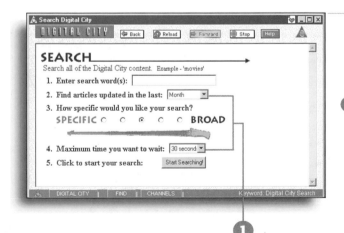

FIGURE 22.15

Learn more about a specific city or its special features using Digital City's Search & Explore feature.

1 Choose the timeframes for your search from the drop-down menus.

You can look up all the available online information about a specific city here, or just focus on a special topic. So in Figure 22.15, I entered Phoenix (as in Arizona) as the search string, just to see what sort of information would turn up. Clicking the **Search** button brought fast results, as shown in Figure 22.16.

FIGURE 22.16

AOL's clever search tool soon brings up the information requested.

Take a look at other Digital City services (refer to Figure 22.13):

- **Local News.** The latest local news is just a couple of clicks away.

- **Movies.** Learn where your favorite flicks are playing, and when they will be shown.

- **Personals.** Meet friends (and maybe your soul mate) when you place your ad here.

- **Chat.** Chatting online is one of AOL members' favorite pastimes. Use this directory (see Figure 22.17) to bring up a list of sessions in your city and elsewhere.

- **Classifieds.** Check out buy and sell ads here, or even place your own announcements.

- **Directory.** Check out the full list of services offered in AOL's Digital City channel.

- **Autos.** The Digital City Auto Guide can help you shop for your next vehicle. You'll get a list of dealers offering low prices before you buy.

FIGURE 22.17
Meet and greet your fellow AOL members in a Digital City chat session.

❶ Scroll through the lists to see more.

- **Real Estate.** If you're looking to buy or sell a home in a specific city, check the information here.

- **Feedback.** Have a problem, or do you want to suggest some new services for AOL's Digital City channel? You can send your ideas here. AOL uses this information as a basis to add new features to the service.

SEE ALSO

➤ *For more information about AOL's Entertainment and Games channel, see page 347*

➤ *Planning a trip, see page 471*

AOL's Research and Learn Channel

Visit online libraries

Advance your education

Call on AOL's online teachers

AOL Has Extensive Educational and Reference Resources

You can think of America Online as the largest school in the world. You can learn something about most anything. You have at your beck and call, the vast resources of major encyclopedias, home study schools, libraries, museums, and dozens of other information centers, including many that are Internet-based.

In the previous century, your resources for learning were confined to written material (such as books, newspapers, and magazines), or verbal descriptions. The 20th century brought audio and visual media into play as well. Interactive learning capabilities have come into their own with the advent of online services such as AOL.

Because of the extent and scope of the educational resources available on AOL, a separate chapter would be needed to fully describe the services of each of the learning and reference forums. Consider this chapter a get-acquainted visit. You'll also find that the Research & Learn channel is vast, with many links to other AOL channels (such as the Influence channel).

SEE ALSO
➤ To learn more about the Influence, Interests, Lifestyles, and Health channels, see page 357.

Exploring the AOL Research & Learn Channel

Keyword: Research & Learn

The Research & Learn channel is your gateway to many of the areas that provide information on AOL (see Figure 23.1). Many of the services available are, no doubt, familiar to you. You'll find references to online magazines, encyclopedias, Internet databases, degree granting courses, and more. Now let's take a brief look at this channel.

SEE ALSO
➤ Searching the Internet, see page 286.

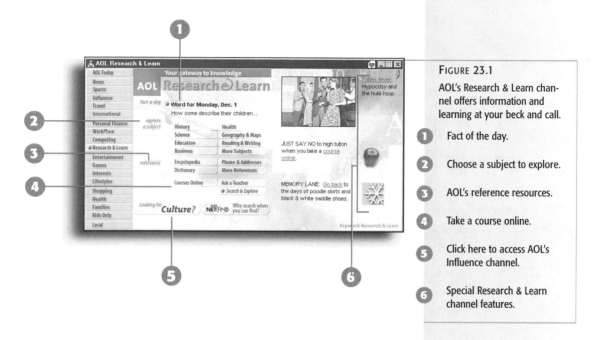

FIGURE 23.1

AOL's Research & Learn channel offers information and learning at your beck and call.

1 Fact of the day.

2 Choose a subject to explore.

3 AOL's reference resources.

4 Take a course online.

5 Click here to access AOL's Influence channel.

6 Special Research & Learn channel features.

- **Fact-a-day.** Click here to check the quote for the day, the day in history, and the day's weird fact.

- **Explore a subject.** What would you like to learn more about? Consult AOL's database resources here for more information (see Figure 23.2).

FIGURE 23.2

You can explore information on a number of fields in this online channel.

1 Click the listed subjects for more information.

■ **References.** AOL provides direct links to online encyclopedias, phone directories, and other reference sources. One example is the online edition of the Merriam-Webster Collegiate dictionary (see Figure 23.3). To find the word you need to check, just enter it in the text field, click **Single Word** or **Full Text** depending on how much information you need, and click **Look Up** to get your answer.

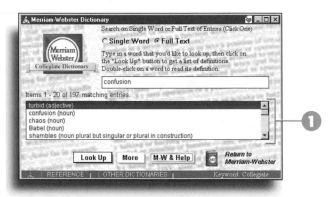

In addition to the information resources shown previously in the list in Figure 23.1, you'll find additional choices when you click **More References** (see Figure 23.4).

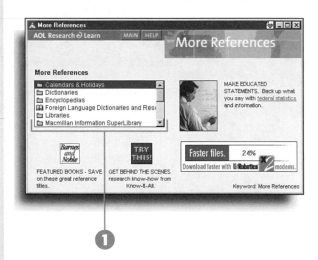

- **Courses Online.** You can take degree granting courses online or get help with your child's homework.
- **AOL NetFind.** AOL's powerful Internet search tool can help you expand your search for knowledge.

SEE ALSO

➤ *Searching the Internet with NetFind, see page 290.*

Teach Yourself: How to Do Online Research

Not so long ago, when you had to do research for a school assignment or a writing project, you had to take a trip to the public library or purchase an encyclopedia. Although you might not want to replace those voluminous, color-filled works on your bookshelves, consider AOL as your second reference resource.

AOL offers rapid access to three online encyclopedias at keyword Encyclopedias (see Figure 23.5).

Let's take a look at one of these reference works—*Compton's Encyclopedia*—which has placed its huge database of information on AOL (see Figure 23.6). All you have to do to tap that database is click the **Search All Text** button, and choose **Open** (or press Return or Enter).

It's easy to search an online encyclopedia

After you bring up the search window, follow these steps:

1. Enter the topic or a description of the information you want in the text entry field near the top of the screen.

2. Within seconds, if articles are available on the subject, you see a list of matching entries (see Figure 23.7). If the entry has a folder icon, it means that the entry contains a number of text reports on the subject.

Is the truth really "out there"?

The amount of information available on AOL and the Web seems almost endless. Many libraries and publications around the world offer free access to a great percentage of their material (on AOL or the Internet) when it's converted to electronic form. Others require that you just set up an account without paying anything, and a few insist on charging for their services. You should find all this clearly spelled out when you first enter a new area.

FIGURE 23.5

Choose the encyclopedia you want to consult.

1 These encyclopedias are available for online research.

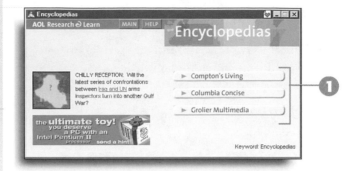

FIGURE 23.6

The resources of a huge encyclopedia are at your fingertips.

1 If you have problems searching for more material, click **How to Search**.

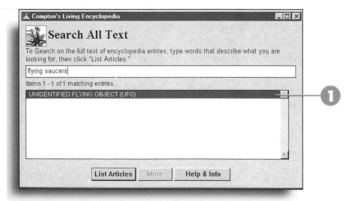

FIGURE 23.7

Searching your virtual encyclopedia is an easy task.

1 Double-click the article to read it.

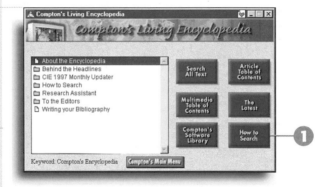

3. In the directory listing, double-click the entry you want to explore (or highlight it and choose the **List Articles** button), and you see the names of all the articles related to the subject. You can view each article online (see Figure 23.8), or you can save or print the article to read at your leisure.

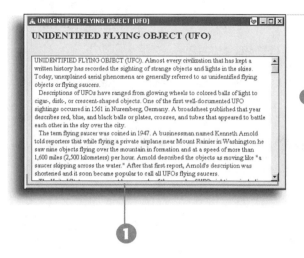

FIGURE 23.8

A typical article you can find on a single topic—in this case, flying saucers.

① This text can be printed for later review.

Teaching Yourself Online

Keyword: Courses

In addition to providing a mountain of research opportunities, AOL offers online instruction on a host of subjects (see Figure 23.9). You can join classes run by AOL's own teaching staff or enroll in extra-cost classes run by the University of California's Extension program.

Let's explore some of the learning options:

- **Online Campus.** This is AOL's own school (see Figure 23.10). Classes are offered in a variety of subjects, ranging from self-improvement to mathematics. Each class has its own classroom and a message board where you can share information with fellow classmates and instructors.

Want a copy to read later on?

Remember that all text you see in an online document window can be saved or printed using the appropriate File menu commands.

Getting images online

Many online photos are available in GIF or JPEG format, which allows for quick downloads and fast screen display. You'll be able to see them with your AOL software within just a few seconds. You can find images to download in the Research & Learn MAPS area and the Computing channel graphics forums.

FIGURE 23.9

Start here to attend school on AOL.

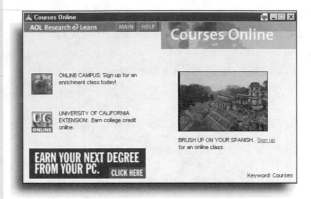

FIGURE 23.10

Choose your subject here and enroll for your class here.

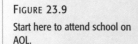 Click here to get the full course listing.

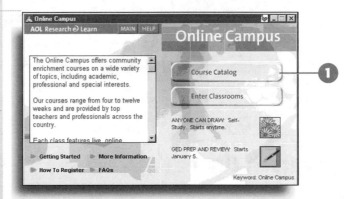

Not all courses are free

Some of AOL's online courses have a registration fee. Before enrolling, you should check course fees, billing information, and whether you must pay a fee if you decide to leave the class.

Take a course to master your PC

AOL's Computing channel (also covered in Chapter 25, "Visiting the Computing Channel") has its own wide-ranging schedule of instructional sessions—all free. You can find out more at the keyword `Online Classroom`.

- **University of California Extension.** These course offerings are wide ranging too (see Figure 23.11). Some of them allow you to earn credit toward your college degree. In addition to checking and registering for an online classroom, the UC AOL area also includes links to a number of popular online information resources.

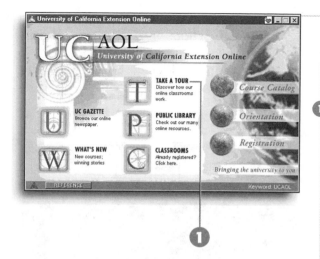

FIGURE 23.11

Some of the courses offered by University of California Extension Online include college degree credits.

1 Before signing up, take a tour of the campus.

Teach Yourself: Ask-A-Teacher Online

Keywords: Ask-A-Teacher, Homework Help

Suppose your child has to write a term paper or complete an assignment that is due tomorrow. Your child has worked for hours trying to pull it into shape, and still questions remain that need to be answered. Don't despair. AOL offers a way to get interactive help from a staff of online teachers. It's called Ask-A-Teacher (see Figure 23.12).

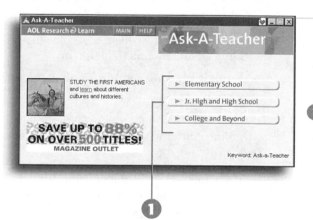

FIGURE 23.12

You can call on an online instructor to help you with homework or other instruction problems.

1 Choose the grade here to receive help.

You have three choices: help for **Elementary School**, **Jr. High and High School**, and **College and Beyond**. The feature covering elementary school takes you to the educational resources run by AOL's Kids Only channel (see Figure 23.13).

SEE ALSO
➢ *To learn more about the Kids Only channel, see page 115*

FIGURE 23.13

Help for students of all educational levels is provided via AOL's Ask-A-Teacher feature, where you can pose the tough questions.

1 Before calling on a teacher, you could try looking it up.

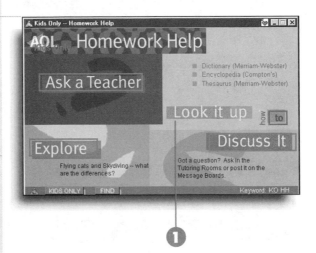

From here, your child has four ways to get the information needed:

- **Ask-A-Teacher.** Questions are emailed to one of the AOL educators who then responds with an answer.
- **Explore.** You're a click away from an area that AOL's Kids Only channel wants to highlight.
- **Look it up.** Consult AOL's online references for the information needed.
- **Discuss It.** Visit an online chat room and talk with an online educator, or leave a message in one of AOL's message boards.

As briefly mentioned in the previous list, when you use the Ask-A-Teacher function, you'll have your child's message emailed directly to one of AOL's educators who emails a response in a short time (but don't expect the response to be immediate).

It works like this: Suppose your child, a grade school student, asks a common question, "How do you add and subtract numbers with more than a single column?" You or your child enters the question, and then enters the topic in which the question fits (in this case, **Math**), as shown in Figure 23.14.

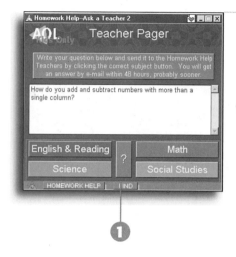

FIGURE 23.14

Enter your question here, and an answer is emailed directly to your mailbox in a day or two.

1 Be sure to click the correct topic when you send your question.

SEE ALSO

➤ *For more entertainment information, see page 347.*

➤ *For financial guidance, see page 452.*

Give your kid a screen name

To customize your child's access to AOL, you'll want to give your child his or her own screen name. You'll learn more about this feature and how to customize access in Chapter 7, "Parental Issues and Internet Access."

Visiting the News Channel

AOL is Your Source for the Latest News

Your daily newspaper is updated once or twice a day. AOL's online news department brings you the latest happenings from all over the world as they occur.

When you first log on to America Online, one of the selections offered to you on the **Welcome** menu is the **Top News Story**, which is the equivalent of the lead headline in your daily newspaper. If you click that icon, you'll open the pages of America Online's own online daily newspaper, a publication consisting of many pages and many sections.

Reading AOL News

Keyword: News

The Top News Story of the day is always featured on the opening (Welcome) screen when you log on (it may change from hour to hour, depending on new developments, but you won't see the change unless you log off and log on again). You can see the major headlines by clicking the **Top News Story** button, which opens the AOL News screen (see Figure 24.1). The AOL News screen is organized much like the sections of your daily newspaper.

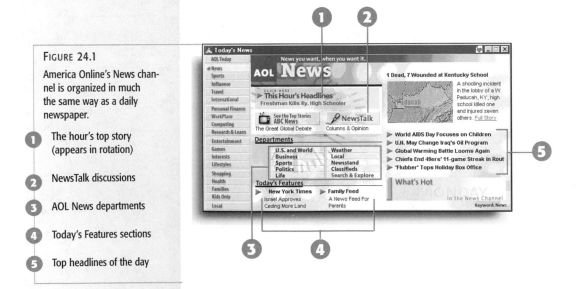

FIGURE 24.1

America Online's News channel is organized in much the same way as a daily newspaper.

1 The hour's top story (appears in rotation)

2 NewsTalk discussions

3 AOL News departments

4 Today's Features sections

5 Top headlines of the day

When you bring up the AOL News screen, you'll see a brief summary of the headline story at the right side of the screen. Double-click the **Full Story** label to read the full details. AOL receives news updates minute-by-minute from the major wire services. Figure 24.2 shows a typical news story; the text is the same as the reports you find in your daily newspaper, only you get it immediately.

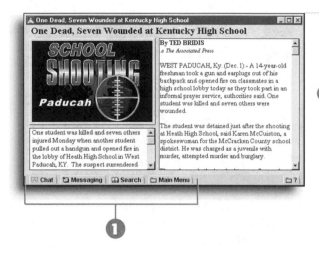

FIGURE 24.2

A news story shown in America Online's News channel.

① Click the buttons at the bottom to access other features.

The News of the Day with Pictures and Sounds

Not all the news you see is limited to just text. Some, like those in your daily newspaper, have an accompanying photograph that illustrates a key element of the story. You'll find many of the stories you select will have photos. Other photos will be offered as Slideshows, complete with sound and limited motion (see Figure 24.3).

Over the next few pages, I'll focus on some of the departments in AOL's News channel. You'll find, as I said earlier, more than a passing resemblance to your daily newspaper.

Ready for a slideshow?

You can find additional examples of how AOL's Slideshow feature runs at the keyword Slideshow.

You need the latest AOL software for online multimedia

To see photos online, you need version 2.6 or later of AOL's Mac software and version 2.5 of AOL's Windows software, and you must have a computer that supports the graphical viewing features. The Slideshow presentations will run with version 4.0 of your AOL software.

FIGURE 24.3

AOL's Slideshow feature adds limited motion video and sound to an information screen. The picture you see here is a bit fuzzy as it was about to switch to another image.

1 Click the **PAUSE** button to halt the presentation.

News customized for different parts of the world

Users of international versions of America Online software will see a selection of news articles devoted to other parts of the world.

U.S. & World News

Keyword: US News

Now that you've read the front page, let's examine the table of contents of your daily newspaper and check out some of the other features (see Figure 24.4). During your online travels, you can set aside pages to read later. The news of the world, for example, is listed by headline, same as your daily paper. If you are seeking information about a particular topic, you'll want to click the **Search** button that appears in many of the AOL News department screens.

As with other searchable databases on America Online, looking for a news item is a simple process. Just bring up the search window by clicking the icon with the appropriate title, enter the topic of your search (notice it isn't case sensitive), and you'll see a display (see Figure 24.5) of the available articles on that subject—if articles are available about your selected topic, of course. Some of the articles may seem unrelated, but you'll find that the name "America Online" is found somewhere in the text.

FIGURE 24.4

Your online newspaper's national and international section.

① Click the arrows to see the full text and more stories.

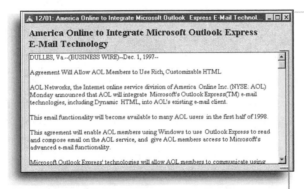

FIGURE 24.5

America Online is always making news, and this is what I found when I used AOL as the search string. It's news about an upcoming AOL email feature.

① Scroll through the window to read the full story.

Note that many of the news-related forums on America Online are linked. If you open one screen, you'll find direct links to other areas with related information.

Weather News

Keyword: Weather

Although you can't do much to change the weather, you can at least be informed about it. By turning to the weather section in your virtual newspaper, you can review both articles and special forecasts not only country-wide (see Figure 24.6), but from around the world.

FIGURE 24.6

When severe weather has a major impact, AOL has the latest information.

1 Enter your location here to see the current weather.

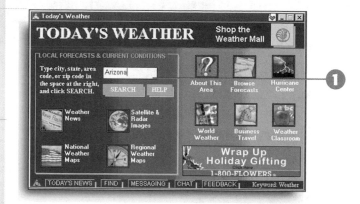

You can also see maps of weather trends directly on your own computer by selecting and downloading them. The forum updates the weather maps daily. You can see them in full color if you have a color monitor. Choose from a satellite view, radar displays, and charts of maximum and minimum temperatures not only for today, but for tomorrow and the next day as well. If you choose, for example, to view the day's weather map, you get the display shown in Figure 24.7.

FIGURE 24.7

See the weather displayed on your computer.

1 You can save or print this weather map for later review.

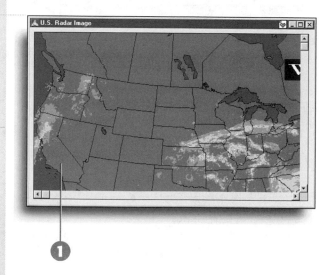

The forum also offers these maps in the cross-platform *GIF for-mat* (short for Graphic Interchange Format). After you down-load the map file to your computer, you can use the latest versions of AOL's software to open and view the file. Just open the **File** menu and choose **Open** to bring the file to your screen.

During the summer and fall seasons, a special area is devoted to tropical storms and hurricanes. You can check this section to see if any severe weather is expected in your area, and what the trends are for the near future (within the limits of the science of weather forecasting, of course).

Visiting AOL's Politics News Department

Keywords: Capital, Politics

After you've reviewed the news of the day, undoubtedly you have some strong ideas about some of the subjects you've read about, especially the goings on in the nation's capital. If you want to examine the issues further, check out AOL's Politics section (see Figure 24.8), where you can immerse yourself in politics and intrigue and get a thorough perspective of the progression of events.

FIGURE 24.8

Read and debate the issues in AOL's Politics area.

1 Click the **More Stories** but-ton for additional items.

This area is configured much like the Today's News area. You'll find stories, photos, and magazine and newspaper links in the main directory screen (see Figure 24.9).

FIGURE 24.9

One example of the sort of news you find in this area—a list of stories about members of Congress.

 Scroll through the list and click **More** for additional stories.

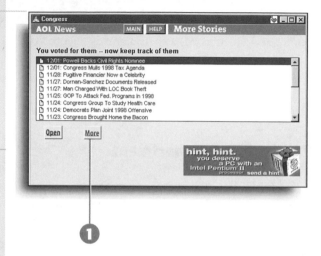

Teach Yourself: Setting Up AOL's Custom News Delivery Service

Keyword: News Profiles

Yet another way exists to get the latest news on AOL, and the technique used is somewhat similar to subscribing to a daily newspaper and having it delivered direct to your home. It's called News Profiles (see Figure 24.10), which is an AOL feature that delivers email containing the latest news on the subjects that interest you directly to your mailbox on a daily basis.

To take advantage of the News Profile feature, you need to create a custom profile, in which you select the subjects of the news stories you want sent, and the sources from which they originate. Let's cover the steps involved in setting up this service. First, click the **Create a Profile** icon to get the screen shown in Figure 24.11.

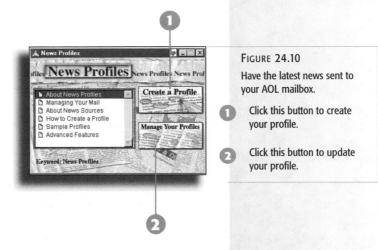

FIGURE 24.10

Have the latest news sent to your AOL mailbox.

① Click this button to create your profile.

② Click this button to update your profile.

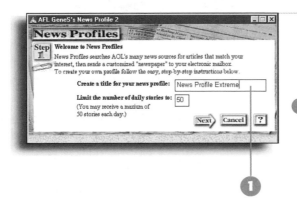

FIGURE 24.11

After you title your News Profile and select the number of articles you want, click the **Next** button.

① Enter the title of your profile here.

The next step in the process is to give the News Profile feature the information it needs to begin to check for articles that interest you. For each step, you'll click the **Next** icon to get to another option.

Setting up your custom News Profile

1. *Find articles containing any or all of these words or phrases.* Enter the words or subjects you want AOL's News Profile database to search for you.

You can refine your News Profile search strings still further with a few handy wildcard characters (not unlike the ones you may use in a word-processing program). The following lists some of the wildcard characters:

- *Asterisk (*).* This letter represents one or more characters and can be used in place of any character to extend the accuracy of your search, such as "computer*," which will include not only the word "computer," but also "computers," "computing," and so forth.

- *At Sign (@).* This character can be used to represent a single character. For example, if you type **a@e** in the Ignore box, News Profiles ignores articles containing the words "ape" and "ate."

- *Plus Sign (+).* This character can be used to represent a single number. For example, if you type **852+0** in the **Find Articles** box, News Profiles finds all articles containing the zip code "85260."

- *Question Mark (?).* This character may represent a single character or a single number in your search string. It has the functions of both + and @ and can be inserted anywhere in a search string.

- *Pound Sign (#).* This character can represent any single word. For example, if you type the phrase **apple #** in the **Find Articles** box, News Profiles can find such phrases as Apple Computer, Apple orchard, and so on.

2. *Require that each of these words or phrases be present in each article.* This is a way to restrict the news report search. You don't have to enter anything in this text box if the subjects you specified are sufficient to identify the topics you want.

3. *Exclude articles that contain any of these words or phrases.* If you absolutely don't want to read about certain items, enter that information here. Again this text box is optional—it's not necessary to enter anything. For example, if you don't want to read anything more about a particular public figure, put that person's name in this list.

4. After the search words are chosen over several screens, click the **Next** button to continue to create your News Profile (see Figure 24.12). Click **Cancel** to stop the process without making a profile.

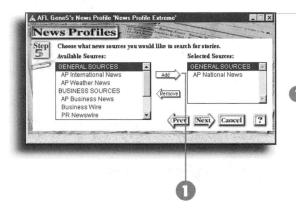

FIGURE 24.12

Choose the sources from which stories will be taken here.

1 Select a news source from the left screen and click the **Add** button.

5. If you want to recheck the search words you included in your profile, click the **Prev** (Previous) button.

6. If you decide not to make a profile at this time, click the **Cancel** button, and all the information you entered will be deleted.

7. If you're ready to create your profile, click the **Next** button at step 5 of the News Profiles setup screen. You'll soon see an acknowledgment message (see Figure 24.13) that your profile has been activated.

FIGURE 24.13

Get ready to automatically receive the latest news on the subjects that interest you.

1 The details of the news profile you just created.

Up to five profiles can be maintained for each screen name. As I'll describe in a moment, it's easy to turn them on or off, day by day, so that a different range of articles can be checked for you by the News Profiles feature.

Within a day or so, you'll begin to receive mailings containing news on the subjects that you've selected for your News Profiles. If you've picked the maximum of 50 items, as I've done, you'll find your mailbox will have a daily avalanche of news items, and you may decide it's just too much to read at any one time. Should this occur (or you just want to select a different range of subject matter), you can always update your profile by clicking the **Manage Your Profile** icon on the News Profiles window. You get the screen shown in Figure 24.14.

Caution: Don't overdo it

The News Profiles feature does its job whether you log on to AOL daily or not. If you want to avoid having your mailbox overflow with outdated news items when you're not going to be connecting to AOL for awhile, be sure to modify your profile.

FIGURE 24.14

Make your changes here whenever you need to change your News Profile.

1   Select a profile and click **Edit** to change it.

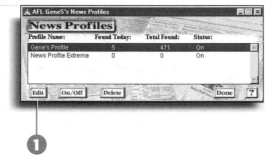

1

News Profiles and Automatic AOL work together

If you use both the News Profiles and the Automatic AOL sessions features, you'll be able to totally automate the process of retrieving online news stories.

The buttons at the bottom of the window shown in Figure 24.14 enable you to configure your existing profiles. First highlight the profile you want to change, and then click the appropriate button:

- **Edit.** Click this button to bring up the same two profile screens described previously, so you can alter your settings as you desire.
- **On/Off.** Click this button to activate or disable the selected profile.
- **Delete.** Click this button to remove the selected profile.
- **Done.** When you're finished editing your profile, click this button to close the edit window.
- **?.** If you need additional online help, click this button.

Now you're ready to enjoy America Online's automated news delivery service. You'll find it can save you money too, because it reduces the amount of time you spend online seeking out news stories on the items that interest you.

Visiting the Newsstand

Keyword: Newsstand

Growing up in the big city, I used to enjoy the visit to the local newsstand to see my favorite magazines and newspapers. Now, I don't have to leave my home office to visit a newsstand. All I have to do is log on to AOL and click AOL's Newsstand channel from the Channels screen (or just use the keyword Newsstand).

When you first visit AOL's Newsstand, you'll see publications highlighted with special icons at the right of the screen (see Figure 24.15). The icons you see here will change regularly, as new publishers set up areas on AOL. A drop-down menu (at the left) takes you to newsstand areas from other AOL channels. The list box at the right contains the rest of the offerings.

FIGURE 24.15

The list of available magazines on AOL's newsstand is increasing rapidly.

Teach Yourself: The Elements of an Online Magazine

The magazines you see on AOL sometimes match the newsstand equivalent, word for word. Other magazines just present highlights of the current issue, hoping you'll be interested enough to buy a copy or become a regular subscriber.

As an example of the sort of publications you'll find online, let's take a look at the *Scientific American* (see Figure 24.16). It's one of my favorites; designed for anyone interested in science, you don't have to have a degree in a specific field to understand the contents. You can quickly access this publication via the keyword SciAm.

Not all the magazines have the same online features. I picked this one because *Scientific American* is typical of a fully featured online magazine. Let's look at the contents:

- **Current issue.** Click this picture to read contents of the latest issue, article by article, in convenient text form.
- **Special features.** This directory list box takes you two clicks away from all the services this magazine offers.
- **SciAm Medical Publications.** Some publishers offer extra books and magazines with comprehensive coverage of a specific topic.
- **SciAm Frontiers—publisher's Web site.** Click this icon to visit the publisher's Web site, where you'll find additional areas to access.
- **More to explore.** Additional online features at the *Scientific American's* online forum. If a publisher has more than one online magazine, you'll frequently find a similar icon to access those publications.
- **Special articles.** This area may offer a special feature article and downloadable photos, sometimes available exclusively on AOL.

FIGURE 24.16

Read an entire magazine online, during your visits to AOL.

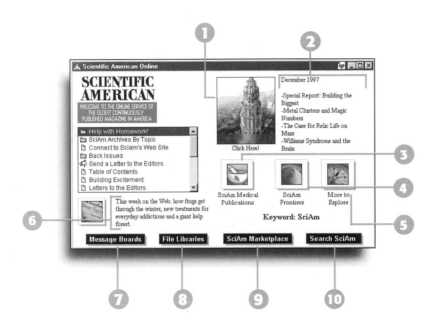

1. Current issue
2. Special features listed
3. Related publications
4. Frontiers—publisher's Web site
5. Additional online features

6. Special articles
7. Message Boards
8. Software libraries
9. Merchandise offerings
10. Search the magazine

- **Message Boards.** This feature separates the online magazine from the printed version. You can use the publisher's message boards to comment about subjects in a particular issue or about the field the magazine covers in general. It's not uncommon for a magazine's editors or writers to actively participate in such an area.

- **File Libraries.** Some magazines offer special image files that illustrate an online article. Computer magazines may even offer a full-featured selection of software in a library such as this.

- **SciAm Marketplace.** You can take advantage of a special subscription offer, or check out a publisher's line of special merchandise. Some of these products may include T-shirts, cups, or specialty products from a variety of manufacturers.

- **Search SciAm.** You can find articles about a special subject here. Just click the **Search SciAm** icon, enter the search information in a text box, and AOL's powerful search engines will find the information you want, usually in just a few seconds.

SEE ALSO

➤ *To learn all about the entertainment-related resources available on AOL, see page 347*

➤ *To explore additional entertainment and special interest resources online, see page 357*

➤ *To learn more about locating sports information on AOL, see page 367*

➤ *To explore online educational resources availabe to you, see page 389*

➤ *To discover sources for tips and tricks on how to make your dollars go farther, and where to seek further assistance at tax time, see page 451*

Some popular publications are not on AOL yet

Not all the publications you'll find on AOL are provided as part of the service. Many others are available that you can easily access via AOL's versatile NetFind feature (see Figure 24.17). You can access NetFind's newspaper search window via the button in the Newsstand channel. You can use the search feature to locate other publications, both on AOL and the Internet.

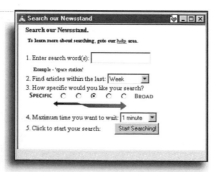

FIGURE 24.17

AOL's NetFind feature will locate still more online publications for your reading pleasure.

Visiting the Computing Channel

Get Computer Help on AOL

There's an AOL computing forum covering every facet of personal computing, from games to the latest hints and tips about using the Mac operating system or Windows 95. You'll find active message boards, huge listings of helpful information, and ready answers to the questions you have. In addition, these forums hold regular conferences, featuring the people who run the forums, as well as industry experts who often come by to tell you about a new product, or to hang out and chat with you about a variety of computing subjects.

Exploring the Computing Forums

Keyword: Computing

If you want to learn to use your computer more effectively or just want to talk computers with fellow AOL members, visit America Online's Computing forums often. You can access this area either by clicking the **Computing** icon on the Channels menu, or by using the keyword Computing. You see the Computing channel screen in Figure 25.1.

The following sections highlight many of AOL's computer-related forums. Because a picture truly is worth a thousand words, look closely at the figures throughout this chapter to see many of the services that the forums offer.

- **Computing Superstore.** Choose from a wide list of computer-related merchandise here. You'll find a new modem, that RAM upgrade you need, an extra hard drive, or a new scanner. It's covered by AOL's special online merchandise guarantee, which I describe in more detail in Chapter 30, "Secrets of AOL's Shopping Channel."

- **Daily Download.** Each day, AOL's Computing forum leaders select the most popular software for you to download (see Figure 25.2). You'll also be able to purchase commercial products during your online visit.

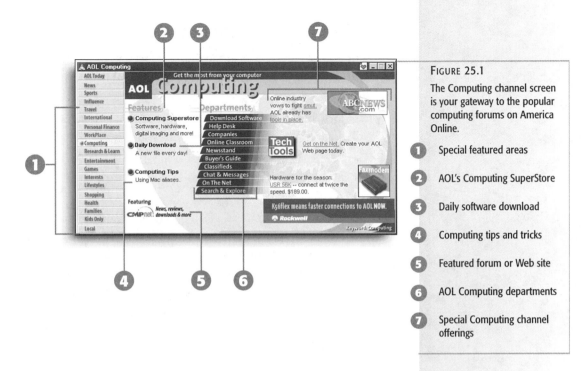

FIGURE 25.1

The Computing channel screen is your gateway to the popular computing forums on America Online.

1 Special featured areas

2 AOL's Computing SuperStore

3 Daily software download

4 Computing tips and tricks

5 Featured forum or Web site

6 AOL Computing departments

7 Special Computing channel offerings

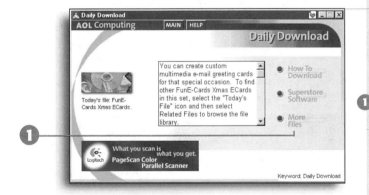

FIGURE 25.2

Choose from thousands of software products, free and commercial, from AOL's Computing channel.

1 Click **More Files** for additional offerings.

- **Computing Tips.** Learn how to deal with a system crash, make your computer run more quickly, and more. Sections for PC Tips, Mac Tips, and AOL Tips are available.

- **Featuring.** A special forum is highlighted here; the selection changes on a regular basis.

Computing Channel Departments

The following list covers the major departments available in the Computing channel. Each of these items will bring up a list of further choices:

- **Download Software.** This is the same Daily Download area described previously, where you can find the best from AOL's software libraries.

- **Help Desk.** If you run into a problem with your PC or with AOL, come here first.

- **Companies.** You can get free technical support from major computer and software makers. I'll cover this area in more detail later in this chapter, in the "Teach Yourself: Secrets of Using America Online's Company Connection" section.

- **Online Classroom.** If you want to hone your skills, sign up for a free online course here (see Figure 25.3). Offerings include topics from the basics of using your PC or Mac, to scanning, Web authoring, and desktop video production.

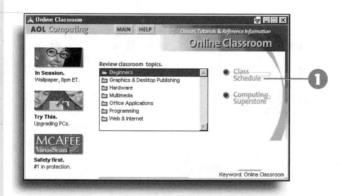

FIGURE 25.3

Sign up for a free online class to learn about your favorite computing topic.

1 Click here to check out the class schedule.

- **Newsstand.** This section takes you directly to AOL's magazine shop, where you can read your favorite computing publications. I'll cover this in more detail later in the "Reading Computer Books and Magazines Online" section.

- **Buyer's Guide.** If you're looking to buy a new computing product (computer, modem, monitor, or scanner), you'll be able to see how the major computing publications rate those products here.

- **Classifieds.** This button takes you directly to AOL's popular Classifies area. I'll cover that section in more detail in Chapter 30.

- **Chat & Messages.** AOL's message boards and chat rooms are always active. You'll learn more about both in Chapters 10, "Chatting Online" and 11, "How to Use AOL's Message Boards."

- **On The Net.** The Internet is just a click or two away from most any AOL forum. You can check out popular Web sites (from AOL members and commercial choices), download popular Internet software, and exchange messages with your fellow members (see Figure 25.4). For more coverage on AOL's Internet services, read all the chapters in Part III, "AOL as an Internet Service Provider," and Chapter 18, "Become a Web Publisher on AOL."

> **Finding online computing chats**
>
> To get a list of online conferences in the Computing channel, use the keyword CompLive. You'll see a listing of the day's chats, and information about upcoming special events.

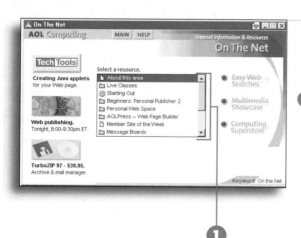

FIGURE 25.4

This area offers information to help make the Internet simple and accessible.

1 Scroll through the list to find more information.

- **Search & Explore.** Where you can't find the topic that interests you, let AOL's NetFind feature help you out. Read Chapter 16, "How to Search for Information on the Net," for more coverage on this subject.

Caution: Read before you post!

Before you post a question in an AOL support forum, read older messages in the same message folder or in other message areas that deal with a similar topic. You may find a response and a solution to a question much like yours.

AOL's Computing Channel—Anatomy of a Forum

Each area of computing has its own forum on AOL. To make them all accessible and easy to navigate, these forums have a consistent look and feel and a similar roster of features. For example, let's take a look at a typical forum, the Mac Animation & Video Forum, shown in Figure 25.5. A PC equivalent is available, by the way.

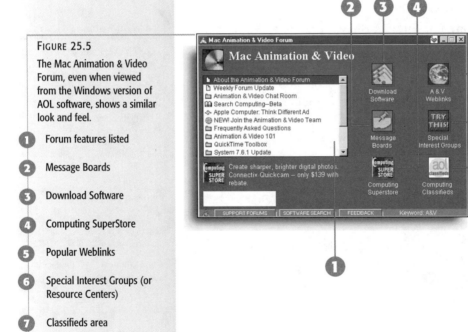

FIGURE 25.5

The Mac Animation & Video Forum, even when viewed from the Windows version of AOL software, shows a similar look and feel.

1 Forum features listed

2 Message Boards

3 Download Software

4 Computing SuperStore

5 Popular Weblinks

6 Special Interest Groups (or Resource Centers)

7 Classifieds area

Let's dissect this typical AOL support forum, and see what it offers:

- **About the Animation & Video Forum.** Double-click this item to learn about a forum's focus, special features, and perhaps a brief profile of the AOL community leaders who run it.

- **Weekly Forum Update.** Learn about special forum features, new areas, and upcoming chats.

- **Animation & Video Chat Room (or Conference Center).** Most computing support forums have a regular schedule of online chats, where you can meet the forum staff, interact with other members, and frequently talk to industry experts.

- **Search Computing.** Check for text-based information on a number of topics. This feature was under development when this chapter was written.

- **Join the Animation & Video Team.** From time to time a forum will seek out knowledgeable volunteers to get involved in helping other members and checking out new software uploads. It's a way for you to get active on AOL.

- **Frequently Asked Questions (FAQs).** Get a quick online tutorial about a specific aspect of personal computing, or fast answers to common questions.

- **Download Software.** Software libraries are the reason many people first visit an online forum. You'll find thousands of software files on AOL. I'll tell you more about this subject in Chapter 26, "Tips and Tricks on Finding Software."

- **Message Boards.** Tens of thousands of messages can be found in AOL's Computing forums. You'll find questions, answers, advice, chit-chat, debates, and more. One of the most popular pastimes is comparing one computing platform to another. When Mac and PC users get together to discuss the merits and problems with their favorite operating system and product, watch out!

- **A & V Weblinks (and Newsgroup links).** It's a sure thing that you'll find many of the areas you seek on AOL, but the Internet also has thousands of sources to tap. AOL's computing forums have fast links to popular Web sites and Internet newsgroups. Read Chapters 12, "Using AOL's Internet Services," and 13, "Using the World Wide Web," for more on this subject.

- **Special Interest Groups (or Resource Center).** These are mini-forums, devoted to a computing specialty (see Figure 25.6 for one example). You'll find special interest groups (or SIGs) devoted to such topics as desktop video production, word processing, scripting, and combating computer viruses.

FIGURE 25.6

A Special Interest Group
(or SIG), such as The Video
Zone, caters to a computing
specialty.

1   Scroll through the list for
more offerings.

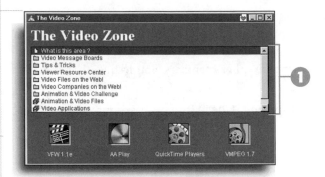

FIGURE 25.6

A Special Interest Group
(or SIG), such as The Video
Zone, caters to a computing
specialty.

1   Scroll through the list for
more offerings.

- **Newsletter subscriptions.** AOL's Computing & Software channel has a weekly newsletter, *Byte*, available to anyone who requests a copy. It's filled with hints and tips to help you get better performance and more reliable operation from your Mac or PC.

AOL's Computing Support Forums—From A to Z

Keyword: Forums

Whatever your computing interest, no doubt an AOL support forum exists where you can find material that you want (see Figure 25.7). Now that you've read about how these forums are organized, let's briefly describe them all (well with the exception of the Animation & Video Forum, which is covered in the previous section):

- **Applications (Mac and PC).** The keyword Apps takes you to a forum that supports your favorite programs, ranging from word processors to database creation tools.

- **Business Applications (PC).** The keyword PC Business will bring you to a support center catering to popular productivity programs.

- **Communications (Mac and PC).** The Mac keyword MCM or PC keyword Telecom takes you to an active support forum that covers networking, modems, and how to get the best possible online connection. Sometimes they're referred to as the Networking and Telecommunications forums.

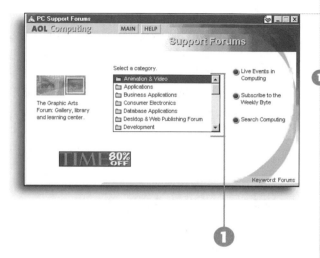

FIGURE 25.7

The roster of AOL's computing support forums is shown here.

1 Scroll through the list to find more forums.

- **Consumer Electronics (cross-platform).** Use the keyword CE to visit an area that covers such things as home theater systems and cameras.

- **Database Applications (PC).** The keyword Database takes you to a forum that covers such programs as Microsoft Access, Paradox, and, of course, the year 2000 issue that may affect many computer users.

- **Desktop & Web Publishing Forum (Mac and PC).** The Mac keyword MDWP or PC keyword PCDWP takes you to AOL's center for document creation software. Whether it's for print or Web use (or both), you'll find advice and software here.

- **Development (Mac and PC).** If you're an experienced computer programmer, or just want to learn the ropes, this is the right place. Use the Mac keyword MDV or PC keyword PDV. Because it's important for software to work cross-platform these days, you may want to visit both areas.

- **DOS Forum (PC).** The keyword DOS brings you to a forum that shows that DOS is not dead, but is still in active use by millions of computer users.

Crossing platforms is easy on AOL

Most PC computing forums have direct links to their Mac counterparts. You can also switch from one to the other via a list box item in the Forums directory available at keyword **Forums**.

- **Education Forum (Mac and PC).** The Mac keyword MED and the PC keyword PCED takes you to a place where you can discover educational software, and advice for educators, parents, and students.

- **Family Computing (cross-platform).** The keyword Family Computing brings you to AOL's Family Computing Resource Center (see Figure 25.8). You'll find direct links to AOL's Parental Controls area, plus forums devoted to family-style computing.

FIGURE 25.8

This is AOL's center devoted to family-oriented personal computing.

1 Choose the family computing forum that interests you.

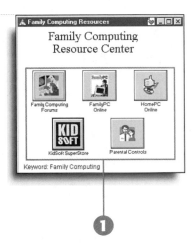

- **Games Forum (Mac and PC).** Many of us enjoy computer games for recreation, especially at the end of a long work day. The Mac keyword MGM or PC keyword PCGames will give you fast access to these areas. As you see in Figure 25.9, they look quite different from the regular computing forums.

- **Graphics Forum (Mac and PC).** Learn about drawing software, CAD creation tools, and more in these forums. The Mac keyword MGR or PC keyword PC Graphics takes you there.

- **Hardware/OS Forum (Mac only).** The Mac keyword MHW takes you to a forum that focuses not only on the latest hardware from Apple and Mac OS clone makers, but on the operating system itself. You'll learn the latest about Apple's new operating system software and how to use it to its best advantage.

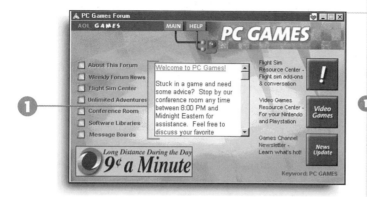

FIGURE 25.9

The PC and Mac Games forums are set up differently from the other computer-related online areas.

1 Scroll through the text screen to learn more about this forum.

- **Hardware Forum (PC only).** Use the keyword Hardware to get to an area where you can learn how to get your PC running to its best advantage. Also, discover the latest about Intel's new Pentiums with MMX and even what some other CPU manufacturers are planning.

- **Home & Hobby (PC only).** This area is accessed on your PC by the keyword PCHH. The coverage includes specialty software, devoted to such things as astronomy, health and fitness, travel, and more.

- **Home Finance Applications (PC only).** You can access this forum via the keyword PCFIN. Download the latest finance-related software, learn to track your investments, and discover tips and tricks on using your favorite personal finance programs. I'll cover this subject in more detail in Chapter 27, "Using the Personal Finance Channel."

- **Lotus Notes (PC only).** This forum can be reached by the keyword Notes. It's devoted to the popular groupware program, and offers both advice and updates.

- **Music & Sound Forum (Mac and PC).** Add a few sounds to your PC, or download shareware sound editing software. The Mac keyword MMS and the PC keyword PC Music will get you there. Areas are also devoted to budding composers who want to use their computers to edit musical compositions.

- **OS/2 (PC only).** IBM's OS/2 system gets the attention here. You'll learn how to run AOL for Windows on OS/2, discover tips and tricks to tame this huge operating system, and find a huge array of useful software. The keyword for this forum is OS2.

- **Personal Digital Assistants (Mac and PC).** They come in all shapes and sizes, and bear the names Newton, OmniGo, Zoomer, Magic Cap, Psion, Pilot, Zaurus, and the Windows CE HPCs. Whatever sort of handheld computer interests you, the keyword PDA will take you to a forum where you can learn what to choose, how to use it, and find software to run on it.

- **Productivity & Spreadsheet Applications (PC only).** These forums are reached via the keywords Utils and Spreadsheet. The former covers popular add-on enhancements to your PC. The latter covers such programs as Microsoft Excel.

- **Windows Forum.** Whether you use Windows 95 or you're sticking with an earlier version, you'll want to visit this forum often. The keyword is Winforum and it will take you to the area where you can get knowledgeable online support. You'll also find an information center covering Windows NT.

Reading Computer Books and Magazines Online

Keywords: Newsstand, Magazine Rack

When you want to learn more about how your computer works, find out how to use a specific piece of software, or just sneak a preview of upcoming products, you are likely to venture into your local bookstore and purchase a book such as this one.

America Online gives you a chance to preview some of those publications before you buy them. You can even search through back issues of many of your favorite computing magazines for a specific article. Additionally, you can participate in online forums run by the producers of several popular computing-related radio and TV programs.

For your convenience, all these resources have been gathered together for access in AOL's Newsstand area (see Figure 25.10).

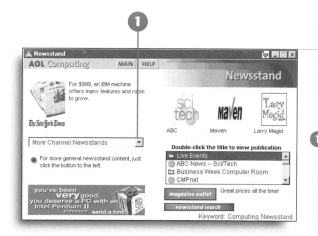

FIGURE 25.10

AOL's Computing Newsstand area is an online media center for computer-related information.

1 Click the drop-down menu for more offerings.

Before you visit the individual computer media centers listed in the area's directory, check out the regular highlights. (The highlights icons won't necessarily reflect the same publications that are shown in this book.)

AOL also offers a good way to save money on your favorite magazine. The Magazine Outlet button shown at the bottom of Figure 25.10 will bring up a list of offers. You'll be able to get the lowest rates on many of your favorite publications here.

Teach Yourself: Secrets of Using America Online's Company Connection

Keyword: Companies

If you've ever spent long minutes listening to voice mail when you try to reach a hardware or software manufacturer for some help, you'll appreciate America Online's solution. Hundreds of firms, ranging from small utility-software publishers to major manufacturers of computer hardware, are represented in the Computing Companies area (see Figure 25.11).

Online magazines and print editions are often different

The content of online magazines is not necessarily the same as the newsstand edition. In some cases, features that appear in the print version may not show up in the online version. In other situations, the online edition provides more up-to-date news because of continuing deadlines. In addition, the online magazine will usually offer other features you won't find in the regular edition, such as active message boards and special areas devoted to online conferences. I'll tell you more about the way these areas are organized in Chapter 24, "Visiting the News Channel."

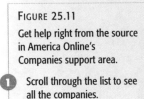

FIGURE 25.11

Get help right from the source in America Online's Companies support area.

1 Scroll through the list to see all the companies.

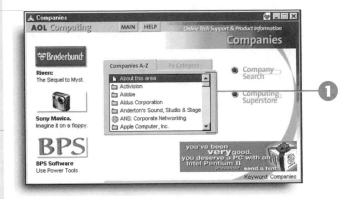

These support forums are places where you can get advice on using a company's product more effectively and solving problems when they arise. The companies' own support personnel usually staff the forums; often, they are ably assisted by knowledgeable America Online members.

Software publishers often provide free maintenance updates for their products in their support areas, so you don't have to wait for a product update to be mailed to you. You also should check the software libraries often, in case the libraries contain an update that you need.

Finding a Company

Not every firm is represented on America Online yet, but more are being added regularly. You can find computing-industry support areas in the computing and software forums catering to the kinds of product that the companies support. Suppose you want to access a modem manufacturer in the hardware and communications forums. You'll see an icon or a list box representing companies with products in that category in the appropriate forum. Just click that icon or double-click the list box to bring up the roster of companies.

If you can't find the company that you're looking for in a computing forum's directory, the Company Search feature in the Companies area (refer to Figure 25.11) will let you see if a particular firm has an AOL support area. In some cases, you'll find direct links to their Web sites.

The fastest method, however, may be using a keyword to go directly to the firm that you want. If you want to find U.S. Robotics, the large manufacturer of computer modems, for example, type the keyword USR. In just a few seconds, you are transported directly to the front door of the company's America Online support forum (see Figure 25.12).

FIGURE 25.12

U.S. Robotics has set aside this area to support users of its modems.

1 Scroll through the list to see more offerings.

Using Company Connection Help

A technical support person can't solve your problem if you don't provide enough information about your setup and the difficulties that you're having with the product. The following letter is typical of the letters that often appear on the message boards in the regular forums and the company support areas:

Question: Help! My computer is crashing all the time. I can't get any work done when I use your software. I need help.

Signed: **Harried Harry**

This sort of letter is only going to delay the process of getting help, because the letter lacks any information that would help a technical support person to diagnose and, if necessary, try to reproduce the problem. Remember that the only information a manufacturer has to go on is what you provide in your letter, because the support people aren't present at your work site to see what exactly is going wrong.

Caution: Please don't repeat yourself!

Don't *cross-post*—that is, don't post your message in more than one message folder in a single forum. America Online members don't always take kindly to reading the same message over and over again (because they're spending extra time reading the messages again and again). Before you issue your plea for help, take a few moments to find the right place to post it. Look for an appropriate computing forum or a company support area (the Hardware forum, for example, for a malfunctioning printer), and leave your message there.

Caution: Don't give out personal information in a public message board!

When you describe your installation in a message, please *do not* include your phone number, address, credit card number, or a software product's serial number. This information could compromise your credit account and give potential software pirates a chance to use software without paying for it. If a computer company needs any of this information for support purposes, they'll contact you privately and request it.

The following list provides some helpful hints on how to ask a company support person for help:

- Describe the kind of computer that you have, including the model number.
- Briefly describe your setup, including the operating-system version and the amount of installed RAM. Also list the accessories attached to your system, such as a video card, sound card, or an additional hard drive.
- Identify the manufacturer's product by model or version number. Often, a problem affects only a single version of a program or piece of hardware.
- Describe, completely and concisely, the problem that you're having. If your computer is crashing, report whether an error message appears on your computer's screen and quote the message (as much as you can). That kind of message may be crucial to figuring out what went wrong.
- If the problem can be reproduced, describe the steps that you took to reproduce it. That way, if the problem is unique to your setup, the steps can help the support person reproduce the problem.
- If the problem started after you made a change in your setup (such as a hardware addition or a software installation), mention that, too. The new installation may have caused your troubles.
- Finally, don't expect miracles. These products are manufactured by human beings who have the same shortcomings as the rest of us. No hardware or software product is perfect; you just want to get it to work as efficiently as possible in your home or office.

Sometimes, a problem is too complex to deal with by email or message board. In such cases, companies invite you to contact their technical-support people directly, by telephone.

SEE ALSO

➤ *Learn to harness the power of your software during your online visits, see page 17*

➤ *Discover all the major features of the latest AOL version, see page 509*

Tips and Tricks on Finding Software

Where's that file?

Shareware? Freeware? Demoware?

Downloading software

Uploading software

What's wrong with that file?

Internet-based software

AOL's Software Libraries Often Come First

For many, the first thing to do when you log on to AOL is to check out the software libraries. It's one of AOL's most popular features. You can choose from literally tens of thousands of Macintosh and Windows files. Whether it's an arcade game, a program that lets you create a to-do list, or an update to commercial software you own, America Online is the place to find it.

Visiting AOL's Software Libraries

When I first joined America Online in 1989, I was the owner of a brand new computer, and I wanted to stock up on software. As a firmly established software junkie, I was a frequent visitor to AOL's vast software libraries. It took me awhile to discover the rich array of information services available elsewhere online.

Before you go on, study these computer terms you'll see often in this chapter:

- *Downloading* a file is the act of transferring a file from America Online's host computer, through the telephone lines, to your computer by way of your modem.

- *Uploading* a file is the process of sending a file from your computer directly to America Online.

Protecting Yourself from Computer Viruses

Online information about computer viruses

If you want more information about computer viruses and how to protect your computer against them, visit AOL's Virus Information Center (keyword **Virus**). You'll also find a selection of virus software updates and evaluation versions of some virus detection programs.

Because the danger always exists that a file can be contaminated by a computer virus, America Online's forum staff members (community leaders) check all uploaded files with an up-to-date virus detection program before posting them online. You should still install and use the latest virus detection software, however, so all your files are safe.

Using File Search

The fastest way to locate software you want is to let America Online's host computer do the search for you. To bring up America Online's File Search window, follow these steps:

Searching for software on AOL

1. Press Ctrl+K (⌘+K for Macintosh) and type the keyword File Search to bring up the search window. You'll see two icons, one to shop for software from AOL's Computing Superstore, the other to download software from AOL's regular libraries. Click the **Download Software** icon to bring up the screen shown in Figure 26.1.

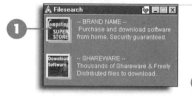

> **Caution: Be careful what you download!**
>
> Files downloaded from FTP or World Wide Web sources are not checked by America Online for the presence of viruses. Please use virus detection software to check files you've downloaded from Internet sources to be sure they are in good shape before you attempt to use those files.

FIGURE 26.1

Your gateway to America Online's convenient software database.

1 Click the icon to access that area.

In seconds, you see a large window on your computer that gives you a number of search options (see Figure 26.2). The categories shown will be different, depending on whether you're using the Macintosh or Windows version of AOL's software (the Windows version is illustrated here).

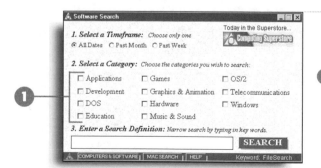

FIGURE 26.2

Find the software you want by category or filename.

1 Check a box to restrict your search to a single category.

You can search for software in several ways. You can limit your search to a specific category, such as Games or

Finding both Mac and Windows files

If you want to search for files on another computer platform, no problem. Click the **MAC SEARCH** or **PC SEARCH** button (depending on which platform you're using) at the bottom of the search window to get you there.

Be precise with your search text

AOL's search engine can only display 250 matches, regardless of how many are actually there. If more than 250 files are shown as available, you should refine your search by describing the file with more specific information.

Graphics. You can even restrict the search to a specific time frame; perhaps you only want to find a file that was posted in the past month.

2. If you want to locate a file by name or subject, enter the information in the **Search** text box. If you want to find a screen saver, for example, enter screen saver as the subject of your search.

If files matching your description cannot be found, a window notifies you.

If files meeting your description are found, you see a File Search Results window onscreen (see Figure 26.3). A file might be listed more than once if it's in more than one library on America Online. Because only 20 files are loaded to the File List at one time, you may need to click the **List More Files** button to see additional entries.

FIGURE 26.3

Success! The files you are looking for are listed here.

1️⃣ Double-click the filename to learn more.

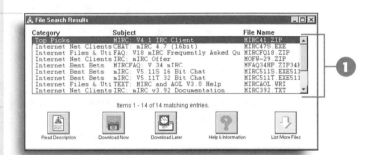

In this example, you'll try to locate a copy of the popular Windows Internet chat client discussed in Chapter 17, "How to Join and Participate in Internet Newsgroups and Mailing Lists," known as mIRC.

Caution: Downloading Mac files on a Windows computer can be a problem

Downloading a Mac software file from the Windows version of AOL can be a problem. A Mac program's file characteristics, which consist of a data fork and a resource fork, are not properly detected on a Windows-based computer. Only files in *binhex* format (converted from binary code to ASCII text) come through unscathed. Such files will usually have an .HQX file extension added to their name. Document files (such as a word processing file or picture file) will also generally come through in usable fashion, if you follow PC file-naming standards (with the proper extension for the file type).

To learn more about the file that interests you, either double-click the filename, or choose the **Read Description** button, either by clicking it or by pressing Return or Enter. You see a window similar to the one shown in Figure 26.4.

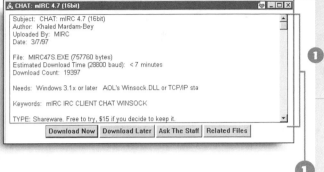

Teach Yourself: Download Your Files Fast

Now that you've found a file you'd like to download, the next step is to start the download process. The **Download Later** option will create a file *queue*, which is a list of files to download. That list or directory will be stored in America Online's Download Manager. This feature can be checked at any time from the **My Files** drop-down menu on the toolbar (it's all described in more detail a bit later in this chapter). If you want to download the file immediately, choose **Download Now**.

The steps that follow cover the typical downloading process. The illustrations shown will be slightly different in the Macintosh and Windows versions of AOL's software (and will probably be altered a bit as software is updated), but the steps you follow will be the same:

To download files from AOL

1. The default selection in the software list, at the bottom of the window, is **Download Now**. Choose this to bring up a window that enables you to indicate where you want to store the file that's being transferred to your computer (see Figure 26.5).

2. Rename the file, if you want.

3. Click the **Save** button or press the Return or Enter key to begin the download process.

It's easy to change the listing order

Click the **Sort Order** drop-down menu at the bottom of a software library directory display to change the order in which the files are listed. To see all the files available, you may need to click the **More** button a number of times.

Caution: *Read* **before you download**

Before downloading a file, check the file description. This description not only tells you more about the file, but also contains information about what kind of computer it works on.

How to get files faster

To speed up file transfer times, you might want to log on to America Online at a non-peak hour, perhaps early in the morning, when network traffic is less busy.

FIGURE 26.5

Select the place where you want the file sent.

① Click **Save** to start the file transfer.

When your file download begins, you see a progress bar showing approximately how much of the file has been sent, and an estimate of how long it will take to transfer that file to your computer (see Figure 26.6).

When the file has been transferred, America Online's friendly narrator will announce (if the sounds are enabled), "File's done!"

FIGURE 26.6

The file download is in process.

① Click **Cancel** to end the file transfer process.

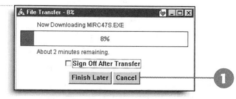

What to do while you're downloading

While the file download is in progress, just click the Taskbar or press Alt+Tab to switch to another program. (If you're a Mac OS user, just click the desktop or another program from the application menu to accomplish the same result.) You should avoid CPU-intensive tasks, such as calculating a spreadsheet, while downloading. Doing so can slow down or even interrupt the download process.

Using AOL's Download Manager to Your Best Advantage

You can build a download queue or list by using AOL's convenient Download Manager. You can start the download at any time during your online session or when the session ends. When you add a file to the list, you see the acknowledgment shown in Figure 26.7.

To use the Download Manager, choose the second option available to you when downloading a file—**Download Later**.

The Download Manager is available by clicking the **My Files** icon on the toolbar and choosing it from the drop-down menu.

You can check it at any time after adding files to the queue to see whether you want to make changes in the lineup before downloading begins.

America Online's Download Manager lets you manage the entire download process from a single window. You can open the Download Manager window when notified that a file has been added to the download queue by selecting the **Download Manager** button in the acknowledgment window, or you can use the My Files icon on the toolbar. The Download Manager displays all the files you've selected for downloading (see Figure 26.8).

The following options are available to you in the Download Manager window:

- **View Description.** The first option in the lower-left corner of the window gives you the chance to check whether you really want to download the file. If the file transfer process will take a long time, you probably should review the file descriptions before beginning a download.

- **Download.** Enables you to immediately begin the download process for the files you've selected.

- **Show Files Downloaded (or Show Completed Downloads for Mac users).** Enables you to view a list of recent files that you've downloaded. You can check the file description again or remove the file from the list.

When you don't really want that file

If you decide you don't want to download the file after all, click the **Cancel** button on the download progress bar (this option doesn't appear on the Mac version). In a minute or two, the download will stop. If you decide you actually want to resume the download at a later time choose the **Finish Later** option instead and *don't* delete the partial file that has been transferred to your computer; if you do, the Download Manager cannot resume downloading at the point where it left off.

Caution: Download Later isn't always available

If you log on to America Online as a guest using another member's software, the Download Later function will not work, nor will you be able to use the Automatic AOL feature to run automated AOL sessions.

FIGURE 26.8

The Download Manager lists the files that will be transferred to your computer.

1 Double-click a filename (while online) to get its description.

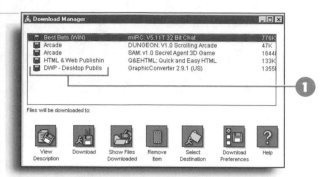

Print the text for later review

Any text window on America Online, even a file description, can be printed or saved to your computer's drive. If you're new to America Online, you'll want to read Appendixes A, "The First Steps to Get Online" and B, "Setting Up AOL's Software" for more information on the basics of setting up your software.

Troubleshooting: Already downloaded?

Help! I'm getting a message that I've already downloaded the file. What's wrong?

AOL tracks the files you've downloaded, so if you try to download the file a second time, you get a handy reminder. If something went wrong with the original downloaded file, or you just need another copy, go ahead and click the **OK** button in AOL's reminder window, and proceed with the new download.

- **Remove Item (or Delete List Item for Mac users).** Enables you to remove a selected item from the Download Manager's queue if you decide you don't want to download the file after all.

- **Select Destination.** Enables you to select a new default location (folder or directory) on your computer's drive in which to store the downloaded files. All files selected for downloading by the Download Manager will always be sent to this location.

- **Download Preferences.** Enables you to set your download preferences for the best performance.

- **Help.** Produces America Online's comprehensive **Help** menu, which includes instructions and quick tips to help you get the most efficient use of your online visit (see Figure 26.9).

The Download Manager window lists the total size of the files you've selected for transfer to your computer and gives an estimated transfer time at your modem connection speed. Downloads can take a little longer than the estimate during the evening prime-time period or when noise is on your phone line. At other times, you may find your downloads moving more swiftly than estimated.

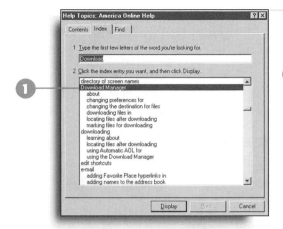

FIGURE 26.9

Getting online Help about a download-related problem.

1. Double-click a topic to read the Help text.

Watch Out for Unsolicited Files!

Although AOL's software libraries are as safe as modern technology allows, you should be careful about downloading files attached to email—especially if you don't know the person sending you the file. It's a sad fact of life that some folks use email to send files that are really Trojan Horses. They claim to provide information or a useful program, but in reality, the files contain macros or programming code designed to steal your password from your AOL software or do other sorts of harm (such as corrupt files on your hard drive).

The best way to protect yourself is to look at the name of the person who sent the email. If it's someone you know, it's probably fine. If you don't know the source, *don't download the file*. When a downloadable file matches the category of software that has the potential of being harmful, AOL puts up a warning (see Figure 26.10).

This warning doesn't mean anything is wrong with the file. It's just a caution for you to check the source of the file carefully before you decide to receive the file.

If you run Automatic AOL sessions, it's a good idea to turn off the option to download files attached to email. You can always retrieve those files later, if you feel they are safe, by logging on,

---

Logging off after file transfers

If you want to end your AOL visit as soon as the file transfer is done, click the option to log off AOL at the end of the download process—it appears in the file transfer progress bar.

opening the email from your Offline Mail drawer (available by clicking the **My Files** icon), and then choosing the **Download Now** option.

Note for Mac Users: Right now, most of the harmful files are in the DOS and Windows world, but that doesn't mean the situation won't change in the future, so please be careful.

FIGURE 26.10

AOL puts up this warning to be careful about downloading files from unknown sources.

① Be certain you really want this file!

Now That I've Downloaded the File, What Do I Do Next?

Why can't I open this file on my Mac?

If you get a message on your Macintosh that the application that created your downloaded file can't be found, log on and check the file description, or view it offline in the Download Manager's list of Completed Downloads. You might need other software to use the downloaded file, either to decompress it or to run it after it's decompressed.

Did you waste time online getting the wrong files?

If you pay for AOL by the hour, and you make a mistake and download a file you can't use, use the keyword Credit to request a rebate to your account for the time you wasted online.

Most larger files in America Online's software libraries are compressed to save disk space and to reduce transfer time, thereby reducing online charges for those of you still using AOL's hourly pricing plans.

Both Macintosh and Windows America Online software can be set to automatically expand (decompress) files that you've downloaded, as soon as you log off. Because some files might be compressed in a format that isn't supported by the software, those files will have to be expanded before you use them.

Before you pick a file to download, read the file description carefully to make sure that your computer, operating system, and software setup are compatible with those of the file.

If you get a message that the file has been damaged after downloading, you need to remove the file from your computer and download the file again. Although files are not damaged often, sometimes a file might not arrive in perfect condition due to noise on the telephone lines or to a network-related problem.

PART **V**

What Types of Software Are Available?   CHAPTER **26**   443

What Types of Software Are Available?

Before you begin to fill your software library, let's discuss the types of software that are available and what software you can find on America Online.

Commercial Software

Commercial software is a retail product. You can find it at your local computer store, in a user group, or by mail order. You can even order commercial software on America Online through a publisher's company support area or through forums devoted to shopping (see Chapters 25, "Visiting the Computing Channel" and 30, "Secret's of AOL's Shopping Channel"). One example is AOL's Computing Superstore (keyword Superstore).

You won't find commercial software in America Online's software libraries, but you can, from time to time, locate a free update program. The author or publisher of a software product can make an update program available so you can revise your copy of the software to a newer version, usually to fix some bugs.

Like most software, commercial software is covered by a license agreement. Although licenses vary from product to product, in most cases, the license states that you are not buying the software itself, but the right to use it. The agreement spells out what those rights are. For most of you, those rights include being allowed to use the software on a single computer at a time and to make backup copies in case the master disks are damaged.

Because many use laptop computers for travel, some software licenses enable you to install the software on both your home or office computer and a portable, assuming that not more than one person will use the software at the same time. If you're going to install the software on multiple computers, you need to buy a site license from the author or publisher.

SEE ALSO

➤ *To learn more about the Computing channel, see page 417*

➤ *To learn more about the Shopping channel, see page 481*

Troubleshooting: Lost files

I can't find the file I just down-loaded. Where is it?

When you first install your AOL software, the program designates a folder or directory for downloaded files. In the Windows version, it's in the America Online 4.0/Download directory. In the Mac version, it's in the Online Downloads folder. You can change the destination to another location, if you prefer, using the Download Manager. You can click the **Select Destination** icon in the Download Manager window, but most users just leave the setting where it is.

Demoware

Demonstration software is designed to let you try out all or most of the features of a software product before you buy it. *Demoware* (the most common term for these files) can be either a commercial or a shareware program. In most cases, you can use the software for a limited period of time, ranging from a few days to a week or two. It then expires and you cannot use it again until you buy a copy. Some demoware might lock out some program features (such as the capability to save and print a document), which become available in the version you buy or by typing in a password on the demo application.

Shareware

Shareware is a modern-day equivalent of the original try-before-you-buy concept. The author or publisher of a software product gives you a fully functional version (although a feature or two might be restricted). You can try it out on your computer for a period of up to a month. When that period expires, you are asked to pay the author or publisher a small fcc for a license to continue to run the program.

Shareware is one of the last vestiges in our society of an honor system. The publisher has no way of knowing whether you are still using the software. If you decide to continue to run it, consider the time and energy the author put into writing and testing that software. Also consider how you would feel if you were not paid for your work.

Shareware is often less expensive than commercial software because it lacks fancy packaging, manuals, and a fully staffed technical support department. Some shareware, however, has become commercial, such as the compression software America Online uses for its Macintosh version, StuffIt. StuffIt was first written by a 15-year-old high school student. It's now published in shareware form, as StuffIt Lite, and as a more fully featured commercial product, StuffIt Deluxe (published by Aladdin Systems).

Freeware

This category covers a wide range of products. *Freeware* is available to you without cost, but the author retains all rights to the program, including how it is to be distributed. Freeware can include a fully functioning program or an update to an existing product. Don't attribute cost to value. You can often find many useful programs in this category.

Public Domain Software

Public domain software can be used and distributed freely. The author has given up all rights to this program.

Teach Yourself: How to Upload Files to AOL

America Online's computing forums have a special software library labeled Free Uploading or Upload Here. This area is set up so you can upload software directly to America Online's software libraries. If you're on an hourly billing plan, "Free Uploading" signifies you won't be charged (except for AOL access numbers that incur extra charges, such as an 800 or 888 number).

Where to Upload

You should do a little research to find out where the appropriate place to upload the file is and to verify that you have the right to send a file. Each computing forum has an information file that tells you its purpose and the kind of software it requires. Rather than waste your time and the forum's by uploading to an inappropriate location, read the description files to be sure that you are uploading your software to the most suitable forum. A screen saver, for example, will likely go in an application or utilities forum.

Before uploading the file—especially if you are not the author—use America Online's File Search feature (described in the

---

Finding the latest software online

The Computing Software Center tracks all the newest file uploads. To see the latest offerings, use the keyword **Hot Software.** The area also offers a Weekly New Files section, where you can see recently released files grouped by category.

Caution: Be careful what you upload

Demoware and shareware can contain restrictions on whether they can be uploaded by anyone other than the author, so read the instructions that come with the software before you decide to upload it to America Online. In general, commercial updates, such as system-related software from Apple Computer and Microsoft, may be uploaded to America Online only by the publisher. In addition, if you upload files with content that violates AOL's Terms of Service (such as a nude or revealing photo), you may risk a bad mark on your AOL account or possible loss of your account.

Check other file descriptions first

Before filling out the Upload information window (the actual name in the title will change from forum to forum), review the descriptions of other software available in that area to become familiar with the way descriptions are written and the kind of information that is required.

section "Using File Search," earlier in this chapter) to make sure that the file you want to send isn't already posted somewhere on America Online.

How to Upload

When you visit a computing software library (see Chapter 25), you'll see an **Upload** button at the bottom of the software file directory. When you want to send your file, click the **Upload** button, which opens the window shown in Figure 26.11.

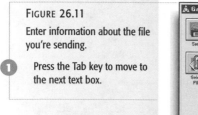

FIGURE 26.11

Enter information about the file you're sending.

1 Press the Tab key to move to the next text box.

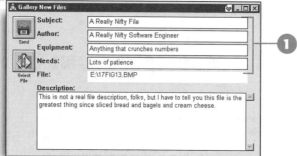

Caution: Uploading limits what you can do on AOL

You can't multitask within your AOL program while a file upload is in progress (that is, you can't switch to another online area as you can when you're downloading a file), so either prepare to switch to another program, or relax until the file upload is completed.

An AOL file upload information window has several text boxes that you need to fill out.

To upload files to an AOL library

1. Enter the subject of the file, which is usually the title of the item you're sending.

2. Enter the author or publisher of the file in the **Author** text box.

3. Describe the kind of equipment used to create this file, and the equipment required to make use of it (this is important).

4. List the operating system and software required to run your file in the **Needs** text box. For example, you may indicate Windows 95, if the program is a 32-bit Windows application. This is also an important requirement.

5. Give a brief description of the file you're sending. Try to limit it to no more than two or three paragraphs, but be as

thorough as you need to be to explain what the file is. The forum staff will edit it if necessary.

6. After the description is entered, click the **Select File** icon, and choose the file you want to send.

7. Finally, click the **Send** button to send it on its way to AOL's host computer network.

When you upload the file, you'll see a File Transfer window that's much like the one displayed when you download a file (refer to Figure 26.6). After the file is received, it is reviewed by forum staff who decide whether it's suitable for their forum. As I said, the file description you give is apt to be edited in accordance with the forum's own library standards.

Because most of the staff members who review these files are volunteers, expect several days to pass before you hear of the forum's decision. If posted, your file will turn up in a forum library specifically devoted to the type of file you've sent.

Using AOL's NetFind to Search for Files

AOL has built an advanced Internet search system to help you locate the kinds of files you want via the World Wide Web. It's called NetFind (see Figure 26.12). You can access this feature directly from AOL's home page by clicking the **Internet** icon on the toolbar and choosing **AOL NetFind** from the drop-down menu. You can also type the keyword NetFind to get the same results.

The next step is simple. Just enter the item you want to look for in the search text box, click **Find** or press the Return or Enter key and AOL's NetFind will get to work to find items that match the description. The process usually takes just a few seconds to complete.

To learn how to customize your information search, read Chapter 16, "How to Search for Information on the Net," especially the section titled "Quick Tips for Using a WWW Search Tool."

Making files smaller

To reduce download time and your online billing time (for those of you still paying for AOL by the hour), many of the files on America Online are compressed, a technique used to make a file smaller. The latest version of America Online's Macintosh and Windows software contains tools to expand compressed files in many formats, such as ZIP and StuffIt. Files saved in other formats are provided in self-extracting form, which means that executing the file (choosing **Run** or double-clicking a file icon) will start the expansion process.

FIGURE 26.12

AOL's NetFind feature uses technology licensed from Excite to find the information you want fast.

1 Type the search text and then click Find.

Troubleshooting: Check the file description

The software I just downloaded won't run on my computer. What's wrong?

Before you download a file, please check the file description carefully. Usually, the description lists the kind of computer the software runs on, along with the version of the operating system, and any additional software you might need. You won't, for example, be able to run a Windows program on a Macintosh, unless you're using an add-on DOS expansion card or a program such as SoftWindows from Insignia Solutions or Connectix VirtualPC. Also, a Windows 95 program won't run under Windows 3.1 (although Windows 95 can usually handle programs made for the older Windows versions). Although Mac and Windows programs may look and work much the same, the programming requirements are quite different.

Finding Popular Web-Based Software Libraries

When you search for a file, choose the option to use AOL NetFind Reviews as the basis of your search by clicking various categories in the NetFind screen. That way you can refine your search for material that has gotten a thumbs up rating from AOL's NetFind team.

With the help of NetFind, I unearthed a number of sources for shareware on the net. As you continue to explore AOL, you'll no doubt find many resources that will provide the software selections you want.

SEE ALSO
➤ *To learn more about the Computing channel, see page 417*

Troubleshooting: When the Software Just Won't Run

I'm lost. I can't get the software I downloaded to run, and no help text is available. What do I do next?

If the publisher or author of the program cannot be contacted, you can try the Mac or PC Help Desk (keyword Help Desk). These forums are set up to help members who can't get online assistance anywhere else. The forums also provide a number of information texts that you can review to enable you to better deal with problems of this sort. Between these help resources, and the information in the forums that make the files available, you should be able to find quick advice to handle most problems.

If you encounter any difficulties using the software you download, consider the following:

- Read the documentation that comes with the program. In many cases, a troubleshooting section is provided that may detail exactly the problem you're having and suggest a solution.

- If the problem cannot be solved by reading the documentation, contact the author or publisher of the software using the screen name, mailing address, or phone number shown in the documentation or online file description.

- If you cannot get help with the previous two options, contact the staff who runs the forum you downloaded the software from. Maybe they can help you get in touch with the author or publisher.

Troubleshooting: Crashing from time to time

Whenever I try to run the software I downloaded, my computer freezes or I get a system error message. Why?

It's the nature of personal computers to crash from time to time. Although the authors or publishers of software may rigorously test their products before release, there's always the possibility of a conflict with someone's setup at one time or another. If you encounter a crash or strange behavior with a program, discontinue using it and contact the author or publisher right away to report the situation.

Using the Personal Finance Channel

AOL's financial forums

World Wide Web financial resources

AOL's Tax forum

Computers and Finance

Computers and personal finance go hand in hand. We prepare checks on our computers, do our tax returns, and manage an investment portfolio. If you own a business, the computer is an indispensable tool.

If you use your computer for any sort of financial purpose, you'll want to visit the Personal Finance channel on America Online. There you'll find a wealth of useful financial information.

This chapter covers AOL's Personal Finance department and its many-layered gateways that extend from business news to an online real estate office.

Personal Finance

Keyword: Personal Finance

In Chapter 24, "Visiting the News Channel," you read about AOL's handy online newsstand, where you can find news and publications about a host of subjects. Now you'll delve more deeply into the world of business. America Online's Personal Finance channel, shown in Figure 27.1, isn't just for your business activities, however. You'll find resources that help you take charge of your personal finances too. Some of them are covered in the final section of this chapter.

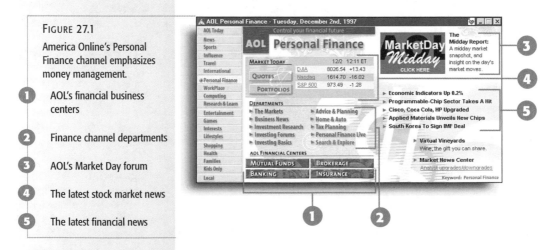

FIGURE 27.1

America Online's Personal Finance channel emphasizes money management.

1 AOL's financial business centers

2 Finance channel departments

3 AOL's Market Day forum

4 The latest stock market news

5 The latest financial news

Here's a brief look at some of the Personal Finance channel features:

- **Market Today.** Up to the minute information from the financial world, brought to you from the major news centers. You'll also be able to check the latest stock quotes and your investment portfolio (I'll cover this area in more detail in the next section).

- **The Markets.** Track your favorite stocks, and get valuable investment tips from AOL's roster of online experts.

- **Business News.** From the major wire services and financial publications, you can read the latest stories and informed speculation about the future in specific industries.

Caution: Look before you leap!

Please take note of the disclaimer that is posted in various forums in AOL's Personal Finance channel. The purpose of these areas is to give you information about various aspects of financial management. The forum staff and contributors to those areas are not responsible in any way for the way you use that information to conduct your personal finances.

FIGURE 27.2

The Business News section is also a part of AOL's News channel (discussed in Chapter 24).

1 Click the **More Stories** button to see more features.

- **Investment Research.** Get comprehensive information about a company before you make your investment decision.

- **Investment Forums.** Some popular forums on AOL are devoted to your investments (see Figure 27.3). The one you hear about often is the Motley Fool, a source of irreverent yet often accurate information.

- **Investing Basics.** Not all of us are financial wizards and if you're looking for a route into the maze of often confusing and contradictory information about personal finance, this is the area to check (it's a place I visit often).

- **Advice & Planning.** The best way to a secure financial future is careful planning. You can get some sage advice in this area (but remember that little warning I wrote earlier about being extra careful before following anyone's financial advice).

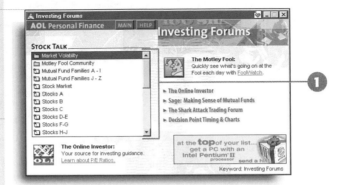

- **Home & Auto.** Whether you're buying a new home, selling the one you have now, or looking to replace that old car, you'll get information to help you make a more informed decision. You'll find links to the AutoVantage online buying service and *Consumer Reports* magazine here.

- **Tax Planning.** April 15th isn't the time to begin planning for taxes. It's a year-round endeavor. When tax time is near, you'll be able to download tax forms and get last-minute advice to review before you file your return.

- **Personal Finance Live.** Online conferences are a big factor in your AOL experience. You'll learn about special chats with a financial slant.

- **Search.** AOL has a custom Web-based Search tool (see Figure 27.4) you can use to locate information about a specific financial issue.

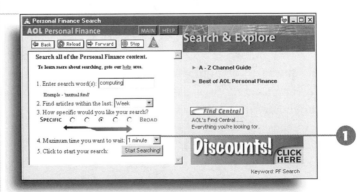

- **Mutual Funds.** Before you invest in a special fund, you can track their progress here. You can also trade with a specially selected group of firms that handle these investments.

- **Banking.** Major banks, such as Bank of America, Chase, and Wells Fargo let you conduct your transactions on AOL. You benefit from AOL's special security features so that you can bank online from the comfort of your home or office PC.

- **Brokerage.** AOL has teamed up with major stock brokers so that you can do your trades online.

- **Insurance.** AOL's Insurance Center (see Figure 27.5) helps you wade through confusing information about the insurance policies you need. You'll also be able to contact some of the major insurance companies online, to check out their policy offerings.

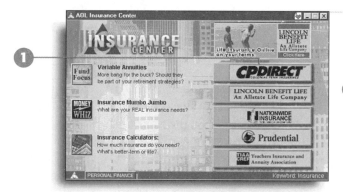

FIGURE 27.5

AOL's Insurance Center offers advice and direct links to major firms.

1   Click the company's name for more information.

Teach Yourself: Using the Online Stock Forums

America Online offers you a vast range of helpful investment information that guides you toward managing a stock portfolio. You also can check the latest stock prices within 15 or 20 minutes after they are posted so that you can see how your favorite stocks are doing.

A little later in this chapter, I'll even show you a sample investment portfolio that I assembled.

Check Your Stocks Online

Keyword: Quotes

How well is your stock portfolio doing? Is your stockbroker's phone busy, or do you just want to see how your favorite stocks are doing before you decide whether to invest? Check out AOL's Quotes & Portfolios center (see Figure 27.6).

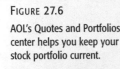

FIGURE 27.6

AOL's Quotes and Portfolios center helps you keep your stock portfolio current.

1   Enter your stock's symbol here to get a quote.

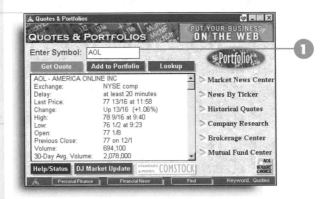

Because America Online's stock is quite popular, I decided to check its present value. Figure 27.6 shows its price and related statistics. Checking the value of stock is easy. First you have to enter the stock's symbol because market entries are usually identified in abbreviated form. The Lookup Symbol feature lets you quickly find the correct symbol. The Add to Portfolio feature is a convenience measure so that you can easily track your favorite stocks, whether your interest in the market is from an armchair or as an active investor.

After you've built your stock portfolio, real or imaginary, you can click the **Display Portfolio** icon (which brings up the screen in Figure 27.7) to see just how your investments are doing, and how much money you've made or (perish the thought) lost in these transactions. As you can see from my choices, I would have made a small profit had these investments actually been made.

If you want to learn more about a company, look at the Company Research area (shown earlier in Figure 27.6). The **Market News Center** button takes you to AOL's business news area, the online equivalent of a newspaper's financial pages.

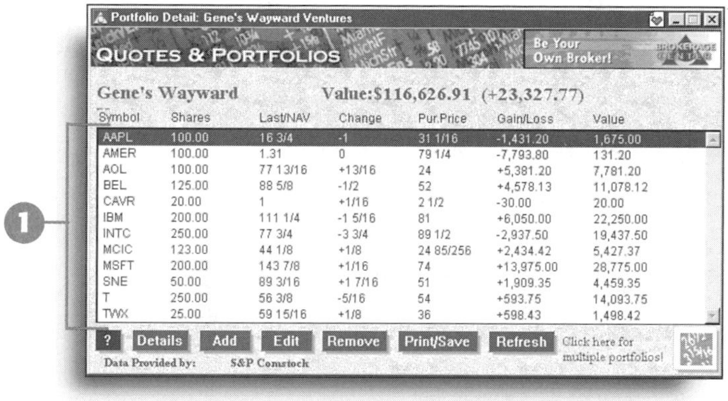

FIGURE 27.7

A sample investment portfolio of popular and not-so-popular stocks. Remember, this is just a sample, and doesn't represent my actual profile.

1 Scroll through the list to see the entire portfolio.

Teach Yourself: Find Online Tax Assistance

Keyword: Tax

The final part of this chapter briefly covers some of the tax forums available on America Online. Remember, however, that AOL and forum staff can't actually fill out your tax returns for you. Only you or your tax preparer can do that. The forums are designed to provide information that helps you over some of the hurdles and eases the process of accurately filling out your tax return. Although forums such as the one run by Intuit, publishers of MacInTax and TurboTax, are available year-round, other tax-related forums only appear during the tax season.

First, let's take a brief look at AOL's Tax Planning forums (see Figure 27.8). The lineup shown here changes frequently, so expect the forum screen to look somewhat different when you call it up. Because it was April 15th when I wrote this chapter, you'll see lots of last-minute advice on how to handle the pressure and get your return out.

- **Tax News.** Keep up-to-date on the latest IRS rules and congressional action.
- **Forms and Schedules.** Download the tax forms you need from AOL. They're all available in Adobe Acrobat format (also available online) so that you can get clear, accurate printouts on a variety of printers.

FIGURE 27.8

At tax time, AOL's Tax Planning area is populated with lots of resources with valuable information to help you prepare your return as quickly and accurately as possible.

1 Scroll through the list box for more offerings.

- **IRAs and Keogh's.** Learn valuable tips on setting up your own retirement plan.
- **Tax Software.** Link up with the major publishers of tax software, to get the latest updates and helpful advice from their online representatives.
- **On the Web.** Although it's difficult to think of the IRS as warm and fuzzy (even with all those promises that they will improve their customer service in response to Congressional complaints), they do maintain an up-to-date Web site where you can get the latest tax information and forms as shown in Figure 27.9. Other helpful Web sites with tax information are available from the IRS Web site.

FIGURE 27.9

Even the IRS has joined the Information Superhighway with a Web site.

1 Click the photo to enter the IRS Web site.

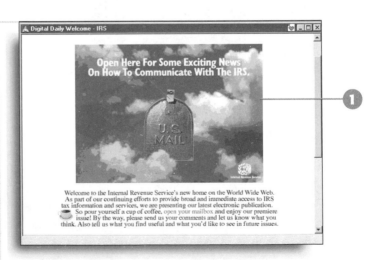

- **Tax Logic.** Visit an online tax preparation service and file your return via modem.

- **Tax Help Live.** Figure 27.8 had a direct link to the NAEA Tax channel, where you can enter an online conference room at tax time and get instant advice.

SEE ALSO

➤ *For more informaton about AOL's online newspapers, see page 402*

➤ *For more information about educational resources on AOL, see page 390*

➤ *For more information about shopping online, see page 482*

AOL's WorkPlace Channel

Internet commerce

Exploring AOL's PrimeHost

AOL's business resources

Business information on the Web

AOL is for Business Users Too

A recent survey, done just before this book was written, has shown that about 28 million Americans surf the World Wide Web, and a healthy percentage of them are AOL members (in fact 10 million as of the end of October, 1997).

A great majority of these folks (perhaps you) explore the Internet on a daily basis, up to two hours or more per week. It's a sure thing that a lot of this Internet access is done just for fun. You want to read your favorite magazine, learn about a new computer game, or participate in an online chat.

Fun is foremost on the minds of most AOL members. As I've explained in previous chapters, thousands of AOL members visit the service for no other reason than to hang out with friends in a chat room or exchange instant messages. Others want to write email to their friends, or play a new online game in the Games channel.

Many of you also use AOL for your business, however. You send email or important business documents to your business associates. You may examine AOL's financial forums for guidance and information. In this chapter, I'm going to introduce you to some of those business-oriented features. I'll even touch briefly on AOL's own Web hosting service, PrimeHost, where you can build a professional Web site, and benefit from expert promotional services.

Visiting AOL's WorkPlace Channel

Keyword: WorkPlace

I introduced you to AOL's financial services forums in the previous chapter. You discovered ways to manage your stock portfolio, check the latest information on your investments, and receive help with your taxes. To start this chapter off, visit AOL's WorkPlace information center (see Figure 28.1).

FIGURE 28.1

AOL WorkPlace is your resource for business information and support.

1   Your Business center for small business

2   Your Career information center

3   AOL professional forums

4   AOL Business Departments

5   Special WorkPlace features

6   Business-oriented merchandise

Let's examine some of these WorkPlace channel features in more detail:

- **Your Business.** This area includes a compendium of information and forums designed to help you make your business more successful.

- **Your Career.** If you are looking for a job, or want to choose your first career or a new one, you'll want to visit this area. In addition to advice on advancing in your chosen career, you'll also find quick access to AOL's own want ads and perhaps find just the job you need.

- **Professional Forums.** AOL has set aside a forum for a number of business categories (see Figure 28.2). You will find areas devoted to most anything, from the legal profession to landscaping.

Caution: Don't follow advice blindly!

Please take note of the disclaimer that you'll find posted in various forums in AOL's business-oriented forums. The purpose of these areas is to give you information about various aspects of financial management. The forum staff and contributors to those areas are not responsible in any way for the way you use that information to develop and manage your business.

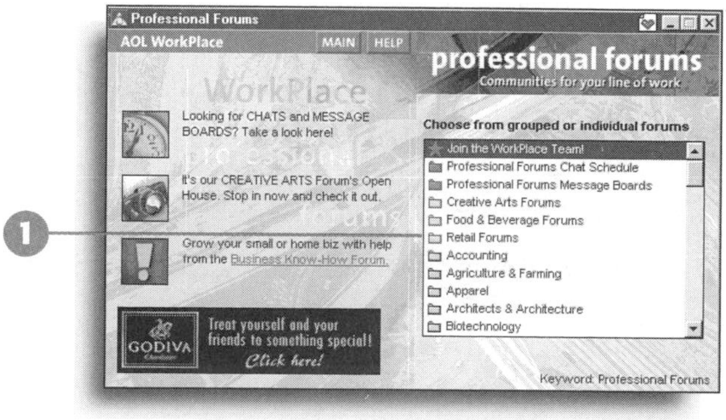

FIGURE 28.2

AOL offers forums for a number of professions here.

1   Scroll through the list for more topics.

■ **Products and Services.** Online commerce is always a major part of AOL (see Figure 28.3). In this area, you can check out some of AOL's offerings, such as PrimeHost (covered later in this chapter), and the AOL Office Store, or you can check on merchandise and services from a host of companies on AOL and the Web.

FIGURE 28.3

You can use this area to locate the product or service you need for your business.

1 Scroll through the list for more products.

■ **Business Research.** You can call on AOL's vast resources and Internet-based databases to find the information you need.

■ **Classifieds.** AOL's Classifieds area offers both free and fee-based ads for your product or service.

■ **Search & Explore.** This is AOL's NetFind search engine, ready to search AOL's business-related resources for additional material.

SEE ALSO

➤ *To learn more about AOL's Shopping Channel, see page 482*

Using AOL's PrimeHost to Build a Commercial Web Site

Keyword: `PrimeHost`

Internet commerce has its advantages over a storefront. You can keep it open 24 hours a day, seven days a week, without incurring higher labor costs. Your audience is not limited to any one service or locality. Anyone in the entire world with interest in the product or service you're offering, and with the money to buy it, can be your customer.

I've already described how you can make your own Web page in just five minutes flat, in Chapter 18, "Become a Web Publisher on AOL." The Web pages you create there are limited to 2MB to cover the space for your document and linked graphics. That's just fine as a personal Web site, and maybe even for a small business. It may also be useful for test marketing, so you can explore the possibilities of Internet-based sales without making a full commitment in terms of development costs and other expenses.

If you want to extend your Web commerce capabilities beyond that level, however, check out AOL's PrimeHost (see Figure 28.4). In addition to offering Web publishing tools, you can take advantage of AOL's own marketing apparatus to help promote your business. One thing AOL is good at, considering its rapid-fire climb to the top of the online service world, is marketing.

AOL's PrimeHost promises a turnkey solution to setting up and maintaining a Web page, and offers tools to help you build your first site in just 10 minutes. This brief list shows the available information:

- **PrimeHost Member Services.** This section details the features offered by the PrimeHost service (see Figure 28.5). You'll learn how to make your own Web page using free online authoring tools (such as the AOLpress software outlined in Chapter 18), and receive advice on promoting your site to get better sales. You'll also find a troubleshooting section, in case you run into trouble getting your site to look right and work properly for your customers.

- **Template Gallery.** You may want to get skilled Web authoring services, especially if your artistic abilities are in any way close to mine. On the other hand, AOL makes it easy for you to get started by supplying a set of ready-made templates (see Figure 28.6), that you can use to make a Web page in just a few minutes by entering the right information in the spaces provided. It's similar to the templates you find in popular word processing or desktop publishing programs in terms of simplicity.

FIGURE 28.4

AOL provides the tools and marketing assistance for your business-oriented Web site.

① Information text about PrimeHost services

② List of available Member Services

③ Template Gallery for fast Web authoring

④ Need More? promotional information

⑤ Why a Web Site?

⑥ The price structure for PrimeHost services

⑦ List of Prime Host features

⑧ AOL's marketing assistance detailed

⑨ Four steps to creating your own Web site

⑩ Sign Up Now ordering form

FIGURE 28.5

User's of AOL's PrimeHost service can get assistance here.
The listings update when you
click a specific topic button at
the center of the screen.

1   Scroll through the list for
    questions and answers.

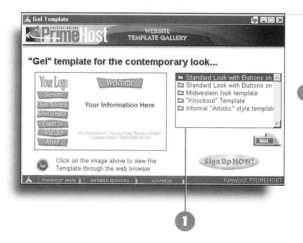

FIGURE 28.6

PrimeHost offers a set of templates to help you get started
with your Web site.

1   Double-click a list box entry
    to see another template.

- **Need More?.** This is just your regular sales pitch. AOL gar-
  ners a list of customers and recommendations for you to
  check and see how their businesses have faired. Marketing
  information is also included, comparing PrimeHost with
  other Web hosting services.
- **Why a Web Site?.** Information on the advantages to setting
  up your business on the Web.
- **What does it cost?.** Consult this area for updated pricing
  information for the service.

Tell your friends you're on the Web

Whether you use AOL's PrimeHost service or not, you'll find valuable information there–telling your customers that you're on the World Wide Web.

In addition to getting listed in a business directory, you'll want to put your Web address on your stationery, your business cards, your product literature, and ads, so folks know where they can find you on the Internet. You'll even notice such information at the bottom of TV ads, movie previews, and in your daily newspaper. It's clear that the Internet has pervaded all elements of our society.

- **What You Get!.** A list of the services AOL is offering you via its PrimeHost service.

- **Exposure on AOL & the World Wide Web?.** A description of AOL's business directory and a list of the marketing resources they offer.

- **4 Easy Steps.** As the salesman say, this is the deal closer. It shows you what you have to do to sign up with PrimeHost and make your Web page.

- **Sign Up Now!.** Just your regular service order form.

Business-Oriented Web Sites

The following sections give you information on a couple of Web sites that cater to business. Many more sites exist that might prove equally interesting. You'll find a number of them listed in AOL's WorkPlace channel and PrimeHost areas, both described in previous sections of this chapter. You can also search for additional business-oriented sources using AOL's NetFind Web search feature, available at keyword `NetFind`.

CommerceNet

URL address: `http://www.commerce.net`

Think of CommerceNet (see Figure 28.7) not just as a single business resource, but more as a huge shopping mall, containing Web pages from various businesses. You'll find areas devoted to such firms as California's Bank of America, Apple Computer, Dun & Bradstreet, and a number of smaller firms, too. CommerceNet is very much a work in progress. Some firms represented at this site provide product catalogs, and others even let you place electronic orders for merchandise. Best of all, if you're looking to gain access to the Internet for your business, this might be one resource you'll want to consider joining so you can click your way to your own Web site.

FIGURE 28.7

CommerceNet is practically a shopping mall in cyberspace.

1 Scroll through the page to see more headlines.

Small and Home-Based Business Links

URL address: http://www.ro.com/small_business/homebased.html

An increasing number of people have found comfort and sometimes wealth in working at home. This site (see Figure 28.8) is devoted to providing information about setting up and running such a business. You'll find information about franchises, business opportunities, reference materials, and advice on how to make your business successful. Of course, whenever you read about a potential business opportunity through this resource or anywhere else, you'll want to check it out thoroughly before getting more involved in the enterprise. This is a good place for you to get started, however.

SEE ALSO

➤ *For more information online about stock quotes, managing your investment portfolio, and getting help with your taxes, see page 452*

➤ *Discover resources for AOL's online newspapers, see page 402*

➤ *Read about resources for education, including online schools, and ways to search for the information you need, see page 390*

FIGURE 28.8

You'll find information about home-based businesses of all sorts.

Secrets of AOL's Travel Channel

AOL is now worldwide

Book a trip

Use AOL's reservation services

Check flight schedules and fares

Using AOL for Travel Planning

I covered investments and saving money on your taxes in Chapter 27, "Using the Personal Finance Channel," so let's devote this chapter to one way of doing something with some of the money you may save. This chapter and the next are devoted to shopping of one sort or another; this chapter covers shopping for a vacation. Instead of visiting the neighborhood travel agency, you're going to an agency located in cyberspace, available through the friendly interface of America Online.

Using AOL's convenient Travel channel, you can pick a spot for a family vacation and gather information about the place you're going to visit without ever leaving your home or office. You can select a hotel, make reservations, and even rent a car.

Suppose, for example, that you've never taken your children on a trip to California, and have wanted to go there for a long time. This chapter uses Los Angeles and San Francisco as sites for a sample vacation plan. Of course, you can travel virtually anywhere in the world by using the same techniques discussed in this chapter.

Visiting the Travel Channel

Keyword: Travel

Your first step in preparing for this vacation is to pay a visit to AOL's Travel channel. To access this area, click the **Travel** icon in the **Channel** menu or use the keyword Travel. You then see the screen shown in Figure 29.1 (or the latest version, because it's updated often). Some of the online areas available in this department are described in the next few pages.

The vast array of AOL travel resources can only be glimpsed in these capsule descriptions:

- *Where to Go, What to Do.* Information to help you choose the location for your next trip.
- *Travel Bargains.* Save money on your next vacation or business trip.

A source for related information

Some of the areas shown in the Travel department are also available as part of AOL's Shopping channel, which is discussed in more detail in Chapter 30, "Secrets of AOL's Shopping Channel."

FIGURE 29.1

AOL's Travel channel provides the resources you need before making a business or vacation trip.

1 Click here to switch online channels.

2 Click here to check travel plans.

3 Click here to book your trip.

4 Travel channel information centers.

5 Special online offers.

- *Reservations Center*. Use AOL's online travel agencies to plan your trip and make flight, car, and hotel reservations.

- *Preview Travel*. Visit AOL's featured travel agency, where you can check the lowest prices before you make your plans.

- *Resource Center*. Consult AOL's information centers on the best places to visit.

- *Messages & Chat*. AOL's message boards are always enjoyable and informative.

- *Travel Store*. Whether you need a backpack for a mountain climbing expedition or scuba gear for diving, you'll find advice and offers here.

- *Classifieds*. You can place your own buy/sell ads or search for ones that interest you.

- *Business Travel*. Planning that business trip is easy on AOL.

- *Search & Explore*. Tap AOL's huge database centers to get the information you want as quickly as possible.

Teach Yourself: Make Travel Plans on AOL

Keywords: Travel Reservations

AOL offers a complete travel agency (see Figure 29.2), where you can seek out special tours, check local conditions, and make plans for your next trip. Each time you visit the Travel Reservations Center, you'll find a different set of offerings, and you'll have a full opportunity to make reservations via several online agencies.

FIGURE 29.2

Visit AOL's Reservations Center to check out information that will help you get the best value on your next trip.

1 Double-click the list box categories to make your reservations.

One popular resource for your online travel plans is AOL's Preview Travel agency (see Figure 29.3). In addition to making travel plans at the best available price, you will want to check this area regularly for special deals on car rentals and special tours. You'll even find a message board where you can learn about the experiences of your fellow AOL members when visiting a specific city, and contribute your own remembrances and advice, too.

FIGURE 29.3

AOL's Preview Travel agency provides travel advice and an easy method to make your reservations at the lowest possible price.

1 Click the Click Here! button to get started.

Take a few moments to click the colorful icons in the Preview Travel center to learn about special offers and featured trips. To make your travel plans, follow these steps:

1. When you're ready, click the **Book Travel HERE!** icon to set up your profile.

2. After agreeing to the agency's terms, you'll be asked to give yourself a password so that your online transactions are secure.

3. After you become a registered user, you'll be able to create a profile in the screen that appears when your password is entered.

4. Then you set up your profile (see Figure 29.4). You can select your preferred airlines here, your departure city, the kind of seats you want, and the cuisine you prefer (but remember, this is still airline food). The seating class you prefer can also be selected.

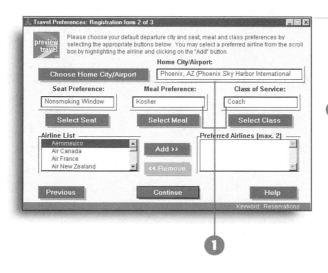

FIGURE 29.4

Your travel profile makes it easier to have your airline reservations entered accurately.

1 Enter your travel preferences in the text fields.

You can create several profiles if you'd like, to cover your travel plans from different cities, or for home or business purposes.

The process from here on takes only minutes. Let's assume you've selected Air with Car or Hotel as your reservations option:

1. In your first Itinerary Planning screen, enter the **Departure City** and **Arrival City** (see Figure 29.5).

2. After your planning information is entered, click the **Continue Flight Selection** button to bring up the list of flights around the time you selected.

Choose the correct airport

Some cities, such as New York and Washington, DC, have more than one major airport. You may see a verification screen asking which airport you prefer before you see the flights that match your request.

FIGURE 29.5

Enter your planning information on this screen.

1. Type your travel itinerary in the text fields.

3. When the available flights are shown (see Figure 29.6), you'll just have to double-click one of them to have it included in your travel itinerary.

FIGURE 29.6

Your list of available flights is shown at the top of this window. At the bottom is the flight you've selected.

1. Scroll through the list to see more flights.

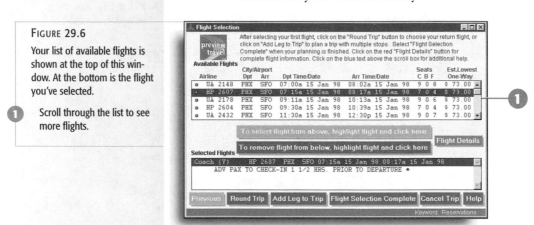

Don't forget your seating and meal preferences

If you have a special preference for seating, such as a window seat, or you're on a special diet, you need to list those preferences in your application. Getting correct reservations is much easier that way.

From here, just follow the information screens to add additional flights or car and hotel reservations. At the end of the process, you can actually have AOL's travel agency make reservations for you and bill it to your credit card. You can also take the information and bring it to your own travel agent or even book the flights directly.

Places to Check Before You Travel

In addition to actually making your reservations, you can check AOL's huge reserve of travel information before you fine-tune your plans. The following sections describe a few online areas you'll want to visit. Many more are just a mouse click or two away.

A Trip to Travel Corner

Keyword: `Travel Corner`

The next stopping point in this tour is the Travel Corner (see Figure 29.7). This forum is hosted by the editors of *Weissman Travel Reports*. The Corner's main focus is the comprehensive profiles about major U.S. and international destinations. You get a brief overview about the high points of a specific city and a list of its main attractions. The report not only describes these attractions, but also suggests the kinds of people who would most like to visit them. This information is especially important if you're taking your children with you.

> **Get more information about a hotel**
>
> Before you choose a hotel, you may want to have its reservations department send you a brochure. The larger hotel chains and tourist spots offer elaborate color booklets describing all the features available and the various room options.

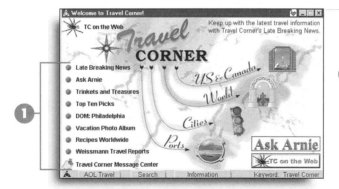

FIGURE 29.7

The Travel Corner profiles your favorite travel spots.

1 Click these buttons to bring up the information you want.

The profiles contain lists of do's and don'ts so you can learn more about the local culture and etiquette of your destination. This kind of help is especially useful if you're traveling to a foreign country where local customs might be different from the ones to which you're accustomed.

AOL text screens can be printed or saved

As with all AOL text windows, you can save the window by using the **Save** command (in the **File** menu), or you can print the text window by using the **Print** command.

Can you connect to AOL from your hotel?

If you are traveling with your laptop computer and plan to stay at a hotel, be sure to ask in advance for a computer-ready room. Many hotels are happy to offer you a room with an extra phone jack for your modem. If your hotel does not have special rooms for computer users, in most cases, you can remove the cable for the phone from the phone jack and insert your modem cable. Before you do that, make sure the hotel staff won't object.

The Travel Corner screen includes separate icons for the kinds of profiles you want to review—domestic or international. You'll even find a message center that describes exotic destinations you might want to visit. You can stop over in this area to learn about the experiences of other online travelers, both AOL members and *Weissman Travel Reports* editors. You also can use this message board to post your own personal reports of your travels, so you can share the information you've discovered with other AOL members.

Visiting the Independent Traveler

Keyword: Traveler

The Independent Traveler consists of a wealth of resources that contains much of the information you need to know before planning your trip (see Figure 29.8). The main window of this forum contains useful articles on many travel-related subjects. If you're going to travel by air, you receive up-to-date information on the lowest fares. When you travel abroad, you need to know specific things about the country you are going to visit, and you'll find them here.

FIGURE 29.8

AOL's Independent Traveler offers special tours and advice on how to get the most from your vacation.

1 Click the **Travel Channel** button to return to the screen shown in Figure 29.1.

Consult the State Travel Advisories

Keyword: `Travel Advisories`

Because the world situation is apt to change at any moment, you'll want to view the official U.S. State Department travel advisories, shown in Figure 29.9. You can tap into a huge database of information that covers the entire world, and learn about any special considerations for traveling to a specific country.

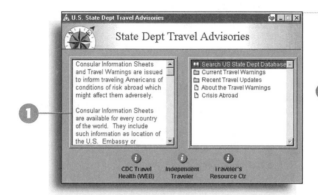

FIGURE 29.9

The U.S. State Department's travel advisories can be searched on AOL.

1 Scroll through the text screen to learn more about this feature.

The U.S. State Department Warnings folder contains the latest alerts about problems and limitations of traveling to specific parts of the world. You'll want to review these text files before you plan your travel itinerary.

A Visit to a Digital City

Keyword: `Digital City`

When it comes to visiting another city, nothing compares to being there in person, but when you make your travel arrangements, it's quite helpful to be able to preview that city and learn more about it before you leave on the trip. AOL's Digital City enables you to search for information on your own hometown and hundreds of cities around the world (see Figure 29.9).

SEE ALSO

➤ *To learn more about AOL's International Channel, see page 376*

FIGURE 29.10

AOL's Digital City channel is a fast and convenient way to tune in any city you want to visit.

1   Click the city's name to see its forums.

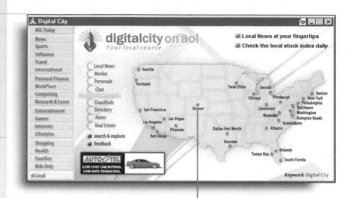

Secrets of AOL's Shopping Channel

Find the merchandise you want

Place your order

Save bucks

Advertise on AOL

Secrets of online commerce

Online Shopping

The description of an average shopping trip is typical these days. You have to fight traffic and search for parking places at your local shopping mall or endure long waits at the checkout lines. You waste time going from place to place to find the best prices. Yes, shopping should be fun, but more often these days, it's not all that enjoyable. A better way to get your shopping done exists with the help of your computer and America Online (of course).

Do you want to save a few dollars on your next purchase? Perhaps you just want to get the most up-to-date information about a particular product or service before you decide whether to buy. America Online is the place to do both.

In this chapter, you'll go on an enjoyable shopping tour by way of the Information Superhighway. You'll make several brief stops at different shops in an online mall, and you'll even buy a few items along the way.

A Tour of AOL's Shopping Channel

Keyword: Marketplace, Shopping

America Online's Shopping channel, shown in Figure 30.1, is a gateway to AOL's huge shopping mall.

Before you go on, you should realize that AOL's Shopping channel, as with other online areas, is definitely a work in progress. Artwork is always being updated, and new shopping features are regularly being added to the mix. So, the Shopping channel you visit might look a little different from the one shown here.

FIGURE 30.1

The Shopping channel is your gateway to AOL's online mall.

1 Click here to select another AOL channel.

2 List of featured items in the AOL Shopping Mall

3 List of offerings grouped by category

4 Special daily offers

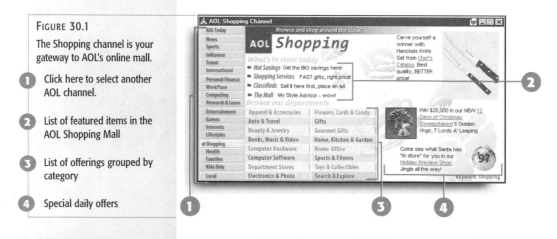

Teach Yourself: Order Merchandise from AOL

Keyword: `AOL Store`

Let's see how easy it is to order something on AOL.

For this example, we'll visit the AOL Store and look at America Online's custom line of logo merchandise, which you can add to your personal wardrobe, send as gifts, or just keep as souvenirs.

To see what's available, click the **AOL Logo Merchandise** icon (on the AOL Store screen 1) to get the window shown in Figure 30.2.

It's only as good as your monitor

The quality of the image you see on your computer screen depends on the size and quality of the monitor, and the capabilities of your computer to display an image at a specific resolution. The image is sent in full color, but whether it appears in black-and-white or clear, crisp, full color varies from installation to installation.

FIGURE 30.2

Choose the product that interests you from the directory listing.

1 Double-click a list box item to see more choices.

The featured item at the AOL Store is illustrated in the picture. If you want to know more about this item, click the picture, and you'll see the screen shown in Figure 30.3.

FIGURE 30.3

A full description of the product you selected appears in a description box.

1 Scroll through the text window to see the entire description.

The descriptive window gives you the same sort of information you find in a mail-order catalog. The description is enticing enough to give you a good picture of what the shirt looks like. I think I'm going to order one of these jackets, so let's select the **Click Here to Order** button to bring up the screen shown in Figure 30.4. Choose the shirt size you want by double-clicking the entry in the directory window.

FIGURE 30.4

Ready to order? I'll take Large.

1 Click **Continue** to select that item.

In the next screen, you can choose the number of shirts you want. After you select the merchandise you want to order, you will probably want to double-check your shopping cart to make sure that you selected the correct item. AOL's software does this automatically for you by displaying a confirmation that the product you want has been added to your shopping cart (see Figure 30.5).

FIGURE 30.5

AOL confirms your selection as you add items to your shopping cart.

1 Click a button to activate its function.

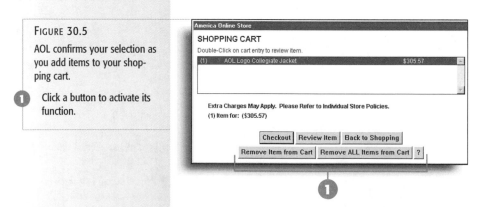

Click the **Checkout** button to bring up a window that enables you to enter billing and shipping information, and then place your order (see Figure 30.6).

After you enter your billing information, type your correct shipping address. By default, the address recorded for your online account appears as the billing address (see Figure 30.7). You can have the same address automatically entered for shipping or enter a different shipping location. Click the **Continue** button to add your shipping information.

Get that credit card first

Before visiting your online shopping center, have your credit card handy so that you can enter your billing information without delay.

America Online Store

CREDIT CARD ADDRESS

Must match CREDIT CARD statement.

First Name	James		Last Name	Kirk
Street 1	Starship Enterprise			
Street 2				
City	San Francisco			
State	CA	Zip	94100	Country	UNITED STATES
Daytime Phone	555-555-5555		Evening Phone	777-555-5555

Continue   Previous Screen   Review Cart

Back To Shopping   ?

FIGURE 30.7

Complete the order. The second Street line can accommodate a longer street address.

Secrets of Internet Commerce

You'll find that AOL's own shopping areas are only a part of the picture. AOL's easy Internet access provides you with a wealth of shopping opportunities, ranging from direct access to large shopping malls (such as Santa Barbara, California's La Cumbre Plaza shown in Figure 30.8), to major mail-order houses that are

It's easy to print the information

As with all online information, feel free to save and print the text window whenever you want. Just choose **Save** or **Print** from the **File** menu (as appropriate).

happy to take your direct order. As you travel the World Wide Web, no doubt you'll come across a number of places with attractive merchandise for sale.

FIGURE 30.8

A shopping mall in California is just one of the sources of Internet commerce.

 Scroll through the screen to see the rest of the page.

AOL software upgrades are free

From time to time, AOL upgrades its software to add new features and offer better performance. Whether you use a Mac or Windows-equipped PC, you can choose the software version you want and download either (or both, for that matter) from AOL's software upgrade center. So, when you're doing your electronic shopping, don't forget to "shop" for the latest AOL software as well. After all, you don't have to pay for these software upgrades.

Before you start your shopping spree, however, you'll want to check the "Tips for Online Shopping" section at the end of this chapter. In addition to the tips noted, AOL has set up a special program to certify its own merchants, called the AOL Guarantee. It's designed to make sure your online transaction is safe, that you'll get the product you ordered, and that you're satisfied with it.

When you seek out a product on the Internet, however, no such guarantees exist. If you take a few precautions, however, you can reduce the possibility of problems.

The following are a few guidelines for safe Internet commerce:

- *Protect yourself against credit card sniffing.* When you send a credit-card number across the Internet, it is possible that someone may be able to tap into that information. The latest versions of AOL software use an SSL (secured) Web browser, which encrypts the information you exchange with your Internet-based merchant, so third parties can't retrieve that data. If you haven't upgraded yet, the keyword Upgrade brings you to AOL's download area to get the latest version.

- *Check the merchant.* Before you order any product, especially a big ticket item, make sure the dealer is reputable. If you don't know anything about the dealer's reputation, contact the Better Business Bureau or consumer agency in their city to see how they rate. You may also use the experiences of other customers as a guide. Some firms may even give you references if you ask.

- *Don't let them rush you.* If the dealer is reputable, they'll still be there tomorrow. Don't be pushed into making a big financial decision on the spot, without checking out the dealer or the offer further.

The vast majority of the dealers who have Web shopping services are honest and will deliver the goods precisely as advertised. A few aren't, however, and you should always check them out before giving out your credit-card number or sending a check.

Your Ads on AOL

Keyword: Classifieds

The Classifieds online forum is the place to post your own ads or check out advertisements from fellow members and commercial outfits (see Figure 30.9). You aren't limited to just computer-related merchandise; you can also place ads for home appliances, electronics, and other types of merchandise.

FIGURE 30.9

America Online's buy/sell/trade center, where you can place your own ads.

1 Click the category icon to see different choices.

Check the dealer first

If you plan to buy merchandise from an AOL classified ad, don't be hesitant about asking the seller for some references. Remember, it's your money and you have a right to spend it carefully.

Caution: Not all ads are free

AOL's Classifieds area offers both free bulletin board ads and ads that carry a special fee. Before placing your ad, be sure to consult current advertising rates and compare the advantages of free versus paid ads; the latter, for example, are searchable, enabling members to locate your ad faster. As with any other online transaction, you can always cancel before your order is sent, if you change your mind.

The guidelines for this area are few and simple. When you post an ad, describe the merchandise you are selling as accurately as possible, including the warts (like that little scratch on the side of the case). Review other ads of the same sort of merchandise to set a fair price, or do as I have done in the past when I've offered merchandise for sale—let your fellow members make their best offer.

Thousands of ads are placed in the Classifieds message area. Most of them are placed by well-meaning firms and individuals; in most cases, you receive the exact merchandise you order. As with all mail-order transactions, however, approach the deal with some healthy skepticism. It's a good idea, for example, to use a credit card when you make your purchase. That way, if you are not satisfied with the product or service, the credit card issuer usually investigates the transaction on your behalf and even credits your account, if necessary.

Tips for Online Shopping

Consider your online shopping tour a modern day equivalent of browsing through a mail-order catalog. Although you can learn a lot about a product or service from the descriptions, sometimes the product you buy just doesn't meet your requirements or the merchandise you've received just doesn't work as it should. Before placing your order, you should keep the following in mind:

- Read the product description thoroughly. If you have further questions, contact the staff of that particular shopping area (not AOL's customer service department unless it's their product).

- Read any posted terms and conditions carefully, in case you need to return the product for an exchange or refund for any reason.

- Merchandise sent via mail or package delivery service usually includes a shipping charge of some sort. If you're comparison shopping, be sure to include the shipping charge (and local sales tax, if it applies) as part of the total price.

- Check the product description for estimated shipping times. Remember that shipments can be delayed as a result of conditions beyond the vendor's control, such as late delivery of merchandise from the manufacturer or delays on the part of the shipping agency (let's not forget the UPS strike in the summer of 1997).

- If you're ordering a product for a special occasion or as a gift, allow extra time for it to reach its destination.

- Make a copy of your order so that you can refer to it later in case you have further questions about the merchandise you ordered.

- When you receive your package, examine the box and contents for signs of damage. If the box seems ruined beyond repair, contact the online vendor immediately about getting a replacement.

- If you have a problem with the merchandise you received, follow the instructions posted in the vendor area about whom to contact for customer service.

- If the product you ordered needs to be repaired, review the warranty information that came with the package. Quite often, service must be done through a manufacturer's own authorized service center and not the vendor.

- Bear in mind that you are ordering the merchandise directly from the vendor, not from America Online. An AOL Certified Merchant guarantees satisfaction, however, and offers special return and refund policies in the event you aren't happy with your new purchase.

- If you use a credit card to make your purchase (and, in most cases, you will), you might also contact the card issuer to assist you if you run into problems dealing with a particular vendor. Remember, too, that some credit cards provide extended warranties and other benefits when you use them to purchase big-ticket items.

SEE ALSO

➤ *Planning a trip, see page 472*

➤ *Finding newspapers and magazines, see page 402*

Printing the order form doesn't always work

Some online order forms consist of multiple text fields, and choosing the **Save** option in the **File** menu might not save the complete text of your order. If this is the case, enter the full details of your order in a text document using AOL's memo feature, or use a screen image capture program to record the actual order screen. The **Print Screen** feature of Windows or the Command-Shift-3 feature of the Mac OS captures the screen, all of it, and this may make for a large file.

Watch out for credit card thieves!

Although online shopping is safe, you should carefully guard your credit card and AOL password. Remember that *no AOL employee* will ever ask you online or by email for any of this information. If you get a request for this sort of information, be sure to report it directly to AOL's Community Action Team for action. Use the keyword `Notify AOL` for information on how to report this sort of conduct.

PART

VI

Appendixes

The First Steps
to Get Online

Installing the software

Join AOL

Getting started

Your first visit to AOL

If You're Not an AOL Member

The purpose of this book is to take you beyond, way beyond, the simple instructions available online. I've filled it with power-user tips that make your online visits more productive and more fun. But I realize some of you haven't joined America Online yet, so I've designed this appendix, and the next one, to serve as a tutorial on joining America Online and using the software. So, I assume you've followed through on my suggestion in Chapter 1, "Getting Past the Opening Screen," to read this section next.

Whether you are using an Apple Macintosh or a PC equipped with Windows, America Online software is easy to install and use. But despite the simplicity of these programs, AOL provides an extraordinary set of tools that makes your AOL visits informative and enjoyable.

Before You Install the Software

Before you learn how to install your America Online software, I want to give you a couple of quick shortcuts that take you around the online community quickly and enable you to get direct online help if you need it.

The first shortcut is a *keyword*. This is a keyboard command that you can use *only* while you're connected to America Online. A keyword can take you just about anywhere on America Online, even if you don't know the exact route.

To use keywords, press ⌘-K if you're using a Macintosh or Ctrl+K for Windows, then enter the keyword in the entry text box of the Keyword dialog box displayed on your screen (see Figure A.1). Now press the Return or Enter key—in just a few seconds, you'll be transported to the place you want to visit. (Of course, if the keyword is wrong, you'll get a message to that effect; you can then click the **Search** button to view some suggestions that might match your quest.) You'll learn more about keywords in Appendix B, "Setting Up AOL's Software."

FIGURE A.1

A keyword is the fastest way from here to there on AOL.

① Click **Go** to access the online area.

Whenever you're logged on to America Online, you can visit an online support area to get direct assistance with any problem you might have. To get there, call up the **Help** menu and select **Member Services**, or use the keyword Help (yes, keywords do come in handy).

Okay, with the preliminaries out of the way, let's get ready to join the online community.

Ordering Your America Online Software

America Online disks are often free with your new software or computer purchase. If you don't have a disk at hand, or you got a CD, but your computer doesn't have a CD drive, no problem. Just call AOL at 1-800-827-6364. Tell the operator the kind of computer you have so you'll receive the correct software—be sure to explain whether you want the CD or disk version. You will get your AOL software in a couple of weeks. In the meantime, you can review this section and the next about installing your software, establishing your personal online account, and mastering all aspects of the America Online program.

Even if you already have telecommunications software installed on your computer, it won't help you connect to AOL. America Online uses its own proprietary software to provide a unique graphic environment and efficient performance. You need America Online's special software to use the service. You can, however, visit AOL's home page on the World Wide Web at http://www.aol.com and download a copy. Whether you install direct from a disk or from the software you downloaded, AOL usually offers free online time to try out the service.

Another way to use keywords

You also can invoke a keyword by entering the place you want to visit in the text box on the bottom row of your AOL program toolbar and clicking the **Go** button. You'll get there just as quickly.

Teach Yourself: Installing Your America Online Software

The steps involved in installing the Macintosh and Windows versions of America Online software are similar. Where they differ, I'll explain those differences and provide illustrations to show the process. The basic system requirements are similar, too (in terms of comparable Mac and PC model support).

Knowing What You Need

To use version 4.0 of AOL software on a computer running Microsoft Windows, the requirements are as follows:

Windows 3.1:

- 486-based or better PC
- 12 megabytes (MB) RAM
- 30MB available hard disk space
- A monitor capable of displaying at least 640×480 with 256 colors or better
- A 14,400bits per second (bps) or faster modem (28,800bps recommended)

Windows 95:

- Pentium-based PC
- 16MB RAM
- 30MB available hard disk space
- A monitor capable of displaying at least 640×480 with 256 colors or better
- A 14,400bps or faster modem (28,800bps recommended)

To use version 4.0 of AOL's Mac software, you need the following:

- A Mac with a 68040 or PowerPC CPU
- 12MB RAM
- Mac OS 7.1 or later
- 30MB available hard disk space

- A monitor capable of displaying at least 640×480 with 256 colors or better

- A 14,400bps or faster modem (28,800bps recommended)

I wrote this section with the assumption that you are comfortable performing the basic functions of using your computer, such as installing new software from a CD or disk onto your hard drive, performing basic file management chores, opening applications, and using your mouse. If you need a quick refresher course, review the instruction manuals that came with your computer or operating system disks.

If you received your software on disk, you'll want to make a backup copy for installation. You should do this with all your software and disks. Then tuck away the originals in a safe place, in case your copies are damaged. If you have the CD-ROM version of AOL's software, just keep it in a safe place and it should last indefinitely. I still have perfectly running audio CDs that date back to the early 1980s.

You need one more thing, of course, and that is a Hayes-compatible modem with a speed of 14,400bps or greater (28,800bps is highly recommended). If you don't have a modem, you can buy one at your favorite dealer. If you've never used a modem before, let me just briefly explain that a *modem* is a device that converts the digital information from your computer into analog tones that can be transferred through your telephone lines.

Because America Online has been expanding its high-speed access service throughout the world—and prices for high-speed modems have dropped—buy the fastest modem you can afford. You won't regret it. (If you have Internet-based TCP/IP access, you can access America Online at even higher speeds; I'll tell you more about that in Chapter 12, "Using AOL's Internet Services.")

I'll tell you more about modems and fine-tuning them for best performance in Chapter 4, "Secrets of High-Speed Access to AOL."

Installing the Windows 95 Version—The First Steps

Again, if you have the disk version, be sure to make a backup copy. After you've made the backup, you're ready to get the software up and running.

Get your billing information and modem ready

Before installing AOL software, have your software's registration certificate and your credit card or checkbook handy. Be sure that your modem has been turned on and is hooked up to your computer and to your phone line.

Installing AOL's Windows 95 software is easy

1. Insert the America Online CD-ROM into your PC's CD drive (or the disk into your PC's drive—A or B).

2. Using the **Start** menu, choose **Settings**, **Control Panels**, and then double-click the **Add/Remove Programs** utility.

3. On the first screen of the Add/Remove Programs Properties screen, click the **Install** button.

4. When the AOL program installer is located, click the **Finish** button to start the installation process.

Installing the Windows 3.x Version—The First Steps

The following steps can, with minor modification, also be used for Windows 95 users.

Installing AOL's Windows 3.x software is also easy

1. Insert the America Online CD-ROM into your PC's CD drive (or the disk into your PC's drive—A or B).

2. In the Program Manager, go to the **File** menu and select the **Run** command.

3. Depending on which drive you inserted the disk in, type either a:\setup or b:\setup (or indicate the drive that has your installation CD). Then press Enter (see Figures A.2 and A.3).

FIGURE A.2

America Online's software installation and setup is easy to follow.

1 Check your installation option.

FIGURE A.3

A progress bar shows the status of the America Online Windows installation process.

1 If you need to stop the installation, click **Cancel**.

AOL Software—Decisions, Decisions

Before the installation continues, you'll have to tell the Installer whether you have an existing AOL version on your computer's drive to update, or you want to do a fresh, clean install of the new version. Because I'm assuming you're joining up as a new member when you read this section, you'll want to check the first option, which installs AOL software without updating from any other copy.

Installing the Windows Version—The Next Steps

At the tail end of the Windows 95 installation process, you'll see a dialog box asking whether you want to put your AOL software on the **Start** menu. You'll want to **OK** this. The next steps of your AOL software setup process are as follows:

Setting up your AOL software

1. When your installation is complete, you return to your Windows 95 desktop. The AOL icon appears in its own application directory; a startup icon is also placed on your Windows 95 desktop. Double-click the icon (or the new America Online entry on your Windows **Start** menu) to open your America Online software.

2. As soon as the program opens, you're guided step-by-step through the process of setting up your America Online software to work with your modem and telephone. Before making a selection, read the instructions carefully. As America Online software is updated, the information is likely to change.

Don't forget your Windows 95 installation disks

It may also be a good idea to keep your Windows operating system disks at hand. Depending on your PC's setup, the AOL installer may need to add files from your Windows 95 Setup disk to enable the program to be set up correctly. You'll see an onscreen message if this is necessary.

A restart may be necessary

If the AOL software installer needs system files from your Windows 95 Setup disks, you will probably be asked to restart your computer. When the process is done, you can continue setting up your new AOL account.

Don't forget the ReadMe

At the end of the installation process, you'll see a ReadMe file displayed on your screen giving you information about AOL's service, and some hints and tips. You'll probably want to print this document while awaiting the installation to finish.

Floppies have a different AOL software version

Depending on whether you receive your Mac AOL software on a disk or a CD, you may see two different versions of the software. Because of the size constraints, disks from AOL include version 2.7 of the program (an older, simpler version with a less sophisticated interface). To get the version of AOL software described in this book, 4.0, you need to use the supplied CD or download the software direct from AOL's WWW site (`http://www.aol.com`) or via its upgrade forum (keyword `Upgrade`) if you're already a member.

Mac users: Don't have a high density drive?

If you are using an older Macintosh that does not have a CD drive or a 1.4MB (HD) drive installed, please contact America Online customer service for a set of 800K (double-density) software disks.

3. If you decide to opt for a custom installation, you can click the **No-I'll select the type of connection myself** option in your first setup window. You'll be guided through several screens that enable you to set up your connection device (your modem or a TCP/IP connection).

   If you are connecting to AOL with your modem and have call waiting on the line to which your modem is hooked, you need to use the option to disable that service so that you aren't knocked offline when a call comes in. Check with your local phone company about this option, however, because dial codes might differ. Some areas might not provide a way to disable call waiting.

4. When you are calling America Online from your office, you might need to have your modem dial **9** or another access number to reach an outside line.

5. You also have the chance to choose the modem profile that best fits your needs—that is, if you decide not to accept the choices made by your software. If your modem isn't listed, however, your best bet is to stick with the profile the software chooses for you; it's smart enough to pick the most popular modem models.

Installing the Macintosh Version

After you've made a backup of your original Mac software disk, you're ready to get the software up and running.

It's easy to install AOL's Mac software

1. Insert the AOL CD into your CD drive (or insert the disk into your Macintosh's drive).

2. Double-click the **America Online** icon, which brings up the Welcome to America Online! screen shown in Figure A.4. Then click **Continue**.

3. You'll next see a ReadMe screen giving you a brief description of the software you're about to install. You can read it now, or print it for later review. When you're ready, click the **Continue** button to go to the main installer screen.

Double-click the AOL icon to begin the installation process and to display this screen.

1 Click **Continue** to bring up the main installer screen.

4. On the main installer screen, you'll have the option to select another folder or hard drive for installation of your software. Your America Online software gets its own special folder and the default location is your startup drive.

After you've decided on a location for the new America Online program folder, the installation process continues. America Online keeps you informed of its progress, as shown in Figure A.5.

FIGURE A.5
You can keep track of the installer doing its work.

1 If you need to stop the installation, click **Stop**.

In a minute or two, you receive a message that the software has been successfully installed. Be prepared for your Mac to restart when you see the restart prompt. (If you have any problems at this point, call AOL at the phone number shown earlier in this chapter, for personal assistance.)

5. If the installation is successful (and it usually is), your Mac's desktop and an open **America Online v4.0** icon will greet you after the restart. Just double-click the **AOL application** icon to display the screen shown in Figure A.6. You then are guided through the steps needed to adjust the computer to your modem.

FIGURE A.6

Your second welcome message from America Online appears at this point. Just click **Continue** to progress through the setup process.

 Choose your setup options.

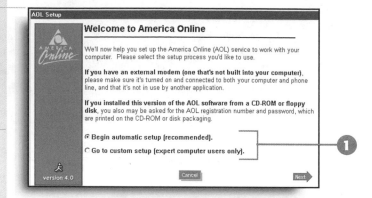

For the next few moments, you see several information windows. As America Online software versions are upgraded, the displays might be different from the ones shown here. Just read the instructions carefully before proceeding. If you have any questions or problems, you can choose **Cancel** to stop the registration process, and resume it at a later time.

If you've opted for the standard setup routine, your modem will now be checked to get basic information (see Figure A.7).

FIGURE A.7

America Online software checks your modem for information about its performance capabilities.

 Be patient! This step takes a few minutes to finish.

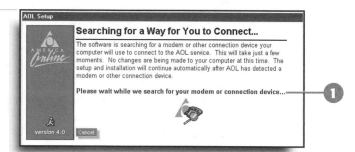

After the modem is probed, AOL software displays its selection for you. If you have a different make and model of modem, choose that instead if it's on the list (as I did for Figure A.8). Make this selection for the best possible hookup to AOL.

If you chose Custom Setup (refer to Figure A.6) at the start of the setup process, you would have been asked whether you want to install the option to disable call waiting services when you are online. If you have call waiting and someone tries to telephone you while you're online, the tones you hear in your telephone quickly terminate your online connection. You might have to check with your local telephone company, however, before choosing this option. Not all services give you the option of turning off call waiting for a single call.

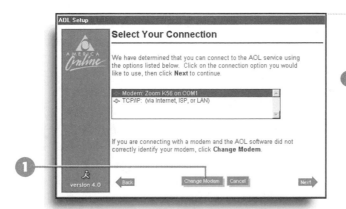

FIGURE A.8

Select the kind of modem you have here, and then click **OK**.

1 Click **Change Modem** if the choice is wrong.

If your online connections are being made from an office, you might have to dial a special number, usually 9, to get an outside line. Be sure to select this option if you need it under the Custom Setup process; otherwise, you can't make your first online connection.

The steps for getting a local connection are similar enough in both the Mac and Windows installation, so they are described together in the next section.

Getting a Local Connection

Now you need America Online's host computer to find a local connection number (see Figure A.9). As soon as your modem setup has been completed, you are asked to enter your area code so America Online can hook you up to the closest and fastest (thus the cheapest) connection in your area.

FIGURE A.9

This screen appears when you're making your first connection.

1 Enter your **Area Code** here.

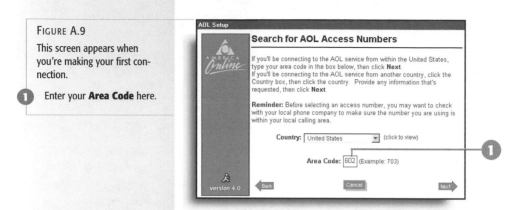

The host computer searches its directory of access numbers for ones that match the area code you entered (see Figure A.10). If you cannot locate a number that's in that area code, you have the option to choose another number from a nearby area code. Because America Online is always adding new connection numbers, you always have the opportunity to change that number later. (See Chapter 3, "Connecting to AOL," for more information about locating and changing your America Online access numbers.)

FIGURE A.10

Select your local access numbers from this screen.

1 Click **Add** to choose the selected number.

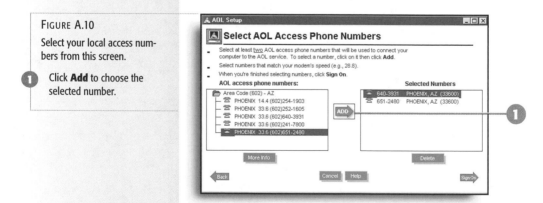

You should select at least two connection numbers if they are available. That way, if your modem cannot make a connection with the first number—perhaps because it's busy or because of line noise—you have another chance to connect to America Online. Each number you add will produce a confirmation screen, which you'll want to **OK** to move to the next step in the sign-up process.

Establishing Your Online Account

From here on, until you log on to the service for the first time, you are guided through several steps that enable you to establish your own exclusive America Online account and set your billing options. (Now you see why I suggested that you have the certificate that came with your software disks, and your credit card or checkbook handy.)

The choices you make now are not etched in stone. If you decide to change your password or billing information later, you can easily do so in AOL's Member Services area.

Setting up your online account

1. First, find the registration numbers on your America Online software package. Enter the certificate number and certificate passwords in the blank **Certificate Number** and **Certificate Password** text boxes. You can use the Tab key on your computer's keyboard to move from one entry text box to the next.

2. Choose the **Continue** button.

3. Enter your name, mailing address, and telephone number.

4. Choose the **Continue** button.

5. Indicate how you want to pay for your America Online service. You can bill your online charges via American Express, Discover Card, MasterCard, or Visa. If you prefer, you also can have your online charges deducted regularly from your checking account (an extra monthly charge is applied for this option).

To protect you, America Online verifies all your billing information. If the program encounters a problem in establishing your account, the account setup process is suspended until you are able to update your billing information. This precaution is taken solely for your protection. After all, you wouldn't want to pay for someone else's online charges.

The setup screens are subject to change

Because the setup screens change frequently, I am not showing them in this book. The instructions are clearly labeled and the steps are easy to follow.

Checking account billing takes longer

If you decide to pay for your AOL bill by a checking account draft, it may take several days for AOL to verify your account. During that time, you will not be able to log on, so be patient.

It's easy to check your online bill!

To check your usage bill for America Online, use the keyword **Billing** (available when you log onto the service). You are then taken to AOL's member support area where you can view your current bill and make changes to your billing information.

Creating Your Online Mailing Address

Next you need to enter your online mailing or email address (log-in name), or *screen name* (which is the way I'll refer to your AOL identity from here on). This is your golden opportunity to be creative. Your screen name can contain from 3 to 10 characters (letters and numbers). You can identify yourself on America Online by your first name, an abbreviation of your name, or even a descriptive word or two that expresses your own unique personality traits, such as TheBear.

The online name you choose for yourself is used for your master account, and the host computer checks that name (along with the password you select) every time you log on to America Online. You can add as many as four additional names to your online account, for use by other members of your family, or for yourself. Remember that you can use only one screen name attached to your account at any one time. If you want to log on simultaneously with more than one screen name, you need to establish separate accounts (and have separate computers, modems, and phone lines, of course).

If someone already has the name you selected, you are given the option of using that name plus a number—the number reflects how many others are using that same name. You may, for example, be offered the choice of using GeneS12345 if a number of people online are already using some variation of GeneS.

An easy way to add a screen name

If you want to add or remove one of your additional names on your account, use the keyword **Names** to access that feature.

As you try to locate an available online address (or screen name), America Online searches its database to determine whether someone else already has selected that name. Because America Online is a family-oriented service, names that use vulgar language or have a vulgar connotation are not accepted.

Your initial sign-on name can't be changed

Because you cannot change or delete your master account name without deleting your account, take as much time as you need to select an appropriate screen name.

After America Online has accepted your screen name, your next step is to select a password. A password is your ounce of protection against someone using your account without your permission, so don't use anything obvious, such as a contraction of your name. Select a unique word that someone wouldn't stumble on at random. A mix of numbers and letters, or even punctuation marks, is a good option. For additional security, you may want to change your password from time to time.

After you've chosen your online address, you're ready to make your introduction to the online community.

Before you are welcomed to the America Online family, you are asked whether you accept the Terms of Service. The Terms of Service (TOS) are the rules and regulations that apply to AOL. Carefully read the information displayed. You also can check the text of it in the Member Services area, but basically it requests that you be a good citizen during your online visits and avoid using vulgar language. For more about the Terms of Service see Chapter 7, "Parental Issues and Internet Access."

Exploring AOL in Your First Online Session

The first time you log on to America Online (and assuming that your sound is working), you hear a friendly voice intone "Welcome," and a few seconds later, you hear, "You've Got Mail." Yes, when you sign onto America Online for the first time, you indeed find a letter in your mailbox. Click the **You Have Mail** icon, and you see your first letter listed in the directory. Double-click that directory listing, and the text appears in a new open document window on your computer's screen. The letter is from Steve Case, the president of America Online. He welcomes you to the service and briefly outlines the special features you may want to examine as you begin your travels through the network.

The first screen you see on your computer, the Welcome screen, is your gateway to all the features offered by America Online (see Figure A.11). Along the right side and bottom of the Welcome screen is a list of special announcements, places to visit, and the Top News Story. Click the icon or button adjacent to the description of the place you want to investigate, and you are instantaneously transported to that area of America Online. The list you see here changes several times per day as different services are featured and the top news stories change.

At the left of the Welcome screen is a triangular icon labeled **AOL Channels**. When you click this box, you'll be taken to the

Save a copy of your password

When you select a screen name and password, write it down and place that information in a safe place. That way, if you forget your password, you can find it again quickly when you need it.

Screen names and real names aren't the same

Please don't forget that all AOL members are known online by their screen names, rather than their real names (which may or may not be totally different). If you decide to write an email message to another member, you contact them by their *screen name* which is the only way they can be reached on AOL (otherwise you may end up writing to the wrong person). I'll cover this subject in more detail in Chapter 9, "Using AOL's Email."

window that lies beneath the Welcome screen (see Figure A.12); this is your gateway to all the major services on America Online.

FIGURE A.11

Read your first welcome message from America Online.

1 Click the **You Have Mail** icon to see the list of unread email.

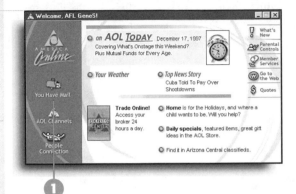

The **Channels** main menu contains three rows of color icons, each of which takes you to a different AOL department (or channel). They are clearly labeled, and you can click any one of them now to explore the service further. These online channels are discussed in detail in Chapter 5, "Exploring AOL."

FIGURE A.12

Consider America Online's **Channels** menu as its table of contents to all the major features of the service.

1 Click a **channel** icon to visit that area.

For now, just take a brief tour of the service. After you've begun to find your away around, you'll want to learn more about your new software.

That takes us to the next chapter, Appendix B, where you'll learn how to harness the power of AOL's sophisticated telecommunications software.

Setting Up AOL's Software

Connect to AOL faster

Keep material for later review

Get there faster

Where are all the program's features?

Customize the toolbar

Getting the Most Out of AOL's Software

I've written this section strictly for those who haven't used America Online's software—or those who just want a little more information about its special features.

Before you begin this chapter, you'll want to make sure you have installed your AOL software, set up your account, and logged on for the first time. After you've done that, you want to get down to the business of learning about your new software.

Your America Online software doesn't come with a manual, although an extensive **Help** menu is provided. But as long as you know how to use your computer to do your everyday tasks, such as moving and clicking your mouse and choosing commands from menus, you shouldn't have any trouble picking up all the ins and outs of using the America Online software. And with this brief guide in your hands, you can become an expert in no time.

Teach Yourself: Changing the Connection and Modem Settings

Mac users: These instructions apply to you also!

Most of the illustrations in this chapter show AOL's software running under Windows 95, but the program runs in basically the same fashion under Windows 3.1 or the Mac OS. Where Mac differences are present, they'll be shown or described.

When you first install your America Online software, the software examines your modem and sets a default modem profile for it based on AOL's own modem profile library. Whenever you buy a new modem, review these settings to make sure the software is set up to work with the new modem. You will also use these settings when you need to change your connection numbers to the America Online network.

Changing Your Modem Settings

Changing your connection settings

1. Click the **Setup** button on the main America Online window. The Connection Setup dialog box appears, as shown in Figure B.1.

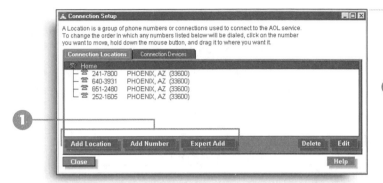

FIGURE B.1

Making changes to your modem and dialing setup is quick and easy.

① Click the button to activate that function.

2. To make a new location setting, click the **Add Location** button. (Keep in mind that you can make these settings only when you're not logged onto the America Online network.)

You can set up one connection profile in each Add Location window (see Figure B.2). Your America Online software uses this profile when trying to make your connection to its access network.

Use the program's **Help** menu

If you have a problem using your America Online software and you need an immediate answer, select **Help** from the AOL application menu bar. You can even print a topic for later review.

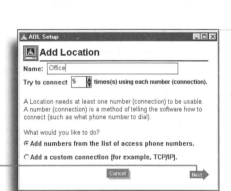

FIGURE B.2

You can change your connection numbers on this screen.

① Click **Next** to save the settings.

3. Give your new location a name in the **Name** text box. It's common to identify the location by its purpose (Home or Office, for example) or city, and even to add the phone number if you have several profiles to set up.

4. Choose the number of redial attempts that should be made if the connection fails (up to 10).

Mac users note

If you're using the Mac OS version of AOL's software, when you click the **Setup** button, you'll see a screen offering automatic connection settings for you. If you want to adjust them in a similar fashion to the way described here, choose the **Expert Setup** option.

Use the Tab key

A quick way to navigate from one data-entry point (text box) to another is to press Tab. To return to the preceding text box, press Shift+Tab.

5. Click the **Add numbers from the list of access phone numbers** option to begin the process of finding phone numbers for your new location. Click **Next**.

6. Enter the area code or country for which you need a number in the Search for AOL Access Numbers screen and click **Next** (see Figure B.3).

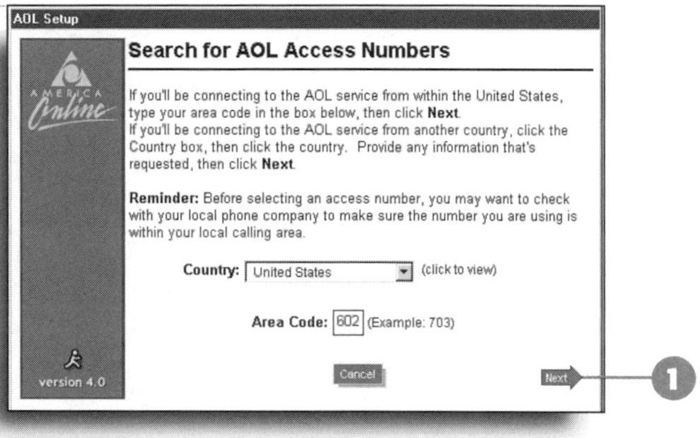

FIGURE B.3

Enter the area code or country here to start the process of finding phone numbers to access AOL.

1 Click **Next** to start the search.

AOL stores many phone numbers on your PC

When you install your AOL software, a database of current phone numbers is included. If the list doesn't include numbers in the area you seek, AOL will be dialed to retrieve additional numbers, and you'll see additional information screens showing the progress of the phone number search.

Would you prefer to do this later?

If you don't want to connect to AOL right now, click **Cancel** then **OK** in the dialog box asking if you want to cancel the setup process. The numbers will still be stored; you just won't log on.

7. In the next screen, labeled Select AOL Access Numbers, click a phone number, and then click the **Add** button to include the setting in your Location profile. You'll receive a confirmation dialog box, which you should **OK**, to include the new number.

8. When the phone numbers have all been selected, click the **Sign On** button at the lower right to sign on to AOL using your new location.

You can create a separate group for each area that you access AOL from. By default, a group is established for the area code you're in. You can move a phone number to a different location or have a different modem choice applied to it.

Moving phone numbers and different modem choices

1. Double-click a phone number in Connection Setup screen, which brings up the screen shown in Figure B.4.

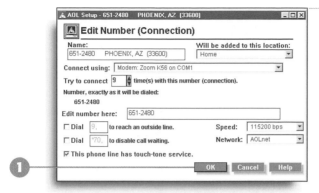

2. If you plan to change the phone number listed, enter the number in both the **Name** and **Edit number here** text boxes.

3. Choose the location to which the number applies from the **Will be added to this location** drop-down list.

4. Choose the modem or other connection method from the **Connect using** drop-down list.

5. The two check boxes with "Dial" options at the bottom left of Figure B.4 control how the software uses your modem to dial the service. Some businesses have special phone lines that require a dial-out code. Usually, it's 9, but you can change that setting if necessary. If you need to dial a special number to reach an outside line, check the first of these two boxes.

6. If you have call-waiting service, when you make your online connection you should disable call waiting using the second of the two check boxes. You should disable call waiting because the tones that sound in your telephone when someone is trying to reach you can cause you to be disconnected from AOL. The number listed in this entry box, *70, is for touch-tone telephones. If you have rotary service, the number is usually 1170. To be certain which number to use, however, call your local telephone company. Sometimes the capability to disable call waiting for a single phone call is an optional service.

Numbers are automatically redialed

If the attempt to dial a specific number fails, AOL will try the number again, up to the total number of redial attempts you've specified for each. Then the second and subsequent numbers will be tried, in turn.

7. By default, the This phone line has the **Touch-tone service** option checked. If you still have rotary (pulse) service, uncheck this option.

8. In the **Speed** drop-down list at the right of the dialog box, set a speed equal to or higher than your modem's speed in the text box. The maximum is 115,200bps (suggested if you have one of those new 56K modems).

9. When you change the number, you also might need to change the Network setting from the drop-down list. This is the service that America Online uses to connect to its host computers. When you get a list of phone numbers from America Online for your area, you see such names as AOLNet, AOLGlobalNet, or SprintNet attached to the phone numbers. Be sure to select the correct name of the service provider.

10. Recheck your settings and if everything is entered correctly, click the **OK** button to save the information to your computer's drive. If you decide not to make the changes at this time, click the **Cancel** button instead.

You've just used the **Add Location** options to change your connection settings. The following paragraphs explain the rest of the options in the Connection Setup dialog box.

- **Add Number.** This option is used to add additional numbers to your existing group.

- **Expert Add.** This option enables you to customize all your connection and device settings.

- **Delete.** If you decide you no longer need a Location Setup, use this option to remove it.

- **Edit.** Click this button to edit the selected Group or Location profile.

Choosing your Connection Device (or Modem)

Now that your phone numbers are set, you need to make sure the proper connection devices (modems or TCP/IP) are chosen.

You can redial each number up to 10 times

If you get frequent busy signals when trying to connect to AOL (and no other access number is available), be sure to specify the full 10 redial attempts in the Add Location and Edit Number windows. Frequent redialing will help you get a connection.

In the Connection Setup dialog box, click the **Connection Devices** tab to change the modem setting and the port to which it is connected. When you choose Connection Devices, the dialog box shown in Figure B.5 appears.

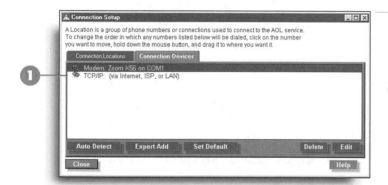

FIGURE B.5

If you've installed a new modem, you can change your modem selection here.

1 Double-click a connection setting if you want to adjust it further.

The Connection Devices window shows the modems you've selected and the ports to which they're connected. If you need to make a change, the options are

AOL does its own modem check

America Online's software does not automatically recognize the modem settings you make in your Modem Control Panel under Windows 95. You must make those settings separately.

- **Auto-Detect.** Click this button to let AOL's software check your PC's serial port and get information about your modem or network settings. For a couple of minutes you'll see the screen shown in Figure B.6, then you'll see a dialog box listing whether you have a modem or TCP/IP network setup. Just **OK** the settings if they match the kind of modem you have and you'll soon have your AOL software configured to work properly with it.

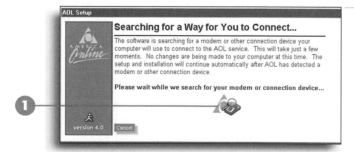

FIGURE B.6

AOL's modem probe goes to work to test your modem and configure the software to recognize it properly.

1 Be patient! This step may take a few minutes to finish.

- **Expert Add.** If the modem you have hasn't been added to the listing in the Connection Devices window, click this

AOL has additional modem profiles

If a modem file that matches the make and model you have isn't offered in AOL's software, you may find one available in AOL's free Members Online Support area. (keyword **Help**) I've explain how to download and install modem files in Chapter 4, "Secrets of High-Speed Access to AOL."

button to choose the modem by make and modem, and the port to which it's connected.

- **Set Default.** Make the selected device profile a default for newly created location settings.

- **Delete.** If you are no longer using a modem shown in the list, select it, and click the **Delete** button to delete its listing.

- **Edit.** Click this button to configure your modem profile. You can use this setting to switch port settings or to edit the initialization string. You can usually find advice on the optimum settings in the manual that came with your modem.

Teach Yourself: Setting Software Preferences

The next thing you want to do is set up your America Online preferences so the software looks and feels the way you want it to. Even if everything looks okay to you right now, trying out a few settings just to see whether you can adjust things a bit better is worth the effort. You can always change the settings back to the way they were originally.

Many of the program's features are shown as drop-down menus accessed from the toolbar. To set up preferences, choose **Preferences** from the **My AOL** icon's drop-down menu. The Preferences dialog box shown in Figure B.7 appears.

FIGURE B.7

You can choose from 14 Preference categories.

1 Click an icon to check or change a setting.

Setting most of your preferences involves the same steps. First you click the icon that represents the sort of preference you want to change. In the dialog box that appears next, you click the check box next to an item to select it, and you see a check mark appear in that box. You click the box again to turn off the feature, at which time the check mark disappears. Figure B.8 shows an example of several options checked in the General Preferences dialog box.

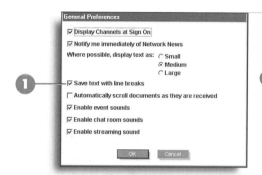

Checking a box changes your America Online preferences.

1 Click the box to change the setting.

Setting General Preferences

The following paragraphs describe the options you find in the General Preferences dialog box, which appears when you click the General icon in the Preferences dialog box.

- **Display Channels at Sign On.** When you first log on to America Online, you see two windows. The top window, the Welcome screen, tells you whether email is awaiting you. It also informs you as to the services being highlighted at that time and the top news headline. Beneath that window is the **Channels** menu, which enables you to jump directly to any one of America Online's channels or other services. To keep your small screen from being cluttered (and speed up screen display), you can opt to keep the **Channels** menu off at sign on. You can bring it up at any time by choosing Channels from the Channels icon.

Not all preferences can be set offline

You have to be logged on to set some of these options. If the preference setting cannot be made until you sign on, you'll see a message to that effect, or all the settings options will be grayed out.

Mac preferences look different

The Mac version of AOL's preferences appears as a dialog box with a scrolling list of labeled icons at the left and the corresponding settings at the right, all clearly labeled. Most of the settings are similar to those offered in the Windows version of the software. (If you've ever used a Mac with System 6, you'll recall that the Control Panels settings had a similar look.)

- **Notify me immediately of Network News.** When America Online wants to send you a special announcement, it normally appears in a small window at the top of your screen. Such announcements might alert you to an upcoming service disruption to perform needed maintenance or a similar service-related issue. If you would rather not be disturbed by these notices, turn off this option, and the network announcements are shut off. It's not something I would recommend, however, because you do want to know if the service will shut down, to avoid suddenly finding yourself knocked offline without knowing why.

- **Where possible, display text as.** This feature gives you three options for displaying your text: Small, Medium, and Large. Choose the option that provides the clearest text display on your computer's screen. The setting takes effect with the window you open after you've chosen that setting. The Medium setting gives you the best all-around display of text, but you might prefer something different. A more complete preference, labeled Fonts, enables you to make a finer level of adjustment. I'll get to that a bit later in this chapter.

- **Save text with line breaks.** This option limits text you save to the breaks you see on the screen, which may be helpful for a small computer monitor. If you want to work with the text in a word-processing program and don't want to bother with the extra line breaks, turn this option off.

- **Automatically scroll documents as they are received.** Turn on this feature, and you see text items scroll on your computer's screen as they are received. The normal setting (with this feature off) just shows the beginning of the text, as many lines as can fill a single text window. You can still scroll through this text, however, by using your computer's scrollbars at the right side of the text window.

- **Enable event sounds.** One of the most attractive features of America Online is its voice messages. When you begin your session, you hear a friendly "Welcome" voice. When you log off, you hear the same voice bid you "Goodbye." If you work in a busy environment, however, maybe you just want to turn those sounds off. If so, turn off this option.

- **Enable chat room sounds.** This feature enables you to hear sounds sent by other America Online members during a chat. For you to be able to hear the sound, however, you have to have the same sound installed on your computer.

- **Enable streaming sound.** This feature activates sounds from AOL's Slideshow feature and from online areas and Web sites that send sound with pictures.

Setting Toolbar Preferences

AOL's elaborate toolbar is the base for most of the program's basic functions (see Figure B.9). The **Appearance** options let you choose whether to reduce it to a text only display or move from top to bottom of your screen (**Location** options). The **Navigation** option lets you control the action of the **Next** and **Previous** buttons at the bottom of the toolbar, and whether to reset the History trail (**History Trail** options). This feature tracks AOL forums and Web sites you've visited on AOL and shows them in a drop-down menu at the bottom row of the toolbar.

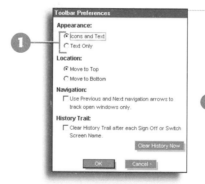

FIGURE B.9

AOL's handy toolbar may be reduced to a text only display to help reduce onscreen clutter.

① Check the toolbar option you want here.

Setting Mail Preferences

The check box options shown in Figure B.10 enable you to decide how to handle your email transactions.

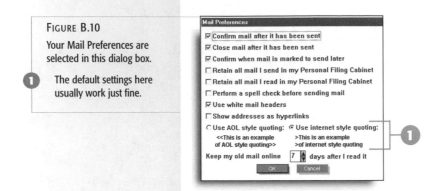

- **Confirm mail after it has been sent.** When you retain this
  option (which is selected by default), you'll receive a confirmation when your email has been sent on its way.

- **Close mail after it has been sent.** This option, also a
  default, closes your email window after the message has been
  sent to its destination. This option helps reduce screen clutter, so it's a choice you'll probably want to keep.

- **Confirm when mail is marked to send later.** This is
  another default option. It gives you a confirmation when you
  choose the **Send Later** option in your email (for example, to
  send during an Automatic AOL session).

- **Retain all mail I send in my Personal Filing Cabinet.**
  The Personal Filing Cabinet is the tool provided in your
  AOL software to manage your email, file downloads,
  Favorite Places (which will be explained later in this chap-
  ter), message board postings, and Usenet newsgroups (see
  Chapter 17, "How to Join and Participate in Internet
  Newsgroups and Mailing Lists"). Checking this option auto-
  matically archives a copy of the mail you've sent; your sent
  email is deleted from your regular online mailbox after about
  a month.

- **Retain all mail I read in my Personal Filing Cabinet.**
  Checking this option causes a copy of the mail you've read
  to be automatically archived. Otherwise, the email you read
  is automatically deleted from your online mailbox after the
  period set in the last preference in this category.

- **Perform a spell check before sending mail.** This option invokes AOL's handy spell checker utility, which checks your email for proper spelling before you send it on its way.

- **Use white mail headers.** This option lets you decide whether to put a shade around the top part of your email, where the sender and other information is listed.

- **Show addresses as hyperlinks.** This option underlines the addresses shown in the mail header. When you check this preference, you merely have to click one of those names to open an email window already addressed to that person.

- **Use AOL style quoting.** You can quote email messages in the online world in two ways. AOL's method involves placing two marks at the beginning and end of the quote. Although this is the default and is common in AOL message boards, if you want to join the crowd of Internet surfers, you'll pick the next option, the one I use.

- **Use Internet style quoting.** The Internet way involves putting a caret (>) mark at the beginning of each line.

- **Keep my old mail online ___ days after I read it.** You can specify the timeframe, up to seven days, after which your email will be deleted from your Old Mail directory. This option is not available with the Mac version.

Setting WWW Preferences

Using the choices shown in Figure B.11, you can decide how to set up America Online's World Wide Web browser feature. This feature enables you to view your favorite Web sites. For more information about the World Wide Web, read Chapter 13, "Using the World Wide Web."

You can make these basic settings by clicking the appropriate tab and checking a few boxes:

- **General.** Choose whether to show pictures and sound, and whether you can play videos. You can also choose text and background colors and how Web links are displayed.

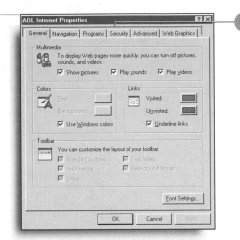

FIGURE B.11

Because AOL uses Microsoft Internet Explorer as its browser, you'll find some of the options shown in the tabbed AOL Internet Properties screen familiar. Some settings are grayed out, because they are not supported within AOL's interface.

1 Click a tab to bring up another setting screen.

Make sure you have enough space for your Web cache

Before setting aside a disk cache for images received from the World Wide Web (or for AOL's own downloaded artwork), be certain you have enough free storage space on your computer's hard drive. If you don't have the small amount of space needed to store these files, you may want to finally get around to the task of archiving all those unneeded files on your computer's drive.

- **Navigation.** The most important option lets you specify which home page to display when you click the globe icon on the AOL program toolbar. By default, it's AOL's home page. If you want something else, you can enter it in the Navigation window.

- **Security.** These options set up the browser's handy content advisor. You can set a password for this option. It lets you limit the display of sites containing revealing photos and other material that you may not want your child to see. You can set additional options via AOL's convenient Parental Controls (as explained in Chapter 7, "Parental Issues and Internet Access").

- **Advanced.** Two settings are available to be considered here. One is whether you'll be warned when entering an unsecured Web site (something to consider if you want to make a purchase there). The other option, under the **Settings** button, lets you establish the amount of space to be used on your hard drive for cached Web artwork. You can use this feature to delete cached artwork too.

- **Web Graphics.** This setting panel lets you specify whether Web-based graphics will be compressed before appearing on your PC. You may get somewhat better quality display if you uncheck this option, at the expense of a slightly reduced performance.

Setting Chat Preferences

Figure B.12 shows the Chat Preferences dialog box that appears when you choose **Chat** from the Preferences dialog box. The following paragraphs explain the options you find in Chat Preferences.

FIGURE. B.12

You can have an online chat organized your way for easier viewing.

1 Click **OK** to save your settings.

- **Notify me when members arrive.** Chats and conferences are often the most enjoyable experiences on America Online. This first check box is turned off by default. If you want to be notified when another member arrives at the chat, however, turn on the option.
- **Notify me when members leave.** When another member leaves the chat, you know about it if you select this option.
- **Double-space incoming messages.** You can have your chat window display text double-spaced so it's easier to read (the normal mode is single-spaced), at the expense of consuming lots of screen space.
- **Alphabetize the member list.** Normally members who enter a chat room are listed in the order in which they enter, but this option lets you display them alphabetically, and helps you quickly locate a specific person in a crowded chat room. I normally check this option.
- **Enable chat room sounds.** You also can decide whether you want to hear sounds that other members might send. This preference is identical to the one provided for General Preferences.

Setting Download Preferences

The capability to download files from America Online's vast software libraries and transfer them through the telephone lines to your computer might become one of your favorite features. You learn some helpful hints on downloading files in Chapter 26, "Tips and Tricks on Finding Software." In the meantime, you want to set your download preferences for the best performance (or just leave them alone as most members do).

Figure B.13 shows the Download Preferences dialog box that appears when you choose the **Download** icon from the Preferences dialog box. The following paragraphs describe the options you find in Download Preferences.

FIGURE B.13

You can fine-tune the software download process on America Online.

1 Move the arrows up or down to change the number of downloads listed.

- **Display Image Files on Download.** This option enables you to actually see some picture files appear on your screen as they are being transferred to your computer. Depending on how fast your PC is, this choice could slow your computer's performance somewhat. If you don't have at least a 486 (and if you're not connected to AOL at 9,600bps or faster), you might choose to turn off this option.

- **Automatically decompress files at sign-off.** Many files you download from America Online are compressed to make them smaller and reduce the time needed to get the files to your computer (and reduce your online charges). America Online software includes a tool to automatically decompress files you've just downloaded. The supported formats include ZIP and ARC on your PC (StuffIt on your Mac). By default, when you end your America Online session, all files you have just downloaded are decompressed automatically (if they're in a format that's supported, of course). You should keep this option checked. It makes using your download files much easier.

If you don't have enough disk space to store all those files, or you want to decide later whether you want to use the files, just turn off this option.

- **Delete ZIP files after decompression.** This option enables you to automatically delete the original file after it has been expanded (on a Mac it'll be a StuffIt file). This option is one you should use carefully, as a protection against the rare occasion when an expanded file might become damaged somehow (yes, it's happened to me). It's useful, however, if space on your hard drive is tight.

- **Confirm additions to my download list.** This option produces a message that a file you've decided to download has been added to the queue.

- **Retain information about my last __ downloads.** The Download Manager enables you to review a list of files you've downloaded to your computer. With this option, you can determine how many entries appear in your download log. Unless you need to track a large number of recent downloads, there's little reason to change the default setting.

- **Use this directory as default for downloads.** The normal setting for downloaded files is your C:\America Online 4.0\Download directory (on the Mac the folder is called Online Downloads). If you don't have enough space on the volume to store the files you expect to download, you may choose another location. Just click the **Browse** button to select that new location for downloaded files.

Setting Graphics Preferences

America Online's software enables you to open and print documents created in some graphics formats, such as GIF and JPEG. You can also observe the download of a picture file while it's in progress. You can use the preference box shown in Figure B.14 to adjust your graphics viewing options.

FIGURE B.14

Choose your online graphics viewing options here.

1 Click the up- and down-arrows to adjust settings.

- **Maximum disk space to use for online art _____ megabyte(s).** This choice enables you to set aside a fixed portion of your hard drive for downloaded art (the fancy graphics you see in AOL's forums). When the block you've set aside for downloaded artwork is filled, the oldest, least used artwork is discarded. Setting aside a larger amount of disk space enables your AOL software to run more quickly if you visit a lot of areas (because the artwork doesn't have to be downloaded to your PC over and over again).

- **Display image files on download.** This choice is the same as the one you can set as part of your Download Preferences (refer to Figure B.13).

- **JPEG compression quality.** This option enables you to choose the optimum quality versus compression of JPEG images. For most purposes, the default setting is just fine.

- **Set Color Mode.** This button brings up the Color Preference display shown in Figure B.15 (it's a Windows-only option). Normally, **Detect Automatically** will do fine. As the text on this screen states, however, some video drivers might have performance problems with the standard setting. If graphics do not display properly, you might prefer to choose a manual color setting.

Wait! What's JPEG mean?

JPEG (pronounced "jay-peg") is a standardized image compression mechanism. It's designed for compressing either full-color or grayscale images of natural, real-world scenes. It works well on photographs, naturalistic artwork, and similar material; not so well on lettering, simple cartoons, or line drawings. Many image files on AOL are provided in JPEG format because of their high quality and small size (making downloads of even large images relatively speedy).

FIGURE B.15

If graphics opened in your AOL software don't display properly, choose the **Set Color Mode** option.

1 Click the option you want to use.

Setting Password Preferences

The Password Preferences feature (see Figure B.16) is one that you should use with caution. It enables the program to store the passwords you select for each of your screen names. That means you can call up America Online and have the program automatically log on for you without first entering your password. If others are using your computer and you would prefer not to risk having someone else use your account without your permission, however, you should not store your passwords in this manner. If no passwords are stored, you are asked to enter your password at the beginning of your online visit.

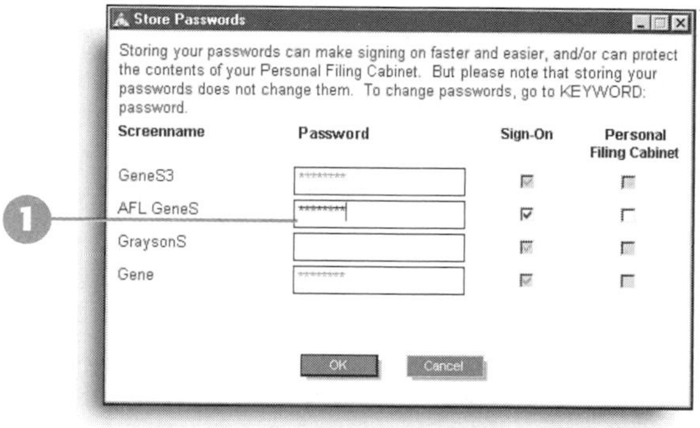

FIGURE B.16

Enter your stored passwords with caution and with no prying eyes around.

1 Enter your password for the screen name you're using.

If, after reading these warnings, you want to store your online passwords, select this option, which brings up a list of your screen names. Enter the correct password in the text box next to the appropriate screen name.

You have two password options. First is Sign-On, in which your password is automatically entered at sign-on. The second, labeled Personal Filing Cabinet, applies strictly to Automatic AOL sessions (you'll read more about those in Chapter 9, "Using AOL's Email").

Windows password limits

With the Windows version of the software, you can only enter a password for the screen name you're now using.

Windows password reminder

When you first install your AOL software, you'll see a reminder dialog box to store a password for each of your screen names after your initial sign on. If you choose not to store a password, ignore this request.

Setting Auto AOL Preferences

Auto AOL (sometimes known as FlashSessions) is a way to let AOL do the work for you. You can set sessions to automatically send and retrieve email, attached files, and message board and newsgroup postings. You have lots of options to select from here. If the feature interests you, you'll want to read Chapter 9.

Setting Personal Filing Cabinet Preferences

The Personal Filing Cabinet feature enables you to customize your ability to archive material from your online visits. You have four options in using this feature, shown in Figure B.17.

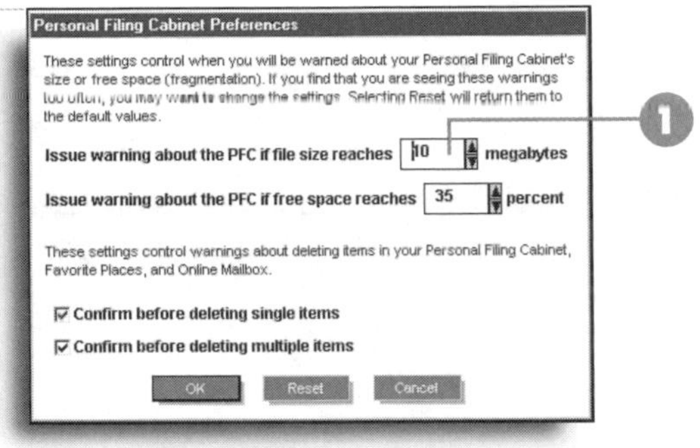

FIGURE B.17

Choose how confirmation messages are displayed in your Personal Filing Cabinet.

1   Set the maximum size for your Personal Filing Cabinet.

- **Issue warning about the PFC if file size reaches _____ megabytes.** To avoid cluttering up your hard drive with Personal Filing Cabinet information, you'll get a warning when the size of the file exceeds the amount specified (10MB is the default).

- **Issue warning about the PFC if free space reaches _____ percent.** As more and more letters and messages are saved in the Personal Filing Cabinet, like your hard drive, it'll become fragmented. This setting puts up a warning notice when it happens.

- **Confirm before deleting single items.** When you check this option, you'll receive confirmation when you delete a single item from your Personal Filing Cabinet.

- **Confirm before deleting multiple items.** When you check this option, you'll receive confirmation when you delete multiple items from your Personal Filing Cabinet.

- **Reset.** This button changes all your settings to the program's default (which is the way it's shown in Figure B.17)

Mac File Cabinet settings are different

On a Mac you can set options as to how long specific items can remain in the Personal Filing Cabinet. In addition, a button is provided for you to click to compact the Personal Filing Cabinet, which reduces unused space and keeps the file size small. The Windows version of AOL software displays a request to do this only as needed.

Setting Spelling Preferences

In addition to spelling errors, AOL's spell checker utility can handle common mistakes as well. You'll see the options shown in Figure B.18. By default, you'll want to check them all.

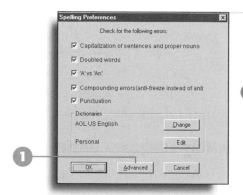

FIGURE B.18

Make your settings for AOL's online spell checker utility here.

1 Click **Advanced** for more options.

You have two choices to consider. One is to change the dictionary used for spelling, by clicking the **Change** button and selecting an alternate dictionary file (which may from time to time be offered by AOL). The other is the **Advanced** button, which gives you a set of grammar checking options, including double negatives, misused words, and others. Each item can be separately selected and turned on or off.

Setting Font Preferences

For users of previous versions of AOL software, this is an all-new option, one similar to the choices available in the Mac version of AOL software. The dialog box shown in Figure B.19 shows you the choices and the following list describes them.

FIGURE B.19

Choose the fonts you prefer for text display on AOL.

1 Choose your font from the drop-down menu.

Don't be too creative with text styling

Not all fonts come with extra style variations, nor do they look good when you add bold or italic variations. Examine your choices carefully to see what looks best on your computer screen.

Did your type disappear?

If you choose light type on a light background, it will seem to vanish. This is a common problem, and is sometimes blamed on a system-related difficulty (it's not).

- **Font.** Select the font for text display from the drop-down list (Arial is the default).
- **Size.** Choose the size for which to display text. 10 point is the default size, readable on most computer monitors. Feel free to experiment. You can change the settings whenever you want.
- **Style.** Pick the style you prefer. Check both **Bold** and **Italic** to get a bold italic style.
- **Color.** Click the reversed "A" icon and the one after it to bring up a color display, from which you can select the color of your text, text background, or page background.

Setting Language Preferences

AOL has become a worldwide service, and the preferences shown in Figure B.20 enable you to choose which language to use to display onscreen messages. Not all these options will work in your software, but if the one you choose is functional, it'll darken the **Add** button when you select it.

FIGURE B.20

If you want to use another language on your AOL session, make the changes here.

1 Select the language at the left, then click **Add**.

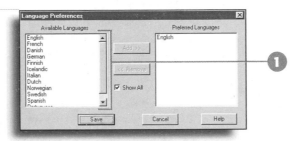

Setting Marketing Preferences

This option lets you choose whether AOL will send pop-up ads on your screen when you sign-on or whether they can give out information about your screen name and mailing address to marketing firms to send you ads. Many folks just opt to say "no" to all these options.

Using the File Menu

America Online's **File** menu, shown in Figure B.21, is much like the one you find in any other Mac or Windows application.

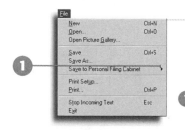

FIGURE B.21

America Online's **File** menu is similar to the File menus found in other programs.

1 A right-hand arrow brings up additional commands.

Most of the commands are familiar to you, but America Online has added a few features to its software that are worth some explanation. The following paragraphs explain the **File** menu's options.

Using the New Option

When you choose **New** or press Ctrl+N (Command-N on your Mac), you see a blank document window, much like the one you would find in a text-processing program.

America Online comes with a basic text editor, kind of a simple word processor. You can use this text editor to write little memos, or write a simple letter, or just to paste text you have grabbed from other memos or message windows online.

The Memo feature is not as full-featured as your word-processing program. Although you have some basic text formatting choices, such as typeface, text style, and background color, you do not have the range of choices available in even the simplest text processor. You can, however, insert a picture into your document and do a spell check.

Using the Open Option

Choosing the **Open** command (Ctrl+O on Windows, Command-O on the Mac) brings up your standard PC Open dialog box. It enables you to open text documents.

Using the Open Picture Gallery Option

The **Open Picture Gallery** command lets you select a folder containing GIF and JPEG image files. Then it builds a display of miniature (thumbnail) images, so you can select which ones you want to insert into your email or instant message. I'll tell you more about these two features in Chapter 9.

Using the Save Option

The **Save** command (Ctrl+S on Windows, Command-S on the Mac) saves the contents of your document window to a file that's written to disk. If you haven't saved the file before, you see a dialog box that enables you to give the file a name.

Using the Save As Option

The **Save As** option enables you to save your document under a new name. When you select this option, you see a standard dialog box in which you can specify the new name of your file.

Using the Save to Personal Filing Cabinet Option

The **Save to Personal Filing Cabinet** option enables you to save the email you've just read or you've just written to both your Offline Mail Drawer and Personal Filing Cabinet. I'll cover the Offline Mail Drawer in more detail later in this chapter, in the "Using the Mail Center Icon" section.

Using the Print Setup Option

Choosing **Print Setup** displays the standard Print Setup dialog box (it's called **Page Setup** on a Mac), in which you can change your page size and orientation (Portrait or Landscape) and select various printer options. These options vary depending on the kind of printer you have.

Using the Print Option

Choosing the **Print** option (Ctrl+P on Windows, Command-P on the Mac) produces the regular Print Document dialog box (see Figure B.22). It enables you to print from any open text window. You can print a memo, an email message, a conference window, a fully formatted World Wide Web page, or any other displayed text on America Online. If a window has more than one text window, such as the opening window of an online department, you should move the cursor to the text file you want to print. You can move the cursor either by clicking the mouse or by pressing Tab.

FIGURE B.22

Printing a text window from America Online is a snap.

1 Click **OK** to print the selected text document.

Using the Stop Incoming Text Option

When you open a text window, the text begins to display in the window as it is received from America Online. If you want to stop this incoming text, from the **File** menu select the **Stop Incoming Text** option, or press the Esc key on your PC or Command-. (period) on your Mac.

Using the Exit (Quit) Option

If you are still online when you choose the **File** menu and select **Exit**, you will be logged off within a few seconds, the America Online application will be closed, and you will return to your PC's desktop or another opened application.

Using the Edit Menu

Five of the first six active selections on the **Edit** menu, as shown in Figure B.23, are much like what you'd find in any application. They are **Undo** (Ctrl+Z on Windows, Command-Z on the Mac), **Cut** (Ctrl+X on Windows, Command-X on the Mac), **Copy** (Ctrl+C on Windows, Command-C on the Mac), **Paste** (Ctrl+V on Windows, Command-V on the Mac), and **Select All** (Ctrl+A on Windows, Command-C on the Mac).

FIGURE B.23

The **Edit** menu is typical of what you see in many Windows programs.

Mac users get the Paste As Quotation option

To use this feature, first open a message board or newsgroup message window. Then copy the text you want to quote. Open your Reply window then press the Option key and from the **Edit** menu choose **Paste**. The function changes to **Paste As Quotation**, and when you paste your quoted text into your message, it is formatted according to Internet styles.

Using the Find in Top Window Option

America Online enables you to search text in the top window (the one you've activated on your computer's screen). By choosing the **Find in Top Window** command (see Figure B.24) and entering the text string you want to look for, you can quickly locate a specific item of text. You can make the search case-sensitive, if desired, by selecting the **Match case** option.

FIGURE B.24

AOL's text search tool lets you find that word again in the document you just read.

1   Click the **Find** button to start the search.

Using the Spell Check Option

Before you send an email or post a message, you'll want to check what you've written with AOL's handy spell checker (see Figure B.25). This utility, as you'll notice, is capable of storing new words, so you can expand its capabilities over time.

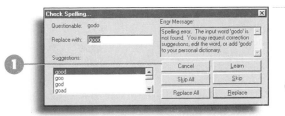

FIGURE B.25

The **Spell Check** option is similar to what you'd find in a word-processor program.

1 Click **Cancel** to stop the spell check.

Using the Dictionary Option

When you choose the **Dictionary** command, you'll bring up an online area that has *Merriam-Webster's popular Collegiate Dictionary*. You can use this feature to quickly check the spelling or meaning of a word before you use it in your message.

Using the Thesaurus Option

The **Thesaurus** command calls up **Merriam-Webster's Thesaurus** (when you're online of course). If you want to fin a better way to express your thoughts, you'll find this handy guide very useful indeed.

Using the Capture Picture Option

The **Capture Picture** option lets you grab a picture from your digital camera, save it to your computer, and send the picture to your friends via email.

Using AOL's Image Tools

When you open a picture file with your AOL software (see Figure B.26) a set of graphics editing tools appears above the image itself. These tools are similar to what you find in an image editing program, although they're not intended to replace one of those programs.

Those tools are described in the following list, row by row, from left to right:

Mac version supports text to speech

Your Mac offers you a **Speak Text and Stop Speaking** option to enable you to use text to speech features with your AOL software. To see these options in your AOL's **Edit** menu, you must have Apple's Speech Manager or PlainTalk software installed. An **Insert** option is also available to let you insert a text file, picture file, or hyperlink into an open text document or email message.

Mac users need another program to edit images

On a Mac, AOL's software doesn't edit images on its own. It does, however, let you link to any image editing program you already have, such as Adobe Photoshop or GraphicConverter (which I used to edit illustrations used in this book), and use that program's tools to provide many of these functions.

FIGURE B.26

AOL's image editing toolbar offers you a set of basic image editing features. The number shown in the picture is the actual image size, in pixels.

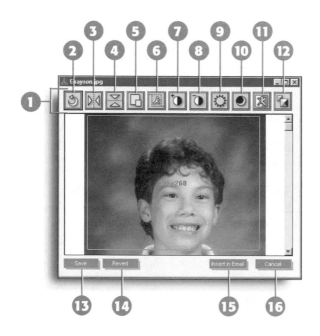

1	Click a tool to activate its function	9	Bright Image tool
2	Rotation tool	10	Darken Image tool
3	Horizontal Rotation tool	11	Invert Image tool
4	Vertical Rotation tool	12	Grayscale tool
5	Fit Image to View	13	Save
6	Crop Image to Selected Area	14	Revert
7	Increase Contrast tool	15	Insert in Email
8	Decrease Contrast tool	16	Cancel

- **Rotation tool.** This tool rotates a graphic image 90 degrees counterclockwise.

- **Horizontal Rotation tool.** This tool flips the graphics image horizontally.

- **Vertical Rotation tool.** This tool flips the graphics image vertically.

- **Fit Image to View.** This tool resizes the image to fit on your computer screen.

- **Crop Image to Selected Area.** This tool enables you to save just a portion of the image.

- **Increase Contrast tool.** This tool establishes a higher image contrast level.

- **Decrease Contrast tool.** This tool establishes a lower image contrast level.

- **Brighten Image tool.** This tool brightens the graphics image by a preset gradient.

- **Darken Image tool.** This tool darkens the graphics image by a preset gradient.

- **Invert Image tool.** This tool makes a positive image negative, and vice versa.

- **Grayscale tool.** This tool removes the color bits from a color image and changes it to grayscale.

At the bottom of the image, you'll see buttons that enable you to insert it in your email message, save it as changed, cancel your changes, or revert the picture to the previously saved version.

If you need to refresh your skills on these and other standard personal computer commands, check the manuals that came with your operating system software.

Using the Window Menu

As you continue to travel through the America Online community, your screen will soon become cluttered with many open windows. The **Window** menu, shown in Figure B.27, is your tool for cleaning and clearing your screen.

FIGURE B.27

The **Window** menu is designed for spring cleaning so that you can clean up a cluttered desktop.

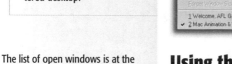

The list of open windows is at the bottom

At the bottom of the **Window** menu is a list of all open America Online windows. After you open this menu, you can type the listed number to bring that window to the front.

Using the Cascade Option

Cascade is another option you can use to organize your online windows. The **C**ascade option overlaps windows in neat form, from left to right, with the title of each window clearly displayed.

Using the Tile Option

As you travel online, you begin to open window after window, and finally your desktop starts getting awfully cluttered. Tiling the windows enables you to place them neatly side-by-side.

Using the Arrange Icons Option

The **Arrange Icons** feature arranges all icons neatly within an active window. This makes it easier for you to locate a specific document title onscreen.

Using the Close All Except Front Option

Everything has its limits, and your America Online software cannot open an unlimited number of windows without the chance that the program will run out of memory. Periodically choosing the **Close All Except Front** option to close all the windows except the one in front is a good idea. It cleans up your workspace quickly.

Using the Add Top Window to Favorite Places Option

The **Add Top Window to Favorite Places** option enables the frontmost forum window to be included in your list of Favorite Places. This feature is most convenient when you are visiting multiple sites across the World Wide Web or when you use other Internet features on America Online. You'll find out more about building a list of Favorite Places in Chapter 2, "Getting the Most from Your AOL Software."

Using the Remember Window Size Only Option

The **Remember Window Size Only** option is similar to **Remember Window Size and Position**, but as you might expect, the position of the window is not saved.

Using the Remember Window Size and Position Option

You might decide that the default size of an America Online message window is too small or too large for your screen. You can use this option to enable the program to recall the size and position of the type of window (email, message, or whatever) you have just chosen so the program always opens that window in the same location and with the same window size.

This feature doesn't work for all America Online windows. If it doesn't work in a window you've opened, the option appears grayed in the **Window** menu.

Using the Forget Window Size and Position Option

If you decide to change the window to its default size and location, choose the **Forget Window Size and Position** option.

Mac version has additional features

The Mac version of AOL software offers two more items in the **Window menu**. The first, **AOL Shortcuts**, brings up a submenu showing commonly used functions, such as finding menus, writing email and instant messages, and styling text. The second feature, **My Shortcuts**, duplicates the feature in the **Favorites** drop-down menu in the Windows version.

Using the Help Window

If you hit a sticking point and need a little more assistance in learning a particular function while using America Online's software, you'll find a lot of useful information in the **Help** menu (see Figure B.28). The **Help** menu works precisely the same way as it does in other programs.

The **Help** menu is divided into four sections, the first of which has two parts. The first part includes Member Services Online Help, which provides a listing of the contents of the Help text. Double-clicking the topic that interests you provides a screen filled with the information you need. You can also use the **Print Topic** command to produce a paper copy of the open Help window.

The second part brings up AOL's Parental Control feature. You'll learn more about this feature Chapter 7.

Help With Keywords and **Accounts and Billing** in the third part provide direct links to AOL member support areas. **AOL Access Phone Numbers** give you access to the latest list of connection phone numbers.

On the final segment of the **Help** menu, **What's New in AOL 4.0**, briefly describes the new features of the latest AOL software. **About America Online** brings up a screen to inform you of the version of AOL software you're using, which is useful if you're online and need additional support.

Using the Sign Off Option

When you log on to AOL you'll see two options. The first, Switch Screen names, lets you check a list of all your screen names on your AOL account, see if email is awaiting by a darkened mail icon, and then sign on to any of those screen names.

The **Sign-Off** command immediately ends your AOL session, but keeps the program running, in case you want to reconnect without waiting for the program to launch again.

Using the Toolbar

America Online's software offers quick access to a specific online channel and allows you to take advantage of the most popular features of your software by using the *toolbar*. The toolbar contains 13 icons at the top, as shown in Figure B.29, each of which represents an online area or command. The second row is used for navigation around the service.

1

Most of the icons shown in Figure B.29 are grayed out when you first launch your AOL program. When you log on, however, the icons become bright and colorful. Any toolbar icon with a down arrow will produce a drop-down menu with additional functions when clicked. I'll get to those in the next section.

Table B.1 lists the special functions and destinations attached to each icon. The areas shown correspond, from left to right, top to bottom, to the icons displayed on the toolbar. All these areas and features are discussed in more detail throughout the rest of this book.

One name at a time

Because all your screen names are part of the same master account, you can't sign on to more than one of these screen names at one time (even with separate computers, modems, and phone lines). If you need to have more screen names than one signed on to AOL at the same time, you would have to establish a separate account for each person.

FIGURE B.29

AOL's toolbar and your mouse are a great combination for activating the most-used features of your America Online software.

1 The icons with arrows have additional functions.

Keyboard shortcuts can be used too

If clicking a mouse isn't your favorite way to navigate around AOL, check Chapter 2 for a complete list of keyboard shortcuts.

TABLE B.1   **Using the toolbar**

Icon	Destination or Function
Top Row	
Read	Check Mail
Write	Write Mail

continues…

Table B.1 Continued

Icon	Destination or Function
Mail Center	AOL's Mail Center (drop-down menu)
Print	Print selected document window
My Files	My Files (drop-down menu)
My AOL	My AOL (drop-down menu)
Favorites	Favorites (drop-down menu)
Internet	Internet (drop-down menu)
Channels	Channels (drop-down menu)
People	People (drop-down menu)
Quotes	Stock Quotes
Perks	Perks
Weather	Weather
Bottom Row	
◄	Previous online area or Web site
►	Next online area or Web site
⊗	Stop display of Web page
↻	Reload Web page
⌂	AOL's Home Page
Keyword	Keyword menu of recently visited places (drop-down menu)
Go	Go to area entered at left
Find ▼	AOL's Find Central feature

Many of the program features are only available via toolbar commands. The ones not previously described in this chapter will be described in detail.

Using the Mail Icon

The mail flag rises whenever new email is present to be read. Clicking this icon brings up a list of New Mail, Old (Read) Mail, and Sent Mail. I'll explain more about AOL's email feature in Chapter 9.

Using the Write Icon

Click this icon to bring up a blank email message window.

Using the Mail Center Icon

When you click this icon, you see a drop-down menu showing a number of email functions (see Figure B.30)

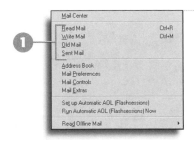

The following sections provide a description of the commands available from this menu.

A Visit to AOL's Mail Center

Most of your mailing options are available from the Post Office window (keyword Mail Center), shown in Figure B.31, simply by clicking the appropriate icon. Each feature will be discussed separately, as it appears on the **Mail** menu.

Using the Read Mail Option

Select the **Read Mail** option to view the email you've just received.

Using the Write Mail Option

Choose the **Write Mail** option to bring up a blank email window.

Using the Old Mail Option

The **Old Mail** option brings up a display of the email you've read over the last few days (up to a maximum of 550 pieces).

Using the Sent Mail Option

Choose the **Sent Mail** option to bring up a display of the email you've sent over the past 30 days (up to a maximum of 550 pieces).

Using the Address Book Option

As you develop a list of regular online friends, you'll want to put their names in your personal Address Book. This list is your own Rolodex that you can use to send mass mailings or merely to look up the name of an individual. To learn more about creating and updating your Address Book, see Chapter 9.

Using the Mail Preferences Option

The **Mail Preferences** option brings up the email preference window described earlier in this chapter, in the section entitled "Setting Mail Preferences."

Using Mail Controls

Use your master screen name

To access Mail Controls, you must connect to AOL using your master screen name. That's the one you set up when you first joined AOL (it's at the top of your list of screen names).

AOL's **Mail Controls** feature lets you deal with a common problem on any online service, junk email. More and more of it is being sent, in the same fashion as junk mail hits your regular mailbox at your home or office.

Selecting Mail Extras

When you click **Mail Extras**, you get a selection of optional (sometimes extra cost) features such as AOL's Card-O-Matic product. This feature lets you send customized greeting cards via email.

Using the Setup Automatic AOL (FlashSessions) Option

Click this item to configure an Automatic AOL session. You'll learn more about this feature in Chapter 9.

Using the Run Automatic AOL (FlashSessions) Now Option

Click this item to activate an Automatic AOL session. I also explain how to set up this feature in Chapter 9.

Using the Read Offline Mail Option

The **Read Offline Mail** feature incorporates one function that enables you to check mail you have received and two for mail you've not yet sent. These functions are

- **Incoming/Saved Mail.** This option enables you to view letters that have been saved to your Auto AOL mailbox. Letters are stored in your offline mailbox until you delete them. This mail is also available to you offline, because it is stored in your Online Mail folder, part of your AOL program's folder, rather than at AOL's host computer. You can save mail that you've read online to this file by choosing the command in the **File** menu and then selecting **Save to Personal Filing Cabinet**. Check Chapter 9 for more information on how to run an Automatic AOL session.

- **Mailing Waiting To Be Sent.** Email is stored in your mailbox before it's sent during an Auto AOL session or while you're online. You can edit or delete your email before it's sent, or attach a file to your message even while offline (because it is stored, like your Incoming Mail, on your own computer).

- **Copies of Mail You've Sent.** Here you can check the email you've sent via the Automatic AOL feature.

Using the Print Icon

Click this icon to print the selected document window (it will be grayed out of you cannot print a specific document).

Using the My Files Option

I've described most of the options shown in the **My Files** drop-down menu (see Figure B.32) previously in this chapter. I'll just list the ones not mentioned so far here.

FIGURE B.32

The **My Files** menu lets you configure a number of program options, and bring up some special features.

Personal Filing Cabinet
Save to Personal Filing Cabinet ▶

Offline Mail
Download Manager
My Web Page
Offline Newsgroups

Log Manager

Using the Personal Filing Cabinet Option

The Personal Filing Cabinet is used to store email, message board postings, and the list of files you've downloaded or are about to download. You can remove individual items and create new storage folders from the feature's convenient file management interface.

Using the Save to Personal Filing Cabinet Option

This feature lets you save individual email to your Personal Filing Cabinet. It may be a better idea than using Mail Preferences to save all your mail, because you're apt to be overwhelmed in short order with unneeded material if you get lots of email on AOL.

Using the Download Manager Option

Downloading is the process of transferring a file from America Online's huge software libraries to your computer. You use the

Download Manager option (Ctrl+D) to choose one or more files to download during your online visit. The files are placed in a download queue or sequence. You can begin the download process at any time during your online session or when you log off.

You learn how to set up the Download Manager to work best for you in Chapter 26. Figure B.10, shown earlier in this chapter, shows the Download Preferences available in your America Online software.

Using the My Web Page Option

As part of your AOL membership, you can make your own Web page. I'll tell you how to do that in Chapter 18, "Become a Web Publisher on AOL."

Using the Offline Newsgroups Option

You can use this feature to check message board and Usenet newsgroup postings. You'll learn about these features in Chapter 11 and 17.

Using the Log Manager Option

During your visits to America Online, you might want to save the contents of a message area or an online conference so you can view and print them later. You have two main logging options in your America Online software, as shown in Figure B.33.

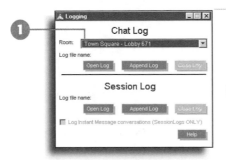

FIGURE B.33

Recording your America Online visit is easy with the program's Logging feature.

1. Choose your logging option here.

- **Chat Log.** During your online travels, you might attend a chat in America Online's People Connection or an online conference. The Chat Log enables you to record the entire conversation.

- **Session Log.** With this log, you can record all the text you read during your visit to America Online. The log doesn't record the mail you send or the messages you post, but you can save those anyway, using the **Save** command described previously. (You also can log instant messages if you check that option at the bottom of the Logging dialog box.)

Logging your AOL session is easy

1. Choose the **Log Manager** option from the **My Files** icon, which opens the Logging dialog box.

2. Select the kind of log you want to record by clicking the **Open Log** button in the appropriate category.

3. Click the **Open** button. You then see a dialog box much like the Save As dialog box, where you are asked to name your file and indicate where it is to be saved (see Figure B.34). The log is given a default name, such as session.log, but you can give the file any name you want, as long as it contains no more than eight characters (and includes the same file extension); this is true even if you're using Windows 95.

FIGURE B.34

Name your Open Log to begin the recording process.

1 Click **Save** to start recording.

4. If you want to end the online recording process, return to the **My Files** icon, select **Log Manager**, and choose the **Close Log** button in the Logging dialog box.

5. When you decide to resume the logging process or add to a previously created log, click the **Append Log** button in the Logging dialog box.

6. When you finish logging, choose the **Close Log** button in the Logging dialog box.

The logging process is flexible. You can open both logs at the same time if you want. What's more, you can append or close each log separately, depending on which one you've highlighted when you make your choice.

Log files have their limits

Remember, America Online's Windows software can read only 64,000 characters in a single text window. When you want to read additional segments of a long file, you need to select the **More** option in your Open dialog box. No such limits exist for the Mac version.

Using the My AOL Icon

I've described most of the options shown in the **My AOL** drop-down menu (see Figure B.35) previously in this chapter. I'll just list the ones not mentioned so far here.

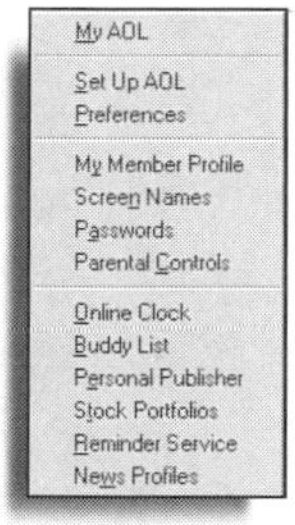
My AOL
Set Up AOL
Preferences
My Member Profile
Screen Names
Passwords
Parental Controls
Online Clock
Buddy List
Personal Publisher
Stock Portfolios
Reminder Service
News Profiles

FIGURE B.35

The **My AOL** menu lets you configure a number of program options and bring up some special features.

- **My Member Profile.** Provide a capsule summary about you, including your likes and dislikes. You'll learn more about this feature in Chapter 8, "AOL's People Connection."
- **Screen Names.** This command brings up a screen where you can add or delete screen names. You'll learn more about this feature in Chapter 8.
- **Passwords.** Use this command to change the password for the screen name you're logged on with. You may also use it to store the password in your AOL program.
- **Parental Controls.** You can access this feature with your master account to customize the online experience for each screen name on your account.
- **Online Clock.** Use this option to bring up a screen showing how long you've been online.

Another logging option for your Mac

On your Mac, you have the option to create a separate log for the instant messages you send, rather than just clicking a check box.

- **Buddy List.** This option lets you configure your Buddy List, that convenient display window showing whether your online acquaintances are logged on. I'll explain more about this feature in Chapter 8.

- **Personal Publisher.** AOL's Personal Publisher feature lets you build your own Web page quickly, without any knowledge of Web authoring. I'll tell you more about this feature in Chapter 18.

- **Stock Portfolios.** This feature lets you display your personal stock portfolio. You'll learn more about it in Chapter 27, "Using the Personal Finance Channel."

- **Reminder Service.** This command brings up AOL's handy Reminder Service, where you can be notified automatically about special events, such as an anniversary, birthday or business meeting.

- **News Profiles.** Access AOL's custom feature to deliver the latest news on the subjects you select directly to your online mailbox. I'll tell you more about this feature in Chapter 24, "Visiting the News Channel."

Using the Favorites Icon

Have you found a cool Web site or online area you want your friends to visit? Just click the **Favorite Places** heart at the upper right of the forum or Web site window to add it to your custom list (see Figure B.36).

FIGURE B.36

This drop-down menu shows your custom Favorite Places directory. Select an item from the menu or submenu to go to that place within seconds.

In addition to adding items to your custom Favorite Places directory, you can do the following:

- **<u>G</u>o To Keyword.** Use this feature to jump instantly to another AOL area.

- **<u>M</u>y Shortcuts.** When you install your America Online software, you have a list in your **Shortcuts** menu of 10 regular spots to which you can travel by pressing two keys (Ctl for Windows, Command for the Mac plus a number from 0 to 9). You can change these destinations by choosing the **Shortcut Keys** option to display the Edit Shortcuts dialog box. (The same option appears in the **<u>W</u>indow** menu of your AOL Mac software.)

    Editing the Shortcuts dialog box is a simple procedure. You can do it whether or not you're logged on.

Adding your shortcuts is easy

1. From the **Favorites** drop-down menu on the toolbar choose **My Shortcuts**. The Shortcuts dialog box appears.

2. In the left column, type the name of the area you want to visit, and type the online keyword on the right. To move quickly from one entry to the next, press Tab. The text box you go to is highlighted automatically so whatever information you type replaces what's already there.

3. After you've made your changes and additions to the **Go To** menu, click **OK**. The changes you've made appear immediately in the **My Shortcuts** menu or through your keyboard shortcuts.

Using the Internet Icon

The **<u>I</u>nternet** drop-down menu lets you easily activate several AOL Internet features (see Figure B.37).

The following list explains what the commands do:

- **Internet Connection.** Accesses all of AOL's Internet features from one convenient interface.

FIGURE B.37

You can use this drop-down menu to choose among some of AOL's Internet features.

- **Go to the Web.** This command takes you to the AOL's home page on the World Wide Web (or any home page you've chosen instead in your Web preferences).

- **AOL NetFind.** This command brings up AOL's handy NetFind screen, which lets you search out information on the Web. I'll tell you more about it in Chapters 13, 16, and 26.

- **Newsgroups.** Internet newsgroups (also known as Usenet newsgroups) are popular message boards where you never know what to expect. You'll discover more about this feature in Chapter 17.

- **Search Newsgroups.** Use AOL's powerful database search tools to locate newsgroups that interest you.

- **FTP (File Transfer).** File Transfer Protocol lets you tap huge numbers of files on the Internet. You'll discover more about this feature in Chapter 15, "Using File Transfer Protocol."

Using the Channels Icon

America Online divides its service into departments, or channels, each of which represents a specific area of interest (although some overlapping of coverage exists, such as the Research & Learn and News Channels). When you log on to AOL, you'll also see a handy display of these channels located just below your Welcome window. In Figure B.38 you'll see the drop-down menu that appears when you click the Channels icon.

FIGURE B.38

Choose an online channel or online support options from this screen.

Using the People Icon

America Online's People Connection is one of the most popular features of the service. You can access thousands of online chats every day, including online conferences featuring famous celebrities. The **People** drop-down menu shown in Figure B.39 lets you access some of the same features available via My AOL. In addition, you'll be able to access online chats, check your Buddy List, and send a message via any one of several popular paging systems.

You'll discover more about the People Connection channel in Chapter 8.

FIGURE B.39

The People drop-down menu lets you learn about members, send them messages, and find online chats that interest you.

Using the Quotes Icon

AOL lets you have quick access to up-to-date stock market information during the trading day. Click the **Quotes** icon to display AOL's Stocks and Quotes screen.

Using the Perks Icon

Learn about special offers available directly from AOL's Shopping channel. You'll learn more about online shopping in Chapter 30, "Secrets of AOL's Shopping Channel."

Using the Weather Icon

Before you go outside or take a long trip, you'll want to consult this feature to get the latest forecast.

Customizing the Toolbar

You can't do this on smaller screens

As you can see from the illustrations, AOL's program toolbar is very wide. If you have a screen with a resolution of 800×600 or less (and these are typical sizes for many users), there won't be enough room to add another icon on the toolbar because it gets wider every time you add something to it. You'll get an onscreen warning, however, if you cannot add an icon.

As explained in "Using the Toolbar" earlier in this chapter, you can move the toolbar to another location on your screen.

You have additional options to customize the toolbar, and also to reduce the amount of space it occupies on your computer's screen. You can place more icons on the top row of your toolbar, to give you one-click access to a favorite online area. All you need do is access an area with a Favorite Places heart displayed.

It's easy to customize the toolbar

1. Click the **Favorite Places** heart and drag it to the position you want on the top row of the toolbar.

2. From the screen shown in Figure B.40 click an icon you like.

FIGURE B.40

Choose the icon to represent the area you want to add to the toolbar.

3. When the icon is selected, click **OK**.

When an area has been added to the toolbar, it'll expand to accommodate the additional icon (see Figure B.41.)

FIGURE. B.41

A new icon has now been added to the AOL toolbar.

How to Restore the Toolbar

If you decide you would rather return the toolbar to its original form, hold down the Control key, select the custom toolbar icon, and drag it off the toolbar. Then **OK** the confirmation message to remove that item.

A Mac option to reset the toolbar

Your Mac's toolbar preferences also include the option to restore the original toolbar.

Using the Tab Key

Suppose you are composing a letter to another America Online member. You can use the Tab key to move from one text box to another, such as from the **Subject** text box to the text box where you write your letter. The Tab key works in any area where more than one text box is available to choose. Holding down the Shift and Tab keys at the same time reverses the process, so you move back to the preceding text box.

Pulling Down a Menu

To use the keyboard to open a menu on your Windows PC, follow these steps:

To use your Windows keyboard power

1. Each menu bar item, such as **File** or **Edit**, has an underlined letter. If you press the Alt key plus that underlined letter, the menu drops down, and a rectangle highlights the first entry in the menu.

2. Use the down-arrow key to move the highlight down to the item you want to use.

3. Use the up-arrow key if you need to move the highlight up to the preceding item.

4. Press Enter to activate the highlighted menu option.

You can get underlined menu bar commands on your Mac too

Connectix has a handy program that underlines the letters of menu bar commands for fast keyboard access (it doesn't work on AOL's toolbar menus, however). It's called Speed Doubler 8 and it also gives you faster 680×0 emulation on Power PC Macs, and improves the speed of file copying, especially over a network.

Getting There by Keyboard

If you want to save wear and tear on your mouse, you can use your keyboard to access many AOL functions. You'll find the full list at the end of Chapter 2.

SEE ALSO

➤ *For advice on logging onto AOL when you're not at your home or office, see page 39*

➤ *For a quick tour of AOL, see page 71*

➤ *To get in touch with fellow AOL members, see page 135*

➤ *To learn how to navigate through AOL's huge software libraries, see page 433*

AOL's Most Popular Keywords

AOL keywords

Where do they take you?

Use a Keyword

The fastest way to get from here to there on AOL (other than the items on the toolbar of course) is a keyword. In this section, I've collected the important keywords you'll want to know as you navigate around the service, and (at least as of the time this book was written) the keywords to some of the most popular AOL areas, as selected by your fellow members. Rather than just list names, I've provided a sentence or two to describe the purpose of the area or service accessed via that keyword.

To use keywords for AOL for Windows

1. From anywhere on America Online, press Ctrl+K (Command-K for Mac users).

2. When the Keyword window appears, type the keyword of the channel or area you want to go to, and choose **GO**.

To use keywords for AOL for the Mac OS

1. From anywhere on America Online, press ⌘-K or select **Keyword** from the **Go To** menu.

2. When the Keyword window appears, type the keyword of the channel or area you want to go to, and choose **GO**.

Keywords are not case sensitive—so don't worry about whether you're using caps or lowercase.

The following listing is, in part, based on material compiled by AOL's Jennifer Watson, to whom I express my heartfelt thanks for the long hours she's spent accumulating this material.

Acc   AOL Community Cares, an organization designed for members to help others in time of need.

Acc Caring Orgs   The organizations that make up AOL Community Cares.

Acc Chat   Accesses chats run by AOL Community Cares.

Acc Help   Help yourself and others via AOL Community Cares.

Access   Check for new access numbers to reach AOL in the United States and around the world.

Keywords change often

The keywords presented here are current as this book is published, but because services are frequently added and changed on America Online, keywords may change as well and some of the ones shown here may be deleted.

Another cool way to use keywords

You may use the navigation bar at the bottom of your AOL program toolbar for keywords. Just enter the keyword you want in the text field, and click the **Go To** button.

When you don't know the keyword, maybe you can fake it

If the keyword for the area you want isn't listed in this appendix, just improvise. Enter a keyword for the name or topic of the area you're looking for. More than likely, if that area exists, you can find it this way.

Can't find that keyword?

If improvising a keyword fails to bring a result, click the **Search** button in the Keyword window, rather than the **Go To** button, to bring up a list of possible matches to the keyword you typed.

Some areas have several keywords

The keywords shown aren't the only ones used to access these areas. I'm just using the most common ones.

AOL Beginners   Reach AOL's Help Desk and get advice on how to deal with common problems.

AOL Gift   Purchase an AOL gift certificate for friends or family members.

AOL Insider   Get the inside track on new AOL features and learn about updated network matters.

AOL Preview   Try out the newest version of AOL's software shortly before it goes into general release (a public beta test of a near-final version).

AOL Store   Buy custom labeled merchandise direct from AOL.

AOLglobalnet   Get a list of AOL phone numbers for accessing AOL from outside the United States.

AOLnet   Get a list of AOL's U.S. access numbers.

AOLPress   AOL's easy-to-use Web authoring software is free.

AOLsewhere   How to stay in touch with AOL when you travel around the world; lists access numbers and international versions.

Apps   Visit the Computing channel's Applications forums.

Ask-A-Teacher   Contact AOL's staff of online instructors and get help with your homework.

Auto Shop   Check the options and the lowest prices before you order your next motor vehicle.

Best of AOL   See a listing of some of the most popular, most important new services.

Beta   Apply to be a beta tester of AOL software.

Billing   Reach AOL's billing services area. Learn about your online bill and change billing options.

Bps   Learn about PowerTools and other useful add-ons for AOL's Windows software.

Buddy or **Buddy List**   Access AOL's Buddy List setup screen to create or edit your own list.

Buddy View   Bring the Buddy List onto the screen if you have closed it by mistake (or to clear screen space).

Call AOL   Access a listing of AOL phone support numbers.

Cancel   I hope you never need to access this area. It's designed to conveniently cancel your account.

Capital   Read the latest politically oriented news on AOL.

Channels   This keyword brings up AOL's Main Menu, which lists all the online channels.

Classifieds   Find or place ads for products and services (some free, some at extra cost).

Clock or **Online Clock**   Check the time of day or how long you've been online.

Ce   AOL's Consumer Electronics forum covers electronic gadgets, auto sound systems, and home audio and video.

Comp Live   Each day AOL holds chats on computing topics. Use this keyword to find out when, where, and what.

Companies   AOL Computing's Companies area provides a direct route to many of the major computing firms.

Computer Class   Sign up for free online courses on your favorite computing topics.

Computing   Get help with your personal computer on AOL; forums exist for all the major computing platforms.

Courses   Sign up and take a class online. Some offer credit toward your degree.

Credit   Request a rebate for connection and download problems.

Critics   See what your favorite writers think, and express your own point of view.

Database   Visit the PC Database forum and learn tips and tricks about your favorite database software.

Desktop Cinema   Access AOL's popular multimedia area to hear sound and see videos.

Digital City   Visit special forums devoted to various cities around the world.

Discover   Learn about some of the best AOL features available.

DOS   The fast route to AOL Computing's DOS forum.

Download 101   Get assistance in downloading files, and read about solutions for common problems.

Encyclopedia   Tap the resources of major encyclopedias and do research for your homework or special project.

Entertainment   Learn what's happening in the show business world, and discover the real skinny about your favorite stars.

Families   Discover the forums AOL provides for you and your family. Read tips and techniques for better parenting.

Family Computing   AOL Computing's Family Computing forums are just a click away.

File Search   Call up AOL's software file search feature and check out offerings of thousands of files.

Finance   Learn how to manage your money in AOL's Personal Finance channel and discover up-to-date investment and tax information.

Forums   Visit AOL's Computing channel forums.

Friend   Have a friend sign up on AOL and get credit toward your account.

Friend In France   Have a friend in France? Use this feature to have them sign onto AOL France and get credit toward your account.

Ftp   Locate software and send files across the Internet.

Gallery   A forum containing thousands of photos of AOL members and their families.

Games   Find shareware games and interactive games, and learn how to win at your favorite computer or video game.

Gfbase   Check out all the stats on your favorite sports players and teams.

Glossary Check out AOL's online glossary and learn the real meanings behind some of that arcane online lingo.

Gopher Call up all sorts of information via AOL's Internet search tools.

GPF PC users can reach this area to get assistance on dealing with system crashes.

Grandstand Visit forums devoted to most every popular sport.

Guide Pager Contact AOL's online helpers for assistance if someone is bothering you online.

Hardware AOL Computing's PC Hardware forum.

Health Learn the road to better health and well-being. Read about new developments in the health industry.

Help Access AOL's Member Services area and get help with billing questions, connection problems, and AOL software programs.

Help Desk Visit AOL's Mac and PC Help forums for general AOL and computer assistance.

High Speed Another route to AOL's telephone access center.

Hobby Call up AOL's Hobby Central, and check out forums catering to the hobby you like.

Homework Helper Another route to AOL's Ask-A-Teacher feature.

Hot or **What's Hot** Discover the major, new online features or an online area with a special service or conference.

Hot Today A list of today's featured online areas.

Hotline Another route to AOL's Member Services forum.

Influence Discover the gossip and inside true stories behind the days events.

Instant Messenger This feature enables you to exchange one-one-one (Instant Messages) with folks who are not AOL members, as long as they have Internet access.

International   Because AOL is now a worldwide service, you can learn about AOL services in major cities and meet your fellow members in other countries.

Internet   AOL's Internet Connection explores all the Internet features offered by AOL.

Interests   Explore forums catering to everything from cooking and sewing to astronomy.

Keywords   See all the AOL keywords in one place, updated regularly (courtesy of AOL's Jennifer Watson). This one is worth illustrating (see Figure C.1).

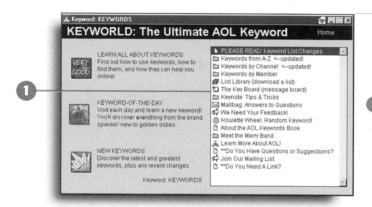

FIGURE C.1

This is Jennifer Watson's Keyword area, where you can find all AOL's shortcuts in one, convenient spot.

1   Double-click a list entry to access that information.

Kids   AOL's Kids Only channel provides a safe online environment for the youngest members of the online community.

KO Help   Where visitors to AOL's Kids Only channel can get prompt online assistance.

La Pub   Visit the People Connection's favorite online hangout to meet friends and enjoy relaxing conversation.

Learn   AOL's Research & Learn channel offers lots of useful information and online courses (some with degree credit).

Letter   Get AOL's community updates from CEO Steve Case.

Lifestyles   Explore AOL communities catering to your lifestyle or religious belief, or discover ways to improve your health.

Live!   AOL Live! offers a regular schedule of online conferences featuring your favorite authors, entertainment figures, and political leaders.

Live Guide   AOL's answer to *TV Guide*. Learn about the latest live events, such as conferences featuring your favorite stars.

Local   Another route to AOL's Digital Cities channel, where you find forums for many major world cities.

PC Apps   Access the PC Applications forum.

Mac Apps   Check out the Mac Applications forum.

Magazine Rack   AOL's online newsstand offers access to dozens of popular magazines.

Mail Gateway   A route to AOL's email information center.

Mailing Lists   Subscribe to any of thousands of mailing lists on a host of subjects, and participate in email discussions.

Marketing Prefs   Tell AOL whether you want to receive online solicitations for merchandise (such as a screen when you log on or you can just turn the feature off).

Marketplace   Find the lowest prices and order top-grade merchandise with special guarantees from AOL merchants.

Mcm   Discuss modems and networking in the Mac Communications forum.

Mdwp   Visit the Mac Desktop and Web Publishing forum.

Mdv   Access the Mac Developer's forum.

Med   AOL Computing's Mac Education forum.

Member Survey   This is where AOL conducts a survey and asks you about the features you want.

Members   Accesses AOL's Member Directory, the list of AOL members who've made a profile.

Members' Choice   Discover the most popular forums as chosen by your fellow members. I'll cover this in more detail in Appendix D, "AOL's Members' Choice."

Mgm   The Games channel's Mac Games forum.

Mgr   AOL Computing's Mac Graphics forum.

Mhm   Access the Members Helping Members forum, where your fellow members answer your questions about AOL service and software.

Mhw   AOL Computing's Mac Hardware forum.

Mms   AOL Computing's Mac Music & Sound forum.

Mm Showcase   AOL's multimedia showcase enables you to access cool, new interactive features.

Modem   Find tips on tweaking your computer's modem for top performance.

Movies   Learn about your favorite flicks and the performers who act in them.

Multimedia Prefs   A feature for Windows AOL users, where you are able to control the display of online artwork.

Music   The road to AOL's popular music forums.

Mut   Access the Mac Utilities forum.

My AOL   AOL guides you through several step-by-step screens showing you how to set up your software for best performance.

My Boards   Check the message boards you set up for offline reading.

My Home PaGE   Call up AOL's Personal Publisher feature and make a Web page.

Names   Add or remove a screen name from your account here.

Neighborhood Watch   Discover the ways AOL can protect your family from unsavory online influences.

NetFind   AOL's powerful Internet search tool makes fast work of finding the information you want.

Net Software   Discover a large selection of Internet software.

New   Check out all the newest AOL features.

New AOL   Another route to accessing the newest AOL software and learning how it works.

New Pricing   Get the specifics of AOL's latest pricing structure and how to change your online billing.

News   AOL's News channel is your online equivalent of the daily newspaper complete with your favorite sections (departments).

News Profiles   Let AOL deliver the latest news right to your email box.

Newsgroups   Enjoy the exciting discussions on thousands of Usenet newsgroups.

Newsstand   Discover online periodicals, some of which are identical to the newsstand versions.

Notes   AOL Computing set up this forum for users of Lotus Notes.

Notify AOL   If someone is annoying you online, or trying to solicit your password, you can report the problem here.

Orientation   AOL's new member orientation area, where you receive online training on using AOL features, and take a brief tour of the service.

OS/2   Get support for IBM's industrial-strength PC operating system from this forum.

Parental Control   Access this feature to give your kids a customized, safe online experience.

Parents   Another route to the AOL Families channel.

Password   Access this area to change your password. *Remember, no AOL employee will ever ask you online for your password or billing information.*

PC Apps   Access the PC Applications forum.

PC Business   Business applications are discussed in the PC Business forum.

PC Games   The Games channel's PC Games forum.

PC Graphics   AOL Computing's PC Graphics forum.

PC Music   AOL Computing's PC Music & Sound forum.

PC Plaza   Discover all the interesting online events and forums run by AOL's People Connection.

PCdwp   Visit the PC Desktop and Web Publishing forum.

PCed   AOL Computing's PC Education forum.

PCfin   AOL Computing's PC Financial software forum.

PChh   AOL Computing's Home & Hobby computing forum.

Pda   AOL Computing's Personal Digital Assistants forum.

Pdv   Access the PC Developer's forum.

Pen Pals   Meet new friends online via email.

Personal Choices   Another way to reach the My AOL area, where you can learn about program preferences and what they do.

Personal Finance   AOL's Personal Finance channel offers advice on money management, and the latest market information.

Personal Publisher   Make your own Web page on AOL in just minutes.

Politics   Read the latest politically oriented news on AOL.

Press   This is AOL's press release library, where you learn about new online services before your local paper or favorite TV network carries a story about it.

Preview   Shortly before a new version of AOL software comes out, you'll get a chance to use a pre-release version. Watch for the announcements online.

PrimeHost   AOL offers a special Web site hosting service for your business.

Profile   Create or edit your member profile.

Questions   It's just another route to AOL's Member Services forums.

Quickstart   Take a fast tour of AOL and learn the ropes.

Quotes   Check on your favorite stocks and follow up on your investment portfolio.

Radio   Don't touch that dial. Learn about your favorite radio shows here.

Random   Your route to finding AOL forums by the service's computerized roulette wheel.

Ref Periodicals   Research information from AOL's large roster of online publications.

Romance   Meet your ideal mate for companionship or marriage, or just find a good friend.

Shopping   Find the lowest prices and order top-grade merchandise with special guarantees from AOL merchants.

Shorthand   Learn all about the little abbreviations used to express your emotions online.

Slideshow   View interactive presentations on the latest events right on AOL (complete with pictures and sound).

Smileys   Another route to AOL's online shorthand information area.

Software Shop   Visit AOL's Software Shop and get the best prices on your favorite programs.

Sound Room   Sample cool online sounds. Works in conjunction with the AOL Desktop Cinema forum.

Sports   AOL's Sports channel provides up-to-date news on your favorite team plus online fantasy leagues.

Sports Ic   Explore Internet sites devoted to the world of sports.

Spreadsheet   AOL Computing's PC Spreadsheet forum.

Stereo   Learn about audio and home theater in *Stereo Review* magazine's online forum.

Steve Case   Each month (or more often when needed) AOL CEO Steve Case presents a letter to members telling about new services and software. It also brings everyone up-to-date on the progress of expanding the service.

Suggest   AOL's suggestion box, where you can give your own ideas on how the service may improve.

Superstore   Visit AOL's Computing Superstore for a large selection of products at competitive prices.

System Response   If you get a system response error of some sort, you can find out why and learn how to deal with frequent problems.

Tax   Get up-to-date tax information year round.

Tech Live   Access AOL's own interactive help service, where AOL staff can help you deal with connection and software problems. Just be aware that getting to this place may involve a complex step-by-step assistance screen.

Telecom   Check out information on modems and networking in the PC Telecom forum.

Tnpc   Visit The National Parenting Council and learn helpful information about child-care.

Today   A listing of the feature attractions of the day on AOL.

Top Tips   Discover the most popular tips for making your AOL experience faster and more fun.

TOS   Learn about AOL's Terms of Service, the rules of conduct that govern this service. You can also use this area to report harassment from other members.

Tour   Take a brief, guided tour of AOL's most popular features.

Travel   Check out prices and book your trip through AOL's online travel agencies, and learn more about local culture in the cities you're visiting.

Travel Advisories   Get U.S. State Department Travel Advisories and learn about worldwide trouble spots before you take your trip.

Travel Corner   Get fully researched reports before you travel to many cities around the world.

Travel Reservations   A fast route to AOL's online travel agencies.

Traveler   The Independent Traveler offers lots of travel-related information for you.

TV   Visit forums devoted to your favorite TV networks and shows.

Upgrade   Get the latest release version of AOL's software.

US News   Read the latest news from all corners of the United States.

Utils   AOL Computing's PC Utilities forum.

Viewers   Choose from a large variety of image and movie viewing software for both Mac and PC users.

Virus   Access the Virus Resource Center in the Computing channel. Learn how to combat computer viruses, and download the latest protection software.

Weather   Check the current forecasts and weather maps for cities around the world.

Windows   Call upon a forum that caters to users of all flavors of Microsoft Windows.

Workplace   Check AOL forums catering to your business or profession.

WWW   Brings up AOL's home page on the World Wide Web.

AOL's Members' Choice

Finding the Most Popular Forums

Even Members' Choice sites change fast

The Members' Choice areas presented here are current as this book is published, but because services are frequently added and changed on America Online, don't be surprised to see some of these areas replaced by other choices when you want to check them out.

AOL has thousands and thousands of forums, and it seems it can take a lifetime to see them all. Well, your fellow AOL members have selected their favorites by the number of times they access (or *hit*) those areas. In the following pages, I'll cover the 50 Members' Choice selections offered at the time this book went to press. As you travel around AOL, no doubt you'll develop your own top 50, but this is a good starting point.

To check the latest Members' Choice selections, use the keyword Members Choice to bring up the screen shown in Figure D.1.

FIGURE D.1

AOL's Members' Choice lists the most popular forums on AOL.

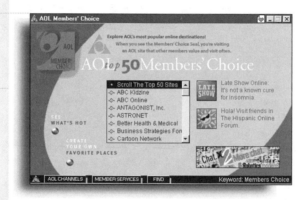

AOL's Members' Choice Selections

ABC Kidzine   Read ABC Online's popular newsletter, designed for younger members.

ABC Online   The popular forum run by the ABC Network. Learn about your favorite programs and about chats featuring the network's top stars.

ANTAGONIST   Access AOL's popular gaming forum, run by Antagonist, Inc.

ASTRONET   Access AOL's forum devoted to those interested in astrology and similar subjects.

Better Health & Medical   The Better Health & Medical Network provides a wealth of information about new developments in the health care professions, as well as message boards and chats.

Business Know-How Forum   Discover hard-won tips on making your business run better. You'll also be able to subscribe to several free newsletters from various business-related AOL forums.

Cartoon Network   Cartoons are not just for kids. This forum is a place for those young and old who appreciate this art forum.

Christianity Online   Access the Christianity Online forums from AOL's Religion & Beliefs area.

Consumer Reports   Read the latest issue of the popular magazine and learn about new products before you buy.

First Call Earnings   If you are interested in building an investment portfolio, or you're just curious about the prospects of a particular company, you'll want to visit this forum regularly.

GamePro Online   A forum run by the popular gaming magazine.

Genealogy Online   Visit this forum and learn how to explore your own family tree. The Beginner's Center helps you get started.

Grandstand   The Grandstand is for dedicated sports fans, and includes AOL's popular Fantasy Leagues, where you can field your own team and compete with fellow members.

Grateful Dead   A forum designed for fans of the Grateful Dead, whose memory lives on despite the death of band leader Jerry Garcia.

Hecklers Online   Hecklers Online is a forum that's brash and controversial, and definitely a place that's different from the usual online area.

Hispanic Online   A popular forum in the Lifestyles channel.

Independent Traveler   One of the most interesting forums in AOL's Travel channel provides both advice and tips on getting the best prices for your next vacation.

Jewish Community   Many members of AOL's Jewish community congregate here for information and discussion.

The Late Show Online   Read David Letterman's always funny "Top Ten" lists, and discover what he has up his sleeve for his next CBS show.

Love@AOL   Access AOL's romance connection, post your personal ads and read ads from other members.

Mac Games Forum   Find the latest shareware games, updates to your favorite gaming software, and get hints and tips from fellow players and experts.

Mac Graphics Forum   The Mac Graphics and CAD Forum is a place for budding graphic artists and professionals.

Mac Music & Sound Forum   Download sound effects and sound editing software, and learn how to make pro-quality sound productions on your computer.

Market News Center   A wealth of business news, all available from a single forum. Check stock prices, currency markets, and more—direct from AOL's worldwide resources.

Marvel Comics Online   Marvel Comics Online is the gathering place for fans of such comic book characters as Spiderman and the Incredible Hulk.

Military City Online   A forum run for those in the armed services and their families.

Moms Online   A popular forum in AOL's Families channel. Learn how to deal with childcare problems, work-related issues, and more.

Morningstar Mutual Funds   A part of the Personal Finance channel, where you can download research reports on many companies.

Motley Fool   An investor's forum that takes an irreverent approach to the financial world.

NetNoir   This area is subtitled "the Soul of Cyberspace." It's a popular center to learn about Black culture and entertainment.

The New York Times   Discover the interactive edition of New York's newspaper of record. You'll see stories from the daily editions, plus exclusive online features.

NICK at NITE   Learn about the nighttime schedule from Nickelodeon, where vintage TV shows are presented.

Nickelodeon Online   Nickelodeon Online provides some extra visual and audio features as part of its AOL forum.

NTN   The NTN Games Studio offers an interesting menu of online games and other features.

Online Psych   Because they have psychologists and psychiatrists on radio, it's no surprise to find a similar resource on AOL.

onQ   An information area run by AOL's Gays & Lesbians forum.

Parascope   Explore the frontiers of science and beyond, and learn about such things as UFOs and strange things that go bump in the night.

Pet Care Online Forum   The Pet Care Online forum offers advice and discussions for pet lovers.

PlanetOut   An online community sponsored by AOL's Gays & Lesbians forum.

Preview Travel   Visit AOL's travel agency, get the lowest prices and make your reservations.

Quotes & Portfolios   This area provides up-to-date market quotes and lets you check your stock portfolio.

Real Fans Sports Network   If the latest sports news and views gets first priority when you open your daily paper, you'll definitely want to check out this area.

Seventeen   An online forum run by the publisher of the well-known magazine for teenagers.

Sporting News   Read the latest issue of the *Sporting News* or check out exclusive online features, such as articles, messages, and chats.

STATs, Inc.   Part of AOL's Sports Channel, STATS, Inc. provides all the latest information about your favorite teams and players. A great place to check your sports knowledge against the actual figures.

Stock Talk   This forum has a large collection of message boards where you can talk about investment possibilities, and share experiences with other members.

Tarot To Go   Okay, can you use those colorful cards to predict your future, or tell about your personality? You'll learn more about it here and you can also check out your daily horoscope.

Thrive   Thrive@AOL provides a forum for health-related issues and frank discussions about human sexuality. You'll find the talk often skirts the edge of AOL's rules of the road, so be careful before you visit this area.

Writers Club   If you're a writer or just plan on becoming one, visit the Writers Club to help you hone your skills and learn about possible markets for you work.

WWF   The World Wrestling Federation's forum offers news of your favorite stars, schedules of upcoming bouts, and as with other online areas, message boards, and chats.

AOL and Compuserve— What Does the Alternative Offer?

AOL & CompuServe—is there a difference?

CompuServe's Internet features

Before AOL Came CompuServe

AOL wasn't the first popular online service. That honor belongs to CompuServe. CompuServe was the largest service too, well at least before AOL overtook it in 1996. As AOL's membership continued its meteoric rise, CompuServe's membership growth stagnated, as did their profit margins. In the summer of 1997, through a complex deal with WorldCom (a large communications company), AOL acquired CompuServe's membership, but pledged to continue to run it as a separate service (in the manner of the MTV and VH-1 cable networks, which are also under single ownership).

Although AOL has worked hard to attract a wide variety of computer users, from the "newbie" to the business user, CompuServe has tended to cater toward experienced PC owners. Before AOL's graphical interface showed the way, in fact, CompuServe was largely text-based. That is, you entered text commands (often just a letter or a word) to navigate around the service. Although CompuServe has migrated toward a more modern interface with the software I'm going to show you in this chapter, some of its origins are text based.

CompuServe continues its emphasis toward the business and professional user, and if you decide to become a member, you'll find that the organization of its forums are not all that different from AOL's. It was, after all, the standard-bearer among online services for many years.

Beyond the Computing forums, you'll find CompuServe's entertainment and lifestyle offerings are not quite as vast as AOL's. This reflects the emphasis on business and professional members. CompuServe excels in its business services. For example, you can take advantage of such features as Dun & Bradstreet's Business reports and TRW Business Credit Profiles.

On AOL, it's the keyword that gets you from here to there when you don't choose to select a toolbar command or colorful icon. On CompuServe, you move around with a "go" word (so it's not all that hard to get used to).

The atmosphere is different

The flavor of AOL and CompuServe is different in many respects. AOL, for example, has long prided itself for being a service for families (even though some members try to ignore the limits). On the other hand, CompuServe offers an adult area, with custom member controls to prevent child access.

CompuServe is Cross-Platform Too

You'll find that CompuServe matches AOL in its support of the major computing platforms. Versions of the software exist for Windows 95, Windows 3.1, and the Mac OS, and all have a similar interface.

A case in point is the opening screen, shown in Figure E.1. It has a passing resemblance to AOL's Welcome and Main Menus, offering the major features of the service in a single, point-and-click screen.

As far as the World Wide Web is concerned, CompuServe is similar to AOL there too. It comes with Microsoft Internet Explorer, and the browser is, to some extent, integrated into the service's interface (as you see later in this chapter). You can change the default browser if you prefer, however, even to Netscape Communicator.

How to Join

CompuServe's ads are nowhere near as common as AOL's, nor do their disks litter your mailboxes quite as much. They turn up often in your new computer equipment purchase, and a CompuServe installer is included on the Windows 95 desktop, smack in the middle of the Online Services folder.

If none of these installers or disks are at hand, just call CompuServe at 1-800-848-8990 and request their sign-up kit. You may also download the latest software from their FTP site, `ftp.compuserve.com/pub/dist/cim`.

Making that First Connection

In case you are interested in trying out CompuServe, I'll help you get set up through that first connection. First, you want to get yourself a CompuServe disk or CD, or, if you have the latest releases of Windows 95, consult the Online Services folder. The steps involved in setting up are the same.

Watch out for extra cost features

Although CompuServe offers a flat-rate option (a little higher than AOL) extra cost options exist throughout the service. Fortunately, they carry warning signs, so you should be aware of the situation. An example is those TRW Business Credit reports. The initial search fee is $5, and the complete report starts at $35.

FIGURE E.1

When you first log on to
CompuServe, you see this screen.

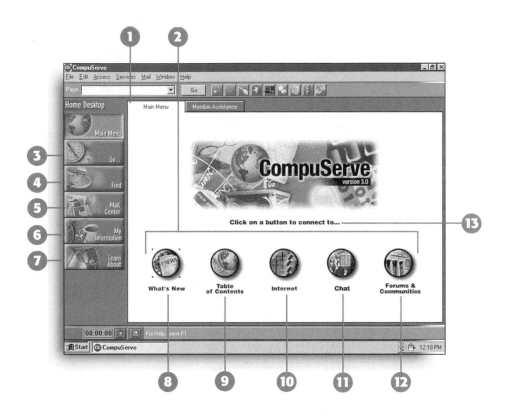

1 **Main Menu** (shown here)

2 Home Desktop buttons

3 **Go...** (to access another area)

4 **Find** CIS content

5 **Mail Center**

6 **My Information** (your personal
settings)

7 **Learn About** (the CIS help menu)

8 **What's New** on CIS

9 **Table of Contents** showing feature list

10 **Internet** access

11 **Chat** rooms and online conferences

12 Forums and CIS Communities

13 **Click a button to connect to...**

Installing CompuServe's software

1. Double-click one of the CompuServe installer icons, either **E**xpress or **Cu**stom, as shown in Figure E.2. The installation process will be complete in minutes.

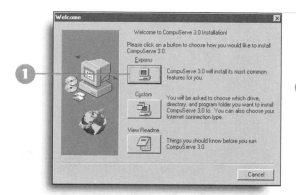

FIGURE E.2
CompuServe's handy installer easily guides you through the setup process.

① Click **Express** to install the software needed for most installations.

2. A new directory or folder is created for the software. Double-click the program icon ⊕ to start the process of establishing your account.

3. Follow the information prompts to continue with setting up your account.

Extra Services

Unlimited access on CompuServe has more limitations than on AOL. Extra-cost services can be found everywhere, such as Computing Pro (see Figure E.3).

High-Speed Access on CompuServe

As this book was written, AOL had not begun to take advantage of CompuServe's large high-speed network, but AOL has already installed hundreds of access numbers for each of the two competing 56K technologies. In contrast, CompuServe had only begun a limited trial of x2. You learn more about the two contents for 56,000bps access in Chapter 4, "Secrets of High-Speed Access to AOL."

Have your billing information handy

Your CompuServe account may be billed to your credit card or checking account. You want to have your billing information handy when you sign up, along with the registration and password information on your installation disk.

Give yourself a name…

At first glance, CompuServe doesn't seem as friendly as AOL. That's because you are given a number, rather than a name. You can also give yourself a nickname, however, similar to the screen name on AOL. To access that service, use the shortcut ("go" word) `Personal Address` to call up the area where you can create a more personal address for your CompuServe email.

FIGURE E.3

CompuServe's Computing Pro is one example of the add-on services that are offered.

1 Click the labeled item to access additional features.

Moving from one place to another is slow on CompuServe

If you opt for an hourly payment plan for CompuServe, be fore-warned. You cannot just zip along from one forum to another as you can on AOL. Most often, you see a status message, stating, `Accessing Service. Please Wait`...when you go from one forum to another; and that can add up over a long session.

If you want to try ISDN, however, you're in luck. CompuServe has hundreds of nodes available, but you'll want to check with your local phone company to see what ISDN will cost you. CompuServe also hasn't been troubled with the connection problems that afflicted AOL. It's a rare, rare occasion for a busy signal, and even then the second time you try, you'll usually get through.

Although AOL has had its share of problems with flaky customer service, the situation at CompuServe has not been as difficult. Their Member Assistance area is well staffed, and you can usual-ly get through to a knowledgeable support representative with-out delay. In fairness, however, AOL has added thousands of customer support representatives, and the last time I called (without identifying myself as a forum person or book writer), I got pretty good service.

CompuServe's Internet Features

Little doubt exists that CompuServe's origins as a text-based service can be found here and there. At times, you'll bring up a forum or feature, and see a terminal window appear on your computer's screen to access the service. Then, just as quickly, you'll jump to a Web-based interface as you try another feature (see Figure E.4).

FIGURE E.4
CompuServe has learned from AOL and has been working to integrate Web-based access.

1 Click the underlined items to reach another forum.

Another case in point is CompuServe's Internet area (their equivalent of AOL's Internet Connection). The "go" word Internet brings up the screen shown in Figure E.5.

Other features, however, seem to bring up an entirely different software interface. If you want to try CompuServe's Newsgroup feature, you'll get one sort of interface. If you want FTP, for example, you'll get still another, as you'll see in Figure E.6.

CompuServe is like AOL in enabling you to use third-party Internet software. If you prefer another Web browser, FTP client, or want to try out an Internet Relay Chat for size, it's no problem. Just begin your CompuServe session, then fire up your Internet program. As with AOL, however, you're not able to run other email software (except for Claris Emailer, which supports CompuServe as neatly as AOL).

FIGURE E.5

This is another example of CompuServe's growing effort to bring Web-like features to the service.

❶ Click the titles on the left side of the screen to access another area.

If you choose to join up with a regular Internet provider, such as EarthLink or Netcom, you'll be able to access CompuServe seamlessly. At the time this book was written, however, there was no equivalent to AOL's "bring your own access plan." You won't get any discount if you use another carrier for your connection to the service; of course with AOL in the driver's seat now, that could change.

FIGURE E.6
When CompuServe discovered
the Internet, they made this
FTP interface.

1   Click the icons on the right
side of the screen to connect
to FTP sites.

SEE ALSO

➤ *Learn more about AOL's features, see page 71*

➤ *Learn how to get the best high-speed modem access, see page 51*

➤ *Learn more about how AOL compares to CompuServe, see page 223*

Index